WESTMAR COLLEGE

THE MIRROR OF BRASS

A special study for the Commission on College
Administration of the Association of American Colleges
directed by Mark H. Ingraham of the University of Wisconsin
with the collaboration of Francis P. King of the
Teachers Insurance and Annuity Association.

The Mirror of Brass

The Compensation and Working Conditions of College and University Administrators

MARK H. INGRAHAM

with the collaboration of
FRANCIS P. KING

THE UNIVERSITY OF WISCONSIN PRESS
MADISON, MILWAUKEE, AND LONDON, 1968

Published by
The University of Wisconsin Press
U.S.A.: Box 1379, Madison, Wisconsin 53701
U.K.: 27–29 Whitfield Street, London, W.1

Printed in the United States of America by
Kingsport Press, Inc., Kingsport, Tennessee

Library of Congress Catalog Card Number 68–98321

PREFACE

THE background of any study is as varied as its impact and just as illusory. This study is no exception. For some projects, however, one can tell in whose mind chaos first becomes cosmos. Carter Davidson, struck by the increasing burdens imposed upon college presidents and by the comparative neglect of their welfare, urged that greater consideration be given their total compensation, including not only salary but also such items as housing, leaves of absence, vacations, and expense allowances. Twenty-eight years of educational leadership as the president of Knox College and of Union College, culminating in service as president of the Association of American Colleges (AAC), not only gave him deep insight but made others heed his words. I deeply regret that his death deprived me of his advice and that he could not have had the satisfaction of seeing the study finished. It was undertaken with his encouragement, carried forward with the hope that it would fulfill his wishes, and completed with the fond memory of an educator and a friend.

If Carter Davidson suggested the study and approved its expansion to cover certain administrative officers other than the president, and their general working conditions as well as compensation, it was William C. Greenough, chairman of Teachers Insurance and Annuity Association, who suggested that Frank King and I, having recently completed a report on faculty benefits, collaborate again.

The Esso Education Foundation provided the major part of the financial backing that made the study possible. We are grateful to the foundation and its officers, especially its executive director, George M. Buckingham, and its associate director, Frederick de W. Bolman, for their interest and support.

As in the case of *The Outer Fringe*,* this is the report to the Commis-

* Mark H. Ingraham, *The Outer Fringe* (Madison: University of Wisconsin Press, 1965).

sion on College Administration of the AAC. It is not a report of that commission (here the reader may insert the usual remarks re credit, responsibility, and blame). The members of the commission were helpful in formulating the questionnaire and, along with certain other presidents, gave its semifinal draft a trial run. The chairman, President Sharvy Umbeck of Knox College, followed the work through all its stages and read, at my request, certain portions of the manuscript.

The officers of TIAA cooperated as well as encouraged. In particular, William C. Greenough, Thomas C. Edwards, Jr., and William T. Slater discussed with me the work as it developed, and as it neared completion they read the manuscript and made valuable suggestions concerning it. Many of the staff of TIAA aided greatly in the work. Special appreciation is due Larry Mahoney and Pat Hanbury who programmed and processed an enormous amount of data, and to Miss Janet Szalus and Mrs. JoAnn Mahoney who administered the preparation, testing, and final production of the questionnaires, supervised the editing of returned questionnaires, maintained project records, and completed and assembled the computer-prepared tables.

My deepest gratitude goes to Francis P. King of TIAA. As in our previous study, he was the chief designer of the questionnaire and directed the coding of the answers and the summarizing of the replies. It is hard to believe that anyone can be so constructive, so meticulous, so patient, and such a good companion all at the same time.

The University of Wisconsin made substantial contributions of space, equipment, and staff time. The office work was intelligently supervised by Mrs. Helen Guzman. She and Miss Catherine Goddertz read the manuscript at several stages, righting my desultory punctuation, making the subject and verb agreeable to each other, seeing that tenses were consistent, and persuading me to clarify the prose. What raggedness persists is a small fraction of what was there before this scrutiny. Mrs. Julie Meyer and Miss Judy Baerwald not only typed various drafts of the manuscript, but skillfully assisted in organizing the selection of quotations used in the text.

Miss Peggy Heim, economist *par excellence* of the American Association of University Professors, made many useful suggestions and helped by reading certain portions of the manuscript. The criticism of the manuscript by F. L. Wormald of the AAC was not only useful but also witty.

Besides all these colleagues who made my work a pleasure, I especially want to thank the 6,276 administrative officers who replied to the questionnaire. Not only were the facts they furnished important, but their comments, both those quoted and those assimilated, were of the essence. Incidentally, a little arithmetic indicates that the time used answering the questionnaire converted into salary dollars is of the same order of magnitude as the grants supporting the project.

The first solemn title given to the study was "Total Compensation of Academic Administrators." This had three faults: First, "academic administrators" might be misunderstood to mean administrators, such as deans, in contrast to those on the business side of the institution; second, the total compensation of an administrator has a major psychic component very inadequately studied by us; and third, as the study developed, working conditions as well as compensation received significant attention. Hence our subtitle now is "The Compensation and Working Conditions of College and University Administrators."

The study from the first was dubbed "The Care and Feeding of Presidents," but presidents were not the only persons considered, and "The Care and Feeding of College Administrators" has no zip. For quite a while we thought it would be called "Polishing the Brass," a title that on King's suggestion was improved to "Burnishing the Brass." My wife still likes that title best. Greenough suggested "The Brass Menagerie." I will not repeat here the delightfully scurrilous chapter headings that would flow from its adoption, for instance, "The King of Beasts," containing quotes under the heading "The Lion Roars!" or "The Cocoon—A Worm Wrapped in Red Tape."

The large proportion of this report which consists of quotations suggested a mirror. So we considered "The Brass Mirror." This, however, did not have the desired ambiguity of the title we have finally chosen—*The Mirror of Brass.*

MARK H. INGRAHAM

March, 1968

CONTENTS

APPENDIX

THE MIRROR OF BRASS

CHAPTER 1

INTRODUCTION

THE American college or university endeavors to turn its administrators into overworked drudges. They are overworked, but they are not drudges. They remain men of vigor and intelligence. Moreover, they do not lose their zest for life or their devotion to education. Generally, they grow in wisdom, often in humor, sometimes in wit.

However, few institutions can claim that the circumstances under which their chief administrators work either maximize the administrators' effectiveness or are attractive enough to persuade the ablest young persons to follow their footsteps. Clearly the problem of developing optimum conditions is a local one, which must take into account not only factors peculiar to the institution but also the individual characteristics of the administrators. Yet, it is hoped that information concerning what others are doing, accompanied by analysis, may be useful to each institution.

It is the aim of this report to describe the compensation which the chief administrators in American colleges and universities receive, the conditions under which they work and their attitude toward them; and to give their suggestions, as well as mine, toward improving these conditions in order to make their work both more effective and more pleasant.

Information and comments were solicited by means of a questionnaire sent to the presidents of universities and of those colleges listed in the 1965–66 *Education Directory** of the U.S. Office of Education as offering a four-year liberal arts and general program. Institutions of higher education offering less than four years of work, professional and teacher-preparatory colleges not offering a liberal arts and general program, theological schools, and technical institutes were excluded. Similar questionnaires were sent through the presidents to the holders

* "Part 3: Higher Education" (Washington, D.C.: U.S. Government Printing Office, 1966).

of the following positions: academic vice president, dean of the liberal arts college, dean of the graduate school, director of libraries, chief business officer, dean of students, director of admissions, registrar, and director of development.

This report is divided into two parts and has a bipartite Appendix. I shall explain the Appendix first.

In the first part of the Appendix the questionnaire which was sent to the presidents is reproduced, and the differences between it and the questionnaires sent to other officers are indicated. All officers except the president were asked identical questions. Certain additional information was sought from the president. In particular, the salary information (1965–66) concerning the various positions was supplied by the president. In general, the information gathered may be classified under the following broad headings: (1) monetary compensation, (2) retirement and insurance provisions, (3) individual well-being and development, (4) housing, (5) special allowances (including those concerned with children's education), and (6) facilities for work.

The second portion of the Appendix consists of 63 tables, summarizing the responses to many of the questions. Tables in the Appendix are numbered from 1 to 63. Those in the text are designated by capital letters. Most of these tables break down the replies according to whether the institution of the respondent is publicly or privately controlled and whether it is a university or a college. The stringent definition of a university falling under Class IV of the *Education Directory* (1965–66) was adopted. In a few tables, institutions are classified by size rather than by type and in a few others the replies are divided into the salary ranges of those replying. For a number of questions, no summary tables of replies are given, but the gist of the findings is included in the text.

Part I of this report deals with the various benefits about which information was requested in the fact-finding portion of the questionnaire. Beyond reporting and analyzing statistics, it attempts to reflect the opinions of administrators about these benefits, to assess the different types of compensation, and to make suggestions concerning many of them.

Part II deals with the incumbents of the ten positions considered, their work, the conditions under which it is done, and their reactions to their situations. The larger portion is devoted to selected quotations taken from the questionnaires. A few persons resented the query in the questionnaire on "improving the attractiveness of the position" as belittling the dedication of educators to their cause. They felt that this introduced a sordid note into the study. In self-defense, I can say that it was the intent of those who planned the study to help the cause of American education, not to besmirch it with crass materialism, and that the questionnaire generally was answered in the same spirit.

Throughout, but particularly in the concluding chapter, I make a few expanded remarks and draw certain conclusions. Without this privilege I would explode. A man should try to be an accurate reporter; he need not be a passive one.

Table 1 gives the number of respondents consisting of 813 presidents and 5,462 other officers (but excluding the dean of students who replied in January, 1968). These replies came from 877 institutions, representing at least one reply from 79% of the institutions to which questionnaires were sent. The variation in the number of replies, according to positions, does not indicate greater willingness to answer by one set of officers than by another, but rather the fact that many institutions do not have certain positions; for instance, there may be no graduate dean or not both a vice president and a liberal arts dean, or the director of admissions and the registrar may be the same person. There seemed to be little reluctance among those replying to answer any question, except that some presidents were unwilling to give data concerning salaries—sometimes their own, sometimes their colleagues, and sometimes both. These omissions of salary information were not numerous enough or concentrated enough in any class of institution to invalidate the findings.

The high level of response, somewhere between two-thirds and three-fourths, was gratifying, but not without its penalty. We asked for comments throughout the questionnaire and gave opportunity for administrators to suggest improvements and to detail the drawbacks of their positions. I had not expected that busy men would make much use of such a chance. I learned. I even suspect that some individuals answered the factual part of the questionnaire in order to feel justified in using the privilege of describing their frustrations. I read thousands of these comments. They not only enriched my point of view but helped develop, alter, or confirm my judgments. Many of them are quoted at the end of chapters in sections entitled "Reflections." Reading the comments and selecting those to be quoted, or to be noted for other use, took five to six months.

An explanation concerning the "Reflections" is in order. In our report on faculty benefits entitled *The Outer Fringe*, many respondents were quoted under the heading of "They Say." I judge from what readers have told me that these quotations added interest and life to the report. This, however, is not the only reason why the current report uses a much larger number of such quotations. Two other considerations entered in: First, on several topics, strongly varied opinions were expressed. A notable example concerns whether it is preferable to have a fixed or a flexible retirement age. It seemed best to give much of the content of the arguments on these subjects by means of quotations. Secondly, in addition to the typical differences between positions, there is a wide variation in the personalities of those holding a particular post. The flavor of these differences could only be given by extensive quotations. Anonymity was guaranteed and the quotations have been identified only by position and type of institution. The title used is that on the questionnaire returned and may differ from the official local title. Thus, chancellors may be listed as "presidents" and some deans of women as "deans of students." A few choice opinions are omitted where it seemed likely that they could be identified by circumstance or by style. A far greater risk actually taken is that twenty presidents will each be convinced that a single quotation came from their institution. I will regret if a well-worded remark gets a score of innocent registrars into trouble. But I at least protect the guilty.

In a few cases, we have corrected the grammar or the spelling of those who believed the questionnaire deserved filling out but that proofreading was not merited. Most of us could be proved illiterate by many "*sic's.*"

A few other matters need clarification.

English is a local as well as our national language. A previous questionnaire should have taught me that the providing of a definition for a familiar word will change no one's usage, and that if a word, though familiar, has different local uses, the replies will have different meanings. Let me illustrate:

1. The vice president who refers to himself as the dean.
2. The director of development whose function it is to determine the location of buildings, parking lots, and the connecting sidewalks.
3. Leave without pay. Question: Without any pay or just no pay from the institution?
4. 100% reimbursement for travel expenses. Is the cost of liquor included?

5. I learned that "a religious" is a currently used phrase in exceedingly good circles.

Speaking of the religious, they found that much of the questionnaire was easy to answer, being nonapplicable to them. A large portion of the "No Responses" to some questions is due to this fact. Many of those in religious orders were most helpful, however, in indicating what was true for their lay colleagues or what would be desirable. We have attempted as far as possible to eliminate any bias in the figures due to the number to whom certain questions did not apply. Even if not completely successful, we believe that we have been substantially so.

At several points in this report, I have discussed faculty benefits. At first glance these discussions might not appear relevant to this study. Frequently, however, what is done for administrators is patterned after what is done for faculty members. Hence, in many areas wise decisions concerning faculty benefits will engender wise decisions concerning administrative benefits. Even when contrasting actions seem desirable, careful comparisons are useful.

I have frequently, consciously, repeated myself out of consideration for the readers who may read only portions pertinent to their interests. Surely other repetitions have crept in unbeknownst.

At the start of the study, consideration was given to whether or not the questionnaire should be sent and returned through the president. Because of the variety of titles used for somewhat similar positions, it became clear that the questionnaire had to be sent through the office of the president. A few presidents desired that it be returned through their offices; many of those who wished them to be returned directly to us still believed the choice of the mode of return should be left to the president. We therefore advised that they should be returned directly by each officer, but did not specify that this was necessary. By far the larger number were returned without going through the president's office. Sometimes when the replies went through the president's office, complaints were registered either in the questionnaire or to me personally. Certainly, no important statistical aberrations resulted from the methods of return.

REFERENCES TO APPENDIX

Summary Table 1.

PART I   SPECIAL TOPICS

CHAPTER 2

SALARIES

THE most important financial compensation that an administrator receives is normally his salary. This chapter deals with:

1. The magnitudes of the salaries of administrative officers and the variations of these magnitudes with the types of institutions.
2. The relationships commonly found in various types of institutions of the size of the salaries of various positions to one another and to the salaries of professors. This I consider more important, though less precise, than 1 since it cannot be found readily in other sources nor, as will be indicated later, can it be derived from 1.
3. The opinions of administrators concerning their salaries and the salary policies of their institutions.
4. Various special salary provisions such as supplementary payments, deferred benefits, and the purchase of tax-deferred annuities.

But first, we must describe the evidence we have for our statements.

THE NATURE OF THE DATA

Presidents of colleges and universities were asked to state their own salaries, the salaries of the other chief administrative officers, and the average salaries of the full professors in their institutions. A large majority of the presidents replying to the questionnaire provided this information, although some thought it inappropriate to furnish salary data. I found no evidence of a strongly differential willingness to do so by type of institution or even by geography. A somewhat smaller proportion of the presidents of private universities than presidents of private colleges replied to the questionnaire. The opposite was true for public institutions.

To secure a ratio of salaries for a pair of positions of course requires that salaries for both positions be known. The number of such ratios which are known for a pair of positions is less than the number of salaries known for either position since some presidents were willing to state their own salaries but unwilling to do so for other officers, and vice versa. Sometimes the average faculty salary was omitted. However, these omissions did not significantly reduce the size of the samples.

Some of the figures given for the average salaries of professors are clearly in error, being unbelievably low. By checking with the AAUP salary report, it was found that in a number of such instances, the salaries of all full-time faculty members had been used, instead of the salaries of full professors. (Electronics showed no ability to discriminate in this regard.) The number of such cases was small and probably does not seriously affect averages or medians, but might throw off the ninetieth percentile figures for the ratios of various administrators' salaries to professors' salaries.

Another matter must be borne in mind when interpreting the data. In some institutions certain positions do not exist. In particular, many colleges do not have vice presidents and some that do, do not have deans of liberal arts. Many colleges unite the registrar and the admissions officer in one person. The position of director of development is ill-defined. In most private institutions he is, next to the president, the chief money-raiser; but in many public institutions this or a similar title is used for the campus planner whose background is either engineering or architecture. The most important variation, however, is in regard to the graduate dean, who is present in almost all universities and in a large majority of public colleges but in only a few private colleges—and then chiefly in the larger and more well-to-do institutions. Hence, overall averages should not be used to form judgments as to the relative salaries paid those holding various positions within the institutions; but the conclusions based on aggregates of comparisons of salaries within given institutions yield interesting and, I believe, valid insight into the salary structures of our colleges and universities.

In Catholic universities and colleges, administrative services are often "contributed," no salary being paid but an estimate of the contribution frequently being given. Apparently the desiderata determining what these estimates should be are somewhat different than when cash payments are being determined. These figures are omitted from tables concerning salaries.

THE RANGE OF SALARIES

There are a number of tables in the Appendix detailing the salaries of various positions. However, the following table will give some idea of the magnitudes involved. These figures are based upon the salaries of the administrative officers who work on a full-year rather than on an academic-year basis and report salaries in effect in the spring of 1966.

The average salaries run somewhat above the median salaries, but their order is the same.

TABLE A
Salaries of administrative officers in reporting institutions

	Lowest Decile	Median	Highest Decile
President	$14,000	$20,000	$30,000
Academic V. P.	12,500	18,000	25,100
Liberal Arts Dean	10,725	15,600	22,000
Graduate Dean	13,000	17,000	23,700
Librarian	7,500	10,800	16,600
Business Officer	9,200	13,756	21,500
Dean of Students	8,400	12,000	17,772
Dir. Admissions	7,500	10,500	14,622
Registrar	6,200	9,000	13,280
Dir. Development	8,700	13,200	20,000

The figures given for the graduate deans are artificially high compared with those for other positions. As explained above, the average salaries for institutions having graduate programs are higher than those for other institutions. When institutions are compared by size and type of control, the salaries of liberal arts deans run slightly higher than those of graduate deans; and, as will appear later, the same is true if only institutions having both positions are considered.

For presidents, vice presidents, business officers, and directors of development, the highest median salaries occur in private universities and the second in public universities. For the other six positions, the highest median salaries are in public universities and the second in private universities. In all cases, the public colleges come third and private colleges fourth.

If we consider the highest decile, the private universities rank first, except in the cases of the dean of liberal arts, the dean of students, the admissions officer, and the registrar, where the public universities are first. The public colleges are third, except for the president and the chief business officer in which cases the private colleges are ahead of the public colleges.

The relative variations of salaries in private institutions, especially private colleges, are greater than in public institutions.

There is a significant tendency for larger institutions to pay higher administrative salaries.

It should be recalled that these figures are for 1965–66 and are perhaps 10% to 15% too low for 1967–68. However, the rank order has probably not changed greatly since that time.

INTERNAL SALARY STRUCTURE

I fear it is natural for people to ask, "Who gets paid more than I do, and how much?" Perhaps even morbid curiosity should be satisfied. Moreover, the salary structures of educational institutions are a subject of important concern.

In order to make comparisons of professors' with administrators' salaries on a full-year basis, I have used as a base 11/9 of the average salary of full professors on a nine-month basis. This alone puts me in jeopardy. Dean X of the graduate school will assert that professors in his institution get considerably more than 22% of their academic-year salaries for summer research and have opportunities for consulting which he forewent when he became dean. Professor Y in French will point out that his institution does not have a summer school, that he does no consulting, and that NSF does not have summer institutes for high-school teachers of French which might provide him with employment in the summer; hence, it is outrageous to multiply his salary by 11/9, so that the president gets only 1.52 times his salary when the multiplier is 1.86 even if his, the professor's, salary were up to the average, which it isn't because the dean—whose salary is really 37%, not 12%, above the professor's salary—favors the department of chemistry. Yet I hope there will be many people who will conclude that I have used as good a base as can be found. (If a nine-month salary of professors were used as a base, all other indices should be multiplied by 1.22, or the professors' index reduced to .82. This would not change the relative salary positions of any administrative officers but would considerably reduce the position of professors.)

In order to arrive at indices typical of the relative salaries for different positions within an institution, I combined the results of data giving the medians of the ratios of the salaries of various positions to the average salary of professors in the same institution (Table 5) with that giving the medians of the ratios of the salaries for these same positions to that of the president (Table 6). If all presidents had furnished all salary figures, and if no services were contributed, these tables would have been based on identical data; but since this was not the case, it was necessary to develop combined indices differing only slightly from those which either table would yield.

TABLE B
Index of median salaries of administrative positions with salary-rank order in parentheses (Full Professors' Average Salary = 1)

	Public Institutions		Private Institutions	
	Univ.	Col.	Univ.	Col.
President	1.77 *(1)*	1.47 *(1)*	2.04 *(1)*	1.52 *(1)*
Academic V. P.	1.40 *(2)*	1.20 *(2)*	1.48 *(2)*	1.16 *(2)*
Liberal Arts Dean	1.29 *(3)*	1.14 *(3)*	1.17 *(5)*	1.12 *(3)*
Graduate Dean	1.28 *(4)*	1.08 *(4)*	1.12 *(6)*	1.00 *(5,6,7)*
Librarian	.99 *(9)*	.88 *(9)*	.93 *(8)*	.75 *(9)*
Business Officer	1.24 *(5)*	.98 *(7)*	1.40 *(3)*	1.03 *(4)*
Dean of Students	1.06 *(6)*	.98 *(6)*	.92 *(9)*	.86 *(8)*
Dir. Admissions	.88 *(10)*	.82 *(10)*	.76 *(10)*	.74 *(10)*
Registrar	.80 *(11)*	.73 *(11)*	.73 *(11)*	.66 *(11)*
Dir. Development	1.04 *(7)*	.96 *(8)*	1.22 *(4)*	1.00 *(5,6,7)*
Full Professors	1.00 *(8)*	1.00 *(5)*	1.00 *(7)*	1.00 *(5,6,7)*

The ranks in Table B are consistent, within sampling errors, with a count of the number of cases within a large sample where the salary of the given position exceeded that of another. I consider these ranks more significant than those that could be derived from Table A.

One word of special warning. The number of private universities involved is small, and hence there could well be a larger degree of error in the indices developed for them than for other types of institutions.

It is worthwhile to point out that the great variation in the relation of salaries for the different positions from institution to institution is hidden by this table. In a few cases, 11/9 of the average salary of professors is greater than the salary of the president, and among the private colleges it would exceed the liberal arts dean's salary in about

20% of the cases. Librarians' salaries exceed those of the development officers in about 40% of the public universities, but in less than 20% of the private colleges. The concept of the various positions varies among institutions. The ages and abilities of incumbents differ. These are important factors in determining the individual's salary. Moreover, some presidents take pride in holding down their own salaries, to the distress of their administrative colleagues but with the admiration of the faculty.

The low index for the chief business officer of public colleges, and for some of the other officers in these colleges, is partly due to their salaries more frequently being regulated by the state than are the salaries for the academic positions. Some Protestant church systems have salary scales even more restrictive than state systems.

WHAT THEY SAY ABOUT THEIR SALARIES

The above title started out as "What They Think About Their Salaries," but was changed to a less telepathic wording.

First of all, and most important, the large majority did not complain about their salaries. Many stated that considering what they knew about the financial circumstances of their institutions, their compensations were fair and gave them livable, though in some cases not comfortable, incomes. However, there were enough complaints to deserve some general remarks and, of course, quotations as well.

There were some statements that income was inadequate to meet the cost of a decent standard of living, but most of the complaints were based on assumed standards or on comparisons with other people within the same group or in another group.

The respondents frequently indicated rules which they believe should be observed in determining their salaries. Librarians, admissions officers, registrars, and some presidents think there are stated professional standards which their salaries should meet. In some cases the interpretations of these standards are somewhat more explicit than the published statements would wholly justify.

A number of presidents stated that they understand the normal salary for a president should be twice the highest salary for a professor in the same institution (I presume the professor's nine-month salary). If we assume that the highest salary of a professor is in the neighborhood of 1.5 times the average salary, the median ratio of presidents' salaries to the highest salaries of professors on a nine-month basis in the same institutions would be about 1.2, and the ninetieth percentile about 1.6. (This assumption represents a range which is probably larger than that in most colleges and smaller than that in most universities.) If the average, instead of the highest, salary of professors were used on a nine-month basis, these figures would be 1.9 and 2.4, respectively. In actual practice, therefore, a president's full-year salary of twice the average nine-month salary of the professors is fairly common. It would be inappropriate for me or anyone else to set down a single figure to represent a desirable ratio of president's to professor's salary. The age, length of service, and ability of the president are all relevant factors. It is well to point out, however, that the highest professor's salary is an extremely unstable standard and that, if any comparison is used, it should be based on the median or on the average salary.

I happen to believe that the presidents in general are not overpaid —in fact, often underpaid—relative to the scale of salaries in our educational institutions; but I also believe that our top scholars and teachers are grossly underpaid relative to such standards, in particular, relative to the average salary of the professors. Newton was far more valuable as a professor than as master of the mint. The fame of the Sorbonne rests upon the renown of savants like Poincaré. Men like Von Newman, or William James, were worth many times the millrun of professors, even at the distinguished institutions they served.

There is no more useful member of the academic community than a really first-class scholar-teacher. Every major university and many other institutions have faculty members whom it would be unfortunate to draw off from research and teaching to be administrators. These persons are scarce, and in my judgment there is every reason why they should receive more than the deans and perhaps the president. There are reasons of administrative orderliness for a salary structure that recognizes the hierarchy of administrative authority and responsibility within the administration. The faculty is not in this chain.

I think an institution is unfortunate when the president and deans are not among its ablest faculty members. Their abilities should be recognized by the budget and perhaps some token provided for extra worry and responsibility. But a university is also unfortunate if it does not have a few scholars who exceed the administrators in distinction. The very top scholars, when they are also splendid teachers, may well receive salaries higher than the salaries of those who are sometimes called their "immediate academic superiors." The quality of a dean is measured far more by the talent, in excess of his own, that he can collect and keep happy in the faculty than by the magnitude of his compensation.

These comments should not be thought of as approval of the "star professor" system. When a genius arises in our midst, he should be recognized, provided with what he needs, and even cuddled a bit. This is very different from trying to buy prestige through a system of professorships where the perquisites of the chair are defined and publicized before the occupant is found. This leads to jealousy within an institution and to a constant turmoil of mind on the part of a group of able men who get on everybody's list.

I would like to see us obtain two somewhat divergent, yet compatible, goals: a wider salary scale, especially recognizing the extremely able when they are young, and greater institutional stability. The possibility of academic mobility must be defended. Too great a use of it is unfortunate.

The following statements occur frequently in respondents' comments:

a) My salary is not up to the average of my position in similar institutions.

b) My salary is not up to what I could get in industry.

c) My work is harder than that of the faculty, but (1) I'm not paid as much, or (2) I'm not paid enough more. (It is interesting to note that far fewer administrators made comparisons of their salaries with those of other administrative colleagues than with the pay of the faculty.)

d) Women are not treated fairly.

We will comment in order on these plaints:

a) The first statement above seems to be based at times on fact and at times on rumor. In the minds of many the average salary is escalated. You all remember the pullman porter who was delighted when for the first time he received a tip as large as his "average." We must remember that by inexorable arithmetic rather than by administrative fiat nearly half of any group will be below the average, and at least half equal to or below the median. Occasionally a salary is outrageously low; but the fact that variations in age and training and the accidents of circumstance will cause discrepancy in treatment must be recognized—even if not accepted—as part of life.

b) The comparison with industry is made most frequently by business officers and directors of development. It must often be a fair complaint, yet in many instances the comparison seems to be made with a few highly paid industrial positions, without considering how many able men in business do not get large remuneration. It is pleasant to note in this connection that some educational officers reported that they had come from higher-paid positions in industry and found their life in a college more rewarding than it formerly was, although often as busy.

c) This comparison with the work and salaries of professors comes from pretty nearly all the positions, but with different slants. Because of its emotional content (a mixture of an outraged sense of justice and of jealousy) and because in many instances its image-picture is found in the faculty, it is a significant matter to be clearly recognized by the president and the governing board. The tension between administrators and faculty not only involves salaries but also vacations, work schedules, authority, and social relations. It often is built on cherished misunderstandings. Some of these attitudes will be described in more detail in chapters on the various positions.

The president, the vice president, the dean of liberal arts, and the graduate dean all are in positions usually held by a person with a Ph.D. degree, and many others of them hold the degree of doctor of education. This is also true of professors. People in these positions customarily have been professors, and this is almost always true of the graduate dean. These administrative officers at least know what the work of a professor is. Misunderstandings between them and professors are largely ones of temperament and of responsibility. The librarian is also a scholar, but with a somewhat different background than the professor and far less experience with the strenuous character of classroom teaching than the graduate dean, for example, would have. To men in the other five positions considered, the world of a professor is often strange; and their world is almost always strange to a professor. Their work serves the work of the faculty, but also to a large degree controls it. Sometimes funds may be granted or refused by the business officer. The registrar sets deadlines for grades, class schedules, and a host of other matters. The admissions officer determines to some degree the quality of the students the faculty teaches. The vacations that administrators do not take are shorter than the vacations that professors do not take. The formal office hours differ widely.

The faculty committees designed to formulate standards often take over the administrative process, or at least add to its difficulty. It also must be admitted that some holders of the Ph.D. degree, especially the less distinguished ones, are a bit top-lofty as regards not only those without the doctorate, but also as regards doctors of education. The "snoot order" can be as important as the "peck order."

d) I found fewer complaints about the treatment of women than I expected, perhaps the strongest one coming from a woman in a women's college with a woman president. It is true that the large majority of academic administrators are men, the smallest proportion among respondents being just under 60% in the case of librarians and registrars; however, in private colleges the majority of these two positions are held by women. The proportion of women in administrative positions is indicated by Table 9. If Catholic colleges were eliminated, the percentage of women administrative officers would probably be still smaller. Circumstances and the attitudes of society that govern what positions are filled by women are probably more potent in determining income than is salary discrimination within like positions.

A number wrote with admiring envy of the effect that the AAUP has on faculty salaries. Some believe that this effect is at the expense of administrative salaries. They are probably in error. A survey of the National Education Association indicates that presidents' salaries, for instance, have been rising at about the same rate as faculty salaries. I believe that the competition for professional personnel, aided by such studies as those of the AAUP, has raised all academic salaries, and that the AAUP studies of faculty salaries have been almost as effective in raising the salaries of administrative officers as in raising the salaries of the faculty. I fear that in the case of faculties they have tended to raise minimum salaries rather than those in the upper level. This may help in a few cases to protect individuals against administrative abuses, but at the same time, and more significantly, it may decrease the emphasis on quality which is greatly needed.

Let us remember that disssatisfaction with one's salary is often a healthy symptom of respect for one's job.

ADDITIONAL SALARY

Administrative officers were asked, "In addition to your regular salary, do you receive any other salary because of your administrative position, or from any other office that you occupy as holder of this position?" Although the proportion giving an affirmative answer ranged from 3% for development officers to 11% for graduate deans, the large majority of replies were not relevant to the subject of additional income based on administrative functions.

Many public institutions, as well as a number of private ones, give professors who are also administrators supplements for performing their non-teaching duties, or for being on a twelve-month rather than a nine-month basis. Certain institutions indicate separately the amounts for these duties so that if a person relinquishes his administrative duties, the financial responsibility of the institution is clearly defined.

These supplements were generally reported by the president as a regular portion of the individual's salary, but a number of individuals reported such supplements as extra compensation or, where the teaching duties were minor, reported the budgetary allotment for teaching duties as extra compensation. Among all the respondents, 75 reported receiving extra compensation of $1,500 or more. In only 19 of these cases was it clear that this was extra compensation beyond payment for their regular full-time duties; in 12 others it may have been; in 44 cases it clearly was not. In 27 of these 44 cases, the amount reported was an administrative supplement, and in 8 of the cases a portion of the budget allotted to teaching. Of the 12 cases that were not clear, 5 gave no explanation of the supplementary compensation, and in 5 it was for teaching which may have been beyond obligations under the regular set-up.

In the 19 cases which reported clearly supplementary salaries, 6 of the supplements were for housing allowance; 5 were for acting as an officer of a foundation connected with the institution; 2 for acting as an officer of an association to which the institution belonged; 1 for teaching not covered by regular salary; 1 for acting as an athletic advisor; 1 for being a bank officer; 2 for other special duties; and 1, although clearly supplementary, was unexplained.

Some other functions for which persons were paid amounts less than $1,500 were: helping a credit union; administering educational tests; acting as treasurer of a special scholarship fund; acting as treasurer of a high school associated with the college; coaching baseball or cross-country; helping in the administration of a pension fund; and assisting the president. Several respondents put housing allowances in this list. (The president's house was seldom so reported and often, in fact, represents an obligation as much as compensation. If listed as compensation, it should be for the "contributed services" of his wife.)

At times there might have been certain informal arrangements that were not reported; but it is clear that the total amount paid for such extra compensation, though important in some individual instances, is not really significant in the general picture. One supplement reported was the receipt of $1,000 so that the individual's salary would not look larger than another officer's.

TAX-DEFERRED ANNUITIES

The Technical Amendments Act of 1958 provides that an employee of an educational institution may have his salary reduced within certain limits, the amount of the reduction being used to purchase a retirement annuity. This sum is not considered current income and is therefore not taxed on a current basis by the federal government, although it may be taxed as income by some states. The total annuity purchased with this amount is taxable when received. Not only may the tax in some cases be paid in a lower bracket but the plan is substantially equivalent to an interest-free loan to the individual of the amount of the tax even if the tax bracket remains the same. The amount of salary reduction that can be made in this manner is strictly limited; and the greater the contribution of the institution toward the present retirement system, the less the tax-deferred reduction of salary that is allowed. However, a very considerable allowance may often be made for past years in which no salary reduction was taken. This is not the place for an elaborate explanation of this legislation. The TIAA publishes information concerning this matter. Of course, information may be secured from the Internal Revenue Service. The use of tax-deferred annuities in plans which include certain minimum guarantees, the so-called "formula" plans, involve greater complications than in the case of "money-purchase" plans; yet the provisions of the legislation can, under most circumstances, be used.

EXTENT OF USE. Table 26 indicates the extent of use by administrative officers of this plan for purchasing annuities on a tax-deferred basis. It is interesting to note that, as one would expect, the ordering of positions by the proportion using the tax-deferred annuity plan is almost the same as the order of the median salaries as shown in Table A, with a slightly greater use by officers engaged in the business side of the institution than the order of the median salaries would indicate.

As shown by Table 27, and as would be expected, the use of this provision rises with the size of the salary. Some replies indicated lack of familiarity with tax-deferred annuities.

Every effort should be made by those who keep the faculty and administration informed on retirement matters to let them know of the opportunities provided by tax-deferred annuities. It would be especially wise to do this at the time of a large general salary increase or when a man is newly appointed, promoted, or placed in an administrative position.

Two words of warning: First, the provisions are highly technical, and both the individual and the institution may be held responsible for their proper use. Moreover, a person making large use of the so-called "exclusion allowance" must make a careful review each year to insure his compliance with the law. Second, it should be understood that sums invested in this way are for annuities only, not for establishing a liquid savings account. In spite of these warnings, this is an important matter and the privileges involved should be more widely known and considered.

DEFERRED COMPENSATION

Administrative officers were asked if they had any arrangement, other than through the tax-deferred annuities described above, by which some of their compensation is deferred until after they leave office. Such a plan is infrequently used. The most frequent use is by the presidents and the development officers, being used by over 5% of these officers. Nearly 14% of the presidents of private universities make use of such a plan; and 10% of the development officers of public institutions have such an arrangement. A few persons answered this question by describing their regular retirement plans—a literal interpretation we should have guarded against.

Though deferred-compensation plans are infrequently used, certain salaries have now reached a level where it has seemed wise to make such arrangements. This is particularly true in the case of presidents.

DISPOSITION OF LECTURE AND CONSULTING FEES

The treatment of lecture fees and consulting fees is so similar that I will make no distinction between the two. Table 28 gives the facts concerning lecture fees.

The number of institutions that require fees to be turned over to the institution is not over 5% for all positions, except that of the president, where it is about 9%. I presume that some presidents in self-protection have requested such a regulation. Public institutions sometimes require that in-state fees be turned over to the institution but not out-of-state fees. A considerable number of officers, especially presidents, give such fees to the institution even though the institution does not require them to do so.

The proportion of colleges having no stated policy about this matter is considerably higher than that of universities. Public institutions have a defined policy more frequently than private ones. To me it was somewhat surprising that a smaller percentage of public than of private institutions required that fees be turned over to the institution. Perhaps one should have expected this, considering the greater diversity of private institutions, so that in most categories of relatively infrequent occurrence we would have a larger proportion of private than of public institutions.

I believe that in most cases where there was no stated policy and no response the question itself had slight import to the individual concerned. This is borne out by the fact that for the vice president and the three deans' positions, where lecture and consulting opportunities are the greatest, the situation is more often defined than for other positions.

Several types of comments occurred frequently: First, there were those who indicated that, with no stated policy or in spite of a permissive policy, their personal practice was either not to accept fees or to turn them over to the institution. Second, a considerable number commented that their involvement in lectures or consulting was so small that the question had little significance. Some compared their small opportunities for such activities with the more extensive opportunities on the part of many faculty members, or even on their own part before having become administrative officers.

Except in the case where an officer believes that it is wise because of his relations with the public or the faculty to be subject to a special rule that fees be turned over to the institution, I believe that administrators should be subject to the same rules, or lack of rules, as are the faculty. I do not feel happy when a person in higher education derives a large income from outside activities carried on while employed full-time by a college or university. Many of these activities are public services and also enhance a man's value as a scholar and a teacher. Some do not. It would be almost impossible for an active man engaged in these desirable activities to refuse all remuneration from them, but I have known many who have given such funds to their institutions, sometimes with conditions that make them more useful than if they were merely given without strings. We need more thought about one's personal responsibilities in these matters, but I hope we do not need more regulations. I believe that the necessity to think about the institutional problems involved, and perhaps occasionally the whole-some effect of limelight, have made administrative officers more care-ful than faculty members not to abuse their privileges in these matters. It would be unfortunate to reward them with more onerous controls.

REFLECTIONS

MERE FACTS

Tax-Deferred Annuities

Our college will not let us do this.—*Director of admissions, private college*

State law does not allow deferred salary provisions as allowed under Technical Amendments Act of 1958.—*Liberal arts dean, public college*

However, our institution is currently considering a plan of this nature and it possibly could go into effect by July, 1966.—*Director of development, public university*

Other Deferred Compensation

Yes—$5,000 a year will be paid for as many years after retirement as will have elapsed between 7/1/65 and retirement. Amount paid will be increased by interest at 4½% compounded annually.—*President, private university*

Yes, $10,000 for each year of service after 7/1/65, payable in 120 equal monthly installments commencing with the first month following termina-tion of service.—*President, private university*

GENERAL COMMENTS

As a general rule, I think that presidential salaries, even including special fringe benefits and allowances, are lower than they should be, at least when you take account of the substantial recent increases in faculty salaries and note the difference between a 9–10 and an 11–12 month year. And by the same token, I believe that most other administrative salaries are too low, especially if the right kind of person is to be attracted to adminis-trative positions. I happen to think that the best person for most administra-tive positions in a college or university is one who is drawn directly from the ranks of the teaching faculty, and that more often than not the best potential administrative officer is one who stands relatively high on the faculty salary ladder because he is also a very good faculty man. If this be true, the financial attractions of an important administrative post may not be sufficiently strong to induce him to leave his faculty position for administrative work. In brief, he might not even be able to afford the change. — *President, private college*

Compensation is adequate, but there is no provision in Trustee operation to compare salary *progress* of administrative officers with salary progress of the faculty. In general, the latter have moved ahead much faster. — *President, private college*

I think that I and others in similar positions should be paid more. The recent advances in faculty compensation have not been matched by advances in administrative salaries. This does not seem equitable, for in the modern American university the demands made on the time and energy of administrative officers are far greater than those made on the teaching staff. Administrative officers, especially in the higher echelons, are also expected to maintain a standard of living substantially higher—and more expensive —than that of faculty members. Because they work harder and under much greater pressure, administrators should be paid well enough so that making ends meet will not need to concern them as much as it often does now. A little pampering would not hurt. — *Graduate dean, private university*

Minor irritant appeared last year when raises for administration were smaller than for faculty. In the eyes of the faculty, this appeared as a deliberate lowering of prestige of the deans by the Chancellor's office, and it weakened our position "vis a vis" the faculty. This apparently will be repeated this year. — *Graduate dean, public college*

To the younger administrator the direct take-home pay is one of the most important considerations. The benefits of retirement, etc., are of limited interest. Too often the latter takes precedence over the former in the fiscal scheme of the institution. Such fringe benefits as entertainment budget, homes, etc., are helpful but generally impose limitations on the administrator who seeks flexibility in determining his fiscal destiny. — *Dean of students, public university*

As compared with a scientist's summer compensation or with summer school salaries, the total financial compensation for administrative work is utterly inadequate, with the result that a Dean's total compensation for the entire year (minus four weeks' vacation) ranks very low indeed among members of the faculty.

On the other hand, any substantial increase of the administrative stipends would carry with it the danger of attracting persons to administrative posts for reasons of financial considerations. This would be a real tragedy. It, therefore, seems sensible to limit the total financial compensation to a respectable medium between a full professor's salary plus double summer school stipend on the one hand, and a distinguished scientist's 11-month total compensation. — *Liberal arts dean, private university*

Compensation should be ¼ (25%) higher than the highest-paid faculty member. The President of a college should receive a minimum of 50% above the highest paid faculty member.—*Liberal arts dean, private college*

What They Say about Their Own Salaries (a biased sample)

The salary provisions of the president have not kept pace with the increase for the faculty.—*President, private college*

Compensation subject to governor's recommendation and approval. No real appraisal of job and its proper compensation made. Many of my deans or faculty earn greater compensation.—*President, public college*

I am underpaid and overworked, especially in comparison with salaries and working conditions of the faculty. A generation ago, administrators argued that the president's salary should never exceed twice that of the highest-paid faculty member. Today, the president is lucky if the salaries of faculty members, at least on a calendar-year basis, do not exceed his. And occasionally this is justified. In addition, the institution gets two persons for one salary. Not so the faculty! Few if any faculty, incidentally, are so consistently overworked as is the president. But I see no possibility of any real change.—*President, public university*

My annual salary is satisfactory, but I regret that salaries of conscientious faculty members with excellent preparation are not more closely approximate to the salary of the President. The freedom enjoyed by Presidents of the State Universities is most appreciated in conferences with other Presidents who are much more restricted by policies of their boards. In short, I am well satisfied with the compensation and working conditions.—*President, public college*

My compensation is relatively low, but this is at my own insistence.—*President, private college*

I should note that my relatively low salary was set at my request thirteen years ago and kept there, again at my request, during that period.—*President, private university*

The compensation for this office is based directly on the top step of the full professor's salary multiplied by 1.333; in other words, it is pegged to this salary level, which in itself may have merits. However, the time one is *required* to put in versus the time a full professor at the top of the salary schedule is *required* to put in, measured in number of days per year, is closer to a multiplier of 1.45. This still would not take into account compensation for additional responsibilities.—*Vice president, public college*

Differential between full professors and Academic Dean should be more pronounced.—*Liberal arts dean, private college*

In general, I feel well treated by the University. My only major gripe has to do with salary differentials. The University is now paying faculty members and department heads as much as or more than deans. I am not satisfied that this is a wise decision. I think the long-term result will be a poorer class of people in college administration. I do think that the opportunities, problems, and responsibilities of college administration call for the best talent we can find. I don't believe such a policy will procure it. At least a dozen department heads are receiving as much for nine months as I receive for 12 months. In addition, they may earn, if they can, two months additional salary from Federal grants. I should have remained a department head!—*Graduate dean, public university*

Yet there are administrators who pay librarians for eleven months work at the same salary that they pay a teacher for nine months work. The result is that many librarians leave the college field, enter industrial or special libraries, work for twelve months and are paid for twelve months work. Librarians' salaries must be determined on nine months with summer months as extra or optional, using the same salary schedule as used for teachers.—*Librarian, private college*

For one of the most important positions on campus, the pay is inadequate. This might be tolerable if the fringe benefits made up for the low pay. They do not. But pay and fringe benefits cannot in any way make up for the unwillingness on the part of the college administration to accept their roles as the chief advocates of the library and its program.—*Librarian, private college*

Compensation is now slightly less than full professor. It should be 2½%–5% higher than for full professor.—*Librarian, public college*

I have understood, or attempted to understand, the entire financial picture at the college. In so doing it has been my conclusion that better salaries were not possible.—*Librarian, private college*

Compensation for this job should be second only to that of President and it is not.—*Business officer, public college*

In all of my professional career I have never demanded or even suggested to my employers to increase my salary. That has, in every case, been left to the discretion of my employer.—*Business officer, private college*

Compensation—I believe that the compensation is not what it should be. I am a firm believer that a professional person in the area of student services is as important (if not more so) to the University campus as is a faculty member or a college dean. I believe that a personnel dean should be paid on a comparable basis as a college dean and have equal opportunity for office space, secretarial help, and other benefits as the college deans. To my knowledge, this is *not* true on this campus.—*Dean of students, private college*

Compensation is inadequate due to high cost of living in this city. In fact I am just existing and not really living; every cent is spent and none saved and we are not big spenders in any sense of the word.—*Director of admissions, private college*

I have been a teacher and administrator for 27 years. It is difficult to believe, but I have been at the top of my salary grade for nine years. There has been no increment except where one was granted to everyone at this institution. Why have I put up with it? Promises that for some reason never were kept. Dedication to this institution is another reason. These things should not happen.—*Director of admissions, public college*

The salary for the position of Registrar is computed as the annual salary of an assistant professor plus 20 per cent. The 20 per cent is to compensate for the time when the teacher is off duty, since the Registrar is expected to be on duty the entire year except for twenty-two days. This method of compensation in effect is a reduction in salary of the Registrar as compared to the assistant professor in view of the long working hours required and the extra working hours necessary to even partially meet the demands of the job. Furthermore, to equate the responsibilities and importance of the position of Registrar to that of an assistant professor, who has no basic responsibilities beyond teaching, is a major inequity.—*Registrar, public college*

The job deserves higher pay, but really is only comparable in salary to a full professor's 11-month contract. More pay should be provided with a full month off.—*Director of development, private college*

In retrospect, I realize that the salary which I accepted when I began my tenure in this position was low. As a result, my present compensation is low. This prevails in spite of generous increments in the past several years.—*Director of development, private college*

Influence of President's Salary

The compensation of . . . tax-supported college presidents is a "line item" in the legislative appropriation. Some boards set the "take home pay" of the President as the absolute top which can be paid to any administrator, department head, or distinguished professor. The result: Some distinguished professors are lost! The governor's salary has served as an "effective lid" on other administrative and executive officers' salaries throughout all branches of the state government. However, some colleges' regents pay higher salaries to distinguished personnel than to the president.—*President, public college*

Administrative increments, which at this time place the salaries of deans, directors, department chairmen, slightly higher than most full professors' salaries, are not competitive when one is seeking a top echelon administrator or professor. Part of the picture, of course, is the fact that our president is *very* underpaid and scarcely earns any more than some of the people he hires. His salary should be immediately doubled.—*Liberal arts dean, state college*

Because the Chancellor has not had an increase for six years, and as I am near his salary, I too have had no increase for several years. There is too much compression at the top and the Board has not done anything about it. Meanwhile my associates are receiving increases annually.—*Business officer, private college*

REFERENCES TO APPENDIX

Questionnaire, Sections B and F.

Summary Tables 1–6, 26–28.

CHAPTER 3

RETIREMENT PROVISIONS AND PRACTICES

THE provisions which determine when a man will retire and what post-retirement annuity he will receive are usually, next to questions of salary, the most important financial arrangements between an institution and a staff member.

In 1959 Greenough and King published their excellent work, *Retirement and Insurance Plans in American Colleges.** A new edition containing more complete information concerning the retirement provisions for administrators than did the 1959 edition is being prepared by the same authors for publication in the spring of 1969. Both the former and the new edition give details not only of retirement plans with TIAA but also of public systems, arrangements with other life insurance companies, and self-administered plans.

Since the academic community has such a satisfactory source of information about this subject, we limited our study to a few topics. We sought information about provisions governing the retirement age of administrators, whether it was mandatory, and whether, when extensions were allowed, there was an age beyond which these extensions could not go. We asked if the retirement age and post-retirement financial arrangements were the same for the faculty as for the various administrative officers and whether the administrators belonged to the regular faculty annuity plan. We invited administrators to give their judgments as to whether a fixed or a flexible retirement age was better for persons in administrative positions, and we were neither surprised nor unhappy that the comments of many went beyond this limited application. We also asked if a man who left an administrative post

---

* William C. Greenough and Francis P. King, *Retirement and Insurance Plans in American Colleges* (New York: Columbia University Press, 1959).

before the normal faculty retirement age could continue until that age in some other capacity in the same institution.

Related data concerning the length of time persons serve in certain administrative posts and on the tenure status of administrators are given in Chaper 13.

AGE OF RETIREMENT

REGULATIONS GOVERNING AGE OF RETIREMENT. There are four categories into which the regulations governing retirement age may be divided:

1. No stated retirement age.
2. A fixed retirement age with no extensions allowed.
3. A normal retirement age with extensions permitted, with no set upper limit for these extensions.
4. A normal retirement age with extensions permitted, but with a set upper limit to the length of such extensions.

On the surface, 1 and 3 are much akin; but 3 may be administered very loosely permitting administrators to remain in office into their mid-seventies, or the exceptions may be rare and short, in which case 3 may be more restrictive than 4 where the limit of the periods of extension may tend to become the normal retirement age for those who wish to continue in office.

The analysis of replies to questions on the retirement age is complicated. Regulations in private universities are usually more formal than those in private colleges. A higher proportion of public institutions than of private institutions have fixed retirement rules. The arrangements are less frequently stated for the president than for other officers. There is also considerable variation among the replies for other positions, but I believe this reflects the varying frequency of a position among the types of institutions and the reliability of the respondents rather than different treatment of various positions within the same institution, with the exception of those institutions where certain positions come under civil service or are filled by members of a religious order.

Table C indicates the approximate percentage of presidents, librarians, and business officers under the four types of retirement-age provisions listed above. These figures are based on all cases where the responses were complete and hence differ from the figures of Table 17.

TABLE C
Retirement age provisions for three administrative positions; percentage of retirement systems in various categories

	All Institutions			Public Institutions			Private Institutions		
	Total	Univ.	Col.	Total	Univ.	Col.	Total	Univ.	Col.
President									
No stated retirement age	36%	16%	40%	8%	8%	7%	50%	32%	52%
Stated retirement age; no extensions	22	31	20	40	34	44	13	26	12
Stated retirement age with extensions, with no stated limit	18	28	17	18	29	13	19	26	18
Stated retirement age with extensions and stated limit	24	25	23	34	29	36	18	16	18
Librarian									
No stated retirement age	17	6	20	5	4	5	24	12	25
Stated retirement age; no extensions	26	38	23	45	46	45	16	23	16
Stated retirement age with extensions, with no stated limit	17	11	18	8	10	7	22	14	23
Stated retirement age with extensions and stated limit	40	44	39	42	41	43	38	51	37
Business Officer									
No stated retirement age	21	9	24	5	4	6	29	19	30
Stated retirement age; no extensions	25	34	22	46	43	47	14	17	14
Stated retirement age with extensions, with no stated limit	19	15	20	12	11	12	23	23	23
Stated retirement age with extensions and stated limit	35	42	34	38	42	36	34	41	33

Perhaps 15% of the cases are omitted, but their distributions would probably differ only slightly from those included and would not alter the figures in any significant way. The business officers' responses are probably the most accurate of any from the ten positions.

The table indicates the basic similarity of the regulations governing the librarian and business officer and the dissimilarity of the situation of the president from that of either of these two. The data for librarians and business officers are so similar to those for the other seven officers as to make it unnecessary to publish, or even to carry out, such an analysis for each position.

In the cases where there is an established retirement age, with or without extensions, it is 65 in about 60% to 65% of the public institutions and in about 75% to 80% of the private. Most of the rest, especially public institutions, use age 70. For private institutions, nearly as many use age 68 as age 70.

If an institution allows extensions beyond the normal retirement age and sets a limit on these extensions, that limit is age 70 in about three-fourths of the cases. Age 68 is the second most frequent limit, occurring in about half of the remaining cases.

For librarians, as an example: Eleven percent are under systems with a retirement age of 70 or over (mostly 70); and 27% are under systems which, though stipulating an earlier retirement age, allow extensions to 70 or over (again mostly 70). If we add to these figures the 17% under systems with no retirement age and the 17% in systems that allow extensions with no stated upper limit, we find that about three-fourths are in systems that (on the books at least) might allow for service as late as age 70. The same four figures for librarians in public institutions would be 20%, 31%, 5%, and 7%, respectively. These figures are fairly typical except for the president.

It would perhaps be fair to estimate that half of the administrators and half of the professors in American institutions of higher learning, if in good health and if they desire, might remain in their positions until 70. Of course, either the health or the desire is often absent.

A similar analysis for the presidents leads to quite different figures. Here, 11% are in institutions that have a normal retirement age of 70 (or over), and 19% in those that have an earlier normal retirement age but allow retirement extensions to 70 or over. However, 36% are in positions with no stated retirement age, and 18% in positions which allow extensions with no stated upper limit. Clearly, less formalized arrangements are more frequent for presidents than for other administrative officers.

The evidence presented in Chapter 13 shows that the services of most chief administrators in their administrative positions are not terminated by retirements because of age but by taking other positions, most frequently not at the same institution.

COMPARISON WITH REGULATIONS GOVERNING THE RETIREMENT OF FACULTY MEMBERS. Except for the presidents, about 70% of the administrative officers report that they are governed by the same retirement age regulations as are faculty members. The proportion is slightly higher in colleges than in universities and is not markedly different between public and private institutions. In the case of presidents, 60% in public institutions and 50% in private institutions are under the same regulations as the faculty.

In describing the difference between the regulations for the faculty and for the administrators, the most common remark was that the administrators either had a slightly earlier retirement age, at least as administrators, or were granted extensions less frequently than the faculty. In the case of presidents, it was also quite often pointed out that there were no rules governing their positions although there were rules governing the faculty. There are a few instances of terms of administrators being for a fixed number of years, possibly with reappointment. A few persons pointed out that the faculty have tenure while the administrators do not.

The thing I really learned from this question: If you want to sleep well, ask for data from only one person at each institution; your answers will then at least be consistent. Time and again two, sometimes three, and once, I think, four persons in a single institution gave different answers about the regulations that govern their retirements, but said that they were the same as for the faculty.

OPINIONS REGARDING REGULATIONS GOVERNING THE RETIREMENT AGE. We asked each administrator whether he believed in a fixed or in a flexible retirement age for his position. It is interesting that only about 5% did not express opinions on whether the retirement age should be fixed or flexible, whereas about 10% failed to answer the factual question as to whether or not they were governed by rules that govern the faculty. We also asked for the reasons for their opinions. This elicited wide response and resulted in many modifications of the categorical replies "flexible" or "fixed" to the first question. In fact, considering the comments, there were four basic replies—"flexible," "flexible but," "fixed but," and "fixed." I would judge that the two middle classifications were most often approved. The "flexible but" ran somewhat as follows. There should be a normal retirement age beyond which extensions are allowed in unusual circumstances, such as a project in mid-stream which should be finished by the person in charge, great difficulty in finding a successor, or a remarkably vigorous incumbent. The "fixed but" were only slightly stricter, but retirement age is considered fixed and the exceptions rare and on special invitation of the governing board. The sort of exceptions considered were most often for part-time projects. The two "buts" may at times be distinguished only by which preference box the respondent marked. A spectrum cannot really be divided into infrared and ultraviolet.

The number who believed in a flexible retirement age exceeded those who believed in a fixed age. Table 20 summarizes these results. It will be noted that in both public and private universities the majority of presidents, vice presidents, and liberal arts deans believed in a fixed retirement age for administrative officers. This is also true of librarians and business officers in public universities and of vice presidents in public colleges.

As mentioned above, many administrators, I believe most, find that neither "flexible" nor "fixed" really describes their opinions.

The arguments for both flexible and fixed retirement ages are sound; and it is largely the weight that one gives to certain considerations, not their validity, that governs one's conclusions.

Those who advocate a flexible retirement age point to the variable physical and mental conditions of persons at any given age; to the waste of human resources when vigorous persons are not used, and many are vigorous at 65; to the value of experience, if not handicapped by decreasing vitality; to the scarcity of first-class personnel; to the fact that at times certain projects, for instance, a fund-raising campaign, demand completion by the person in charge; to the difficulty in finding a successor; and to other relatively unusual, but not infrequent, circumstances that may make it advisable to retain one person longer than another. Some wish flexibility only to the extent of making it possible to retire some people earlier than usual. A few persons suggest that when retirement is postponed, a physical examination should be compulsory, with its findings available to those considering the matter.

The proponents of a fixed retirement age believe that in practice when flexibility is allowed, decisions often are made on a personal or sentimental basis; that campus politics may enter into the matter; that the exception becomes the rule; and that under a fixed retirement age fewer feelings are injured. Moreover, many say that a fixed retirement age forces both the institution and the individual to plan for the future, and that this is desirable.

New blood, of itself, is considered good; and some advocate terms of fixed length with possible reelection. There was one complaint that younger men were having to overwork to carry the superannuated on their backs.

It is interesting to note that administrators did not discuss the relation of fixed or flexible retirement age to academic freedom, a matter some faculty members stress. Only a few even hinted concerning this.

MY OPINION. If I had to vote one way or another, it would be for a fixed retirement age, not earlier than 68, for all except possibly those in certain administrative positions.

Since the majority of our institutions pattern the retirement provisions for administrators after those for the faculty, the provisions for retirement of faculty members are relevant to this discussion, even if certain modifications in these provisions may at times be made for administrators.

Doctors tell me that man's health and vigor in his later years have probably increased more significantly than his longevity. In the majority of American colleges, 65 has for some while been the normal faculty retirement age, often with extensions possible. If, when these age limits were fixed, 65 could be justified, 68 now could be and still leave a time margin before senility. Some believe that by retaining 65 as a normal retirement age, retiring at that age those who have become or always have been ineffective and extending the services of others, one can have the best of both worlds. I believe the few years of poor service thus eliminated are more than offset by uneasiness and decreased morale on the part of the faculty, as well as by accusations of favoritism, and by the occasional mistakes of judgment that inevitably will be made.

If a retirement system is adequate to provide reasonable economic security for those retiring at some fixed age, say 68 or 70, it is my belief that the institution need pay them no further salary, but should furnish those who wish to work after retirement laboratory and office space, library privileges, and, when a case can be made in the same manner as for a faculty member before retirement, secretarial and research help. Moreover, the institution should be willing to be the agency for the fiscal management of programs involving retired staff members which outside agencies, such as foundations, wish to support. Such provisions, in fact, set up a system of selection, partly self-selection and partly extra-institutional selection.

Given a retirement age of perhaps 68 or 70, reasonable provisions for retirement annuities, and facilities for post-retirement scholarly work, I believe a fixed retirement age is desirable. With the increasing public health, the fixed retirement age should be reviewed regularly with the hope that it can legitimately be made later.

I also believe that administrative officers who hold faculty positions are wise if they relinquish their administrative duties and return to teaching and scholarship before age 68 or 70. Holding a faculty position is much more common for administrative officers, such as the deans of the colleges, the deans of graduate schools, and the deans of students, than for those in other positions. If an institution believes it wise for administrative officers holding certain positions to retire from administration at an age as early as 65, it would seem that it should either provide opportunity for other employment until the normal faculty retirement age or make special annuity provisions for these officers.

There may be a good case for flexible retirement provisions for administrators giving contributed services as members of a religious order which determines what their services will be. With the advent of large lay representation on the boards of these institutions, the strength of the arguments may diminish.

CONTINUATION AS A FACULTY MEMBER

As is to be expected, the assurance that an administrative officer may continue as a faculty member if he retires from administration before the normal retirement age differs greatly among positions. In this regard, as elsewhere, a graduate dean is identified with the faculty; to only a slightly lesser degree so are the dean of liberal arts and the academic vice president. Less than 1% of these are sure that they could not serve on the faculty after leaving administration. Since there are graduate deans only in certain types of institutions, it is wise to compare them with other administrators only within categories of institutions rather than by using total figures. In the majority of cases, presidents and deans of students could remain on the faculty, but a number of presidents indicated they would not desire to do so. A large proportion of administrative officers do not know if they could continue on the faculty; in every position except that of the business officer, these outnumber the persons who are sure they could not remain on the faculty. Some positions are such that faculty appointments for the incumbents might not be appropriate, but other employment in the institution would be possible if they gave up their present functions.

Here, as elsewhere, public institutions have a somewhat clearer status for their employees than do private institutions, the "don't know" answers being in smaller proportions.

COMPARISON WITH FACULTY RETIREMENT PROVISIONS

Table 21 indicates the proportion of administrative officers in each position who belong to the same retirement annuity plans as the faculty.

The overwhelming majority belong to the same plan as the faculty, the figures ranging from 73% for the deans of students to 88% for graduate deans. These figures are particularly striking when one remembers that for many positions in Catholic institutions this question is not relevant because those who contribute their services do not belong to the plan covering the lay faculty but are cared for in their old age by their religious orders and that in some institutions new appointees who may not be covered by the retirement system until after a specified period replied they did not belong to the plan. Moreover, in some cases, officers, especially presidents who are ministers, are allowed to continue with the church plan to which they belong even when the college plan is not the same; and in certain public institutions, officers such as the registrar and business officer belong to retirement systems different from those of the faculties. At some colleges, membership in a retirement plan is optional and a few administrators did not join, sometimes because of other provisions, such as being covered by an army retirement plan. In one instance, a librarian replied, "My husband, being an investor, felt that it was not advantageous in my case."

After taking into account the variations described in the preceding paragraph, there remain a few institutions where there is a different contribution made for some administrators than for faculty. The most frequent of these special arrangements (remembering that any special arrangement is rare) is for the institution to contribute toward an annuity for the president an amount equal to a larger proportion of his salary than the proportion contributed for a professor. The president usually, but not always, makes the same percent contribution that a faculty member does. In a few cases the president is guaranteed a certain percent of his salary as a retiring annuity even when this is not true for faculty members. It should also be remembered that in those instances described in Chapter 2 where an officer is to receive deferred compensation, this is an additional financial protection for his old age.

Considering how often, when a man leaves an administrative position, it seems to him or the institution that it is desirable for him to go elsewhere, the vesting of rights in his annuity plan is of even greater importance to him and to the institution than in the case of a faculty member where indeed it is of major importance.

The subject of retirement annuities for administrative officers in positions that are apt to lead to earlier retirement than for the faculty needs rethinking. This is especially true for the president.

RECOMMENDATIONS

I believe that a good retirement system should satisfy at least three criteria:

1. It should provide for persons to conclude their services in a dignified manner at an age which minimizes both the loss of talent
   through too early retirement and the retention of ineffectiveness
   because of too late retirement. My suggestion is a fixed and relatively late retirement age.
2. The financial provisions should be such that there is no loss in the
   amount of the retirement annuity derived from service already
   performed by a man when he leaves an institution because of either
   early retirement or accepting another job. Moreover, the value of
   this future benefit should be available as a death benefit if a man
   dies before starting his retirement annuity.
3. The retirement annuity should be adequate.

We have discussed the first of these criteria at length and, in the "Reflections" at the end of this chapter, shall present the pros and cons of a fixed retirement age as expressed by administrative officers. The means for providing for the second and third criteria are discussed in detail in Greenough and King, *Retirement and Insurance Plans in American Colleges.*

I wish to stress the importance, especially for administrative officers, of the second criterion. There are few things that are as bad for an institution as an ineffective or dissatisfied administrative officer. A board or an administrative superior will be reluctant to dismiss or even suggest the resignation of an administrative officer if it involves him in large financial sacrifice. A man desiring to leave will hesitate to do so if it jeopardizes his future or that of his family. The money-purchase plans of the type provided by TIAA, which vest both the individual's and institution's contributions in the individual, as well as similar plans provided through other life insurance companies, admirably take care of the matter. There are, however, many formula plans in public systems that provide little, if anything, aside from the man's own deposits to the retirement provisions of a person who leaves relatively early in his career. Such plans are bad for a faculty member, worse for an administrator, and perhaps worst of all for an institution. Some formula plans, though not completely adequate in this regard, do vest in the individual considerably more than the accumulation from his contribution.

There is no way by prepayment for an institution to guarantee adequate retirement allowances for those who retire. Inflation might destroy the value of any such scheme. However, a plan that involves in the neighborhood of 15% of the salary (contributed either jointly by the institution and the individual or by either separately) including Social Security, in which half of the amount not required by Social Security goes into a variable annuity, will (if past experience is a mirror of the future) allow men to retire at around 68 with the expectation of being able to live in a manner to which they are accustomed.

Since the variable annuity, though existing since 1952, is nevertheless too young to have had its full effect and since most institutions have had programs dependent upon contributions well below the 15% mentioned above, many institutions are faced with making special provisions for older staff members, especially for those who will be retiring in the next decade. Administrators not only should initiate such steps but should share in their benefits. These steps should involve either the use of a variable annuity or, if in the form of direct grants, take into account future changes in the cost of living.

A retirement system needs watching; and even if its structure remains unaltered, changing conditions—inflation, longevity, interest rates, and Social Security, for example—will alter its parameters.

REFLECTIONS

FLEXIBLE VERSUS FIXED RETIREMENT AGE

A few votes were paired:

Flexible	*Fixed*
Some old goats are young, and needed.—*Liberal arts dean, public university*	No one's indispensable. Give the kids a chance to bring in new ideas. —*Director of admissions, private university*
Mandatory retirement at a fixed age is an invidious distinction.—*Director of admissions, private college*	To avoid invidious comparisons when some are retained and others not.—*Academic vice president, private college*
Consistency with faculty policy.— *Liberal arts dean, private college*	The administrative personnel is part of the faculty and no differentiation should be made.—*Dean of students, public college*
In Registrar's work, experience is important. Many people are still mentally alert and active at 67. An experienced Registrar can make valuable contributions to an institution.—*Registrar, public university*	You can grow too old to present a proper image to students as Dean of Students.—*Dean of students, private university*
Obvious, I trust.—*Graduate dean, private university*	No particular reason.—*Registrar, private university*

And from the same institution:

Many still mentally and physically able to function as administrators after 65.—*Director of libraries, public college*	My experience has shown that after 65 the capabilities are limited.— *Director of development, public college*

THESE VOTED FOR A FLEXIBLE RETIREMENT AGE

Principles

Ability to perform the work should be the chief criterion for employment. —*Dean of students, public college*

Where excellence and experience are combined, it should be possible to continue to use them.—*Dean of students, private college*

Some individuals, I think, have ceased "growing" many years before the national norm for retirement (age 65); others are still receptive, alive, active at eighty or even ninety. Of those in the latter category, I think students should have the opportunity to benefit from their unique combination of "todayism" with roots in the past.—*Director of libraries, private college*

Every attempt should be made to salvage human resources where available.—*Business officer, private college*

It takes so long to prepare, a man should be permitted to serve as long as possible.—*Graduate dean, public college*

Some men have too much ability, knowledge, experience, and youthful zest to be shelved automatically.—*President, private college*

The institution should have the option and the courage to get rid of tired old men, and *keep* energetic and useful old men.—*Graduate dean, private college*

I do not believe in "fixed" ages for anything; example: six years as the time that all children begin school, or sixty-five as *the* age of retirement.—*Registrar, public college*

Variation of Ability with Age

Generally a man's effectiveness in this work is enhanced yearly by the additional contacts and friendships he makes. It is not affected by age.—*Director of development, private university*

Individual differences in aging and institutional needs are such great variants that arbitrary policy is unintelligent.—*Graduate dean, public college*

The position is unique and individual capacity to fulfill it at various ages is unique as well. Therefore, a fixed retirement age makes little sense unless it is extraordinarily high, e.g. 75.—*President, private college*

The effects of age are not equally felt by all individuals. Frankly, some people should retire at 40—some should never retire!—*Librarian, public college*

Would you have retired Churchill at 65?—*Liberal arts dean, private college*

Senility

Some of these remarks are comforting to this septuagenarian:

Not everyone becomes senile at 65!—*Director of development, private college*

Individuals begin to lose effectiveness at different ages. Some are more senile at 60 than others are at 70.—*Vice president, private college*

Some presidents are both "bright and influential" beyond age 70, while others "lose their marbles" and/or their health earlier than age 65!—*President, private college*

Is difficult to balance sentiment and senility without guidelines.—*Dean of students, private college*

Flexible. Senility is not a constant factor. Administrators should stand for election every so often like politicians.—*Liberal arts dean, private college*

Scarcity of Competence

Trained people are too scarce to use an automatic scale. — *Business officer, private college*

An effective dean is hard to find. As long as he does a good job, keep him. — *Liberal arts dean, private college*

Many of our faculty and staff are in good health at 65. Since they most likely have the Ph.D., they are badly needed to sustain a graduate program which we are beginning. — *Dean of students, private college*

A flexible retirement age could benefit the college especially in the area of retaining doctorates where health and mental alertness permit. — *Director of admissions, private college*

In a small college the services of a capable older man are often badly needed and his continuance is understood. — *Vice president, private college*

Finding a Successor (this was often mentioned)

Eliminate interim appointments. Make selection of successor more flexible. — *President, private college*

Financial Considerations

Until adequate retirement is available, the fixed age of retirement should be flexible. — *Director of development, public college*

I think an option should be open from age 62 on. Possible retirement should bear a direct relationship to social security options. — *Dean of students, private college*

Improving Longevity and Vigor of Population

Mortality tables and changing practices now make age 68 more appropriate than was age 65 when that age was generally adopted. Some deans are highly efficient administrators after age 68. — *Graduate dean, private university*

Life spans are becoming longer, and medical science is now able to keep older people in better health than was once normal. Aging is also an individual matter. Some people are old at 60; others are still vigorous at 72. I should also like to see more experimentation with partial and gradual retirement in academic institutions. — *Librarian, public college*

Medical advances and political experience (cf. Chancellor Erhart of West Germany) strongly suggest flexibility. — *Graduate dean, public college*

Prerogatives of the President and of the Board

Age alone is a poor criteria. Ability and energy vary greatly at different age levels. A mutually advantageous extension of employment should be permissible. It would not require board action, but that of the Chancellor or chief administrative officer. — *Business officer, public university*

Invitation to remain should come from the president, not be initiated by the individual concerned. — *Director of development, private college*

I believe the president of the institution should, in each and every case, have the authority to hire and retain the best talent possible for each position within the university without limitation.—*Director of development, public university*

Board should never tie its hands completely.—*President, public university*

Flexible—In an organized society there must be regulations. In a democratic society there must be procedures to alter regulations so that justifiable exceptions can be made.—*Director of admissions, private college*

Returning to Teaching

I favor required retirement from administration at age 65, but I believe retirement at an earlier age should be possible. Good administrators are also usually good teachers. I believe our finest contribution can be through teaching.—*Librarian, public college*

Some administrators are more effective if continuing as administrators than if going back to teaching.—*Vice president, private university*

One's Personal Position

I am young at 64; others I know are old at 50.—*Director of development, private college*

Certain offices by nature differ from others. There is a great difference in individuals holding offices. It is time for *me* to move at 58.—*Dean of students, private college*

Flexible. This answer is, of course, prejudiced. (1) College benefit. I am still head and shoulders above my replacement in ability, experience, and results produced; and (2) Personal. I created out of chaos. It would be pleasant to enjoy what I sowed, now that we have a good staff and budget, and I am still not senile.—*Librarian, state college*

We're getting too much improvement to break it up; resources trebled in five years.—*President, private college*

Presidents have an elder statesman's role. They can often serve with utility up into their 70's—or am I being prejudiced?—*President, private college* [Age 51.]

Some presidents can give good service until 70, etc. (not me—I'll abide by 65 if I make it that far . . . .)—*President, private college*

Flexibility for Early Retirement

A flexibility to permit early retirement is more likely to be wise and used than is flexibility to permit extension.—*President, public university*

Use of Judgment

1) Many a *good* man could continue his work past a stipulated and admittedly arbitrary age. 2) Many a *poor* man wants to continue past the time when he should retire and is not the best judge—a joint determination is advisable.—*Dean of students, private college*

Fixed age needed so that there is a fair way to eliminate personnel no longer capable. Possibility of extensions desirable to make use of those still judged capable.—*Business officer, private college*

Valid judgments can be made in this area as well as for salary and other areas.—*Liberal arts dean, private college*

Two from Many Miscellaneous Comments

Certain professions—medicine, law, politics—don't require this and can be strong competing professions for bright people.—*Librarian, public university*

Flexible—Is the question pertinent? Officers do not have tenure. They may be retired at will or may assume a faculty teaching position where retirement regulations govern.—*Vice president, private college*

Flexible, But

Term in office also critical. Appointees at age 40 should not serve excessively long terms.—*President, public university*

Should depend on what programs under way should be completed by man who started them. At any rate, should not be on more than a year or so.—*President, private college*

At the option of the University, it can make use of exceptional professional abilities but should be only on an annual basis at the request of the University after reviewing the man's report on health. One-half time or one-fourth time often helps the University as well. Extensions must be used with care.—*Vice president, public university*

A "normal" age, with extensions possible *when needed*, seems to serve best. Needed, of course, by the institution.—*Liberal arts dean, public university*

The physical and mental stability should be the prime factor for retirement. However, I feel that 70 years of age should be mandatory retirement irrespective of ability to perform duties.—*Business officer, private college*

Fixed—Fixed age with reservations is my choice. Stated as: May retire at . . . . Must retire at . . . . —*Business officer, private college*

A Few Last Dicta

Flexible. It would be this way no matter what the rules, if the person is needed.—*Dean of students, private college*

Flexible in small institutions. Rigid in larger institutions.—*Liberal arts dean, private college*

Use as long as useful, then discard.—*President, private college*

Don't shoot a good horse.—*Business officer, public college*

THESE VOTED FOR A FIXED RETIREMENT AGE

Institutional Planning and Morale of Younger Person

A terminal date provides both the institution and the individual an opportunity for appropriate planning.—*Dean of students, public university*

Faculty-Staff morale is measurably improved when definite retirement is foreseen for unpopular administrators. This also requires planning for change which can be put off if retirement age is not firm.—*Director of development, private college*

If definite date is determined, someone can be trained for the job, and a good man will not be lost not knowing when he will have an opportunity to move up. —*Business officer, private college*

1) Need for new blood. 2) Give younger men a foreseeable time when they can expect openings in administration. —*Graduate dean, private university*

To enable younger men to move up. —*Director of development, public university* [Age 33.]

Young Blood is Needed

Change in administration is generally good for an institution. —*Dean of students, private college*

New presidents bring new looks. They prevent errors from becoming permanent. —*President, private college*

There is need to make way for younger men, with a new outlook, unabated energy, and a closer association with the margin of development where the problems are being stated. —*Vice president, public college*

A Fixed Term in Office Desirable

The Board should have the option of continuing a vigorous and alert president beyond retirement age. However, this question misses a more important point: whether any president, no matter how vigorous and alert, is capable of serving effectively in the post beyond a ten- to fifteen-year period. —*President, private university*

Fixed. Colleges should have a change in chief administrative officers at least every 10 years. By the time a president has reached retirement age, he has usually served that length of time and he has probably exhausted his capacity for creative leadership in that situation. —*President, private college*

In general, I believe it is wise for administrators to serve for limited terms (10 years, for example). Setting a retirement limit is the next best way to handle the question. —*Graduate dean, private university*

No man should hold the same administrative position too long. He tends to identify the institution as himself. Hubris is not good for university administrators. —*Graduate dean, private university*

Saves Hurt Feelings

The complications raised by extensions are a hazard to the serenity of the small college. —*Director of development, private college*

Politics and sentiment interfere if policy is flexible. Dangers are charges of favoritism and hurt feelings. —*Dean of students, private university*

Fixed. I was a strong advocate of a flexible policy until, as the person chiefly responsible for administering the policy, I learned first-hand the many problems and heartaches created when decisions to retire individuals against their will had to be made, while others were invited to stay. —*Director of development, private college*

Retirement is always difficult. A fixed age avoids grounds for feelings of rejection, etc. —*President, private college*

In my opinion, failure to extend will be regarded as a rejection of a man at a time when he should feel honored for his years of service. — *Director of development, public college*

A Graceful Exit
A fixed age should be adhered to so that incumbent may leave honorably and not so exhausted that the institution is glad to see him go. — *President, private college*

Easy and graceful exit for those who should retire; and there is room for other services in church and community for those who can still contribute creatively. — *Librarian, private college*

You should leave gracefully while you're still ahead of the game. — *Registrar, private college*

The Board Acts for Wrong Reasons
A flexible retirement age makes retirement dependent on the whim of a superior officer. — *Librarian, private college*

Flexible rules make possible poor decisions due to sentiment, unwillingness of Boards to act, and fear of an entrenched incumbent. — *Director of development, private college*

Good men slow down and are retained because of prior service. — *Vice president, public college*

Trustees will "take easy route" and try to persuade President to remain — contrary to institution's best interests. — *President, private college*

Fixed. Board inclined to grant extensions, though institution's welfare probably requires retirement. I do not hold this opinion regarding faculty retirement, for which extensions are desirable. — *President, public university*

There is a tendency for a flexible policy to be no policy. Positive appointment in a different position avoids this and allows competent person to continue in service. — *Liberal arts dean, public university*

Individual flexibility systems *often* seem to be ineffective and merely raise the retirement age. — *Registrar, public university*

Otherwise sentiment and emotion will interfere with the welfare of the institution, and the ultimate stature of the individual president. — *President, private college*

A Man is a Poor Judge of Himself
Often pressures to stay on are exercised by those who should retire earliest. — *Business officer, private college*

Fixed — Beyond 65, Presidents do not do as good a job as they think they do. *Panta rei.* — *President, private college*

Experience indicates that presidents are not inclined to retire until required to do so. — *President, private college*

Administrators are worse than anyone else about not recognizing their need to retire! — *Liberal arts dean, private college*

Some people don't know when to quit. — *Dean of students, public college*

At What Age

I would prefer a lower retirement age for the dean of students—perhaps 60. For a ten-year period after retirement the Dean of Students could teach or serve as an assistant to a younger person.—*Dean of students, public college*

65 is old enough for an administrator. After this "elder statesmen" roles might be devised, but real power should pass to younger men.—*Liberal arts dean, private college*

Type of responsibility makes beyond 65 hazardous for the school.—*President, private college*

If a president has not completed his program of policies by the age 65, he will never complete it.—*President, private college*

Most deans, probably all, have had their major impact on the institution before age 65.—*Graduate dean, public university*

By age 65, the Development Officer who has really done a job should be too worn out to continue.—*Director of development, private college*

Too much chance for argument about whose time should be extended exists with a flexible retirement age. I am wondering about the magical attributes of age 65. Why not 66, 67, or 68?—*Director of admissions, public college*

But the age should be 68 not 65!—*Librarian, private college*

Anybody should be ready to retire at sixty-eight!—*Graduate dean, public college*

Provided mandated age is not below 70. I can't think of anyone in his right mind wanting to continue these tensions and pressures beyond age 70.—*Registrar, public university*

At present, the mandatory retirement age is 72. I believe this to be the maximum age at which the persons services are valuable to the college.—*Librarian, public college*

Most individuals begin to deteriorate to some degree physically in their seventies and eighties—according to my observations.—*Director of admissions, public university*

Retirement Age for Faculty Members and Administrators

Flexibility for the president would make enforcement of faculty retirement difficult.—*President, private university*

Conviction that experience indicates administrators do not wear as well as faculty after 65.—*Librarian, public university*

Retirement for an administrative position should be 65; however, retirement age for a faculty member should be 70.—*Graduate dean, public college*

Administrator's position is full-time position. Professors may lighten their teaching loads. Position too demanding for one over 65.—*Dean of students, private college*

Should be same as faculty for reasons of amity; almost more important for president to retire on age than for a professor.—*President, private college*

Post-retirement Work

Fixed—Much easier to administer. Some people do not know when to retire; easing them out is a problem. Those whose minds are active usually have other things they would like to do—write, travel, read, relax, take another position that is less exacting or closer to most recent interest, or of an advisory nature.—*Director of development, public college*

If person still productive, he can and should go elsewhere at retirement age. Otherwise what should be exceptional tends to become the rule.—*Director of development, private college*

A good scholar on retirement need not retire from his discipline—only the daily routines of meeting schedules.—*Dean of students, public college*

Financial Considerations

Retirement should be possible at an earlier age than 65, and with an adequate pension.—*President, private college*

I further believe that some system of retirement should be developed so that regardless of the number of years of service, if the man serves beyond a given age, he could retire at at least half his final rate of earnings. A man ought to leave the presidency before there is any serious diminution in his resources in terms of energy and drive, but he may in some cases be obliged to stay longer than he should in order to qualify for a substantial retirement income. He ought not have to cut his standard of living on retirement.—*President, public college*

Some Personal Reactions

No one is quite as good as he thinks he is at retirement. I may, of course, change my mind on this.—*Registrar, private college* [Age 41.]

I favor a fixed age now. I shall favor a flexible age as I grow older.—*Graduate dean, public university* [Age 44.]

Miscellaneous

Our Board controls nine institutions, and there must be a common principle.—*President, public college*

A man trying to prove his right to a position is not a good executive!—*President, private college*

A president who stays on the job lives on inventory from the day he starts on the job. Everybody suffers when he runs out of inventory and if mandatory retirement at a fixed age catches him with some inventory left, so much the better for him, and the institution loses little or nothing.—*President, public university*

Exceptions May Be Made

It is easier to make an exception to a "hard and fast" rule when circumstances really warrant, than to have a flexible regulation that could be very difficult or awkward to apply.—*Liberal arts dean, private college*

Retirement at a fixed age would eliminate any question regarding the matter. If, after retirement, the university and the individual agree that continued service would be in the best interest of both parties, this could be accomplished by rehiring.—*Director of development, public university*

If Board actually needs the services of a president emeritus, the arrangement should be that of consultant.—*President, public college*

Two-year leeway should be granted for convenience of institution only. [Retirement age 65.]—*Dean of students, private college*

Our fixed normal age is 65. I believe that annual extensions should be possible, if advisable, to 70 but not beyond.—*Business officer, private university*

The expectation should be retirement at a fixed age to avoid the problems created by a *stated* discretion. The Board should have an implicit discretion.—*President, private college*

Some Dicta

Fixed—Persons beyond a certain age are usually too opinionated to be flexible enough for this position.—*Business officer, public university*

Administrators are peculiarly susceptible to ossification.—*Liberal arts dean, private college*

Fixed. The President's office is not the place for old men.—*President, public university* [Age 73.]

Deans dry up.—*Liberal arts dean, private college*

Standard reason . . . only way to remove us.—*Business officer, private college*

A specified retirement age also prevents interference of personal feeling about the older men who want to stay on and no one wants to tell them they cannot have an extension of time.—*Registrar, public university*

While it is probably true that good men should not retire at 65, it is also true that a mandatory retirement age is an indispensable protection against incompetence and autocracy.—*President, private college*

And this man did not vote:

I am too close; I have no perspective on this problem.—*Librarian, private college* [Age 65.]

One questionnaire was answered by an assistant who believed that his chief should have been retired.

REFERENCES TO APPENDIX

Questionnaire, Section D.

Summary Tables 17–21.

CHAPTER 4

LIFE INSURANCE

WE asked administrators whether they were covered by a group life insurance plan and, if so, whether it was the same plan that covered the faculty. We also inquired as to whether they were covered by travel accident insurance to which the institution contributed and if the institution contributed to any other type of life insurance for them.

GROUP LIFE INSURANCE

PARTICIPATION. By far the most important means by which life insurance is provided by the institution for the administrator is through participation in plans of faculty group life insurance. Roughly 80% of the universities, both public and private, 60% of private colleges, and somewhat over 50% of public colleges have a life insurance plan covering the faculty in which administrative officers almost always participate. It must be remembered that Catholic colleges may have a faculty insurance plan that does not cover religious personnel and that some plans have a waiting period; hence, the proportion of institutions with group life insurance plans is probably a little above the proportion of administrators covered by such plans.

Group plans are normally required by law to cover a certain proportion (frequently 75%) of the eligible group. For this reason, they are often compulsory for personnel employed after the initiation of the plan. A large institutional contribution naturally encourages its acceptance; paying the total contribution ensures it.

TYPES OF GROUP PLANS. Most of the group insurance plans are for term insurance, some with a residue—often paid-up—continuing for the individual's life. The more important types are described below:

1. *Insurance with Fixed Benefits.* This plan, usually on a term basis modified to provide for decreasing insurance after a given age, is used

quite frequently, sometimes as a floor beneath a collective insurance program or some other type of decreasing insurance. Often it is the relic of a long-established system that has not been brought up-to-date, the amount of benefit sometimes being as little as $2,000. (I almost used the spelling "relique" as appropriately archaic for such insurance.)

I do not recommend this type.

2. *Benefits Proportionate to Salary.* This plan is in common use, especially in public institutions. The multiples used go from about one-half to two-and-a-half times salary. Where the benefit is more than the salary, there is frequently an upper limit (often necessitated by state insurance laws), such as a benefit of twice the salary with a limit of $40,000. When established, these limits usually affected very few persons and those only slightly; but as salaries have risen they have become more important, especially in the president's case. Since one of the strong arguments for this plan is that it keeps up with inflation, it is unfortunate to have outdated checks upon this inherent advantage. A rather interesting example of such a plan in a public institution starts with a benefit of one-and-a-half times salary at age 21, rising to two-and-a-half times salary for ages 35 to 50, and then decreasing until it is equal to salary for ages 60 to 65. (This would be a rather generous plan if it were not limited by legislation, in this particular case to a maximum benefit of $20,000. Moreover, its greatest impact is later in life than it should be.)

Many institutions using a plan dependent on salary still provide for decreased insurance after a given age and a paid-up residue for life. Of course, many institutions use a bracket system for their benefits instead of an exact multiple of salary. In some cases, the amount of insurance depends on rank, and in others on salary and length of service.

Sometimes, unfortunately, there are waiting periods after the start of employment before coverage is effective; these may range up to five years.

3. *Collective Life Insurance.* The following quotation from Greenough and King, *Retirement and Insurance Plans in American Colleges* (p. 116) describes collective life insurance:

Under collective life insurance the covered staff member receives an individual life insurance policy. Collective life insurance is issued without medical examination to cover all or designated groups of a college's staff members. It provides decreasing term insurance, thus concentrating the greatest amount of protection at the younger and middle ages. The premium for each participant's insurance remains the same from year to year, and the protection, at any age, is the amount of one-year term insurance purchased by the premium for that year. Dividends as declared are applied as additional insurance protection for each participant. If the employee leaves the institution he may continue his policy in force on his own until it expires at age 70.

Nearly all institutions that use this form of insurance secure it from TIAA. Dividends have markedly increased the benefits until they are now practically twice the guaranteed amount. This insurance is sold in units for which about a dollar a month per unit is paid. The benefit decreases with age, approximately in inverse proportion to the mortality rate at each age, the guaranteed amount for one unit being $5,860 at age 25, $4,480 at age 35, $3,040 at age 40, decreasing to $330 at age 65. An institution may arrange for one or more units to cover a given group; but, of course, if varying numbers of units are used, they must be in accordance with an established rule not adversely selective as to mortality risks. The number of units may vary with the individual's salary, but not with his state of health. Some institutions with this plan use as high as eight units, which is the maximum currently allowed. A number of institutions use this type of insurance combined with an insurance for either a flat amount or an amount proportionate to the individual's salary.

Collective life insurance makes a lot of sense. It dovetails admirably with fully vested annuity plans where the accumulated contributions are available as death benefits in case of death before retirement.

There is one drawback. There is no built-in adjustment to inflation unless the number of units depends on salary.

Other forms of group insurance are not only variations and modifications of the above types, but frequently combinations of them.

In spite of the length of the questionnaire, we did not ask for enough details to discover the full picture of how the amounts of benefits are determined. The new edition of Greenough and King will give much information on this matter.

A sample of the replies to the questionnaire for the current study indicates that in nearly half the cases salary is involved in the benefit formula, that in somewhat under a quarter of the cases collective insurance is used as a portion or as the whole of the program; and that the principle of the insurance decreasing with age is observed in many

other cases, including a large number of those based on salary. Some
flat component is often included, but a strictly flat amount is seldom
used except in cases where, by present standards, this amount of
insurance is almost nominal.

The number of institutions with a mixture of types is great, sometimes as a result of new programs having been added to those already
in existence and sometimes due to a clearly conceived plan. A number
of plans take marital status into consideration; a very few also cover
the lives of the wives of faculty members, and sometimes the lives of
their minor children.

Although we did not ask for data on who pays for group life
insurance, we received a good deal of information on the subject.
Several arrangements are in use, including: all premiums being paid
by the institution; the institution sharing the cost of premiums with
individuals; or, the individual paying the whole cost. One plan calls
for the individual to pay a flat amount, or a flat amount per $1,000 of
insurance, with the institution making up the difference. This may
result in a young man paying the entire annual cost, or even more than
the entire annual cost, of his insurance, while the older person pays a
minor fraction of the expenses incurred for his coverage.

CONCLUSIONS AND RECOMMENDATIONS CONCERNING GROUP LIFE INSUR-
ANCE. It is desirable for an institution to recognize its stake in the
welfare and peace of mind of its staff members and of their dependents to the extent of establishing and contributing to group life insurance for them. There are tax advantages in the institution paying the
full cost of such insurance. However, group insurance has advantages
for the faculty not dependent on contributions by the institution. The
premiums of group insurance, because of lower sales costs, are less
than those for individual insurance. The medically poor risks will be
covered. The morale of the community is enhanced.

I recommend that an institution provide group life insurance
for its faculty; that this insurance be dependent on salary but with age
be a decreasing multiple of salary; that it be independent of length of
service, marital status, or rank; that it may be continued on an individual basis at as near the same premium as possible if a member leaves
the group; and that administrators be included in the group. (For that
matter, I believe the whole full-time staff should be included.) My
first choice of type would be collective life insurance with a number of
units sufficient to give at age 35 a coverage (when dividends are

included) of approximately twice salary. This would be accomplished (considering dividends) if there were three units of TIAA collective insurance for those under $12,000 salary; four units for salaries from $12,000–$16,000; five units for salaries from $16,000–$20,000; and so on. This would give a coverage about equal to salary at age 43 and to about one-half of salary at age 50. In some cases such a schedule is approximated in other forms of group insurance by a formula based on salary and age. If the institution itself does not have a retirement plan with substantial death benefits at the older ages, the insurance program should provide greater benefits and decrease less rapidly than the one just indicated.

Of course, an institution should review its program frequently, remembering that if salaries increase 7% a year as they have recently been doing, insurance benefits should be doubled about every decade to keep pace.

NON-GROUP LIFE INSURANCE

Table 25 indicates the percent of institutions that provide insurance, other than group life or travel accident insurance for their administrative officers. It must be understood that in most of these cases it is in addition to a group plan, but in some it is the only life insurance provided by the institution. In a few cases a general plan, but not technically a group plan, may have been described in these responses. It should be noted that for most positions universities are more likely to provide non-group insurance than are colleges, and private institutions more than public. In private colleges, the president is more likely to be covered by this insurance than are the other college officers; this is not true in private universities or in public institutions.

The average amount of non-group insurance, when it exists, is very much larger for presidents than for other officers. In the case of presidents it is about $70,000, the next highest coverage being for business officers and development officers who average about $20,000. In the case of presidents, the highest amount was a "keyman" insurance of $1,100,000, with the wife as beneficiary to the extent of $100,000 and the institution to receive $1,000,000 in case of his death.

Sometimes making special provisions to protect the dependents of a key person, such as the president, if he comes to the institution without substantial vested rights in a retirement plan, would seem to be justified.

A number of institutions, 3% of the total, take out life insurance on the president with the institution as beneficiary. I do not understand the logic of this type of lottery, unless the trustees believe that they are working the president so hard that he is an especially poor risk. If an able administrator dies, the institution suffers a loss in educational leadership but it does not, in general, incur expenses; in fact, the interim substitute often receives a lower salary than the president he replaces. It is true that in the midst of a financial campaign the loss of a president might result in reduced income for the institution, but the amount of insurance would scarcely be commensurate with such problematic and undeterminable damages. The number of officers other than the president for whom the institution is the beneficiary is negligible.

TRAVEL ACCIDENT INSURANCE

About half of our institutions either provide travel accident insurance for administrators (see Table 23) or reimburse them for the cost of such insurance. Provision of this type of insurance is more common in universities than in colleges, and in private institutions than in public. Only a small proportion, around 5%, of public institutions will reimburse an individual for the cost of travel accident insurance, while nearly a third of the private ones do so. (I'm afraid that this questionnaire has been expensive for a few institutions since the idea of reimbursements for the cost of travel insurance seemed to a number of persons to be new, possible, and happy.)

As should be expected, the officers by whom the greatest amount of traveling is done—the presidents, the directors of development, the admissions officers, and the chief business officers—are more often covered by travel insurance than are the other officers.

The variation in the amount of this insurance is wide, but not as markedly great between positions as in the case of keyman life insurance. For all positions, except the president and graduate dean, it averages—if it exists—from about $50,000 to $65,000; the average for presidents and graduate deans is slightly above $70,000. For all positions (usually also for all types of institutions) the ninth decile is at $100,000.

Within a position (president, vice president, etc.) the higher the salary, the greater the probability that an individual is covered by a travel accident policy provided by the institution.

In about 13% of institutions providing travel accident insurance for their presidents, the institution is the beneficiary. This represents about 4% for all institutions. For other positions this practice is of little significance.

The reasons for travel accident insurance are chiefly psychological. Death while traveling causes no greater financial crisis to a man's family than other forms of death. However, the working schedule of an administrator may be such that he must travel a great deal and he, or his institution, usually believes that air travel is necessary. If either in reality or in his wife's opinion this is a more dangerous form of travel than other ways (certainly any travel involves risks not incurred on the campus), there is apt to be a sense of injustice if the institution fails to afford special protection for the families of those it requires to take special risks. This often can be removed by providing travel accident insurance. It might be more logical to pay for more general life insurance for the individual, but this would be more expensive and would invite more green-eyed comparisons. Moreover, we must also remember that a privilege, even one that does not make too much sense, if it is customary, has negative comparative value when withheld.

ACCIDENTAL DEATH AND DISMEMBERMENT

Under a number of life insurance policies, both group and individual, there is double indemnity for accidental death or dismemberment. I have never understood why a person needs more insurance if he dies from falling off a ladder than if his heart stops while climbing a mountain. The dismemberment provisions may have served a limited purpose before the development of major medical insurance and disability insurance. It no longer seems the way to care for such needs. It is too bad that such a fine product as insurance is sold by gimmicks.

REFERENCES TO APPENDIX

Questionnaire, Section E.

Summary Tables 22–25.

CHAPTER 5

FINANCIAL PROVISIONS
DURING DISABILITY

THE financial provisions made for administrators during disability include:

a) short-term disability (generally cared for by sick leave although occasionally by group insurance; sometimes this is the start of a long-term disability).

b) long-term disability, largely covered, if at all, by group disability insurance or by the disability provisions of public retirement systems as well as, in most instances, by Social Security. This subject will be covered in the new edition of Greenough and King, *Retirement and Insurance Plans in American Colleges.*

SHORT-TERM DISABILITIES

Very few officers reported that they would not receive salary during short-term absences from work due to illness, and about 10% did not respond to this question, often, I presume, because they had never taken the trouble to discover the facts. I believe that some of the few who reported that they would not be paid during a short illness are covered by short-term disability group insurance, some may be in error, and some may be cared for by some agency other than the institution.

Although almost all persons would receive salary during short absences due to illness, institutions differ sharply in the degree of formality of the rules on this matter. Not far from 60% of the plans (70% for presidents) are classified as informal; however, half of the public institutions have formal arrangements, while only about one-fourth of the private institutions do. It must be remembered that in many formal plans which guarantee salaries during a specified period of illness there are provisions for discretionary extensions of such payments.

Only about half of those who stated they were covered by formal plans gave quotable answers as to how long they would receive salary while ill. This is not surprising considering that many of these plans regulate the length of sick leave by the length of previous service by the individual. In addition, many officers, being well, do not bother to find out what would happen to them if they became ill. The range of answers was large. Certain institutions provide for less than three weeks of sick leave; but over one-third of those who stated the length of formal sick leave would be entitled to a half year or more. In this respect I believe gossip as much as I believe formal replies, and I would judge that by extensions, failure to report illnesses when colleagues care for the work, and various laudable shenanigans, the actual workings of the plans are more generous than the stated rules. Moreover, informal plans are apt to be more generous than formal ones. This is perhaps why at many institutions there have been no major drives to formalize their sick-leave plans. I would estimate that at least half of the administrative officers would have their salaries continued for an illness lasting up to six months.

About 8% of our administrative officers are covered by short-term disability insurance. This may be used to supplement inadequate sick-leave provisions and also to dovetail with long-term disability insurance.

LONG-TERM DISABILITIES

Between a third and a half of our institutions had in 1966 a formal plan for income during long-term disability, the figures being slightly higher for public institutions than for private. (The number then considering plans would indicate that the figures would now be considerably larger.) In public institutions, the majority of these plans are a part of the public retirement system, about 20% are with commercial companies, and about 10% with TIAA. There is a sizable scattering of other arrangements. The majority of plans of private institutions are with TIAA, and about a quarter are with other companies.

Since TIAA pioneered in this field and many of the other satisfactory plans are copied after their plan, a short description of it follows. There are minor, but for some institutions important, exceptions to a few of my statements.

A long-term disability, for the purpose of TIAA long-term disability insurance, is one that has existed for six months and is such that the employee is unable "by reason of sickness or bodily injury, to engage in any occupation for which the employee is reasonably fitted by education, training or experience." There are certain exclusions to rule out the results of war, pregnancy, and self-inflicted injury as well as disability resulting from pre-existing injury or illness developing during the first year the plan is in effect. The benefits selected in most plans are the continuation of 60% of the first $1,000 of monthly salary and 40% of the next $1,000 until age 65, and the payments of the premiums toward a retirement annuity available at age 65 at the premium rate existing before disability. For slight extra cost, it is possible to provide that the benefits, both salary and premium continuation, increase 3% a year, thus forming a hedge against inflation. Since the cost of such insurance depends on the composition of the group as to age, sex, and salary distribution, it will vary from institution to institution, and from year to year for a given institution. However, it is much less than many seem to believe, generally being between .4% and .6% of the payroll for those covered, and even less if the desirable 3% annual increase of benefits is omitted. A fuller description is given in the TIAA pamphlet entitled *Group Total Disability Benefits Insurance.*

There are few, if any, disability plans in use by American colleges or universities superior to the TIAA program. Some of the variations from it include:

1. Different benefits, usually smaller.
2. Longer periods of employment before coverage is available. These frequently range from 5 to 15 years.
3. The amount of benefits dependent in part on length of service.
4. Other, sometimes stricter, definitions of disability in some instances involving expected permanency.
5. Payment for only a limited number of years.
6. The continuation of benefits for life rather than to a fixed age when the retirement annuity becomes available. Under some plans, this gives little protection to dependents.
7. The integrating of the system with Social Security so that the plan pays the individual less by the amount or part of the amount he receives from Social Security.

Almost all the comments concerning the TIAA plan were favorable. Many wanted to establish such a plan and others wanted to shift to it. The only complaints I remember were in regard to the size of the benefits, stating that for those with moderate salaries the benefits should be larger. Some of the public plans are quite satisfactory, although many are not; even those with good benefits often require too long a waiting period before coverage becomes effective. Some private companies have imitated the TIAA plan, at times adding a few sales "come-ons."

It should be noted that TIAA started this plan with few precedents and estimated that the cost would be greater than experience proved to be the case. The unexpected savings, of course, resulted in lower costs.

A considerable proportion of the institutions pay the full cost of this insurance. There are tax and accounting considerations that make this a good way of giving a minor, across-the-board salary increase.

In nearly half of the public and in about 15% of the private institutions without TIAA disability insurance, the duration of benefits depends on length of prior service. About one-third of the non-TIAA plans continue premiums toward the retirement annuity, the private institutions running a little above the public in this regard.

More than three-fourths of the administrative officers are covered by Social Security. Excluding those in religious orders, and ministers, and those who elected not to be covered at the times the plans were initiated, I would estimate that almost 90% of the officers are covered.

Some respondents mentioned the protection afforded by workmen's compensation insurance, but more forgot this important protection. A considerable number reported the use of individually secured long-term disability insurance; some of these appear to be in group insurance plans outside the institution.

RECOMMENDATIONS

I recommend that:

1. Institutions participate in TIAA disability insurance with the option providing 3% annual income in benefits or in a program as similar to it as their circumstances will allow, being sure to keep the waiting period as short as possible and to provide not only lifetime income to the individual but also protection to his dependents after his death. This protection is afforded in the TIAA plan through the

continuation of annuity premiums and through the options available for these annuities.

2. Either by formal arrangement or by understood policy, salary be continued during short-term illness at least up to the time when long-term disability insurance becomes effective.

3. The institution follow a policy that treats generously those few administrative officers who become ill or disabled in the period before they are eligible for the institution's disability insurance plan. (It is only the subject of this report that keeps me from making similar recommendations in regard to faculty and other staff members.)

4. Employees of American educational institutions be covered by Social Security. The mobility of academic personnel, if nothing else, makes uniformity in this respect desirable.

REFLECTIONS

SICK LEAVES

I have been neither ill nor disabled, but my impression is that fair arrangements are made on an informal basis.—*Dean of students, private college*

. . . I am aware of a recent situation which was most unfair and unjust to a long-term employee who became ill for a period of four months. It was only because of great pressure that the man was continued on the payroll. There should be a formally announced program so that every employee, of any rank, knows what his status will be at all times during illness or disability . . . .—*Director of development, private college*

Reasonably adequate, but I would like to have a longer basic sick leave allowance at full pay. We are limited to twelve days a year, non-cumulative.—*Librarian, private university*

After the first six months there is a period of six months at half pay. I believe both periods are much too short.—*Dean of students, public college*

Institution has cumulative sick leave plan. This is adequate for short-range illnesses but once the leave is exhausted, it is the person's responsibility.—*Dean of students, public college*

Informal, but generous based upon experiences of faculty members recently suffering extended illness.—*Graduate dean, public college*

Poor, at least because of lack of stated policy.—*Director of development, private college*

Short-term disability should be covered for 6 months to dovetail with TIAA long-term disability.—*Business officer, private college*

They appear adequate. The present administration has consistently demonstrated a most humane and kindly attitude in cases of faculty illnesses. Substitutes are hired and every effort made to assist those ill. Frequently this attitude has exceeded formal or official positions.—*Graduate dean, public college*

LONG-TERM DISABILITY PROVISIONS

Present Plans

Arrangements for short-term disability are adequate. Since there are no arrangements for long-term disability, the provisions are, of course, totally inadequate.—*Librarian, public university*

I believe the arrangements are quite adequate, if one has long service in the state system. To induce presidents to come in from out-of-state, special provisions for counting prior experience elsewhere should be developed.—*President, public college*

I am not clear on the long-term problem. Frankly, I have never asked nor given it much thought.—*Registrar, private university*

I am satisfied with short-term arrangements. Believe the institution should make some type of provision for long-term arrangements.—*Graduate dean, public university* [NOTE FROM PRESIDENT: Dean . . . seems not to have learned about the University's TIAA long-term disability insurance plan.]

Excellent.—*Liberal arts dean, private college* [The institution has the TIAA plan.]

The institution makes no deduction from pay of faculty member (or president) for short-term illness. TIAA provision for long-term is reasonably adequate.—*President, private college*

The long-term disability is really disability retirement. This benefit requires at least 10 years service. It is considered liberal if the 10-year eligibility is established.—*Business officer, public university*

Personnel Provisions

I have made such provision for myself through the American Library Association Group Insurance Plan for members. This arrangement, at least for me, has the advantage that I can maintain it in a position-change situation . . . .—*Librarian, private college*

Not applicable. If a man is disabled, the religious order provides for him. This is done, of course, with funds of the order completely apart from college finances.—*President, private college*

Quite adequate; based on fact I am retired General Officer with over thirty-four years military service.—*President, private college*

O.K. I don't believe in becoming sick or disabled.—*Liberal arts dean, public university*

Need for Plan

There is a weakness here—nine-day sick leave policy is generally adequate and the institution generally would go further—but in case of a long-term illness or disability, our lot would not be good—it would be well to have some provision for this eventually.—*Business officer, private college*

Plan is good and adequate for an employee who has considerable tenure in position. In early years while just getting started disability benefits are inadequate . . . .—*Business officer, public college*

Disability is now a greater risk for the family than death. It is the major financial concern left.—*Vice president, public college*

Our disability benefits are not adequate. Staff members continue on the job even after they can offer little service.—*Director of development, public college*

Cost

Disability income is not provided. It would be a desirable benefit. However, such a benefit would not be feasible unless the institution bore a large share of the cost. Salary deductions are becoming burdensome.—*Director of development, public university*

For long-term disability I don't believe a private university can afford a plan to cover periods in excess of one year, through an insured or self-funded plan.—*Dean of students, private college*

Provisions for long-term illness are considered inadequate. The University has not formally dealt with this problem because of cost.—*Business officer, private university*

The low premium cost of TIAA permanent disability insurance for a group would be a desirable addition.—*Business officer, private college*

Type of Plan Desired

Present plan seems inadequate. A plan based on years of service and annual salary at time disability occurs would seem more to be desired.—*Librarian, private college*

Long-range disability coverage could be higher than the 60%, first $1,000 base.—*Librarian, private college*

Income for young family men should be greater than for man and wife or single member.—*Director of development, private college*

Could be and should be related to increasing cost of living or the dollar index.—*Vice president, private college*

Future Plans

Room for improvement but would have to be done at a statewide university basis and not institution by institution.—*Business officer, public college*

A formalization of our disability plan is proposed for 1966–67. The proposed plan will be TIAA or equivalent.—*Business officer, private college*

REFERENCES TO APPENDIX

Questionnaire, Sections I and J.

Summary Tables 39–40.

CHAPTER 6

HEALTH PROTECTION

WE inquired of administrative officers concerning the various health services available to them through their institutions, and whether or not these were free. We asked if periodic physical examinations were required and if the information derived from them was available to the administration of the institution. We requested information about the coverage of administrative officers by basic group insurance, such as Blue Cross and Blue Shield, and by group major medical insurance. We inquired as to who paid for such coverage, both for the individual administrator and for his dependents. Finally, we afforded an opportunity for individuals to suggest means which "ought to be taken by a college or university to promote the continuing good health of a person with your responsibilities."

To all these inquiries, including the last, we secured a high percentage of responses.

HEALTH SERVICES

PERIODIC PHYSICAL EXAMINATIONS. About 10% of our principal administrative officers reported that their institutions provide for periodic physical examinations for them. The figures run somewhat below this in public institutions. Private universities provide these examinations in a higher percent of cases than do private colleges or public institutions. One-third of the presidents of private universities report such arrangements. In a handful of institutions, about 3% or 4%, these examinations are required of the administrative officers. In a slightly greater number, the information from physical examinations is available to the institution. In more than half of the instances for every position where these examinations are provided, the institution pays for the examination. In the case of several positions, including the president's, this figure is over 70%. The public colleges pay for the

examinations least frequently. We must remember, however, that because of the small number of institutions where provision is made for
periodic examinations (even though most of these are paid for by the
institution) the number providing free examinations is small, ranging
from about 5% to 10% depending on the position concerned. No
cross-check was made to discover what proportion of the required
examinations was free. Probably it is rather large.

There is a distinctly greater tendency for there to be arrangements
for periodic physical examinations in large institutions than in small,
ranging from none for presidents in public institutions below an
enrollment of 1,000 to over 10% in public institutions above 10,000
and from 12% in private institutions below 1,000 to 31% in private
institutions above 10,000.

DOCTOR'S CONSULTATION. About 60% of the institutions have facilities, mostly for students, for doctor's consultation. In about 45% of
these cases this service is available to the administrator, and when
available, is free in about 50% of the instances. Thus, about 14%
(.60 × .45 × .50) of the institutions provide free doctor's consultation
for administrative officers. In the case of the president, the service is
available more frequently and free more often, so that about 20% of
the presidents are provided with free doctor's consultation.

Although a doctor's consultation service is present for students as
frequently in public institutions as in private, it is not as often available or free, to the administrative officers in as large a percent of
public as of private institutions. In all these respects, the proportions
are higher in private universities than in other types of institutions.
Hence, only 13% of presidents in public universities and 16% in
public colleges have doctor's consultation available at no charge,
while 22% of the presidents in private colleges and 38% in private
universities have this privilege.

EMERGENCY MEDICAL TREATMENT. The availability of emergency
medical treatment is more important than who bears the cost. Here
there is little discrimination between positions. A little over 75% of the
institutions have provisions for emergency medical treatment, and in a
little under 80% of these cases it is available to the administrative
officers; thus, in somewhat over 60% of the institutions the administrative officers have this protection—although registrars seem less aware
of it than others.

This service is more usual in large institutions than in small ones.

REGULAR MEDICAL TREATMENT. Unlike emergency treatment, where immediacy is the prime consideration, in regular medical treatment the cost is of major importance. It is true that when the university has a medical school or when a college has the best medical service in a small town, the quality of the treatment may loom large; but in most cases the lower cost of the treatment through the medical services of the institution and its convenience are the chief factors. From 4% of vice presidents, graduate deans, and admissions officers, up to 8% of deans of students and 9% of presidents reported that free regular medical treatment was provided. In about 15% of the cases (about 17% for deans of students and presidents) service was available, either free or with a charge. Presumably the charge is often somewhat less than it would be elsewhere.

The variation with size of the institution is not marked, but the private institutions are more likely to make these services available to administrators and provide them free somewhat more often than do the public institutions. It is perhaps a general rule that private institutions can encroach on private enterprise with greater impunity than can the public institution. It is certain that in many instances members of the local medical profession resent use by the staff of regular medical services furnished by the institution, though I do not know of any opposition to emergency treatment.

INFIRMARY BEDS. It would seem that somewhat under half of our institutions have infirmary beds. About one-fourth to one-third (varying with their positions) of the administrative officers in institutions with infirmary beds may use them, though the proportion is considerably less than this in public institutions. In somewhat under 10% of all institutions infirmary beds are available and free to administrative officers, though this is less often true in universities than in colleges, and in public institutions than in private.

MEDICAL GROUP INSURANCE. Since this is group insurance, we may assume that when the institution provides it for administrative officers the privilege is shared by the faculty, although occasionally certain officers may belong to the same insured group as the clerical staff.

In many Catholic institutions administrators who belong to a religious order or who are priests are cared for by the order or the church and do not participate in a plan which covers the faculty.

BASIC INSURANCE. From 85% to 92% of the administrators, depending on their positions, are eligible for Blue Cross, Blue Shield, or some other plan of basic hospital-surgical-medical insurance carried through the institution. The lower figures are for those positions which have a higher instance of religious administrators—chiefly Catholic, but sometimes Protestant ministers covered by a church plan. Because of this, institutional coverage is more complete in public than in private institutions. The incidence of expense differs slightly from position to position, but greatly by type of institution. About 5% of public institutions pay the total cost; about 25% of private institutions do so. Of the private institutions which do not pay the full cost of this insurance, about half share the cost with the individual and in about half the cost is borne by the individual. The cost of covering dependents is shared by the institution and the individual in about a fourth of the cases and borne by the individual in almost all other instances in public institutions. About 7% of private institutions bear the full cost of the dependent coverage.

MAJOR MEDICAL INSURANCE. In my judgment this protection against those medical expenses which may be catastrophic to one's personal budget is more important than the basic insurance which to a much greater extent meets expenses that could be planned for by the individual. The record of our institutions in arranging for major medical group insurance for their faculties and administrative officers, though good, is not as good as it should be. For most positions, the percent covered by major medical insurance runs from 75% to 80% of the officers. To a greater extent than in the case of basic medical insurance, the institution either pays for the insurance or shares in its cost; for instance, of the 88% of business officers covered by basic insurance, only 19% have it paid for wholly by the institution, whereas of the 78% of the business officers covered by major medical insurance, 33% have it paid for by the institution. Thus, 17% of the business officers receive free basic insurance and 26% free major medical insurance. Major medical insurance is more prevalent in public institutions than in private, but only a small fraction of the public institutions meet its total cost, and a somewhat lesser proportion of public than of private institutions share in the cost. In considering all of the above figures, it should be remembered that there are a number of institutions with one or more religious officers whose medical care is provided for in other ways.

An excellent discussion of the desirable provisions of a major medical insurance plan is published by TIAA in a pamphlet entitled *Group*

Insurance for Major Medical Expenses. I would like to emphasize a few points: (*a*) There should be no—or only a short—waiting period before a new staff member becomes eligible for the plan. (*b*) The upper limit of expenses covered should be high. This adds little to the cost but much to the protection in the rare case where insurance is particularly needed. (*c*) The cost should be kept down by a "deductible" threshold and by the individual paying a portion of the total expense, for even in the academic world the free-rider is not unknown. (*d*) Some extension of the insurance into the post-retirement period should be provided.

At the time our questionnaire was sent out, Medicare was not available. (Soon thereafter I was in the throes of proving that my wife was as old as she claimed, of even proving that she was born at all.) It is, of course, important that any major medical plan be dovetailed with Medicare to provide complete protection while avoiding double benefits for overlapping coverage. It seems quite possible that continuous adjustments to federal medical-care programs will be in order for some time to come.

SUGGESTIONS BY ADMINISTRATORS

As mentioned above, administrative officers were invited to suggest measures they believe ought to be taken to promote their continuing good health. The invitation was accepted by a large proportion of respondents. The flavor of these suggestions is given later through quotations, but I will comment briefly upon them here.

Among the most frequently given suggestions were periodic physical examinations and relief from the pressure of overwork.

A very large number believe that provisions for periodic examinations, usually annually, are desirable. Many believe these examinations should be required; some specify that the resulting information should be available to the institutions while others wish it to be confidential. Almost all believe that the service should be free, or at least provided at a cost less than the usual doctor-hospital charge. It is probable that the rather detailed questions concerning physical examinations stimulated some of the thinking in regard to this matter. Many respondents would like other medical services, either free or at reduced cost. The desirability of free "shots" is often suggested. Moreover, the problems of dental and optometrical care are listed by some.

Administrators realize that they are badly overworked. To alleviate the situation, many of them advocate more adequate vacation provisions, recognizing that the present provisions are often not fully used; forced vacations are often recommended. But vacations are not the only solution. Many point out that more adequate clerical help and staffing to make delegation of duties feasible are needed before the tension of overwork can be relieved or vacations taken.

On the theory, I presume, that any irritation is bad for the health, this rubric was used to promote cherished reforms or to plead for the eradication of pet peeves.

It was also the heading under which a considerable number of persons declared their annoyance with the tendency of institutions to take over responsibilities that they held should be those of the individual and also their opposition to any further steps in this direction.

RECOMMENDATIONS

1. I believe that the most important step that many institutions should now take in regard to health programs for the administrative personnel is to provide major medical insurance.

2. The question of periodic medical examinations is not easy to deal with. I do not believe that it should be required as often as once a year, especially during the younger ages. Constant attention to one's health is not the surest way of protecting it. If a physical examination is required, it should be free. Moreover, it would seem only fair that if physical examinations are free, their results should be available to the administration. Some of the objections to a policy of shared information which (considering how easily faculty-administrative tensions may be created) apply to the faculty should not apply in the case of administrative officers. I find myself rather ambivalent on this question; but if I had to vote at this moment, I would require administrative officers to have a physical examination, as detailed as the doctor recommends, once every two years, with the information available to the president, or in his case to the chairman of the board. These examinations should be free, and when deemed necessary, given more frequently than once in two years.

3. Emergency medical treatment should be available to the staff.

4. Whatever medical services are furnished to the students should be available to the staff, but the question of charges must be decided on the basis of many matters peculiar to a given institution. Applecarts should not obstruct traffic, but to be upset is not their chief purpose.

REFLECTIONS

The following quotations are a small sample of statements elicited by the request, "Please suggest the measures, if any, that you believe ought to be taken by a college or university to promote the continuing good health of the persons with your responsibilities."

The most frequent suggestions dealt with periodic physical examinations. Next to these, and more important, was some relief from the constant pressure of overwork and, as a part of this, more time spent on vacations. The unreasonable burden of work is also stressed in other portions of the responses.

Certain quotations that might seem to be more appropriate to other chapters, such as those on vacations and leaves or on office and staff, are placed here since they are in response to the above question.

The selection of quotations was made with more concern for variety (especially of opinion) than of balance. For instance, many more desire increased medical services than believe that the institution should not be involved. The quotations do not make this clear.

PHYSICAL EXAMINATIONS

Type of Examination
Require an annual physical paid by the College but using doctor of your own choice. — *Director of development, private college*

Should be required annual physical examination by a doctor of the institution's choice. — *Business officer, public college*

Annual physical examination. It is practically impossible for a person to obtain a good checkup on his own. — *Academic vice president, public university*

An annual physical checkup at some outstanding clinic with reports sent to the Board of Trustees would be a safeguard to the college. — *President, private college*

Just don't believe in that periodic "search" for loose gears in my works. — *Librarian, private college*

Age and Frequency
All faculty should have required physical exams when hired. — *Dean of students, public university*

Annual physical report over 40 years of age. — *Dean of students, private college*

Annual physical examination should be encouraged after age 45. — *Dean of students, private university*

Annual physical examination without charge required of all who are 50 or older. — *Business officer, private university*

Annual physical after age 60.—*Director of development, private college*

They should pay for annual physical examination every three years to age 30; every two years from 30–40; and every year over 40.—*Director of development, private college*

I think a physical examination could be required every 2 or 3 years and paid for by the college.—*Director of admissions, private college*

I think a biannual physical exam would be desirable—my own doctor suggests this, instead of an annual one.—*Librarian, public college*

The college ought to be responsible for medical and dental check-ups semiannually.—*Liberal arts dean, private college*

Required quarterly physical examination.—*President, private college*

The questions of requirement of payment and of whether the results are reported to anyone but the individual are related:

An annual physical examination should be encouraged. However, this examination should not be mandatory, nor should the results be available to anyone other than the examinee.—*Dean of students, private college*

Annual physical examination should be available to all top-level administrative personnel, at expense of institution.—*President, private college*

Compulsory annual physical examination, at institution's expense, would be most desirable.—*Liberal arts dean, private university*

Most of the major industrial firms in our nation require an annual physical examination (at company expense) of their key administrators. It seems to me that colleges and universities could very well follow the patterns set by industry and protect the health of their key administrators by requiring annual physical, paid for by university funds.—*Vice president, public university*

Require the individual to take an annual physical examination. Results should be available only to the individual, unless he elects to use them in his own behalf.—*Registrar, private college*

A required annual complete physical examination, cost shared 50–50, and results available to staff member, personal physician, and appropriate University official.—*Registrar, public university*

VACATIONS

There should be a clear understanding that the president is free to take time off for rest or travel whenever he feels that the pressures of his job are taxing his health or effectiveness. (We have such a written understanding . . . but in practice I have not availed myself of it during the past five years.)—*President, private college*

College should insist that President take a vacation annually—be encouraged not to appear on campus unless some emergency occurs during the vacation.—*President, public college*

I should be required to take my month's vacation. (I've never taken it.)—*Graduate dean, public university*

Two months annual vacation—mandatory.—*President, private college*

Mandatory physical absence for periods commensurate with longevity and the age of employee involved. In all cases, a specific mandatory absence.—*Business officer, public college*

Institution should insist on people taking the vacation time to which they are entitled, rather than encourage major staff members to forego vacation under the press of business.—*Director of development, private college*

Required annual vacation. (A religious can easily pass up vacation and not be noticed.)—*President, private college*

Some provision for a break in tension, only briefly but regularly, no less frequently than every six weeks.—*President, public university*

A two to three day vacation during each of the three terms to provide Registrar with a break from the continuous routine. During faculty and student vacations, the Registrar has no vacation but instead much overtime work must be done. Other than one day at Thanksgiving, 1 or 2 at Christmas and Good Friday, there is no relief from a Monday through Saturday schedule.—*Registrar, private college*

Afternoon off each week without feeling that duties are being shirked.—*Vice president, private college*

Planned times for retreats with other administrative personnel and faculty.—*Director of admissions, private university*

Normal vacations . . . nothing special . . . . The man must set his own pace, be free to call his own rest periods, and cannot be forced out of his own routine.—*President, private university*

STAFF

Adequate professional assistance so that this need not be filled out at 11:20 P.M.—*Vice president, public college*

More staff, enabling me to work a 40-hour week rather than 60–70, to get some sleep. Fire me for smoking, drinking, and raising hell.—*Liberal arts dean, public university*

Don't fire me.—*Liberal arts dean, private college*

Give him plenty of help. Teach him how to use it. And the constituencies which demand his time a willingness to accept it instead of him in person.—*President, private university*

HEALTH SERVICES

Cold shots, flu shots, etc., through the College infirmary.—*Librarian, private college*

. . . has a full-time college physician but supposedly faculty and staff members have his services or that of another doctor at their own expense. In practice the College physician gives a great deal of free service to faculty and staff members.—*Liberal arts dean, private college*

Make the resource of our infirmary open to all faculty and administrative personnel as it is to classified employees. Also, since physicians are scarce in this community, permit the college physician to utilize infirmary facilities for faculty and their families. —*Liberal arts dean, private college*

. . . the services of college physician at no cost to employee. (Admittedly a large request.) —*Director of admissions, private college*

Special discount in optometric service to faculty. —*Liberal arts dean, public university*

Dental insurance plan. —*Dean of students, private college*

EXERCISE AND SPORTS

I zealously put time aside for physical exercise (e.g., swimming, golf, platform tennis). Provides good contact also with students and faculty. —*President, public university*

PHYSICAL SURROUNDINGS

Better lighted campus. —*Librarian, private college*

Temperature, humidity and air circulation in the office should be carefully controlled. —*Registrar, private college*

Improve working condition by air-conditioning; increase office space so as to afford privacy. —*Liberal arts dean, private college*

A place to rest for ½ hour a day and possibly nap. — *Business officer, public college*

MISCELLANEOUS

A comprehensive life-health policy with provisions for regular medical examinations should be provided. If the president remains until retirement, it should become his property. —*President, private college*

I favor comprehensive insurance coverage under the auspices and partial support, if necessary, of the Federal government. Sweden, England, and certain Canadian provinces have dealt with this problem effectively. In the meantime, major medical insurance would help. Those who are likely to need it most are often unable to secure such coverage. —*Librarian, public college*

Additional point: Not yet possible to ascertain whether Medicare is going to be adequate for retired faculty members. College could be more concerned about medical insurance for retired members and their dependents who may not be eligible for Medicare. —*Dean of students, private college*

Return to a semester calendar or—more free time to help relieve the pressures of the trimester calendar under which we operate at present. —*Director of admissions, private college*

Less rigid office hours—fewer administrative meetings. —*Graduate dean, public college*

Increased salary would help. —*Librarian, private college*

N.A. Vacationland! —*Dean of liberal arts, public university* [In a scenic state.]

. . . and no questionnaires. —*President, private college*

THREE PACKAGE DEALS

Not distribute questionnaires. Pay all . . . medical premiums. Make sure I have the assistance I need. Compel one to take a vacation.—*Dean of students, private college*

1) A sympathetic and supportive board; 2) Financial support to relieve financial worries; 3) Strong first line executives; 4) A "rustic hide-out" for regaining sanity; 5) Provision for travel abroad; 6) A first-rate security.—*President, private college*

1) Require evidence of good health at time of appointment; 2) Encourage some outside activity not directly connected with position—research training, educational service; 3) Require an annual period of change of pace —vacation, education service, research, professional service.—*Liberal arts dean, public university*

YES, NO, AND YES-AND-NO

A free medical clinic for all students, faculty and staff.—*Librarian, private college*

I think this should be the responsibility of the individuals and not the college.—*Director of development, private college*

Pay adequate salary and retirement and let the individual provide for his own medical care (excepting Major Medical, which is hard to buy individually).—*Business officer, private college*

I feel that personal health problems are a personal not an institutional responsibility. I do believe, however, that the University lags somewhat behind other institutions in the proportion of the health insurance premium met by the institution.—*Director of development, public university*

The individual is responsible for his *own* health and the care thereof!— *Dean of students, public university*

I believe that it would be wise policy, economically and, as well, in terms of maximum intellectual output, for a college or university to support a regular program of health maintenance or preventive medicine. This could include regular health examinations and opportunities and facilities for recreational programs (and perhaps approval of time expenditures for such purposes). There is much evidence to demonstrate the soundness of such programs as a means of obtaining full potential over extended periods of time from populations of highly paid and scarce personnel.—*Graduate dean, public college*

None: I am old fashioned and independent to the point that I want the privilege of taking care of my own health. Also, I can't believe that any of us are so valuable and indispensable to an institution or to this world.— *Dean of students, private college*

I believe that Christian church colleges ought to be exemplary in establishing all or many benefits for their employees. Adoption of major medical —pension plans—travel accident insurance, etc. All discrimination between faculty, clergy and laymen, as well as staff laymen should be eliminated.

Some church colleges in this relation are more *secular* than secular colleges. This ought not to be. — *Director of development, private college*

I believe that this is entirely my own responsibility and I would not welcome any assistance from anybody — college or government. — *Liberal arts dean, private college*

Health services provided the students should be made available to faculty and administration. — *Dean of students, private college*

If I am competent to do this work I should be competent to take suitable care of myself. — *Director of development, private college*

The next two are from one college:

The college should provide all health services for the faculty and staff without charge where possible. — *President, public college*

I do not think that it is the responsibility of the College to do more than to see to it that working conditions are as favorable as possible, that employees are not subject to more stress than necessary, and that they are not overloaded to such an extent that health is threatened. I feel that . . . College meets these criteria very well. — *Graduate dean, public college*

WORKING CLIMATE

Not too many years ago college work was attractive to some people because of the relaxed nature of the work. This characteristic of college work is fast disappearing, however, and formal recognition needs to be given to this fact. — *Registrar, private college*

Since we are a Catholic college and short of clergy, the priests are given one and sometimes two extra near full-time jobs beyond their administrative or faculty work. A man can go at this pace only for so long before he breaks down. — *Dean of students, private college*

Complete backing when great pressures are applied by alumni, parents and "friends." — *Director of admissions, private college*

All the checkups in the world won't help without some relief from the pressures which get greater every year. — *Dean of students, public university*

I find that state of health depends primarily on smoothness of job operation, lack of tension, and decent regard for the performance and abilities of the persons in question. These conditions can be provided by an alert and humane administration, and such provision is a primary administrative function. — *Librarian, public college*

If the attitude prevailed that some things could be done tomorrow or even the day after and that everything would not fall apart as a result, the whole administrative situation here and elsewhere would be healthier. The game in too many academic communities seems to be: How fast can you wear your deans out? — *Liberal arts dean, public college*

I can think of only two measures [to promote continuing good health] and neither of them can be taken by a college or university, though they are vitally important. The first is to change the nature of the public expectation of a college or university president: the second is to harden the president's heart so that he protects himself. Neither seems to be working well at the moment; I would suggest that both for the sake of the president and his institution, we should take this problem fairly seriously. —*President, private university*

REFERENCES TO APPENDIX

Questionnaire, Section H.

Summary Tables 31–38.

CHAPTER 7

VACATIONS AND LEAVES

Learn to labor and to wait. —LONGFELLOW
*'Tis better to have loafed and lost than never
to have loafed at all.* —JAMES THURBER

AT the beginning of this study, it was clear from talks
with many administrators, especially presidents, that leaves are desirable when practicable and that much attention should be given to
making or proving them so. However, I was not prepared to discover
how critical the situation is in regard to the annual vacation and the
occasional holiday.

VACATIONS

Although the time officially provided for vacations differs from
position to position, with the arrangements more often informal for the
president then for the other officers, the picture in broad outline is as
follows.

Ninety percent or over of the institutions provide guidelines as to
the length of vacation for all positions except that of the vice president
and the dean of students, 88%, the dean of liberal arts, 82%, and the
president, in whose case less than two-thirds have any formal arrangements. Informal policies are much more frequent in private than in
public institutions. In fact, the vacation provisions for the majority of
presidents in private universities and for over 43% of those in private
colleges are informal, whereas for public institutions the corresponding figures are about 16% and 24% respectively.

In a good many institutions, although we have no exact measure of
the number, the length of vacation to which one is entitled depends
upon the length of previous service. As a reward, this may seem
logical; but in the interests of effective administration it is better to

keep men fresh than to try to revive the weary. If any rule of this sort were to be used, it should be based on age rather than length of service. This would at least have the logic of being tied in with the presumed decrease in recuperative powers that comes with advancing years. My own belief is that no such distinction should be used and that the habit of taking reasonable vacations should be established early in one's career. This habit is a physical and mental protection, and a guard against the psychological arrogance of assumed indispensability.

The provision in Catholic institutions for their non-lay officers is somewhat confused by the mixture of religious retreats with vacations. The formal provision for these officers is often quite short or nonexistent.

Although vacation provisions of only two or three weeks per year are not unusual, especially in the South, and for those with short previous service, a considerable majority of the institutions that have formal rules make provision for a vacation of four weeks or a month. In some institutions, especially public ones, strict accounting of time off is kept—for instance, for the Friday after Thanksgiving or the day before New Year's. In other cases, a few days off during winter vacations, or in connection with attendance at meetings, are allowed without question.

The formal regulations for administrators, though not as generous as for the other faculty, are not the chief obstacle to adequate vacations. The dismaying fact is that in almost all positions where the vacation is officially four weeks or a month in length, less than half of the administrators take this much. In the case of presidents, only one-third take a four-week vacation in any given year. Even fewer take their allotted time off regularly each year.

Table 41 indicates the length of vacations to which administrative officers are entitled, and the vacations actually taken. The "no vacations reported" category includes those who did not respond as well as persons in their first year of service, and of course persons who have not taken a vacation. It would appear from this table that, except for librarians, one-third or less take a vacation as long as four weeks, and only about one-fifth of the business officers do so. Rules clearly have little to do with this matter. The feasibility of leaving one's position for a given length of time and the desire to do so are the controlling factors.

For all positions, except director of development, the likelihood of a vacation as long as four weeks is greater in universities than in colleges; the difference exists for both public and private institutions. In most positions a slightly greater proportion take a four-week vacation in private than in public institutions.

There are both structural and psychological causes for the failure to take adequate vacations.

It is usual for administrative officers to be selected because of the high quality of their previous records, resulting from both ability and hard work. Except for the presidents, they seldom have had much experience in delegating responsibility (often this is also true of the president). They are do-it-yourself men. Most of them have worked in jobs which, even if absorbing, could at times be laid aside. The deadlines of grades, publications, and application for grants, though occurring, were not ever-imminent. The year had many periods without classes. Their energy and interests may have made vacations scarce and short, but not the sense that their own work and that of others would suffer severely if time off were taken. As a matter of fact, however, many of them never developed the vacation habit.

When starting a career as an administrator, it is natural personally to undertake everything that one's position requires be done by one's office, and once in the groove, a chance for let-up is rare. In chapters devoted to the various administrative positions some of the demands on the principal officers of the college or the university are described. For most of these offices there is no time in the year when they cease to function even for a few days. If there is not enough staffing in depth at a high level, or if a secretary is not encouraged to use her full competence, an administrative officer will decide he cannot take a vacation. He is trapped by his own ability and past habits of performance. The college also is trapped.

This is recognized by many who recommend a "required vacation," which is, of course, an oversimplified and usually impossible solution, but does represent a genuine cry for succour.

Let us analyze for a moment the barriers to a vacation. Some of these are:

1. The psychological barrier already described.
2. Lack of adequate help to carry on even for a short time without "the chief." This may be because of (*a*) the financial problems of the college, or (*b*) the unconscious underrating of the ability of subordinates and hence the failure to give them responsibility.

3. Lack of communication, so that the policies of the administrative officer are not understood both by those to whom he reports and those that report to him.

4. Fear of the overcrowded desk upon return.

For the board of trustees to tell the president he must take a vacation, or for the president to tell the dean that he must, is of course not feasible. It does not remove any of the barriers mentioned above, and if strictly enforced, would be an intolerable abridgment of a man's independence. I did once tell a department chairman he would not get a raise until he took a vacation. He took one. I do not know which of us put it over on the other. Strong pressure may be exerted provided help is given in clearing the roadblocks.

In many institutions, more money should be spent on administration even at the expense of other things. Yet, a stand-in dean cannot be kept in mothballs in order to allow the dean to get a four- instead of a two-week vacation.

As yet, utility infielders have not been developed for college administration.

The suggestions that follow, some of them distilled from answers to the questionnaires, will not apply to certain institutions, and yet I believe they will apply to enough to make them worth considering. The vacation problem is not chiefly that of the larger institution. When the administrative load is so great that every office has a large staff and there is usually an associate ready to fill in—not infrequently to the benefit of the work—the habits of the administrator may be in the way but not the structure of the institution. At the other extreme is the impecunious small institution in a small town where even the clerical pool is limited. Often these institutions do not even pretend to give a person more than a two-week vacation, which itself may rarely be taken. Until the situation improves, vacations will have low priorities in these institutions.

In between are many institutions where there is both a need and an opportunity to improve the situation. Here are a few suggestions.

1. Improve the quality, enlarge the responsibility, and increase the pay of the chief secretaries of the administrative officers. In many cases, the first of the triad is unnecessary. It is a delight to read the tributes paid to secretaries by officers, especially presidents. A poor secretary should be replaced; otherwise a poor administrator will have to be. The salary scale of clerical help is notoriously flat. From the

graduate assistant on a full-time basis to a distinguished professor, a salary ratio of one to four or five is not uncommon. The ratio from the graduate assistant to the president would, of course, be much larger. But from a beginning full-time typist to the president's secretary, such a difference in salary would be extraordinary. Moreover, the responsibility given to secretaries of wide experience and sound judgment is often far less than that given rather green and not always carefully selected young men, frequently either without the doctor's degree or, less fortunately, the culls of those who have it.

This, of course, is no criticism of the fine program that some institutions have of involving first-class young scholars in the administration, thereby using talent and developing it for positions of future responsibility, either at home or elsewhere.

2. In many institutions, larger expenditures for "middle management" would be desirable even within current budgetary limitations.

3. In a number of cases, proper communication would not only improve the work of those one echelon below the chief administrative officers, but also would supply substitutes. As illustrations: If a vice president or dean were kept abreast of the president's activities, his own would be improved and the institution would run more smoothly when the president is away. (I do not mean more smoothly than when he is present.) Most libraries have at least a second professional librarian, who could be given greater insight into the total workings of the library. Business offices, with the increasing burden that relations with foundations and government have placed upon them, need more than one man with not only technical accounting training, but with general business capacity. Most coeducational institutions with a dean of students also have a dean of women or a dean of men, and many have a dormitory counseling system employing experienced personnel of good judgment. These should keep in touch with each other. If kept aware of each other's work, the registrar and the admissions officer, when not the same person, can to some extent share each other's burdens.

In other words, if the communication problem were solved—and, as many bear witness, it often cries for solution—the possibility of vacations would be significantly increased.

4. My fourth suggestion will seem almost immoral to many— namely, selective neglect. Not everything one is called upon to do is worth doing. And not everything worth doing is worth doing well.

Some formal duties deserve perfunctory performance. For example, I am grateful indeed to those who carefully answered the questionnaire for this study, but I also sympathize sorrowfully with those who dashed off a reply or decided consciously or by delay not to answer it at all. (I do not agree with their choice, but I understand it.)

FEW LONG VACATIONS VERSUS MANY SHORT BREAKS. It is clear from reading replies to the questionnaire that people's tastes differ on how they wish to take a vacation. Some complain that although they can take off twenty-one working days in the year, these are neither consecutive nor away from home. Hence, there is no period when relaxation is anywhere near complete. To them, a little time at Christmas, at Easter, and around Labor Day is no substitute for the month of August. (I belong to this category, although Sundays in the country mean much to me.) Others feel that what they want most are frequent breaks in the tension of their work. To them a week four times a year would be of far more value than a month in the summer. Circumstances dictate which of these is feasible—often neither. It is most unfortunate, as is not infrequently the case, when rules of the institution stipulate the type as well as the total time of a vacation.

DESIRABLE FREEDOM. The evidence is convincing that the majority of college and university administrators are at least sufficiently conscientious and that many are pathologically so. The problem is not that of curbing a man's desire to have time off, but of helping him get enough vacation. It would seem that there should be few rules in this matter. The attitude of the board or a superior officer should be: "We want you usually to have about a month off per year. Some years it may be a little more; do not make it less. Of course if your work is ineffective, someone else should take your place; but we fear more that you may go stale, become irritable and tense, resent new ideas, and show other signs of overwork than that you will neglect your job. Arrange your work as you think best. But the basic human need behind the advice 'Remember the Sabbath Day to keep it holy' should never be overlooked."

LEAVES

Not only are vacations and leaves closely associated, but they overlap in people's thinking. I am sure that I can make no definition of the two that would be acceptable to a wide range of readers. And yet, some distinction between the two must be indicated. My personal one

would not do, but it is illustrative. On vacations I walk through forests
and climb mountains; on leaves I walk through cathedrals and climb
towers. This is symptomatic. One hopes for vacations at frequent
intervals to maintain one's physical tone and mental bounce. A leave is
less ordinary, and usually has some special purpose: to regain health
after illness; to enhance one's education, whether formal or not; to
serve the public; to teach in another institution; to complete a research
program. Usually the plans for a vacation, within certain rules, need
only be settled with one's own conscience. The leave, even the sabbatical leave, usually takes special authorization.

It is hard to stress too greatly the importance of leaves. The overwhelming consensus of respondents to our questionnaire is that leaves
are of great importance for administrative officers; many, in fact,
believe them more important for administrators than for faculty members. It was often pointed out that one of the difficulties of interesting
faculty members in administration is the lessened likelihood of getting
leaves. There were a few well-written, thoughtful statements discount-
ing the importance of leaves for administrators and pointing out the
injury a college can suffer if the president or some other principal
administrative officer is absent. Such statements come with special
frequency from business officers and directors of development.

A very large number believe that leaves would be valuable for
administrative officers, but do not believe that their institutions are
presently or soon will be staffed in such a way as to make leaves
feasible. This is discussed below under "feasibility," and what has
been said on this subject under "vacations" applies here.

Here I quote at length from a report of a conference on faculty
leaves held between representatives of the Association of American
Colleges and of the American Association of University Professors. It
should be noted this is a report of a meeting, not the formulated
doctrine of either organization. The reader may make proper substitutions and judge how well the quotation fits the case of administrators.
In my judgment the fit is close. The full text was published in the
AAUP *Bulletin* in the autumn of 1967.

The college or university teacher should be a scholar who is constantly
increasing his knowledge and keeping abreast of the development of his
field. Frequently he is an active investigator, and in many institutions
research is a significant portion of his obligations. He should remain a man
of vigor with a fresh mind and broad intellectual interests. Heavy teaching

duties performed year after year may make this impossible. Leaves of absence and special research assignments at reasonable intervals of time are among the means of assuring that institutions of higher learning have the kind of faculty that they need. A well-developed program of leaves is of major importance in enhancing the professional development of faculty members. Moreover, the work done while the scholar is on leave, for example, through the results of his investigation or his public service, often is of immediate value to society. The health of the faculty member is a constant concern of the college, and leaves are one of the means of protecting it.

Hence among the chief purposes for leaves of absence from college teaching are:

1) The protection or recovery of health;
2) The direct usefulness of the work expected to be done while on leave; and most important,
3) The professional development of the teacher and thereby the increased effectiveness of higher education.

. . . .

In the majority of colleges and in many universities by far the chief purpose of leaves is to insure that the individual becomes and remains as good a teacher as his capacities permit. This means that the young scholar should have as early an opportunity as possible to complete his formal education, and to develop his special field of scholarship on his own after attaining a Ph.D. degree. The opportunity to keep abreast of rapidly developing fields frequently is needed. Nor is old knowledge to be scorned; often it is well to dwell in cultivated fields, not always struggle amid the smoking stumps of the frontier. A change of pace, even a change from one set of frustrations to another, is often needed.

. . . .

It is our belief that leaves, though serving both the personal needs of individuals and the interests of institutions, are primarily an investment of society for strengthening higher education as well as in the accomplishments of the individuals while on leave. A sound policy in regard to leaves, adopted by many institutions, will facilitate such investment because institutions can more generously grant leaves when they can expect to gain in the effectiveness of professors who receive these leaves and to attract stronger men into their faculties.

We do not consider leaves as deferred compensation to be furnished to a man by his institution no matter what other opportunities he may have had for professional development, or to be given him in cash if he resigns to go elsewhere to teach or do some other kind of work, or paid to his estate if he dies. However, faculty members do have a right to conditions of work that afford opportunities for their development as teachers and scholars. An institution has an obligation to provide these opportunities; an increase in a teacher's bank account is no substitute for an increase in his experience and his knowledge.

A college should furnish opportunities for growth to all the scholars on its staff. We do not believe that an institution should provide leaves only to those who are expected to remain on its faculty or, for that matter, even in teaching. An educational institution whose chief purpose is to develop the abilities of those who serve the nation, usually in capacities other than formal education, should not resent improving the minds of those few of its staff who may leave the academic profession.

. . . .

Leaves for scholarly or cultural development can be put much more nearly on a periodic basis than research leaves or, of course, than leaves for public service and health. The timing of a research leave is usually related to the state of the project. Neither illness during the working year nor the call of public service comes to all scholars. However, for every teacher the need to learn is constant. Although time may not generate the right to a leave as compensation, it will generate the need for one as opportunity, a need which should be met by an opportunity the faculty member has an obligation to use. The ticking of a clock should be a reminder both to the conscience of the institution and to the conscience of the individual.

. . . .

Of course a leave of absence is not a guarantee that a man will increase his effectiveness and, fortunately, many scholars are able to continue their professional growth without leaves. Nevertheless, we consider a well-thought-out and adequately supported plan of leaves to be a major component of a sound educational policy for a college or university. We recognize that it may well be an expensive component. Leaves must compete for funds with salaries, retirement benefits, insurance, additional staff, and occasionally with buildings and the beauty of the campus. Leaves may not be first on the list but they do deserve high priority.

FREQUENCY OF LEAVES. Table D indicates the approximate percent of administrative officers who have held their present position for more than ten years who have had a leave other than for sickness during that period. In my opinion these figures are probably a little high because of some short absences that most would not have called leaves.

It has not proved worthwhile to break these figures down between universities and colleges except to say that the graduate deans in the colleges seem to take leaves more frequently than those in the universities, and that the reverse is true for librarians. This was to be expected. The persons who filled out the questionnaire of the graduate dean in the colleges were often directors of graduate studies on a part-time basis, with the graduate work of the institution given mostly in the summer and limited to a few departments—especially education. For the purpose of leaves, these persons are essentially on the same basis as the rest of the faculty. On the other hand, a librarian in a college may be the only professional librarian on the staff or one of the very small group of such and have no natural deputy. As indicated by Table D, persons in these two positions have a higher frequency of leaves than those in any of the other positions studied. In most positions the proportion of administrative officers of long service who have had a leave is slightly greater in private than in public institutions.

TABLE D
Officers serving more than ten years; percent who have taken a leave

	Number having served more than ten years in present position	Percent who have taken a leave
President	219	32%
Vice President	58	33
Liberal Arts Dean	110	25
Graduate Dean	45	44
Librarian	287	42
Business Officer	246	9
Dean of Students	110	28
Director of Admissions	132	16
Registrar	214	19
Development Officer	44	7

Some 760 administrative officers reported having had a leave while holding their present positions. This represents about 1,000 leaves, averaging perhaps a little over four-and-a-half months each. The over 6,000 administrative officers replying to the questionnaire have served in their present positions for a total of about 43,000 years, from which we might conclude that they get about three days a year on the average for leaves. Because of the disparity of length of service and the greater likelihood of having a leave after a considerable time in a given position, this estimate may be slightly high. *The Outer Fringe* study made in 1963 would indicate that faculty members would on the average receive twice that amount. If such faculty members had been limited to the upper ranks, the average amount of time spent on leaves would probably have been considerably higher.

LENGTH OF LEAVES. A sample indicates that about 40% of the leaves reported are for a month or less, many of these being military leaves, and some of the others absences that many would not have reported as leaves, such as an absence of four days at the time of the death of one's father or consulting services of less than a week. In a sample of 74 leaves taken, 11 were of about a summer session or of a quarter in length, 12 of about a semester, 5 of about an academic year, and 13 of a year or more.

PURPOSES OF LEAVES TAKEN. For the positions of librarian, business officer, dean of students, admissions officer, registrar, and director of development, the most frequent purpose for leaves is to devote time to graduate study. Most people in these positions do not have the doctor's degree. The great majority of presidents, vice presidents, deans of liberal arts, and graduate deans do hold the doctorate, and few take leaves for formal study.

A moderate-sized sample indicates that some form of public service, frequently abroad, is the chief reason for leaves granted to presidents.

A sample of 55 administrators taking leaves, some of them multiple, had the following purposes: graduate study, 18; research, 7; public service abroad, 7; public service, U.S., 5; military service, 4; teaching elsewhere, 3; official visits abroad, 2; conferences abroad, 2; and study abroad, rest, travel, exchange, workshops, maternity, and undisclosed, 1 each. In this sample, there were no leaves for health.

A striking number of administrative officers have taken leaves for service abroad. The following, although incomplete, gives some idea of the variety of such experiences. Presidents have served the State Department in Poland and Pakistan. "Fulbrights" of various types in the Philippines, India, Germany, Burma, Egypt, Colombia, Iraq, and Korea have been held by a vice president, liberal arts and graduate deans, librarians, a dean of students, and a director of development from public and private colleges and universities. A registrar, librarians, and assorted deans have been academic consultants in Chile, India, Egypt, Turkey, Pakistan, and other countries in Latin America or Asia.

Special mention should be made of the satisfaction expressed by those who have participated in the work of the Center for Study of Higher Education at the University of Michigan and of the desire of others to do so.

Aside from the question concerning leaves actually taken, efforts were made to get at the regulations governing leaves by questions as to the purposes for which a person was eligible to take leaves and whether or not the rules concerning leaves were the same for administrators as for faculty members. We also asked questions concerning the feasibility of taking leaves.

REGULATIONS REGARDING LEAVES FOR ADMINISTRATIVE OFFICERS COMPARED WITH REGULATIONS GOVERNING FACULTY LEAVES. A summary of replies on whether or not the administrative officer was governed by the same rules on the matter of leaves as those which applied to the faculty is given in Table 43. By eliminating those who did not respond, we conclude that for well over half the presidents, business officers, and development officers the rules (or lack of rules) governing leaves are different from those governing leaves for the faculty. This is true for about half of the admissions officers and registrars. For about two-thirds of the vice presidents, deans of liberal arts, and deans of students, and four-fifths of the graduate deans and librarians, the rules are the same as for the faculty. In general, when there is a difference, the faculty is reported by the administrator as having a more generous program for leaves. The practical importance of this lies more in the discontent engendered among administrators than in any effect it has on frequency of leaves, regulations being far less controlling than circumstances.

ELIGIBILITY FOR LEAVES. Administrative officers were asked for what purposes they were eligible to take leaves with pay and also without pay.

1. *Sabbatical Leaves.* Over 60% of the institutions which replied to the questionnaire on which *The Outer Fringe* (1965) was based either had plans in 1963 for sabbatical leaves for their faculties or had plans at such a stage that they would have been in effect by 1966. In contrast, the only administrative position that came near this figure was the graduate deanship, 49%. Vice presidents and librarians had such provisions in 37% and 38% of the institutions respectively, and the other positions were at a level of a third or under, ranging down to presidents, 16%, and development officers, 15%. In all cases these percentages ran higher in public institutions than in private, perhaps largely because the vacations and leaves are on a more informal basis in private institutions than in public. The difference between universities and colleges does not appear to be important.

2. *Research and Study.* It is difficult to be certain how many institutions will grant leaves with pay other than sabbatical for research and study to faculty members. A lower bound to this figure is approxi-

mately one-third. My guess is that it is nearer to 40%. As to administrative officers, the percent who said they were eligible for such leaves ranged from business officers, 7%, and presidents, 9%, to librarians, 24%, and graduate deans, 28%. The proportion eligible to take leaves for these purposes without pay, of course, ran higher than the proportion eligible to take them with pay, but again ranged from the business officers and presidents at 13% to the librarians at 42% and graduate deans at 57%. In the case of deans, eligibility for leaves both with and without pay for research and study was more frequent in public than in private institutions—again perhaps a reflection of the more informal arrangements in private institutions, which in practice might well lead to as generous or more generous treatment of this question by them than by public institutions.

3. *Reasons of Health*. From 12% to 18%, depending upon the position, reported that they were eligible for leaves with pay for health reasons. More reported they could have such leaves without pay. One should not place much significance on these figures, because the answers are confused not only by the general informality of the arrangements in the majority of private colleges but by the nomenclature of regulations concerning continued pay during illness.

4. *Other Purposes*. The fishing expedition as regards eligibility for leaves for other purposes brought only a small catch. The variety of leaves actually taken as detailed above exceeds the imagination of those looking toward the future.

FEASIBILITY OF TAKING LEAVES IN THE FUTURE. Two series of questions were asked the administrators about the feasibility of taking leaves for various purposes in the next ten years and the possible length of these leaves. The questions were asked about leaves both "with" and "without" pay. In the second case the issue was somewhat confused, since some took it to mean that the individual would get no pay rather than that the college would not be doing the paying; hence their replies merely indicated that it would be impossible to be away without any income. Others gave negative replies because they felt it unlikely that anyone would offer them financial support, although the institution itself would not object to their being absent. Still others made their judgments solely on whether the institutions would permit such leaves. Some of my statements are based on my own judgment of what the situation is, after not only looking at the statistics, but also after reading many comments.

Another difficulty in interpretation arises from the fact that these questions were answered by a larger proportion of administrators in public than in private institutions. Hence we are led to such results as 48% of the presidents in public institutions answering that it was not feasible to take a leave without pay for research while 23% said it was feasible, whereas for private institutions the corresponding figures were 37% and 18%. This occurs because 71% of the presidents of public institutions responded to this question while only 55% did so in the case of private institutions.

However, even if many questions cannot be answered, others can. To a large extent presidents have given up the hope of keeping up in their own fields while in office. In the other positions where holding the doctorate is customary, that is, the vice presidency and the academic deanships, as well as in the case of librarians, considerably over one-third believe that leaves for research and study in their own fields are feasible. The proportions are much smaller for the other positions except that of the dean of students, where a somewhat larger number either have or are candidates for the doctor's degree and where such leaves would probably be for formal study.

The purpose for which it is considered most feasible to take a leave is for research or study in college administration. This is true both for leaves with or without pay. In the case of leave with pay, a large number give the expected length as two weeks, probably thinking of participation in workshops and conferences. Those who believe leaves without pay for this purpose are feasible often mention rather long periods ranging up to two years—in contemplation, I presume, of extended formal study or leaves for "apprenticeships" in other institutions.

Nearly one-third of the presidents consider it feasible to take a leave with pay for public service in the next five years. No other administrative officer is as optimistic in this regard. However, when it comes to leaves without pay for the same purpose, the vice presidents (43%), the graduate deans (42%), the deans of liberal arts (35%), and the deans of students (31%) who believe such leaves are feasible show higher proportions than the presidents (30%).

The presidents have evidently given greater consideration to the feasibility of leaves for "rest and renewal" than the other officers. It is probable also that being in close contact with the governing boards they have assurance of approval of such leaves, so that the judgment of their feasibility involves no outside person. So many presidents tell me that their boards urge them to get away more than they do that I feel confident of this interpretation.

REFLECTIONS

Let's start with vacations first.—*Director of development, public college*

Most of the vacations (except those taken abroad) are not true vacations, since my work may follow me, and usually does, to our summer residence. . . . In 18 years I have been completely away from my work for exactly thirteen weeks overall (3 trips abroad). I could have had more had I asked. But I don't like to ask.—*President, private college*

. . . On the rare occasions when I have had a brief respite of two weeks in the winter, or a summer vacation of two or more weeks, I have returned to the campus with renewed vigor and a new view of things, and felt ready to tackle whatever problems might come.—*President, private college*

If some system could be devised whereby I could have an occasional weekend entirely free of responsibility, I believe that I could work more effectively.—*Dean of students, private college*

It is very difficult to schedule a vacation period. The President doesn't; consequently I have difficulty.—*Director of development, private college*

The following form a small sample from those who believe that leaves are desirable:

I think leaves of absence for college presidents are great!—*President, public university*

. . . I am heartily in favor of presidents enjoying leaves of absence. Those presidents I know who age most gracefully in their jobs are those who do back away from the press of their duties for regular vacations and for leaves of absence.—*President, private college*

Workshops ought to be established for college presidents.—*President, private college*

. . . If it is possible to arrange for an entire year of absence for a president, I would see a very great advantage in this sort of arrangement since it would give him time to think through his whole philosophy and to view at a distance what he is trying to accomplish. It would also help other administrators to try their wings.—*President, private college*

I think a leave for a study tour, or tour around the world visiting alumni would be tremendous. I have never had the opportunity of travel outside the continental U.S. and across Canada. At the same time, we have a program of foreign study for our students, many of them come from different parts of the world, many have traveled with their parents, or members of the faculty have traveled extensively and I find myself out of step.—*President, private college*

. . . I believe present-day Deans should have travel sabbaticals. I am educating people who will lead the 21st century, when the world will be very close. I have been in 48 states, but have never been to Europe or Asia. I believe I need to know the world better—very much better—but without some form of financial assistance and some arrangement for traveling time, I will never get that knowledge.—*Liberal arts dean, private college*

An especially fruitful experience for me was a 6 month leave on a Fulbright Research Grant, some years ago. Leaves of this kind are as important for administrators as for faculty.—*President, public college*

Teaching (which we all do) and leaves (for which faculty-administrators are eligible) are essential to maintain academic awareness and to preserve something "to go back to" when retiring from administration.—*Liberal arts dean, private university*

It is clear to me that a leave of absence for at least a semester every four to six years will be an absolute necessity. In a small college in a small town, weekends are not free, vacations are short, interrupted and inadequate. A long period away is absolutely essential.—*Vice president, private college*

Administrative officers need to retain some familiarity with current developments in the fields of previous academic training, as well as in their administrative fields. All too often administration tends to become the shortest route to a kind of illiteracy.—*Graduate dean, private college*

College administrative officers, especially those whose responsibilities are with the academic side of college, should be given the same leave privileges as faculty members. Their work suffers from outdated ideas as much as does a faculty member's who would use outdated lecture notes. Librarians need to know new literature in all fields, new methods of teaching, and new philosophies of education. He teaches as does any other teacher. Does it matter that his instruction is individual rather than in a formal classroom? Often this individual instruction is more effective than formal instruction. I feel that eliminating the librarian from leave privileges is a mistake.—*Librarian, private college*

I believe that administrators get into very deep ruts and need to change their perspective. I think that their positions need to be audited by someone else performing in their area occasionally.—*Business officer, public university*

I believe leaves of absence for college administrative officers to be most desirable—especially fairly early in their careers—to visit, maybe even work in other institutions, is the most effective way to absorb ideas and ways and means of instituting improvements in the conduct of one's office in my judgment.—*Registrar, private college*

In twenty years I have not been away from this institution for more than three weeks at any one time. The continuing grind without significant interruption is wearing in the extreme. I feel strongly that a systematic program of leave-with-pay should be instituted for administrative officers. —*Registrar, private university*

An outstanding institution requires an outstanding faculty, but can it be truly outstanding if it has a second-class administration? I think not, and eventually the faculty's lack of support to administrative endeavors will react to the detriment of the institution's small progress. There are many ways to develop a harmonious relationship between faculty and administration, with each given the respect and responsibility it is due. One such way to reduce harmful distinctions and at the same time improve the level of administration is to promote a plan of six-month or one year leaves for selected administrative personnel. Such arrangements for administrators are long overdue and should no longer be the exclusive province of faculty members. — *Registrar, public college*

The logic which has enabled American colleges to provide periodic recesses for instructional staff, but not for administrative personnel, escapes me. — *Director of admissions, public college*

And in contrast:

Leaves of absence are not as important for admissions people since their program is far from routine. During certain periods of the year there is extensive travel with interviews throughout the United States. — *Director of admissions, private college*

Some note the indispensability complex:

A leave of absence is likely to prove what most deans probably secretly know, that they are dispensable. I think an academic dean should continue an interest in his field of teaching—he ought to teach at least one class— and a leave of absence would help him to stay fresh and original. — *Liberal arts dean, public college*

Administrative personnel sometimes convince themselves that the school "can't get along without me." This is, of course, a myth. — *Vice president, private college*

. . . let you know the school can run without you! — *Dean of students, private college*

Certain special situations are noted:

Leave of absence is a tender subject. I am one of those people with all the course work out of the way but need to find time to do my dissertation for the doctorate. The problems of this growing institution have kept me extremely busy. A 60 hour week from September to April is the norm, so I have not had time to pursue a project. — *Director of admissions, public college*

We need a policy which will grant leaves of absence for employees who have earned their doctor's degrees. At our institution persons who have earned such a degree *never* qualify for a leave of absence with pay. All other conditions are satisfactory. — *Graduate dean, public college*

Business officers should be encouraged to take leaves of absence on an exchange basis with industry, if such arrangements could be made. Industrial management methods can be adapted to college administration in purchasing, physical plant planning and operation, food services, and even in libraries where archaic methods of filing, inventory control, traffic, processing of books, etc., still prevail.

Business Officers should enjoy the same sabbatical privileges as teaching faculty—and even tenure, if desired!—*Business officer, private college*

Deans of Students will always be frustrated as long as discipline problems exist and discipline problems will exist as long as there are students. Because of this I firmly believe that it is highly desirable that a leave of absence, with pay, should be given at least every two years for a minimum of one term to Deans of Students.—*Dean of students, private college*

After a successful multi-million dollar campaign, a two month or so "leave of absence" would have been desirable.—*Director of development, private university*

. . . A sound program assisting younger staff members to move toward acquiring additional professional training and broader experience will better equip them for the serious problems with which they will be faced.—*Director of development, private college*

My experience is limited, but no *one* of the years has approached a condition I would describe as "normal" or "routine." I am therefore approaching the conclusion that if leaves are taken, they must be scheduled even at times which *appear* disadvantageous to the institution.—*Liberal arts dean, private university*

Leaves of absence should be compulsory for administrative officers as well as senior faculty. Perhaps administrative leaves should be briefer and more frequent, but they should involve a substantial change of role.—*Graduate dean, public university*

Administrators are more apt to get into ruts than faculty people and should be compelled to take leaves.—*Librarian, private college*

Many presidents refer to the role of the board of trustees:

It would be highly desirable for the trustees to work out a plan with a new president insisting that he take a semester or a year off at least every seven years. This would necessitate providing adequate administrative personnel to carry on the responsibilities during his absence.—*President, private college*

I have come to the conclusion that presidents should be required to take at least two months each year in rest and refreshment.—*President, private college*

A Board of Trustees should insist that a president take a leave consisting of not less than three months and possibly six months to a year out of each five years of service. If a president waits until he "can afford the time" or until "everything is in order" to take a leave, no leave would ever develop. —*President, private college*

Our Board . . . has urged me for years to take a leave of absence. The present year was the first time, in my own judgment, it was possible to do so. I took a six months' leave of absence, using the period for study. It was a wonderfully refreshing period, and enabled me to see many things with a different perspective on my return. — *President, private college*

Board couldn't care less about vacations. They want the college to reach its stated objectives and, if this is the case, all is well. — *President, private college*

And also from a non-president:

A final comment on point c [leaves] is that provision for succession will be attended to by the officers as a corollary of this practice. As a consequence, the Board is forced to consider succession planning as part of the management process, which, I would guess, college and university Boards rarely do. — *Business officer, private college*

Some doubt the possibility, practicability, or wisdom of leaves:

In a small college with limited staff, leaves for long periods are not really feasible. Shorter leaves of 2–4 months are desirable. In my case one has been granted with salary and expense, the first in 10 years, but the first I have felt it responsible judgment to request. — *President, private college*

Leaves of absence for presidents would be quite desirable, but I consider them impossible. — *President, private college*

I don't see how one can realistically talk about vacation when one is burdened continuously with the over-all responsibilities of an institution. What is needed is periodic diversion and relaxation of the burden, not total escape for a given length of time each year. Possibly a two-month "sabbatical" every four years would be desirable. — *President, private college*

I am of two minds about the desirability of leaves of absence for the college president. Of course, it would be wonderful for him if he were able to detach himself from the cares and responsibilities of office for a six-month period, or a year, and find personal renewal and refreshment in travel or in study. However, if he were to do this and then come back to his job, he would find the unsolved problems and the postponed decisions piled upon his desk to a height that would simply stagger him. It's a fine idea, but somehow I feel that it is rather impractical. — *President, private college*

The duties of the president of the college are incompatible with the idea of an extended leave of absence, say for one year. If the duties of the president's office are placed for long periods of time on the vice-president, then the vice-president, it seems to me, should be advanced to the presidency. — *President, private college*

. . . The intellectual values of a leave are, in my mind, still unquestioned. The emotional release from tension which a president may seek is not, however, available. The telephone will follow him everywhere and, on return, the stockpile of work, even after the most conscientious of help, is likely to drain the reserves of composure he will have gathered in his absence quite quickly. I think my own preference now would be for a brief but regular absence from the desk . . . . — *President, public university*

For the large institutions with sufficient administrative depth, the idea of sabbatical or similar leaves [for presidents] would be excellent, but I do not see how it could be done in the smaller, administratively thin institutions.

[For other officers:] Provide for sabbatical type leaves; make certain that they have all the fringe benefits that regular faculty members have; see that they carry reasonable work loads.—*President, private college*

Leaves of absence for college administrative officers are desirable along with some other dreams of our current Utopia (The Great Society). With the size of the administrative staff we have, they simply would not be practical.—*Liberal arts dean, private college*

Leaves of absence for administrative officers constitute a personally appealing idea, but the idea poses operational problems. A teaching faculty member performs a discrete function in the institution that, when he is on leave of absence, can be postponed for even as long as a year without disturbing operations or that can usually be filled in his absence by his colleagues or a temporary appointee. On the other hand, the responsibilities of a college officer are peculiar to him and his position and the fulfillment thereof cannot be long postponed, nor is there usually a qualified replacement available from within the institution or from outside.—*Business officer, public college*

As to leaves of absence, I am not sold on the need for them for administrators. Vacations are really adequate and I am perfectly free whenever I wish to take a day or two. Perhaps looked at theoretically, periodic leaves of absence do keep an administrator from feeling indispensable, give the staff experience at running things, and enable a successor to be trained. All of this is to the good, but I think that the same ends can be accomplished much more effectively with good organization. So far, I have not felt the need; I'll probably look at it differently in ten years.—*Registrar, private university*

Others believe they can be arranged:

I believe frequent leaves are very important and believe it is possible to arrange the program to make it feasible.—*President, private college*

I certainly endorse a leave for Presidents and I have had a summer leave on the average of one summer in five since 1951.—*President, private college*

In our religious community, we do not take leaves of absence, but I think we should!—*Liberal arts dean, private college*

We confuse consistency with good administration. A change always leads to some inconsistency; hence fears and confusion develop at the thought of an administrator taking a leave. (When this has happened, things go quite well.)—*Vice president, public university*

The inclusion of administrative officers in the pattern of general faculty provision for leaves of absence, without special provision for administrative officers seems appropriate and sufficient.—*Graduate dean, public university*

Some believe in short tenure in office without leaves:

Since the term of office is a stated number of years, I don't believe any extended leave of absence is desirable.—*President, private college*

As to leaves of absence, in my circumstance I doubt their value. The deanship here appears to be held for about five years. At some point I will move over to full-time teaching.—*Liberal arts dean, private college*

These just don't believe in leaves:

I think leaves of absence for university presidents are occupational hazards.—*President, private college*

. . . When an administrative officer takes a leave of absence in most cases he might as well surrender the position to a successor.—*Graduate dean, private university*

I worked in professional consulting life prior to this and I have little sympathy for leaves of absence.—*Director of development, private college*

This panders to man's natural laziness. A month's annual vacation is ordinarily adequate. Cannot see "sabbaticals" for administrative leaders— perhaps some extra vacation for long service.—*Director of development, private college*

I have the old-fashioned feeling that a person is paid for working, and I feel that leaves of absence should be granted only for sickness.—*Business officer, private college*

Leaves should be short and infrequent.—*Liberal arts dean, private college*

REFERENCES TO APPENDIX

Questionnaire, Sections K and L.

Summary Tables 41–44.

CHAPTER 8

HOUSING

IN this chapter, after some general statistics concerning the housing of administrative officers, there is a fuller discussion of the housing of presidents. Knowing that the majority of presidents, but the minority of other officers, are provided with a house, and that to a large extent the president's house is a place of official entertainment, we asked for more details from the president on this subject than we did from other officers.

THE GENERAL SITUATION

Over three-fourths of the presidents are provided with housing by their institutions. In some 7% of these cases (24 public colleges, 19 private colleges, and 1 public university) the president pays rent. Provisions for housing for other officers range from 9% for graduate deans to 28% for deans of liberal arts or deans of students. For these houses, rent is paid by 30% of liberal arts deans, 44% of graduate deans, and 69% of directors of development. Except in the case of presidents, the proportion of housing provided is much less; and the percent of the other officers by whom rent is paid if they live in institutional housing is much higher in public than in private institutions. The proportion of presidents furnished housing (90%) is higher in public universities than in private universities or in colleges of either type; but public universities provide less housing for all other positions than do the other categories.

About one-third of the presidents who are not provided a house are paid a housing allowance. Only a small proportion of other officers who do not receive housing are given such an allowance. In regard to housing, therefore, the picture for the president is entirely different from that for other officers. While seven-eighths of the presidents either are furnished a house free of rent or receive a housing allowance, well under half of the others receive either one. How much under half is hard to determine because of the large number who did not respond to these questions. It should be remembered that religious personnel in Catholic institutions are among those who get free housing, thus accounting for a good many of such cases.

HOUSING THE PRESIDENT

There are 636 presidents of the 813 who answered our questionnaire for whom the institutions furnish housing. Of these, as mentioned above, 44 pay rent.

What goes with the house or, in some cases, apartment? In almost all cases in universities—both public and private—and in public colleges the utilities, heating, maintenance, and repair of the house and maintenance of the grounds are furnished. This is also true in over 85% of the private colleges. The supplying of all or part of the furniture is almost as general, including under "part of the furniture" the case where the institution would gladly furnish all of it but then the president's wife would have no place for her antiques. In 80% of private colleges, 90% of private universities, and 95% of public institutions, when a house is provided a garage goes with it. Air conditioning is provided by most public institutions and private universities and by 40% of the private colleges. The telephone is usually paid for by the institution. Maid service is usual in universities and is provided in about half of the colleges. Providing a cook is less frequent, 27%, although over 50% of the universities do so. About 40% of the universities provide houseman service, as do some colleges. Food is furnished free in about one-fifth of the private institutions, many of these Catholic, and in a few public ones.

Two-thirds of the homes have overnight accommodations for official guests, and in three-fourths of the cases the president considers his home adequate for official entertainment. A number of presidents commented on the suitability of their houses, many favorably. Complaints were common as to location and size, the location often being too central and the size being too small for entertainment or too large for family living. The lack of privacy for guests or family was frequently mentioned.

One president is happy with the homes on each of two campuses.

Presidents are treated well, but required to live in goldfish bowls.

Many of them would rather not. In fact, slightly over a hundred presidents said that they would prefer to live in their own homes, often at a distance from the campus; slightly under a hundred expressed doubts on this question. However, 60% who had official homes are glad of the fact, and many of those who do not have one wish they had.

It might be mentioned here that only a small minority of the other officers without official houses believe that they should have one.

CONCLUSIONS

There are few things considered in this report that depend on local circumstances as much as a wise housing policy for the president and other administrators, as well as for members of the faculty. In some towns, without the interposition of the institution, it would be difficult for a newly arrived administrator to find a suitable home; a housing project of some sort is imperative. In other places there is little need for them.

Too little attention is given to the individual's or his wife's taste and too little consideration to the needs of their children. This is particularly true for presidents.

I believe that:

1. A president should be allowed to decide whether or not to live in an official home and, if his decision is negative, should be given an allowance for housing on an adequate scale, but not on the scale of a house planned for official entertainment.

2. More attention should be given to protecting the privacy of administrative officers, in particular: (*a*) The location of the president's house and that of the dean of the college or the dean of students —if provided by the institution—should not be such as to invite constant intrusion on the private lives of these officers; (*b*) Guests' rooms should be located and have such facilities that both the guests and the host as well as his family have space to themselves; (*c*) Where possible, a place other than a home should be available for the accommodation of official guests.

3. As in the case of faculty housing, help through providing rental space or through the financing of the purchase of homes can be of great use (see *The Outer Fringe*, Chapter 2, especially pages 13 and 14).

4. An institution should not accept the gift of a home to be lived in by an administrator unless there are alternate uses allowed and a date when the gift becomes unrestricted.

There will be more discussion of entertaining as an administrative function in Chapter 9 on official entertaining, which, of course, involves official housing.

REFLECTIONS

Dining and living-room space not large enough, kitchen too small. The house is quite old; was probably adequate for a small family and small faculty, but is much too modest now.—*President, private college*

It would be helpful to the College if we had more adequate space to entertain high-level guests *on the campus,* instead of lodging them in a downtown hotel. Very adequate in most respects.—*President, private college*

Under present conditions, it is not suitable and plans for a new home are underway. It is not suitable because: (*a*) Too old and difficult to renovate; (*b*) Private and entertainment quarters cannot be separated; and (*c*) Too centrally located on the campus—land is badly needed for academic purposes. [Wife would prefer to own their home.]—*President, public university*

Excellent—but located in the center of the campus.—*President, public college*

Excellent for official requirements although a bit difficult for routine living.—*President, private college*

Excellent—couldn't be better!—*President, private college*

Generally suitable but a president's house would be better than sharing a priest-faculty house.—*President, private college*

REFERENCES TO APPENDIX

Questionnaire, Section M.

Summary Tables 45–48.

CHAPTER 9

OFFICIAL ENTERTAINMENT

THE provisions for official entertainment and the opinions of administrators as to its desirable extent vary greatly; and these opinions are not always reflected in the provisions.

ENTERTAINMENT ALLOWANCES

The questions we asked on this subject are in Section N of the questionnaire. Table 49 indicates the percent of administrative officials in the several types of institutions who receive entertainment allowances. A few features of this table merit comment. In the first place the private institution is more likely than the public to provide an entertainment allowance for administrative officers. The great difference in this regard in the case of the admissions officer, who in nearly a third of the private institutions and in only 2% of the public ones has an entertainment allowance, is probably accounted for by the fact that there is more emphasis on the personal recruitment of students in private institutions than in public. Many deans of students entertain student groups frequently and informally. The director of development in a private institution is a money-raiser, a function that entails entertaining. Often in public institutions he is a campus planner.

The availability of entertainment allowances increases with the size of the institution.

About 45% of the presidents of public colleges and two-thirds of the other presidents who have allowances believe that they are adequate. As for the other officers, remembering that only a small minority receive entertainment allowances, we find that over two-thirds of those with allowances are satisfied with them. The happy proportion in private institutions is greater than in public and so are the allowances in institutions of comparable size.

A large sample of replies reporting the amounts of the entertainment allowances gave for the presidents an average of $3,489 per annum in public universities, $1,654 in public colleges, $3,665 in private universities, and $2,222 in private colleges. The allowances that are considered adequate average greater than those that are not. Yet, the overlap is large; one president of a private college considers his allowance of $100 adequate, and another his of $6,000 inadequate. The highest annual allowance in the sample was $9,000, occurring in two public universities. From sampling the replies of directors of development and deans of students, it is clear that not only are allowances given less often to these officers than to the president, but that they are much smaller, perhaps half as large in the case of development officers and one-sixth as large for deans of students as for presidents.

There are varying restrictions placed upon the use of these allowances. In almost all cases the president may use his for entertainment in his home. This is true for only about one-third of the registrars, the proportion running up to three-fourths for deans of students. Almost all persons with entertainment allowances in almost all positions may use these allowances for on-campus entertainment and, almost as generally, for in-town entertainment. Usually, out-of-town entertainment is also covered by such allowances.

Quite a number of persons complained that liquor could not be charged against the entertainment allowance—a complaint sometimes reiterated in connection with reimbursement for travel expenditures. Some mention this regulation with approval. Public institutions more commonly than private ones appeared to have rules against charging for liquor.

In addition to entertainment allowances, many institutions make available their food services, sometimes free, for official entertainment. Sixty-five percent of the presidents may make use of the food services of the institutions for entertainment in their homes, in 70% of the cases without personal charge. Thus, slightly under half of the presidents may use this service free of charge. Such services are available free to about 14% of the directors of development and deans of students down to 3% of registrars. The use of food services for entertaining on the campus is, of course, much more general, ranging from 60% for registrars to 91% for presidents. From 30% for librarians and registrars to nearly 70% of the presidents receive free campus food services for official entertainment. Private institutions are more generous in this regard than are the public ones.

In a number of cases the various administrative officers are provided with free club memberships, obviously often used for entertainment. This provision covers less than 11% of these officers, except for business officers (16%), directors of development (30%), and presidents (38%). Such memberships are less frequently provided by public than by private institutions.

In spite of these allowances and other entertainment privileges, over half the presidents, vice presidents, graduate deans, and deans of students spent their own funds in 1965 for official entertainment. This is also true for almost half of the college deans and directors of development. The registrar, who is supported least in regard to official entertainment, is also least likely to spend his own money upon it. In many cases these personal expenditures are trivial in amount, probably at times representing items for which it is easier to pay than to go through the red tape (perhaps involving receipts) of collecting for them. On the other hand, 63 presidents reported spending $1,000 or more of personal funds for official entertainment in 1965. Some reported several times this amount. Although only 12 officers in the other 9 positions reported personal expenditures for official entertainment of $1,000 or more in 1965, 77 presidents and 97 other officers reported expenditures of between $500 and $1,000. The average annual expenditure of presidents using personal funds for official entertainment and supplying such data is about $615. The director of development is next with $266 per year and the librarian last with $121. The 2,108 officers reporting personal expenditures for official entertainment spent over half a million dollars for this purpose in 1965. Few of them mentioned the savings resulting from being entertained officially themselves.

COGITATIONS AND CONCLUSIONS

In this section I state some rather strong personal opinions which may not be agreed with by the majority of academic administrators but which I believe are shared with a significant number of them. The quotations under "Reflections" sample a wide variety of points of view.

Some might suppose that the statistical description in the foregoing part of this chapter was a build-up for recommending larger allowances and other provisions for official entertainment. This is not so. In fact, I believe that entertainment has often gotten out of hand, at least in the use of time.

First let me set forth my conclusions which are less extreme than some of my discussion.

I believe that:

1. Entertainment is overdone and its importance overrated, and the financial burden and the energy drain that it entails should be diminished.

2. In the case of the president, great effort should be made to decrease his entertainment obligations, but they should be covered more completely than at present both as to financing and as to aid for his wife.

3. In the case of the director of development or other officers who have active responsibilities in fund raising, the financial obligations of reasonable entertainment should be fully met.

4. The dean of students should have certain funds to care for simple entertaining in connection with meeting of students.

5. Unless special circumstances, either temporary or permanent, in a given college demand an exception, other officers should not be furnished with entertainment allowances. If an entertainment allowance is discontinued, some adjustment in salary would seem indicated.

6. There should be a pool, under a single person (a committee only when required by diplomacy), from which substantial costs for special occasions, group visitations, and the like, can be met and this be open for use by the whole academic community—not just by the administration. College facilities that can at times be assigned for the same purpose are desirable. The University of Tokyo has an "official residence" for its president. The president continues to live in his own home. In fact, I believe the official residence has no sleeping rooms, but it has a truly beautiful dining room where delicious meals are graciously served to guests of the University.

VISITORS

Celebrities. Our campus life is greatly enriched by the notable visitors who come to it for speeches, consultation, conferences, and a multitude of other reasons which keep them mobile and us receptive.

They enjoy meeting colleagues if the meeting is informal enough to get somewhere, and we enjoy welcoming them. Only occasionally is a formal affair necessary; but luncheons, dinners, and other group meetings for them are in order and the totality of these on a given campus may be very great. In a large university the departments take care of most of such entertainment. In a small institution the president or dean may often be the host. Frequently, the individual friends of the visitor give a luncheon or dinner for him, but seldom do these fall on the same person so often as to make it financially onerous. Some of the most delightful times I have had were when I was included in such affairs. The colleges may well be grateful to these hosts and gracious hostesses without insulting them by reimbursement. Higher salaries, not more bookkeeping, may well be in order. I recognize that the president will be subject to expenses from performing what are almost ex-officio acts of hospitality, and these should be cared for by the college.

Recruiting. Many speak of the cost of entertaining persons who are being considered for faculty positions. I believe that in most cases this should be left to their future departmental colleagues but not be too great a burden for any one person.

Conference Groups. These should be chiefly supported from funds especially allotted to the conference. When entertainment is provided, it should be by the institution and in the name of the institution.

DONORS

Individual. There is no question that in seeking funds, expenditures frequently must be incurred for entertaining donors, past, present, and prospective. Though any member of the academic community may occasionally meet such an obligation, the president, the development officer, and in some institutions the business officer, must do so regularly. They should be reimbursed for this. The entertainment should be good in quality but not lavish.

Foundation and Government Representatives. In institutions which have many dealings with foundations and government agencies, the normal amenities call for some taking-out-for-lunch and so forth. When this is a frequent occurrence, there should be funds to meet these expenses. Embarrassment will be saved if such entertainment is simple and is in the name of the institution.

Trustees. Trustees or members of the board of visitors get to know each other and enjoy each other's company. They give both of themselves and of their wherewithal. The institutions may well provide luncheons for them and their wives.

Faculty Receptions. These are among the most boring ways of wasting time of which I know. They are usually dreaded by the president, his wife, 90% of the faculty (if attendance is expected), and a large number of wives. They are almost completely useless unless one can get off in a corner and talk shop. I have never known a faculty to judge a president or a dean by the quality or frequency of these receptions. As a means of making genuine contact between the faculty and the administration, they are usually a complete failure. Moreover, the ambiguous statement that is necessary at the end of a dismal evening is repugnant to me! If a college believes these receptions should be held, the responsible officer—whether president or dean— should not be required to pay for them, and his wife should be given every aid in arranging them. If they cannot be abolished at once, a good step in that direction is to decrease their frequency.

Student Receptions. I believe these also have little value. If a student body wishes one, let them arrange and pay for it; but the administration should cooperate by seeing that as far as possible those officials and faculty members whom the students want to be present, attend.

Public Receptions at Commencement. Here my personal distaste for these affairs is overcome by the clear evidence that the public desires them. Year after year I have watched parents of graduating students stand in line for an hour or more, often in oppressive heat, to shake the hand of the president and his wife. The student, if male, is often coerced by his mother to put on a tie and go with her. There is clearly a deep, emotional fulfillment in this and in commencement for many parents. Such an affair should, of course, be arranged and financed by the college. I believe they should be continued, although to me they are painful.

The reader may believe from the above that I dislike all large academic functions. This is not so. I have enjoyed a great many of them. For example, Phi Beta Kappa dinners, and dinners in honor of retiring faculty members. Many of these have both a spiritual and an intellectual content. They have given me the opportunity to speak and to listen, and I have enjoyed both. Besides, in contrast to receptions, these are occasions when one can both eat and sit down.

There are two arguments against the plan of increasing salaries and decreasing entertainment allowances for most administrative officers. First, salaries are a matter of comparison and jealousy. Second, the allowances may be tax-free while deductions on income taxes for official entertainment take a good deal of explaining.

These arguments are cogent but not conclusive.

One does not avoid comparisons by giving people entertainment allowances rather than salaries. Many people, notably the departmental chairmen, do a considerable amount of entertaining that is just as official as that done by the full-time administrators. The belief that someone else has not only a greater salary but also a not clearly justified special privilege can be a source of tension. There is no logical boundary to the system of allowances when it goes beyond the president and a few others, such as the development officer and the dean of students. There can always be a pool to be drawn upon for special functions and group visits.

The tax argument is valid but seldom of great weight. It frequently will not save more than the stimulus to personal economy would produce. I do not readily understand the attitude that encourages spending but considers it almost unethical not to reduce to a minimum what one pays to the government. We should cherish the example of the will of Justice Holmes.

There are other matters to mention.

The president is so much the symbol of the institution, and his entertainment is so customarily at its expense that there is no deceit in his entertaining without explaining who pays the bill. This may also be true of the development officer and sometimes the business officer. Beyond these cases it would seem appropriate, in general, that entertainment paid for by an institution be in the name of the institution.

One insidious facet of an administrative entertainment allowance, if it is used for what appears to be personal entertainment, is that the administrator entertains at the college's expense and is entertained in return at the expense of the individual faculty members.

I am one of those who believe that liquor is not a legitimate item on an expense account, especially in public institutions.

The scale of entertainment can scarcely be controlled by a code, yet there are limits, which if exceeded, should be at private expense. It appears to be true that the more affluent the society, the greater one's desire to spend money other than one's own.

REFLECTIONS

These quotations were selected before I realized what a large proportion come from public institutions. The problem of entertainment funds appears to be more difficult in public than in private institutions.

TYPE OF ENTERTAINMENT THOUGHT DESIRABLE

Allowance should be at least $3,000 per year.—*President, public college*

For entertainment of certain types of visitors to the campus, for candidates for positions on campus; for occasions off campus when representing the institution and see the need to have a person for a drink or a meal.—*Vice president, public college*

Entertain academic department heads, entertain new staff. Reception for graduates and faculty. Entertain selected departments.—*Vice president, public college*

I need at least $1,000 per year to entertain candidates for faculty positions and department heads.—*Liberal arts dean, public university*

I have no need for a specific allotment for entertainment. It would be helpful to be able to tap a fund for small amounts as the need arises.—*Graduate dean, public university*

. . . 1) Entertainment of foundation representatives; 2) Inter-institutional social functions; 3) Governmental agencies visitors to campus; 4) Intra-institutional social functions—for purposes of faculty morale, improving university lines of communications, graduate student morale, faculty-student rapport.—*Graduate dean, public university*

Entertainment allowance desirable for: Contact with booksellers; Potential donors of Friends of Library Group; Informal professional exchange.—*Librarian, public college*

To entertain visiting colleagues, prospective staff members, prospective donors. An entertainment allowance is an urgent need.—*Librarian, public university*

This position could be made more attractive by: . . . Paying for certain memberships in social organizations in the city which would greatly benefit the college.—*Business officer, private college*

The university would likely benefit greatly if staff had financial provision made for picking up tabs for state officers . . . .—*Business officer, public university*

Should be $1500. I am legislative representative.—*Business officer, public university*

To entertain students in home. To entertain staff members in home. To entertain candidates for vacancies on staff.—*Dean of students, public college*

I believe that a small fund for coffee or meals for prospective students and their families and for school [representatives] would leave visitors with a better impression of the school.—*Director of admissions, public college*

Business luncheons and dinners restricted to members of my staff are not considered legitimate expense by the College. Often necessary, however, because of pressures during normal working hours.—*Director of development, private college*

Provisions are quite adequate but would be more satisfactory if first-class rather than tourist-class were permitted; if liquor were an allowable expense in entertaining; and luncheon expense on campus for employees conducting business were permitted as a matter of policy.—*Director of development, public university*

STATUS OF SOME ENTERTAINMENT ALLOWANCES

This office has no fixed entertainment allowances, but small amounts for entertaining visiting dignitaries or candidates for positions will be allowed by comptroller. Alcoholic beverage costs can never be reimbursed.—*Vice president, public university*

We would like to entertain much more frequently. However, the President does not encourage use of college funds for this purpose.—*Liberal arts dean, private college*

Money was provided for a Christmas reception for 200 faculty and wives, but for nothing else. There is obviously other position-related entertaining. —*Liberal arts dean, private college*

Yes; $30 [personal cost]—because the State does not pay for liquor.— *Graduate dean, public university*

A businessman's downtown club—this is only one paid for by institution and other officials can make use of my membership.—*Business officer, private college*

Yes, $500 [entertainment allowance]—*Not* state funds; amount furnished by Alumni Achievement Office; b, Adequate.—*Dean of students, public university*

We entertain every student, all faculty and spouses, trustees and wives at dinner at least once every year, plus teas, receptions, etc.—*President, private college*

Have budget for meetings. More likely to be entertained.—*Director of development, public university*

OPINIONS

I really consider entertaining to be part of my job.—*Liberal arts dean, public university*

I have felt it necessary and desirable to entertain at a reception in my home all new faculty and staff members and wives each year. However, I would not expect the State or college to provide an allowance for this.

There is a state policy against this, and I think the policy is a wise one. — *Liberal arts dean, public college*

When a special occasion arises, such as dedication of a new library, special provision is made for entertainment. This is sufficient. — *Librarian, private college*

On numerous occasions secondary school faculty members make it evident that they are disappointed that the University does not entertain them in the manner followed by private colleges and universities. — *Director of admissions, public university*

Would not recommend allowance for anyone other than the president and development officer because too difficult to control. — *Business officer, public university*

Clear definitions are needed of legitimate entertainment items, and specific provision made for their reimbursement or direct institutional payment. — *Director of development, public university*

Certainly certain types of *pro forma* social necessities and ceremonial duties could be greatly reduced. — *Liberal arts dean, public university*

REFERENCES TO APPENDIX

Questionnaire, Section N.

Summary Tables 49–52.

CHAPTER 10

TRAVEL PROVISIONS

THIS chapter puts within one rather crowded tent five topics, the first three applying to all officers and the last two to the president only. These are:

1. Reimbursement for travel expenses other than by car.
2. The use of institutionally owned automobiles and reimbursement for use of personal cars.
3. Use of institutionally owned or chartered airplanes.
4. Special information concerning the automobile assigned to the president and its use.
5. Travel expenses of the president's wife.

REIMBURSEMENT FOR TRAVEL EXPENSES

We asked about the degree of reimbursement for transportation, hotel rooms, meals, and tips, both when traveling on official institutional duties and when traveling in connection with the officer's professional academic field.

A sample of replies to the query on the adequacy of the travel reimbursement indicates that about 74% of those replying are satisfied with the situation, about 17% are dissatisfied, and about 9% are reasonably happy but with minor reservations. A very large proportion did not comment on this question; probably many of these would join the 9%.

In this sample we received more answers from the business officers than from others, perhaps because they more frequently knew the facts.

TRAVEL ON INSTITUTIONAL BUSINESS. The public-carrier transportation expenses incurred when traveling on official business can almost always be recovered in full. The number of "No Responses" for certain positions, notably librarians, indicates that there are a few officers who have had no occasion to find the answer to this question. Limitations on the type of train or plane accommodations are sometimes imposed, and a few persons said they recover only part of their expenses since they choose to travel more comfortably than they can be reimbursed for. These are a small portion of the whole, but somewhat more significant for public than for private institutions. Some think such restrictions are reasonable; some do not.

Practically all private institutions cover the total expense of hotel rooms, whereas in public institutions from 20% of the presidents to 30% of the registrars and directors of development answer they are reimbursed "in part." This indicates the frequency of some upper limit that may be reimbursed by public institutions on the charge for rooms.

The picture for meals has the same structure as for hotel rooms. A few private institutions are represented in the "in-part" category but still in an almost insignificant proportion, except for librarians where it reaches 7%. For public institutions, from 22% of presidents to 38% of librarians and directors of development answered "in part." Those saying they can get no reimbursement for meals are few, but reach 2% for librarians for private and 3% for public institutions.

Tips are generally paid in full by private institutions. In public institutions about one-third allow them in full, about one-third disallow them, and of the remaining one-third somewhat more answered "in part" than did not respond.

A few persons recognize that there could well be an offset against the expense accounts for amounts that would have been spent at home on meals, carfare, and other items.

There may be a scattering of answers by the totally dissatisfied gloomier than the facts—surmises and not verified. However, considering the distinction made between types of expenses, this would appear to account for very few answers.

TRAVEL IN CONNECTION WITH PROFESSIONAL ACADEMIC FIELD. Although there is no direct evidence, there is a strong presumption that the rules governing the reimbursement to administrators for travel in connection with their professional field are similar to or identical with those for such travel by the faculty. The faculty member is probably more likely to be able to charge such travel to a grant or a contract than is the administrator. The uniformity of answers among the administrators of a given institution would tend to substantiate the above hypothesis.

The number of institutions that pay no expenses for professional travel, in contrast with payments for official business, is far greater; and there is less difference between the policies of public and private institutions. From 7% of librarians to 13% of presidents are ineligible to receive reimbursement for transportation in connection with their professional fields—although I can hardly imagine a trip of the president that would not involve some institutional business.

The number of institutions that make no reimbursement for hotels runs only slightly higher. The same holds in regard to meals. Again, the librarian seems to be the surest to eat or sleep.

About 25% of the institutions, around 40% for public ones, make no reimbursement for tips incurred on professional trips not on institutional business.

Some institutions still have a pernicious practice (for explanation of the use of adjective, see *The Outer Fringe*, p. 98) of paying traveling expenses in full only if one appears on a program.

PER DIEM REIMBURSEMENT. About half of the officers in public institutions state that they are reimbursed for travel expenses other than transportation on a per diem basis; but in private institutions this practice is observed in from 4% for registrars to 12% for graduate deans.

After making this simple statement, semantic difficulties make it hard to say anything more that is not either involved or inaccurate. The difficulties arise from the various ways that "per diem reimbursement" is used. The two arch-types used are: (*a*) A simple claim of so-much-a-day up to a specified limit will be honored without any explanation of the expenses being required. This may be the only way a person is being reimbursed; or he may have the option of presenting details or taking a per diem. At times it is made clear that a man should stick to one or the other method and not select the trips, or even days, on which he is paid on a per diem basis. (*b*) Detailed accounting may be required, but the per diem sets the maximum for the amount to be honored. At times this is broken down into upper limits for meals and for rooms. (One instance was $6 for room, $1 for breakfast, $2 for lunch, and $3.50 for dinner.) Thus, one may not take a small room or go without breakfast to help satisfy a gourmet's palate.

In public institutions, per diem allowance is sometimes different for in-state travel than for out-of-state travel. In all types of institutions it may be somewhat higher for visits to such cities as Washington and

New York than for trips elsewhere. Per diem allowances range from $5 a day to over $35. The average is not far from $15. This statement, as explained above, has little meaning. A given per diem may represent a reasonable option, but justly be considered niggardly if it is used as an upper limit for itemized reimbursement. Satisfaction and dissatisfaction seem about equal in the neighborhood of $20 a day.

Some particular comments dealt with the slowness of reimbursement and the accounting complications, especially in public institutions. Others mentioned the desirability of prepayment. The refusal to cover taxes on travel, which can be avoided—if at all—only by cumbersome methods, was complained about. Still others said that travel insurance either was not covered by the institution or was inadequate.

A large number of persons said the rules governing reimbursement for travel were good but that the restrictions on the total travel budget limited too greatly the amount of travel covered.

A well-justified complaint concerned the cost of the official banquets. For some years I have boycotted most of these in favor of better, less expensive meals elsewhere in the same hotel and with a clear conscience have listened to the after-dinner speeches if they promised to be worthwhile.

AUTOMOBILES

It is a common practice for institutions to own cars which can be used on official business by administrative officers as well as by other members of the staff, and to assign one to the president for his exclusive use—or at least control. For positions other than the president's, from 52% of registrars to 66% of business officers said that an institutionally owned car was available to them. The figure for presidents is 81%. The number of especially assigned cars is under 10% for all officers except: the admissions officer, 10%; the business officer, 10%; the director of development, 15%; and the president, 55%. It must be remembered that many presidents prefer to drive their own cars on institutional business and be reimbursed for doing so.

The cost of operating institutionally owned cars, including gas, oil, maintenance, and insurance, is almost always paid for by the institution. In the large majority of private institutions the president can use the assigned car, without charge, for personal purposes. This is true in half of the public universities that assign a car to the president, but in only about 17% of the public colleges. About 12% of the presidents may use the car for private purposes but pay for the privilege, these instances being mostly in private colleges. For other officers in public institutions the personal use of the car generally is not permitted. A very considerable minority of private institutions, especially universities, allow administrative officers to make personal use of institutional cars, usually free but frequently with a charge.

When a personally owned car is used for official business, the owner is normally reimbursed, at least in part. The basic way that reimbursement is made is on a per-mile basis, although there are rare instances of the institution paying for the auto license, collision or liability insurance, maintenance, and depreciation, or giving a purchase allowance. The per-mile reimbursement is usually within the limits of seven to ten cents. Eight cents is the most frequent figure, accounting for about one-third of the cases. Seven cents is more frequent than nine cents; and ten cents, used in about 16% of the cases, is more frequent than all rates under seven cents combined. The lowest amount that I found anyone thought satisfactory was five cents per mile, and the highest amount considered insufficient was ten cents per mile. Eight cents per mile seems to be about the level where complaints and complacency are in balance. I presume that some have based their opinions as to the inadequacy of the reimbursement rate on carefully kept records; but unless academic (for that matter, general human) nature has changed vastly in this regard, most of these judgments are based on hunch, hearsay, articles (slanted or unslanted) and, perhaps most often of all, predilection toward being satisfied or toward being unhappy.

To shed some light on this matter, I secured the figures from a large state university for the cost of running its car fleet. It must be remembered that there are two major savings that such a fleet affords compared to the use of private cars: it is not subject to state sales taxes on either fuel or the car, and substantial discounts are available to it on the original purchases of cars. The cost per mile (including all costs for gas, oil, maintenance, depreciation, insurance, and administration of a car pool) was, in 1965–66, 5.6 cents per mile. The cars used were mostly medium-priced sedans or station wagons. Certainly this cost, considering the savings involved, would indicate that seven cents per mile is below the cost to the individual. Eight cents per mile might not be far off. Ten cents per mile may be generous.

It is not unusual to pay an allowance per month for the local use of a personal car and a per-mile reimbursement for extended trips of perhaps twenty-five miles or more from the campus. Sometimes distinctions exist between in- and out-of-state travel. At times depreciation allowances are paid with a low per-mile reimbursement in addition. Oil and gas are sometimes furnished directly by the institution to the individual. A number of institutions pay about 5.5 cents if a car-pool car is available but not used, and a higher rate if no pool car is available.

Highway tolls and parking are frequently paid by the institution.

Under local conditions, all of these plans may make good sense.

I believe that those institutions paying less than eight cents per mile should raise their rates and that, with rising costs of maintenance of cars and of safety, those using eight cents per mile might soon consider increasing this rate.

THE PRESIDENT'S CAR. Of the 453 presidents who stated the kind of car assigned to them, the following were most frequently used: Oldsmobile, 19%; Ford, 15%; Buick, 15%; Chevrolet, 11%. The Buicks and Oldsmobiles were tied for the lead among cars of the presidents of universities.

Of the 450 who gave the year of their car, 73% reported either 1965 or 1966 models. These replies were made in the spring or early summer of 1966.

In 35% of the universities and 15% of the colleges where the president has an institutionally owned car available, a chauffeur is provided; but only in a handful of these cases is driving the president's car his only duty.

USE OF INSTITUTIONALLY OWNED
OR CHARTERED AIRPLANES

Evidently somewhat over a fourth of public universities and a scattering of other institutions own airplanes available to the president and certain others on the staff. About a fourth of the universities and not far from 10% of the colleges will on occasion charter a plane for the use of the president or the development officer, and a somewhat smaller portion of our institutions do so for other administrative officers.

A few administrators reported flying their own plane and being reimbursed in a manner similar to reimbursement when they drive their car.

TRAVEL EXPENSES OF PRESIDENT'S WIFE

Few persons are more praised and less provided for than the president's wife.

In considerably less than half of the institutions are the expenses of the president's wife paid when she accompanies him on official business; the private universities do this in slightly over half of the cases. Private institutions on the whole are somewhat better in this regard than are public ones. The same statements hold for the expenses of the wife when representing the president. The president in a number of cases remarked that his wife never officially represented him.

Payment for the wife's travel is one respect in which the situation of the president and, for that matter, of some of the other officers—especially the vice president and academic dean—should be improved. The president is forced to travel a great deal; and when his wife can accompany him, his life will not only be more normal but her presence at social and semisocial functions will add to the value of such occasions. In my opinion, it is outrageous if the expenses of the president's wife are not paid when she represents him, and hence the college, on official occasions, often as effectively as he could himself.

REFLECTIONS
AUTOMOBILES

The question on adequacy was relative to total travel reimbursement, not just reimbursement for use of a personal car. In some cases, such use of a personal car on official business may be so slight that the reimbursement formula is not considered significant.

Some Special Arrangements
8¢ per mile for two persons; 10¢ per mile for more than two.—*Librarian, private college*

9¢ per mile up to 400 miles, ½ that after 400 miles from campus.—*Librarian, private college*

$100 per month for depreciation and travel within 25 miles of college, and 7¢ per mile when traveling beyond a 25-mile radius.—*Business officer, private college*

Auto insurance, auto liability insurance, depreciation allowance $45 per month—mileage reimbursement $50 per month within 25-mile radius plus 7¢ per mile beyond 25 mile radius. Adequate.—*Director of development, private college*

Five cents per mile when college can furnish car. Eight cents if no college car is available . . . .—*Dean of students, public college*

. . . Some provision needs to be made for in-city travel.—*Vice president, private college*

But I am not permitted legally to take it [the car assigned to him] to my home, to and from the campus.—*President, public college*

Opinion re Cents per Mile

Mileage should be 10¢ per mile. [Now 8¢ per mile.]—*Director of admissions, private college*

$0.10 per mile should be raised to $0.12–$0.15.—*Business officer, private college*

I think the rate per mile should be raised to 10¢ now as this is the present government rate and 15¢ by 1967, which I understand is the proposed new rate for that year. [Now 7¢ per mile.]—*Director of development, private college*

TRAVEL REIMBURSEMENT INCLUDING AUTOMOBILE

Professional Meetings

Provisions are adequate for institutional travel, but not for travel related to my academic discipline . . . .—*Liberal arts dean, private college*

Maintaining currency in profession difficult because of partial reimbursement in-state and zero funds for out-of-state.—*Dean of students, public college*

. . . if a paper is given or an office is held, all expenses are reimbursed. —*Vice president, private college*

. . . Reimbursement for trips to meetings where one gives a paper should include more than transportation.—*Graduate dean, public university*

Good Formulas But Not Enough Money To Go Around

Coverage is adequate, but amount available is inadequate.—*Librarian, private college*

Per Diem Payments

Our present per diem is very inadequate. We are required to pay room rate and meals from a $12.00 per day allowance. It definitely needs raising. —*Director of admissions, private college*

$20.00 out-of-state—$10.50 in-state.—*Director of development, public college*

Recommended adequate per diem reimbursement be made to simplify record keeping.—*Business officer, public college*

Public Regulations

Current state allowances for hotel rooms, meals, and incidentals are too low and unrealistic. The method of reimbursement is too slow.—*Liberal arts dean, public college*

. . . Inadequate in larger metropolitan areas . . . or if an expensive banquet charge is part of meeting.—*Business officer, public university*

The amount is fixed by the state legislature for out-of-state and is completely inadequate ($1,000).—*President, public college*

. . . Tips, pressing service, telephones, damaged or lost luggage and the like, while individually inconsequential, add up to a significant amount of unrecoverable official expense.—*President, public college*

. . . Meals eaten out-of-state are not paid for by the state; . . . —*Graduate dean, public college*

Per diem allowance is entirely inadequate. The type of room available at state cost is substandard, uncomfortable, and depressing. Any attempt to use a room for entertaining or interviewing is either embarrassing or impossible.—*President, public college*

State accounting requirement discourages all but minimum travel.—*Graduate dean, public college*

The state comptroller classifies as "institutional business" only a small part of the driving which I have to do, on what is really institutional business.—*President, public college*

Adequate. Accounting procedures are a nuisance, but probably necessary. —*Liberal arts dean, public university*

At times there are echoes from private institutions:

Only complaint might be over comments by non-traveling personnel who review expense accounts. Traveling personnel often feel that non-traveling persons do not understand nor appreciate the problems or expenses of continual travel.—*Director of development, private college*

Particular Set-up

The Association provides the funds and I am expected to use what I need to get the job done.—*Director of development, public university*

[College] can often charge expenses to a grant or contract.—*Vice president, private college*

. . . Meetings west of the Mississippi prohibited.—*Registrar, public college*

Only because air travel includes free meals and frequent trips can be made with little or no lodging involved can I break even on their travel allowance. I think travel expenses should be fully reimbursed.—*Vice president, public university*

Adequacy

Very adequate. All expenses are paid. My budget is $500 per year for travel—not much for some colleges, but adequate for us.—*Vice president, public college*

Limited to one conference per year with so small amount allowed that only local conferences can be attended—Second—it [travel] is not explicitly encouraged!—*Registrar, private college*

I underwrite my 40–60 days off campus on the average of $700 per year. —*Vice president, public college*

Completely adequate and perhaps should be somewhat more controlled, on taxes, for example.—*Business officer, private college*

Special Remarks

Travel, if authorized, should include all expenses to which the traveler becomes liable in excess of what he would have incurred had he remained at home; or a flat per diem should be paid in addition to the economy class air fare and the traveler pay his own.—*Identity lost in a stack of some 6,000 cards.*

Entirely adequate. Even though I am permitted to be reimbursed completely, I never present the full expense as I wish to bear some of the expense because of benefits I feel I derive.—*Registrar, private college*

College pays generously for official travel, but I do little traveling and usually pay my own way (having an independent income).—*Dean of students, private college*

. . . Inadequate in-state during Tourist Season. [From a state with a large tourist business.]—*Vice president, public college*

Fine; however, in view of the frequency that I must travel, it would be very nice if I could, at University expense, take my wife, say, once every six months. [And in the conclusion he asks for:] Some consideration of the pressures the position imposes on my wife.—*Vice president, public university*

There are so many frequent absences from home that the Board has approved my taking along my wife whenever I deem it advisable.—*President, private university*

My wife is a marvelous drum beater for the college—her expenses should be paid when she accompanies me.—*President, private college*

REFERENCES TO APPENDIX

Questionnaire, Sections O and P.

Summary Tables 53–59.

CHAPTER 11

SPECIAL ALLOWANCES

IN this chapter, reports on various allowances or privileges not described elsewhere are brought together. The chief of these is provision for the waiver of the tuition for children of the administrator or the payment of their tuition if they go to college away from home. Other items covered are: moving expenses, professional association membership dues, allowances for the president to make gifts, allowances for miscellaneous expenditures on the part of the president, and aid to the president's wife.

CHILDREN'S EDUCATION

This section very easily could be written in one paragraph if one were willing to assume that it would be read in connection with the report on faculty benefits published under the title, *The Outer Fringe.* It would read as follows: "In the matter of tuition waivers for children of administrators and cash grants toward the tuition expenses of those children who go elsewhere to college, the administrative officers are treated in almost all cases the same as the faculty. The proportion of institutions providing for tuition waivers remained nearly the same from 1963–66. The proportion of private institutions making cash grants for faculty children going elsewhere rose from about 20% to about 30%. My opinions on this question have not changed."

Yet this section should be somewhat more self-sufficient.

Anyone studying the data of the 1963 study and the present one would be struck by the larger proportion of non-responses concerning tuition waivers and cash grants in the present study than in the former. In 1963, the non-responses amounted to about 2% for tuition waivers and 2½% for cash grants, while in the present study non-responses for presidents were 13% in both cases. This is easy to explain, being almost entirely accounted for by the fact that this question is not relevant to presidents of Catholic institutions but does apply to their faculties who were the subject of the 1963 study.

Since most administrators are treated the same as the faculty in respect to children's education, one set of replies will be typical of all; and since the business officers' responses are likely to be the most accurate, and more of them in the case of Catholic institutions are laymen, I have used their replies to compare with those made in 1963.

I reviewed a sample of the cases where the presidents said that the arrangements relative to tuition waiver or cash grants for their chil-

TABLE E
Percent of institutions providing tuition waivers or cash grants for children of business officers and faculty (These figures are based on replies of those who responded to the relevant questions.)

	All Institutions			Public Institutions			Private Institutions		
	Total	Univ.	Col.	Total	Univ.	Col.	Total	Univ.	Col.
Business Officer (1966)									
Tuition waiver	65%	45%	69%	13%	20%	10%	93%	92%	94%
Cash grants	22	12	24	0	1	0	34	33	34
Faculty (1963)									
Tuition waiver	71	53	75	13	22	8	94	92	94
Cash grants	15	10	16	0	0	1	21	23	21
Business Officer same as faculty (1966)	98	99	97	99	99	99	97	100	97

dren were different from those of the faculty. Most of these cases, of which there were very few, were cases where the president explained that being a "religious," the faculty rules did not apply. Most presidents of Catholic institutions did not reply to this question or stated that there was no difference since they were treated the same as faculty members without children. Some gave no explanation for the difference; and some used the space to explain various classes of the faculty that had different treatment from other classes, for instance, those with sons from those with daughters, or those with varying degrees of seniority. It is safe, for all practical purposes, to ignore any difference between the treatment of the faculty and of the administrative officers—even of the presidents—in this matter.

In 1963 we found one institution where the privilege of tuition waivers was extended to the grandsons of faculty members. In 1966 a Catholic institution reported waiving tuition not only for sons and daughters of administrators and faculty members but also for nephews and nieces. Both of these plans help return the pristine meaning to the word nepotism.

Some institutions waive the tuition of faculty wives. (I am glad to report that none stated it paid their tuition to go elsewhere.)

The marked increase in the use of cash grants is probably connected with the diminished use of the "tuition exchange" plan. In this regard I should mention that one institution reported making cash grants for tuition elsewhere only to those who had been refused admission at home.

A number of institutions pointed out that instead of making cash grants to faculty children they made payments directly to the institution the children attended to cover tuition. This, of course, is the practice of many institutions which did not report the distinction on the questionnaire.

There are a number of bilateral or multilateral agreements between colleges for the waiver of tuition.

Even the small proportion of public institutions that reported tuition waivers overstated the case since some of these merely waive out-of-state tuition for the children of staff members when legal residence has not been established, these children being charged the same "incidental fees" that are paid by the residents of the state. The number of public institutions where the administrators' children pay less than residents of the state or city is small. (Incidentally, nomenclature such as "incidental fees" and "out-of-state tuition," used in different manners by public institutions, has been the basis of a good deal of public misunderstanding, for example, in California.)

I now report a few of the conclusions on this matter contained in *The Outer Fringe:*

1. This is an important benefit, highly valued by some of the staff, and is considered by administrators to be important in recruiting and holding faculty.

2. In my judgment, it is not a socially defensible practice and is particularly unfortunate when used by public institutions.

3. If, however, tuition is waived for children of the staff, it is wise also to establish a system of grants for those who go elsewhere. Often

the going away to college is educationally desirable, and in non-coeducational institutions it is necessary for about half of the children. Pressures to vary the admissions practices of an institution in favor of faculty children should be minimized. (In the case of administrative officers, especially the president, the dean, and the admissions officer, there may be elements of embarrassment in having a son or daughter enroll in the home college.)

I therefore welcome the increase in the practice of making cash grants to children going away to college where the institution itself provides them with tuition waivers, although I would welcome even more the doing away with both waivers and grants.

May I add that in *The Outer Fringe* I quoted at length—as a rebuttal to my own arguments—those of an able, experienced, and wise administrator in a private institution who disagrees with me on this subject.

MOVING EXPENSES

The proportion of officers who came to their present positions from other institutions ranged from 26% for graduate deans (20% in universities) to 54% for presidents and 66% for librarians. The moving expenses of the presidents were paid in full in 65% of these cases in private institutions and 28% in public institutions. The percent of other officers whose moving expenses were covered is much less than for the president, but for all positions is considerably higher in private than in public institutions. If any expenses are paid, they are usually paid in full. However, the number of cases where about half of the expenses were paid is not negligible.

PROFESSIONAL ASSOCIATION MEMBERSHIPS

The question concerning membership in professional associations clearly had a different meaning for the president, the vice president, the liberal arts and graduate deans, and the librarian than for the other officers. For the first group it stood for membership in such organizations as the American Physical Society or the Modern Language Association. For the latter it was membership in the society of those people in one's own particular position, such as the Association of College and University Business Officers. The different meanings of course resulted in reporting different practices. For the president, 12%

of the public institutions and 53% of the private institutions pay professional dues. For the vice presidents, liberal arts and graduate deans, and librarians taken as a group, about 5% of the public institutions and about one-third of the private ones pay professional dues. For the remaining five positions, about 40% of the public institutions and 75% of the private pay such dues. (These figures are somewhat larger than is the case for deans of students, and smaller for registrars of public institutions.)

The distinction between the two types of professional organizations is clearly valid. The registrar has an institutional obligation to belong to the Registrars Association, whereas there is more reason, if any, to pay the dues of a professor than of the dean in the American Mathematical Society.

In many Catholic institutions the dues of any organization to which the president belongs are paid by the institution; one president listed 21 such organizations.

ADDITIONAL ALLOWANCES OF THE PRESIDENT

FOR MAKING GIFTS. Some 51 institutions reported that they budgeted funds for gifts in the name of the president, for example, for the Community Chest. A sample indicates that about two-thirds of these are Catholic institutions. Since in many of these cases the presidents have no personal funds, it is clear that the gifts are institutional, but determined by the president. I expect that many of the other presidents who have this privilege also make clear the source of the gifts. The funds for this purpose range up to $5,000 per annum, but most are for $500 or less. The total amount spent in this manner is probably around $50,000.

ALLOWANCES TO COVER MISCELLANEOUS ITEMS. Among presidents, 111 of 813 reported that the institution provides "an annual expense allowance intended to cover the items not reported in normal expense accounting." Such an allowance is a convenient way to cover fully justified expenses. These allowances range up to about $10,000 but the median is somewhere between $1,000 and $2,000. Although the allowance is not always completely expended, the amount spent annually in this manner probably substantially exceeds $500,000.

SECRETARIAL HELP TO PRESIDENT'S WIFE. I am sorry to report that only about 25% of the institutions provide secretarial help for the president's wife. About 5% list it as moderate, and only 1% as substantial;

true, 19% of the presidents, many of them unmarried, did not respond to this question.

REFLECTIONS

CHILDREN'S EDUCATION

Facts

Remission of tuition if parent has been employed by [the college] at least 3 years and if more than 50% of the family income is derived from [the college].—*President, private college*

Full waivers are granted only to the families of a few senior workers. For the rest, the waiver is up to 20% of salary.—*President, private college*

Students who are from faculty or administration families also have free tuition at other state institutions.—*Liberal arts dean, public college*

For non-resident tuition if faculty member is not a . . . resident.—*Graduate dean, public university*

$1,000 per year, per child, but not restricted to tuition.—*Business officer, private college*

No. The bishop frowns on priests having children! Faculty and all married employees may send their children (male) here tuition free. Priests excepted.—*Dean of students, private college*

Wishes

Family or educational allowances in cash rather than service. Attendance of children at institution where parent works poses many problems.—*Business officer, private college*

There is need to provide tuition allowances for children of the faculty and of the administrative officers to attend *other* colleges. This need is more urgent for administrative officers' children than for faculty because of the local involvement of administrative staff members—fairer to the children to attend elsewhere.—*Dean of students, private college*

It would be a great satisfaction to me if the Board would decide to underwrite faculty and staff tuitions for faculty children at other colleges. This is one of the few things that I think they should do that they have so far not been willing to do. Another thing that I would appreciate would be to have available to me a small contingency fund. This year through the generosity of the . . . Foundation, I have such a fund, and it has been a great help to me. Things do come up that one really had no way of anticipating.—*President, private college*

The other fringe benefit which would make a great deal of difference to me and many of my colleagues would be an allowance for college expenses for our children. Since our institution is one with limited focus—not a large multiversity—the provision for tuition waiver in our own institution but nowhere else is a rather dubious benefit. Unless our children want to be teachers, they will likely want to go elsewhere.—*Vice president, private college*

Having no children I am not included in the fringe benefit allotted to those who have children so I am happy to say that I have been able to save the College a considerable amount of money. Those with four to six children (or more) are really fortunate. They are given also activity tickets for every member of their families and it costs the College double for dinners and other activities which include the spouse. We hope that the college appreciates the bargain it has in its faculty which does not get those fringe benefits, for it gives us great pleasure to know that we are donating such large sums in addition to periodic cash donations. So much for that.—*Librarian, private college*

Other Allowances
. . . My college is most generous in providing financial assistance for further education, and, even more important, provides the climate which is supportive of further education. By this I mean that I have the freedom to take time away from the office to work on my doctoral dissertation, attend institutes, etc. Without this kind of understanding, the financial help would be less meaningful.—*Director of admissions, private college*

[Budget for gifts] included in budget for "Goodwill and Favors."—*President, private college*

. . . A discretionary fund would be highly desirable. I have of course various funds, but their use is circumscribed pretty closely.—*Liberal arts dean, public university*

. . . My wife does all the family bookkeeping and personal business work. In addition, she handles our complicated social calendar. She should be on the payroll or have personal secretarial help.—*President, public university*

By my own free choice I spend many evenings and weekends working in my office. I would like an allowance of $2,000 to $3,000 to spend on persons who would take care of the lawns, garden, and help my wife with household chores so that entertaining would not be a burden. An entertainment allowance . . . would also be desirable. I would prefer this to living in a college-owned house.—*Liberal arts dean, public university*

REFERENCES TO APPENDIX

Questionnaire, Question 22, Sections G, Q, and R.

Summary Tables 14, 29–30, 60, 62.

CHAPTER 12

THE OFFICE AND THE STAFF

THE OFFICE

IT would be easy and factual to report that the large majority of administrative officers are satisfied with their offices and their furnishings. This would miss the point. A considerable number are dissatisfied. This is significant both because it is unfortunate to have overloaded keymen work under unsatisfactory physical conditions and because it indicates in how many instances the administrator has placed the working conditions of others ahead of his own. The scope of responses to questions on this subject varied greatly. For example, the president and deans usually interpreted the questions as applying to their immediate offices. The librarian often seemed to consider the whole library.

Queries were made concerning six aspects of the administrative offices: (1) floor space and layout; (2) physical attractiveness; (3) furnishings; (4) office equipment; (5) location on campus; and (6) conference rooms. One was asked to check in each case whether that aspect was satisfactory, unsatisfactory, or not considered important. For a question so near the end of an exhausting questionnaire, the small number who did not respond is remarkable. The president and business officers almost all answered every portion of the question. The librarians had the greatest number of "no responses," reaching 13% for private college librarians in regard to conference rooms. Except for conference rooms all other items were considered "important" by nearly the complete list of respondents; 16% of the registrars and 10% of the business officers, along with a fair number of other officers, did not consider conference rooms "important."

Table 61 is a dissatisfaction table giving the percent of administrative officers in each of the ten positions who believed given aspects of their offices were unsatisfactory.

I tried to write some general comparative statements concerning universities versus colleges and public versus private institutions, and they turned out to be more confusing than a direct perusal of the table.

In general, it must be stated that we have far too many administrators handicapped by the lack of proper office conditions. They share this handicap with the faculty who, in addition, often struggle with outdated laboratories and crowded classrooms. Priorities must be set campus by campus. A luxurious office can readily be a cause for jealousy, but the adequate office is a great educational asset. One should not be showy, but it is equally important not to be quixotic as to one's appurtenances.

A few particular topics concerning offices and equipment should be mentioned. A significant number stated that their offices were poorly located, although occasionally the complaint was that the location was too central—too much in the mainstream of traffic—causing unnecessary and irrelevant interruptions. The more frequent desire was to be nearer to the center of things and closer to other administrators. The development officers often seemed to have particularly valid reasons for being dissatisfied with the location of their offices, one of these being located in the center of the city, miles from the campus.

A number wanted a "hide-out"—some sort of private office in addition to the official one. For years, while a dean, I benefited by having a small office in close proximity to my regular office with an unlisted telephone and a desk calculator. People soon came to know of it, but also to respect its privacy. This was of great value to me. Once while playing billiards at the faculty club, I hung on my back a sign in small type reading: "These are not office hours." The effect was lasting.

The safe storage of records was frequently mentioned, particularly by registrars; fire, theft, and alteration are all feared.

Of course, the location of the phone, the Xerox machine, the secretary, and the computer come in for attention.

To some the computer seems the promise of a simple life. Those who use one realize that although things may be done with computers that are impractical to do in any other manner, it is still true that if used only for a small fraction of their capacity, they are expensive for what is performed, and if programmed to capacity, demand much service and often are used for projects heretofore considered marginal, such perhaps as servicing our questionnaire. There is also little doubt that this will increase the expenditures and the manpower requirements of the institutions. The electric typewriter is a cheaper status symbol.

THE STAFF

We asked:

Do you believe your own office is now staffed in such a way as to enable you to make reasonably satisfactory use of your time? (Please comment.)

and

What additions or changes do you think might be desirable in the organization or staffing of your own office? (Please comment.)

The comments on the first question were as enlightening as the attempts to give categorical answers to it, which averaged "yes, but."

Most of the discussion of the answers to these questions will be given in the chapters on the separate positions. A few general ones can be made here.

More clerical help is needed by many administrators, and frequently the need is more to improve the quality than to increase the quantity. At some places, leaves, unsatisfactory applicants, and rapid turnover and poor pay—particularly poor pay—were cited. Sometimes a college is in so small a community that there is an insufficient clerical pool to draw upon. The civil service system was often blamed— usually unjustly, I believe, except when employing a person at the highest level. My experience is that the civil service system is a boon to both employers and employees. In contrast to these complaints, there were many heartwarming tributes to the devotion, intelligence, and effectiveness of individual secretaries.

Another almost universal desire is for a deputy who can speak for the officer and take over in his absence, perhaps even making leaves feasible. Not only the first team of the Packers is great, but so is their "bench"; it did much to win the championship. A college administration also needs a "bench."

Student help is a source of unhappiness. Some students are able; some are not. All have scholastic duties which take high priority. Scheduling their working time is difficult. However, my own experience with student help has been happy.

In many instances, after stating what extra staff was desired, the administrative officer pointed out that without more space no more staff could be used. Also, in a large number of institutions the staff is being enlarged, often in response to needs of growth and opportunities afforded by new buildings.

The desire may be for either more or better staff in offices other than one's own. The handicap of dealing with an office where the normal flow of work is impeded by inadequate staff is nerve-racking. Every dean can mention some department that has stymied him in this fashion.

Another complaint from every position was that the respondent must do too much routine work because he has no one to whom he could delegate it. There certainly are many instances where this is true. There are also many instances where doing some of this routine work leads to greater understanding and fulfills the psychological function of relaxing the tension while satisfying the puritanical urge, almost universal in administrators, to keep busy. By all means, get secretaries who can do many jobs better than you can, but preserve some areas of routine expertness in which you excel—if for no other reason than to increase your self-respect.

Hardly anyone is unaffected by federal programs. They are of great benefit to our institutions. Sometimes, they are literally lifesavers; but they have greatly increased the paperwork, perhaps unnecessarily. However, much of the red tape is the reaction of the upright bureaucrat (an honorable designation) to the chiseler—even, I am sad to admit, the academic chiseler. There is no question, however, that offices that would have kept up with the increased load caused by more students, are severely taxed by the additional procedural complications connected with government programs, not only those programs that give money for educational purposes, but also those, such as Social Security and Selective Service, that require service from the institution.

Years ago I visited a major university and asked the chairman of the mathematics department about the administrative structure of the university. These, omitting names, are almost his words: "We have an able president, but he is a very busy man; so he appointed a vice president who is also dean of a college, and a very busy man; so he appointed a provost and everybody wished jobs on him, so he became a very busy man; so he got a secretary, Miss. H., who is a very intelligent woman, and things get done."

REFLECTIONS

THE OFFICE

The Dean of Students' Office is like Grand Central Station. The Dean should have an inner office so that persons seeking to have a conference cannot walk past the secretary right into the office . . . . One of the chief sources of frustration is the constant interruptions the Dean of Students experiences. Most people think you are "not busy" if you happen to be writing, reading mail, or pulling material from a file. You must constantly have someone in your office if you want to be considered busy.—*Dean of students, private college*

The arrangement of the registrar's office here is perhaps the source of greatest frustration. It is located so that the Registrar is always available to the public while the secretary is secluded in an inside office.—*Registrar, private college*

Not having a private office, it is impossible to talk with staff, faculty, students, or visitors, confidentially.—*Registrar, public college*

Needed improvements are: (1) Space for visitors to be seated comfortably in waiting room; (2) Space for seating visitors comfortably in private office; (3) Space and furniture to provide "admissions atmosphere" rather than the present "business office atmosphere" which is crowded.—*Director of admissions, public university*

We would like to move our Xerox machine out of the center of the main office, away from the counter where we serve students and faculty and general work area.—*Registrar, private college*

However, now almost all of my letters are dictated through my telephone to our central typing . . . .—*Liberal arts dean, private college*

Severity of space allocations and lack of niceties of a pleasant environment so often found in business situations (drapes, rugs, armchairs, private or even semi-private restrooms, shower facilities, etc.).—*Liberal arts dean, public college*

The building lacks adequate facilities for clerical staff—no rest room for smoking or lunch—no hot water in three summer months, etc.—*Director of admissions, private college*

A genius working full-time could not design a more inefficient layout of administration facilities . . . . Close proximity of academic and business administration is paramount . . . .—*Business officer, private college*

THE STAFF

I have no secretary and must depend on student labor, which is not conducive to efficient operation of the office for the following reasons:
1. Difficult to schedule student time so that I have help all day. At times I have no help, at others too much help.

2. It is difficult to hold any one person responsible, since several students may work on one job before it is finished.
3. So many people in an office tend to cause confusion and distractions.
4. Difficult to secure students who are well qualified.
5. I must spend a great deal of time planning their work for them in advance. — *Graduate dean, public college*

I am not allowed a budget for student help or a free hand to administer it. A central administrative office chooses all student workers and sets salary. I can only accept or refuse individual students as they are sent to me. — *Librarian, private college*

Need for a first-rate assistant. Because I have a relatively long period of service ahead, it is difficult to attract competent individuals when the opportunity for advancement within the office seems so small. Adequate salary is also a problem. — *Registrar, private university*

In a way it is. What I really need is to have a "right hand" man that can do everything I am supposed to do, but is willing to be paid for on a lower scale. — *Librarian, private college*

Policy now prohibits employment of new staff member until person leaving has used all of her vacation time. — *Registrar, public college*

The college classes, and therefore the teaching faculty, are now scheduled on a five-day week, but all administrative offices are still on the 5½ day week. It would provide some needed rest and relaxation for all administrative officers if these offices were closed on Saturdays, at least in the summer months since we do not have summer sessions. If the above-mentioned assistance is secured, the work of the Registrar's Office should not suffer. — *Registrar, private college*

The keen competition by industry, government and other educational institutions, for personnel, makes staffing very difficult. — *Business officer, private college*

Low clerical salaries deny us the type of qualified people we need to do the best possible job. This is a constant irritation. — *Librarian, private college*

Higher salary for my secretary. *Very necessary.* — *Liberal arts dean, private college*

Most of all we need *intelligent* and *educated* secretaries, girls who can be turned loose on a job and who will complete the job in an intelligent and craftsmanlike way. — *Liberal arts dean, public college*

I presently have two part-time secretaries, one of whom works five days a week, the other three days. They are mothers of school age children and are *supplementing* their family income rather than earning it entirely. In the two years this office has been in operation they have acquired considerable competency in their work. For this reason I feel they are quite valuable. It would be preferable perhaps to have one full-time employee, but it is unlikely that one as well qualified and trained as these two could be found because the salary offered would be prohibitive for one who must earn her livelihood. — *Director of admissions, private college*

At times, I am a rather highly paid secretary myself.—*Dean of students, private college*

The chief source of frustration is my secretary who has been here 16 years—unmarried—and who feels that what has been done for the past decade is still the thing to do.—*Dean of students, private college*

Because I am blessed with an excellent secretary, I feel my office is adequately staffed. The efficiency of my secretary makes her in some ways an administrative assistant.—*Vice president, private college*

Too many small colleges overstaff in administration.—*President, private college*

REFERENCES TO APPENDIX

Questionnaire, Section R.

Summary Tables 61–63.

PART II   VARIOUS POSITIONS,
CHIEFLY AS SEEN BY INCUMBENTS

CHAPTER 13

THE INCUMBENTS

THE chief purpose of Part II is to give information derived from the section of the questionnaire on "personal data" and to describe the replies to our request for general comments.

Many of the facts concerning the incumbents of various administrative positions will be discussed in the chapters devoted to those positions. The tables in the Appendix give additional detail as does also Part I.

I suggest that, whether it is as interesting or not, it may be more important to read about the other positions than to read about your own. This is especially true in perusing the "Reflections."

SOME STATISTICS ABOUT INCUMBENTS

Table 9 gives the proportion of women in the various administrative positions. There are few women presidents, vice presidents, deans, business officers, or directors of development except in women's colleges—perhaps most often in Catholic women's colleges. This is by no means true of librarians, deans of students, directors of admissions, or registrars. In fact, in the private colleges, women outnumber the men among librarians and registrars.

Roughly speaking, the presidents tend to be around 55 years of age; the vice presidents, deans of liberal arts, graduate deans, librarians, and business officers, about 50; and for deans of students, directors of admissions, registrars, and the directors of development the median is a youngster of about 45 years. More data on ages are given in Tables 7 and 8.

There is an interesting pattern of educational background as shown in Table 10. Over 70% of the vice presidents, deans of liberal arts, and graduate deans hold the Ph.D. degree. This is true of 59% of the presidents, 21% of the deans of students, and a goodly sprinkling of the rest.

In addition, doctorates in education are held by 11% of the presidents, 16% of the vice presidents and graduate deans, and 18% of the deans of students with a scattering in other positions. Of the 525 officers reporting that they have the degree of doctor of education, 273 (52%) are in public colleges, many of which at an earlier stage were teachers' colleges and before that, normal schools. These institutions account for only 22% of the responding officers. In all positions, except for the director of development, the majority of those without the doctor's degree do have a master's degree.

The distribution of major subjects among administrative officers, although fascinating, is hard to depict. If we divide them among the multitudinous categories which the officers themselves listed, the data become so diffuse as to be meaningless. If we group them by large classifications, essential differences are hidden. We will attempt in the sections devoted to each position to say something about the educational background of the incumbents, but here we will mention only a few points of general interest.

Nearly a quarter listed education as their major. There is a heavy concentration of these among presidents of public colleges, 49%. In all types of institutions, there is a high proportion of education majors among deans of students, 40%, admissions officers, 36%, and registrars, 34%, with even higher proportions in public institutions. In fact, over half of the deans of students and admissions officers in public colleges, and admissions officers and registrars in public universities, are education majors. Aside from these three officers, the number of education majors in the universities in the ten administrative positions is relatively small.

If we lump together the social studies, but exclude from them philosophy, psychology, geography, and commerce, we account for about 18% of the officers. This, in spite of the fact that 65% of the librarians have majored in library science; 49% of the business officers in commerce; and 54% of the deans of students, 44% of the directors of admissions, and 40% of the registrars either in education or psychology, often presumably educational psychology. Perhaps it should be noted that 11% of the presidents and 7% of the development officers majored in religion—many, but by no means all, of these being in Catholic institutions.

It is customary for the vice president, the dean of liberal arts, and the graduate dean to hold tenure positions on the faculty. This is true of just under half of the librarians (considerably over half in the universities). This is also true of over a third of the deans of students, but of even fewer in other positions, being as low as 16% of business officers and directors of development. Lack of formal tenure does not mean that persons will necessarily be treated unfairly, or even with harsh justice. In fact, persons who work as closely with the governing boards as do presidents, business officers, and directors of development will be shown every consideration, except in those rare instances where personal animosities have developed. It should be remembered that holding a tenure position in the faculty does not mean tenure in the administrative position to which a man may be currently assigned. Moreover, it is not unusual to give an administrator faculty rank without granting him tenure in this rank.

Between 40% and 50% of the business officers, directors of admissions, and directors of development who have faculty rank have tenure in such rank; so have 50% to 60% of the presidents, librarians, deans of students, and registrars. Of those with faculty rank, 72% of the liberal arts deans, 77% of the vice presidents, and 89% of the graduate deans have faculty tenure.

This discussion should be compared with that in Chapter 3 on retirement describing the opinions of administrators of the possibility of continued employment if they left their administrative post before the normal faculty retirement age.

Two-thirds of the librarians, more than half of the presidents (just under half in private institutions), less than half of the deans of students, and around a third of the other administrators, except the graduate deans, came to their present positions from other institutions. About a quarter of the graduate deans did so. More details are given in Table 13.

HOW LONG DO ADMINISTRATIVE OFFICERS SERVE?

This is a far harder question to answer than would appear on the surface. We asked administrative officers how long each one had been in his present position and how long his predecessor served. Tables 12 and 15 are derived from these answers.

If we had a static population of institutions, each with a fixed administrative structure, the answers to the second of these questions would give reasonable estimates of the length of administrators' services. However, those who have no predecessors represent the longer surviving group in new institutions or in newly created positions (sometimes only new in title), while those who reported a predecessor draw not only on the normal turnover from relatively older positions, but the short-time turnover from those recently established where the term could not have been longer than the existence of the position itself. For example: If an institution is six years old and the first director of development served for three years, his successor would report the fact; but if the first director of development was still in office, he would have no predecessor and would not be in the group considered in Table 15. Thus, our sample is weighted with short-term predecessors. Table F gives the approximate proportion in each posi-

TABLE F
Percent of officers reporting they have no predecessor

President	4%	Business Officer	20%
Academic V.P.	25%	Dean of Students	25%
Liberal Arts Dean	15%	Dir. Admissions	21%
Graduate Dean	24%	Registrar	8%
Librarian	6%	Dir. Development	40%

tion of persons reporting they have no immediate predecessor. This table was based on a tally that did not distinguish among the types of institutions.

Since almost every institution has a president, we may estimate that about 4% of all responding institutions are not older than the tenancies of their present presidents. In most other positions, except that of librarian or registrar, the figures in Table F chiefly represent restructuring of the administrations of the institutions, or in some cases merely a change of title.

Since only about 4% of the presidents reported having no predecessor, the figures of Table 15 probably give a good estimate of the tenure of presidents; namely, an average of 11 years, and a median of 9 years. However, the figures for the development officer, an average of 4 years and a median of 3 years, are probably far under what may be expected, since over 40% of the development officers are the first incumbents of their positions. The figures for librarian, registrar, and perhaps dean of arts would yield fairly good estimates of length of tenure. The rest would not.

For the same four positions—president, librarian, registrar, and liberal arts dean (where the number with no predecessors is small) — a good estimate of the length of service which the present incumbents will have served when they leave office can be secured by assuming that on the average they have served half their terms.

On the basis of all the evidence, we would conclude that the president probably serves on the average of 11 years, the librarian and registrar about the same, and the dean of liberal arts about 8 years. There should be a small but indeterminate correction upward to these figures, the correction increasing from position to position in this list. The present presidents, when they retire, should have served on the average about 14 years, the librarians about 20, the registrars about 18, and the liberal arts deans more than 12, again with the upward correction. The above paradox is akin to the fact that the average length of the whole lives of those now living will be greater than the average length of all persons born during the period when the living were born.

I hope that St. Peter as a professional statistician agrees that it is better for me to make reasonable guesses on relevant but inconclusive evidence than not to guess at all.

Table 16 gives the median age when predecessors left their offices. Again, where there are many new positions, there is a downward bias in these figures as compared with those for a stable situation. Hence, the more significant figures should again be those for positions of president, librarian, registrar, and dean of arts, except for the fact that the librarians are either less informed about the ages at which their predecessors left office or are more reluctant to give such information than are other officers, since 23% of the librarians with a predecessor did not give the predecessor's age, while only about 9% of the presidents failed to do so. Forty-one percent of the librarians are women. The more pertinent information as to what percent of the librarians' predecessors were women is not available. (My secretary thinks that this whole remark is itself impertinent.) It will be noted that presidents are the only group in which the median age of the predecessors leaving office is anywhere near normal retirement age.

PRESENT STATUS OF PREDECESSOR

Table G gives us the distribution into categories of the present status of the immediate predecessors of the incumbents of various

TABLE G
Present status of predecessor

	Number reporting age and status of pred.*	President elsewhere	On a college faculty	Other position in same inst.	On leave	College position elsewhere†	Other	Retired	Deceased	Av. age of pred. on leaving office	Av. age of pred. now
President	702	8%	10%	...	1%	...	30%	23%	29%	58	65
Academic V.P.	304	...	...	29	2	30	12	15	12	53	58
Liberal Arts Dean	450	...	...	39	3	23	11	14	10	52	58
Graduate Dean	185	...	...	34	4	20	9	18	15	54	59
Librarian	530	...	...	10	1	29	18	22	20	51	61
Business Officer	516	...	...	11	0	18	30	19	22	52	61
Dean of Students	429	...	...	34	4	30	22	7	4	45	50
Dir. Admissions	421	...	...	30	1	22	28	11	8	45	51
Registrar	518	...	...	26	1	15	20	25	13	50	59
Dir. Development	258	...	...	15	0	30	39	9	7	46	50

* The percents are based on the persons who gave both the age and the status of their predecessors. The average age of predecessor now is given here as the sum of the average age of predecessor on leaving the position and the average length of service of the present incumbent. Since some of the incumbents had no predecessors, and hence the populations are somewhat disparate, the results are only approximate and probably slightly low for certain positions. Moreover, these include the ages of those now deceased.

† The presidents' questionnaire did not inquire whether the predecessors had other positions in the same institutions or college positions elsewhere. However, presidents' predecessors reported as being "on a college faculty" were probably mostly but not entirely at other institutions.

positions, as well as approximations to the present ages of these predecessors, whether living or not.

Although the average retirement ages and length of service of the incumbents' predecessors are somewhat greater, position by position, in universities than in colleges, and in public institutions than in private, the differences appear unimportant.

Several items in Table G are worth pointing out. First of all, as expected, the percent retired or deceased is highly correlated with age of leaving office. Second, those on leave are a mere smidgen, except for positions such as graduate dean and dean of students, where leaves may be given for a man to catch up or go ahead in his field after a stint of administration.

Since 8% of the former presidents are now presidents at other institutions, and since some of the more than 50% who are now retired or deceased almost certainly served in such capacity, it would be fair to estimate that nearly 10% of those who leave a presidency go to another. Some leave a presidency to go to one with a later retirement age. Presidents, librarians, business officers, and development officers rarely take positions on the same campus when they give up their offices. The large number of college or graduate deans who go to some other position on the campus probably are composed both of those who take a regular faculty position and those who become presidents or vice presidents; in the latter case sometimes a new title covers the same old job. The interinstitutional mobility of college administrators, who often complain of the mobility of the faculty, is shown by the proportion of previous administrators who hold positions on some other campus.

THE COMMENTS OF ADMINISTRATORS

In addition to asking for much statistical data with comments on specific topics, the questionnaire ended with the following invitation:

The answers to the preceding questions form the substance from which good appendices are made, but the real judgments derived from the study must be the distillation of the wisdom of those who live with the administrative problems of our colleges and universities. Hence we are particularly anxious for you to comment on the topics of this study, including, but not limited to, the following:

a. Your compensation and conditions of work and on any means by which your work might be made pleasanter and more effective.

   b. The chief sources of frustrations and tensions, if any, that arise in the conduct of your office.

   c. The desirability of leaves of absence for the college president.

   d. Suggested methods of improving the conditions of work for the other administrative officers of the college.

   e. The desirable composition of the board of trustees and the ways the trustees can aid the president.

   f. Ways of improving the attractiveness of the position of president.

Suggestions *d* and *e* were omitted from the questions sent to officers other than the president, and the wording of *c* and of *f* was modified to apply to these officers.

Not only did we receive a larger number of replies to the questionnaire than was expected, but the opportunity to write on the above and related topics was taken by a surprising portion of those who returned the questionnaire. These included a few who carefully blotted out certain passages; presumably the mere writing was sufficient catharsis.

The replies to item *c* have been described and in some cases quoted in Chapter 7 on "Vacations and Leaves," and numerous other quotations from the last page of the questionnaire have been used in other chapters, especially Chapter 2 on "Salaries" and Chapter 12 on "The Office and The Staff." Practically all the items that were described in Part I are among those mentioned in these final comments.

Certain statements occurred frequently and seemed to stem less from a particular position than from the circumstances under which administrators, in general, work. The quotations selected from the terminal comments on the questionnaires are contained in the chapters on the various positions.

The academic vice president and the dean of liberal arts are dealt with in a single chapter, and the admissions officer and the registrar in another. In both cases this seemed desirable because of a number of instances where the two positions were held by the same person.

In the Introduction, I mentioned certain ambiguities derived from local variations in the use of English. Some ambiguities are built into the language itself. Three words—"quite," "moot," and "adequate"—were frequently used in replies to the questionnaire. The context did not always make clear whether "quite" meant "rather" or "completely," whether "moot" meant "open to discussion" or "no longer of practical significance," and whether "adequate" stood for "really sufficient," "tolerable but not generous," or "all right because it is of slight importance." The following synthetic sentence is twelve-valued: "Our policy for sick leaves was adequate but in light of our new quite good disability plan our future policy is a moot question." Explanations may leave one more puzzled than their omissions. For example, one respondent referred with a touch of admiration to a colleague as an "S.O.B." with the footnote "used in the business and oil field sense of the word."

The very few vitriolic remarks made concerning colleagues have been omitted.

REFERENCES TO APPENDIX

Questionnaire, Section C.

Summary Tables 1, 7–13, 15–16.

CHAPTER 14

THE PRESIDENT

WE start with details concerning the presidents of American universities and colleges. Many of these facts, along with similar statistics concerning other officers, will be found in Tables 7–13, 15, and 16. Some of the data has been absorbed into other chapters, particularly Chapter 13 concerning the incumbents. Using both the same and additional material, Francis P. King, in an article in *Liberal Education*, October, 1967, entitled "Presidents' Profile," has given a splendid statistical description of the presidents.

The median age of male presidents is 54. Seventy percent of the presidents hold a doctorate; 59%, the Ph.D., and 11%, the Ed.D. The highest degrees of over four-fifths of the presidents were in the following fields: education, 24% (49% of public college presidents); social sciences, 24%; religion, 11% (mostly private church-related institutions); English or journalism, 8%; philosophy, 7% (almost entirely private colleges); physical sciences, 6% (9% of university presidents); and language and literature, 4%.

Of the 813 presidents who responded, 79 were women, practically all in private colleges primarily for women and most of them in Catholic women's colleges.

Over half of the presidents came to the presidency from outside the institution.

The above are pretty dry data about a zestful and interesting group of people.

I presume that I have personally known most of the responding presidents who have been in office for at least a decade; many of them I have known well. This has been one of my great privileges as an administrator. It has even been a privilege to disagree at times with a number of presidents, or even better, to work out agreements when our initial viewpoints may have been quite different. I have always respected their motives and their abilities, though occasionally I was puzzled by the intellectual processes of some of them. Except perhaps for a very select group of our top scholars, some of whom are themselves presidents, there is no more useful group in the academic world.

On occasion, some presidents may act in an arbitrary fashion. It is a tribute to them in general that this is relatively rare; for the circumstances that lead to arbitrary action—great but limited power, and engulfing pressures—are ever present. There has been no controlled experiment, but it is my opinion that a random selection of faculty members, taken from this same age group, would in the position of president be at least as arbitrary or, to use the familiar phrase, be to as great an extent "corrupted by power."

THE PRESIDENT'S WORK

This report is not a job analysis; but if overwork and divergent duties are among the chief afflictions of the president, some note of the nature of these burdens is in order—a note, however, that is intended to be explanatory of parts of the rest of the report and of certain "reflections" and not a complete picture.

One of the most common statements on any campus is: "The president has an impossible job." Actually the success of American higher education belies this statement in any literal sense; but if a president were required to accomplish all that is expected of him under the circumstances of his life, he would have an impossible job.

There are three major aspects of the president's work that must be noted: that of representing the institution to the public, that of internal educational leadership, and that of performing an enormous amount of routine, albeit high-level routine, work. In addition, there are many opportunities, almost obligations, for service that come to a president, in part because he is president but more because he has the abilities and the background that made him president; for example, service on the board of the National Science Foundation or of a private foundation, participation in some of the White House conferences, membership on the committees of the AAC, and work on various state educational commissions. Some of these opportunities also come to deans and other administrators.

Clearly any of these four roles—external representative, internal leader, routine administrator, or extra-curricular activist—could absorb the full time of a vigorous, intelligent man. If one's goal is not only to do work of the highest quality, but also of the maximum useful amount in each of these areas, it cannot be attained. Difficult choices must be made; and the choices are not only difficult but aggravating if deadlines, lack of staff, or pressure from important (or at least importunate) persons lead the president to devote his time to what he considers the less rather than the more valuable, and prevent him from doing that for which he is best fitted by experience, aptitude, or taste.

Many a president, having grown up as a faculty member, knowing the needs of an institution to develop its course offerings, its curricular structure, and its community life, and wishing to make an impact on these problems, is frustrated by having to spend much of his time getting money. I pity even more the man, brought in because he has the talent for fund-raising, who finds himself expected to lead the faculty to a conclusion on the foreign-language requirement, and day by day to help the dean of students concerning outside speakers.

And then the desk! If you spend a week assuring alumni that all is well, you come home to a dean who has not been able to answer the demands of five departments for desirable budget allotments beyond the agreed-upon guidelines. If you attend a riot and its aftermath of consultations and committee meetings, the mail piles up. To some, the desk is the chief frustration.

Reading the complaints on these matters, one begins to feel sorry for the president, until one realizes that presidents—although they, like other human beings, wish to grumble and indeed have something to grumble about—are a happy lot. They are happy because their work is useful, because most of it is not unpleasant and some of it is sheer fun. They are happy because they are where much can be and is accomplished. I presume they are also happy because the persons selected to be presidents are normally healthy, optimistic, and happily married.

Much of the above will be illustrated by quotations, but again the reader must be warned that the quotations do not give a balanced impression. If 40 presidents say how content they are and 15 others divide into 5 groups, each of which bears a single complaint, I probably would choose 10 quotes (two for each complaint) from the 15 malcontents and perhaps 3 or 4 pleasant expressions from the 40 satisfied presidents.

STAFF

Quite naturally, presidents discussed both their immediate staffs and the general administrative structures of their institutions. In respect to quality, there were more expressions of satisfaction than of dissatisfaction; but there were a considerable number of the latter.

As for the immediate staff, need was expressed for additional high-grade secretarial help as well as personal assistants, both general odd-job men and those of a specialized nature, to take care of particular facets of the president's work, such as: dealing with federal programs, institutional research, abstracting educational literature, editorial work, ghost writing, and handling alumni.

Beyond the matter of personal staff, many presidents mentioned the need of creating or filling positions such as those of academic vice president, director of development, director of graduate studies, and director of physical plant.

The general impression one gets is of inadequate staffs made up of competent but overworked people. The inadequacies arise from the rapid growth in size and complexity of the institutions, increasing involvement with government programs, and a laudable but sometimes exaggerated desire to save money so that it can be spent on the academic program.

In connection with the staff, especially in connection with other administrative officers, the question of delegation is often discussed. Sometimes it seems clear that the president does not know how to delegate. In other cases, capable legates are not available. Naturally the president's judgment and that of his subordinates may differ on this question.

THE PRESIDENT'S WIFE

The public expects much from the wives of presidents, and the institutions benefit greatly by the manner in which they fulfill these expectations. Moreover, too often they do this with little institutional help and at the sacrifice of family finances. I believe that public expectations sometimes force the president's wife to do the unneeded. The successful administration of many Catholic institutions by celibates and of other institutions by presidents who are bachelors or widowers point in this direction; yet, we must all be grateful to the president's wife for her unrequited services. Also, we must never forget the great contribution to the institution of the administrator's wife through the companionship, loyalty, solace, and criticism that she gives him. No one needs these four more than a college president.

In the section on "Special Allowances," the secretarial aid occasionally given the wife of the president is noted.

FRUSTRATIONS, SATISFACTIONS, AND SUGGESTIONS

Most of the president's frustrations arise from the nature and the variety of the functions he is supposed to fulfill, as described in a previous section. Others will be apparent to any who read the quotations which follow in this chapter; so will the satisfactions which presidents derive from their work.

In addition to overwork, a few difficulties of the president's position should be mentioned here.

Many a president lacks time for a normal family life and the life of the mind, be it reading, research, or keeping up in his academic field. This is also often mentioned by the deans of the colleges and the deans of the graduate schools.

Vacations and leaves are desired. Some believe that this is just wishful thinking, at least until staff problems have been solved. The number who report actually having taken leaves is significant and is reviewed in Chapter 7 on leaves. We must find some way to break the syndrome of too many duties, too short vacations, inadequate staffs, and no leaves. Most believe the key, if there is one, is the staff; although some indicate that taking a leave, perhaps at the behest of the trustees, and discovering one's dispensability is the secret.

Governmental red tape and, sometimes akin to this, church regulations come in for much criticism. Both private and public institutions find federal relations almost overwhelming. Does a lifesaver have to knock out a drowning man to bring him to shore? At times, yes; but it should not be routine practice.

I have often heard presidents speak of their positions as ones of hazardous tenure, and I sympathize with them; yet, the figures developed in this study and described in Chapter 13 on incumbents indicate a longer tenure than current myths would lead one to believe. In addition, many presidents move on voluntarily. I also have sympathy with the boards of trustees who have high hopes that they have picked a man who is an able leader and will be with them for a long while, but find that either his leadership is deficient or that, though able, he is lured away after a short period in office. It is like having divorces only when the marriage is happy. However, the financial problem of the man without tenure, who has no house of his own, has many financial demands (greater than those incurred by others in the community) for the travel of his wife, for entertainment, for charity, and for a host of incidentals, and who has no president to fight for his fiscal interests, can be severe. Many suggest that the trustees be more systematic in reviewing the compensation of the president.

A number of presidents regret the fact that there is little formal pre-job training for their positions. This is especially true of those who have had no administrative experience above the departmental level. They believe more could be done about this (although a start has been made) by associations, foundations, and universities.

The inability of faculty and administrators to establish communication and the desire of both to step beyond the roles which guidelines have established are frequently mentioned. Often the definitions of the roles have not yet been agreed upon. The recent statement of the American Council on Education, the American Association of University Professors, and the Association of Governing Boards, entitled "Government of Colleges and Universities,"* may help clarify thinking on this matter. Perhaps better practices will follow.

Finally, the attitude of faculty members and of students produces reactions ranging from impatience to indignation. Almost always, complaints on this subject are accompanied by the reservation that only a few faculty members and only a few students cause the trouble; but the presidents believe that, even if the troublemakers are few, many more lack understanding of the president's position. Suggested cures range from more persuasion to more authority. I believe it was Yost who suggested that in certain situations, you should "punt and pray."

ON OTHER POSITIONS

The pay dirt from the request for comments on "suggested methods of improving the conditions of work for the other administrative officers of the college" was not very rich nor full of surprises. Need for more compensation, more adequate staffs, longer vacations, and more frequent leaves, and particularly for more clear-cut delegation and better communications was recognized.

* *AAUP Bulletin* (Winter, 1966).

REFLECTIONS

As an exception, these quotations are not at the end of a chapter but are followed by a section on trustees, with its own set of "Reflections."

On some topics, such as vacations and leaves, compensation, and the president's home, there are quotations from presidents both in this chapter and in others.

Most presidents like being president:

I cannot imagine anything I'd rather do.—*President, private college*

It is customary to say that the job of president is crushingly difficult—that it is often hard to fill presidential jobs, that they wear a man out, change him, or force him to do chores less attractive than those required of classroom professors. I do not agree with this analysis. The work is difficult, the pressure great—but the assignments are varied, usually interesting and often highly important. If one has the ability to make decisions, and a little ability to look ahead, and some talent for working with people, there is no more satisfying position than a presidency in higher education.—*President, public university*

I really can't think of any way in which the attractiveness of the position of president can be improved. It is the most exciting and the most rewarding position in the university. The university is the most exciting and the most rewarding institution within our present-day society. Anyone who has the opportunity to serve as a college or university president should count himself among the most fortunate of men.—*President, private university*

It is full of responsibility, headaches, problems, but it is very attractive for anyone really interested in the education of youth, especially if it is a vocation from God.—*President, private college*

My position is already very attractive, for the last decade—my ten years as a college president—have been my most gratifying and happiest years. Let's leave well enough alone. (This sentence proves, of course, that I am not a good, dissatisfied respondent!)—*President, private college*

I think the job of a college president is so exciting, so challenging, so varied, so rewarding that applicants should pay a premimum for the job. I have been a practicing lawyer, a merchant, a banker, chairman of the board of a manufacturing company, and on the boards of a variety of enterprises. They are all dull by comparison.—*President, private college* [Has held position 8 years.]

With the current salaries being paid presidents of the [system] and the freedoms concerned with local administration, about 100 applicants indicated their desire to fill some of the recent vacancies as presidents in our system.—*President, public college*

Stop talking about it! It is not as bad as it is made out to be!—*President, private college*

I trust it is clear from my answers to this questionnaire that I regard the position of President of this college as extremely attractive. We have generous compensation, a very comfortable home, more than ample fringe benefits of all sorts, and a highly congenial community.—*President, private college*

But most presidents are overworked or find that the use of their time is out-of-balance:

My problem is illustrated by the fact that if I do not answer this question within the next three minutes I will not be able to do so within the reasonably near future.—*President, private university*

On the whole I accept as inevitable that the president will have to spend more time on administrative matters and fund raising than upon academic affairs. Although the theoretically desirable balance might be somewhat different than it is, I can see no real prospect that an institution which is dependent upon outside support for its financial strength is likely to be able to free the president from much that detracts from his attention to academic matters.—*President, private college*

It does seem to me that, if society provided different circumstances, a university officer could spend more of his time on the academic quality of his institution, gleaning thereby greater satisfaction, making a greater contribution, and perhaps, living longer. It seems folly to speculate on whether the circumstances will change in any way to relieve the press of fiscal, social, and protocol obligations. The trend is toward more rather than less. Moreover, some of them, perhaps most of them, are necessary and constructive. It is also true that, if these duties are to be successfully performed, no surrogate is acceptable.—*President, public university*

My impressions are, however, that few presidents have the time for the necessary reading, reflection, visits to other institutions, and the simple expediency of sitting with planning committees sufficiently to give a sense of direction to them, on the one hand, and to learn of the nature of their own deliberations, on the other.—*President, public university*

On the basis of 65–75 hour weeks, I can keep up with my job. The problem is how many years can one keep up this pace on a year-around basis with students underfoot four quarters a year.

The small college president has been assigned a most difficult task. He is expected to participate and be cognizant of everything which takes place in the life of the institution. He obviously must be the chief administrative officer but also the college representative in public. Every donor to the institution wishes to hand his check to the president. He is expected to appear at every alumni meeting or else apologize for his absence. Few new friends are won for the college without his playing a major role. He necessarily must be off campus at least half or more of the time yet he must hide his absences by being seen at a sizable percentage of concerts, plays, chapels, and athletic events. Unless he knows most of the students he runs the danger of losing their support. Meanwhile, he must also appear regularly at community affairs. Even when he delegates most of his administrative responsibilities he still is faced with a work load which begins early in the morning and usually does not end until he retires for the evening.—*President, private college*

A college president is the head of an academic endeavor, yet he is compelled by the circumstances of American higher education to be fundraiser, and public relations man, and a government sycophant.—*President, private college*

There are too many formal types of things requiring the president. They are window dressing types of duties that don't materially improve programs, or assist in a more effective accomplishment of mission.

If you could eliminate the necessity of dedicating college buildings or inaugural ceremonies of college presidents, a lot of time could be saved.

Then, too, if there were some kind of limitation on professional conferences that serve little purpose, more time could be saved.

Lastly, there ought to be pressure against having such a proliferation of professional associations. You almost need a college president just to represent the college at meetings.—*President, public college*

Legal, property, and Federal Government questions and programs should be in the province of a specific staff official.

Fund raising should not be placed so specifically on the office of the President, though presidents should indirectly reflect this responsibility.—*President, public college*

A second difficulty, which contributes to the first, is the problem of maintaining an "open door" without being overwhelmed by minor matters.—*President, private college*

Too much of a detailed type comes to my desk. (1) Approvals of out-of-state travel, (2) All appointments (secretarial, clerical, and other personnel actions), (3) Routine correspondence.—*President, public university*

I spend too much time with problems such as parking, student food service, non-academic employees (including organized union), social-ceremonial affairs, research administration, student publication flare-ups, and office space hassles. I have trouble getting to the more important questions of new academic programs being planned, selection and retention of academic and other administrators, seeking outside support for innovation and improvement, and development of reports and statements of institutional purpose. I am returning to teaching because the imbalance above does not correspond to my professional interests.—*President, public college*

But increasing demands of inter-institutional cooperative programs quickly soak up the liberated time, again at the cost of on-campus relationships.—*President, private university*

Perhaps too often college presidents are asked to perform civic duties that are not in direct line with their collegiate responsibilities.—*President, private college*

The extra, long, tedious hours make the job almost unendurable—when it should be one of inspiration.—*President, public college*

Most of us live in hopes, however, that at some time the task of educational leadership will be the significant responsibility of the presidency.—*President, private college*

It seems to me that the President should be primarily concerned with matters of broad policy and long-range planning. He should be responsible for staffing the College with alert and thoughtful faculty and administrative officers whose general progress he should supervise. He should be as little as possible involved with the solutions of daily problems. Through a combination of luck and good management, we have come pretty close to achieving such a situation here.—*President, private college*

STAFFING

An administrative assistant or similar position with primary responsibility for preparation of agenda material, background papers, minutes, etc., for the Board and its various committees is sorely needed. If such were provided, much additional time would be available to the President for planning and policy matters.—*President, private college*

Somewhere on the staff there needs to be an officer who can write a good letter or statement. I have to correct and rewrite too many official documents and then there is money-raising. Being the management in charge of production and also sales force as well as grounds supervisor I find interesting but it doesn't give me much time to upgrade the food service and interior decoration or research the college portfolio or read a book.—*President, private college*

There are days I think I'd like to have a "speech-writer." But this is impractical and, besides, he could never satisfy me!—*President, private university*

I could use a research assistant to write reports, do detail work (such as 80% of this report).—*President, private college*

A buffer—male; diplomatic; perceptive; intelligent, and *literate.*—*President, public university*

Have been without an administrative assistant for past two years. This was my choice, but a poor one. Such a position has been provided again for next year.—*President, public university*

There is a possibility that the office of assistant to the president will be revived. Particularly in the drafting of proposals to government agencies and foundations is there a need for such a person. The Administrative Dean, if he were given more assistance, could assume these duties, and my present thinking tends toward giving him an assistant and toward releasing more of his time for these purposes.—*President, private college*

My impression is that in a larger institution the president is protected from the administrative detail and routine that comes to the president's office in a small college.—*President, private college*

Provision for a representative of my office on campus during the evening hours—almost 6,000 students attend classes when no representative of the college administration is available for consultation.—*President, public college*

Secretarial help should be available on a second shift.—*President, private college*

My hope is that additional staff in the President's Office would not create an insulation between the President's Office and other members of the Administrative Staff and the Faculty. I am also conscious of the likelihood that some will regard this step as the creation of additional bureaucracy. Nevertheless if additional assistance will spare me some chores and at the same time create arrangements which will use my time more effectively, then I think a gain will have been made.—*President, private college*

The president often also sees the need of additional major administrative staff:

The problem is not that of staffing the office of the president but rather other administrative positions so that more competent operation of these offices will reduce the supervision and involvement of the president in many duties that ought to be handled by someone else.—*President, public college*

I have tried for 27 years to get three or four additional senior administrative officers (vice-presidents or provost?) so that the officers now reporting to me might report to the president indirectly. It is our experience that the budget will provide for additional teachers and clerks as the enrollment rises but relief on the top level is practically impossible (except perhaps in the negotiations with a possible successor?).—*President, public college*

My time would be better used if the Academic Dean and the Treasurer had more adequate staff assistance. We are working on this now.—*President, private college*

There should be an Executive Vice President, or chancellor or other person of position roughly comparable to that of the President himself to be an alter ego to the President, and fully able to represent the institution in various important aspects of relationships with the general public, governmental agencies, foundations, corporations and individuals of special importance to the institution.—*President, private college*

I believe that institutions beyond a certain size or degree of complexity should emulate business and employ a full-time paid chairman of the board as well as President.—*President, private college*

DELEGATION

Too many details and decisions that should be made at other levels, releasing more time for fund solicitation and public relations work.—*President, private college*

A chief source of frustration is the member of the administrative staff who does not get things done on time or who surreptitiously negates a decision of which he does not approve. The solvents here are tact and firmness, coupled if need be with courage. —*President, private college*

Ineffectiveness, careless, and heartless second echelon administration. —*President, private college*

A chief source of tension is those at the lower range of the ladder not solving their own problems. —*President, private college*

These remarks should be balanced by a few remarks from other officers. There are many tributes paid to presidents by their colleagues:

The president of the college is one of the finest men in higher education to work with, and that makes the position especially interesting and satisfying. —*Vice president, private college*

The confidence and approval of the Trustees and the President have made my deanship a most pleasant one, sufficiently so that I have turned down offers ranging up to nearly double my present compensation. If I had to do it over, I would turn them down again. —*Vice president, private college*

The fact is that the College is administered by a great educator and administrator, wise in judgment, clear in thought, a man who when he makes a judgment sticks by it, one who says exactly what he means, a man his chieftains admire and trust. —*Librarian, public college*

I am fortunate to have an excellent working relationship with the Dean of the College, and the President is an understanding, hard working person who needs assistance more than I do. In addition we have a splendid Board of Trustees who are helpful without interfering. —*Dean of students, private college*

Many also comment favorably on the degree of delegation:

The President has granted each of the administrators an almost unlimited authority to perform their duties in the manner which they deem best. The overall relationship with the president could not be more pleasant. —*Dean of students, private college*

Also we deal with parents, alumnae and many others in "pressure" cases. However, the administration stands firmly behind decisions—a great help! —*Director of admissions, private college*

He is a remarkable person in that when he has delegated a responsibility, he does not meddle. —*Registrar, public university*

I am responsible directly to the President who gives me almost complete freedom in operating this office as I see fit. —*Director of development, public college*

But there are others who wish for a greater delegation:

I believe that my chief frustrations and tensions arise from the fact that the President of this institution rather regularly permits individuals to by-pass the regularly constituted channels of authority and appeal to him directly without even any notification of the intermediate officials. — *Liberal arts dean, private college*

Great differences in general philosophy of what a good college should *be* and *do* between my office and the office of the president. The president's office is primarily that of fund promotions; therefore, little emphasis on actual purpose or concept of a college.

President has difficulty in delegating authority and allowing other administrators to perform their functions. Too much a "One Man Show." — *Liberal arts dean, private college*

Too often, college presidents, from Olympian Heights, exercise, in disciplinary matters a final judgment that has been based on a combination of fear of student demonstrations and an attempt to win popularity with students rather than an objective appraisal of the problem and an understanding of its long range effects. — *Dean of students, private college*

Another source of frustration for myself and some of the other administrators in this institution, is the President's practice of hiring individuals without consultation with the person under whom they would be working. — *Dean of students, private college*

There is sometimes lack of communication:

The chief complaint, the chief source of frustration, the chief cause of tension, and the most unattractive feature of my position is the lack of time to discuss and arrive at meaningful decisions with the Chief Executive of the institution. — *Business officer, public university*

A president who is not aware of some of the problems, and therefore acts upon partial or incomplete information! — *Registrar, private college*

And at least one person believes the presidency is worth trying:

Though I am aware I have a good job and am grateful for my relatively satisfying professional life, I am interested in moving up to a presidency. I doubt that job would really offer the advantages of my present one, but I wish to try it anyway. — *Vice president, public college*

FRUSTRATIONS. It is impossible to divide quotations categorically between remarks that describe the frustrations and tensions, and the suggestions made for improving the situation. The attempt to do so is itself frustrating.

The president's life may be lonely:

The buck has to stop here and everyone tries to pass it up here. A president is a lonely man because he has no one in whom he can confide. You are sort of a devil from the standpoint of the Board, a tool of the faculty—from the standpoint of the faculty, a tool of the Board.—*President, private college*

The family life of the president is interfered with:

Means to protect the privacy of the President and his family is always a prime necessity. The children of a college president are particularly likely to suffer as he gives attention that they may formerly have had to other people's children. It is also probably true that a college president and his wife are together at functions much more than formerly, but they are rarely together, except when they are tired and querulous, when they can be relaxed. The president must fight for every opportunity to preserve and cultivate family life and yet at the same time keep it natural and unaffected.—*President, private college*

Here the home is immediately adjacent to the campus and the members of the President's family are subjected to a sort of "fish bowl" existence. The President's Home should be located some distance from the campus in quiet surroundings.—*President, public university*

The president finds little time for reading and keeping up in his field:

I have less and less time for reading and writing, involvement in faculty recruitment, and curricular matters. Instead I am constantly fighting off or dealing with public relations matters and administrative details.—*President, public college*

The lack of time to read some of the books my students and faculty are reading. They have left me far behind. I don't even have time to read the professional material that I receive because of insufficient secretarial help and constant interruptions. Free time for reading good books is essential for a president's mental health.—*President, private college*

Too little time is available . . . for professional research and writing by the president as a scholar and academician in his own right.—*President, private college*

If administrative assistance was available and adequate to enable the president drafted from an academic position to continue teaching even to a limited extent, the position might be more attractive to some persons highly qualified for it.—*President, private college*

It is stultifying to make decisions under such pressure that their bases are inadequately explored:

I think one of the hardest things for someone in my job is to be called upon to make extremely important decisions on very short notice and with insufficient data upon which to base the decision.—*President, private college*

What is particularly frustrating is the necessity of making up one's mind and acting before all the evidence is in.—*President, private college*

The problems of governmental and church relations are often referred to:

State red tape and student-faculty freedom movements.—*President, public college*

Federal support of faculty as individuals, which with other forces at work, caused the institution to get out of control of anyone.—*President, public university*

The problem of communication is often considered, but even more frequently by other officers than the president:

The chief source of frustration is communication. It is always difficult to keep open the routes of information from the administration to the faculty, from the faculty to the administration, from the educational processes to the students, and vice versa, from the University to its public constituency and to the legislature.—*President, public university*

Inability to communicate effectively with the "new breed" generation of students although I am a youthful president by comparative standards.—*President, private university* [Age 44.]

The following illustrate that some duties are particularly distasteful:

I expect my greatest frustrations accompany our land acquisition program (we are in the heart of this small town) where we have to dispossess people of their property. The most difficult part is trying to keep people informed time-wise when we ourselves are not sure how fast the legislature will allow us to expand.—*President, public college*

Perhaps the attitude of a minority of the persons with whom a president must deal caused the strongest protests:

To oversimplify only slightly, basic tension arises from faculty views (and student views) that administrators (1) are generally or relatively unnecessary, (2) have motives that should be suspected, and (3) should have little influence on educational policy. This needs to be resisted as adroitly and continuously as possible, to make the positions of president and other administrative officers satisfying and challenging.—*President, private college*

The chief source of frustration and tension is a new sense on the part of the faculty to want to teach less, want to do research more, want fewer students and more pay, and the fact that dedication to teaching is not as prevalent as it was. Another source of frustration is the fact that trustees grow old and do not wish to be given emeritus status or be relieved of their responsibility and make way for younger men with new ideas.—*President, private college*

I suppose one of the chief irritations facing the college or university president is the stereotyped faculty attitude that administrative officers are whipping boys. This is something of a convention in American academic life. The critical and belittling comments, sometimes snide and intemperate, are hard for a sensitive man to bear and tend to lessen the effectiveness of those whose skin is thicker. One wishes that there were some way of developing greater understanding and tolerance. Such a development would lead to greater cooperation and effectiveness.—*President, private college*

If the academic community continues to harass unduly top administrators, good administrators are going to become more difficult to attract and then the whole community will suffer.—*President, private university*

(1) Complete lack of outsiders understanding the pressures on a Land-Grant College President. (2) Faculty members who get themselves into trouble, but never find themselves to blame.—*President, public university*

. . . but probably the chief frustration is that of attempting to meet these problems in an ultra-conservative and sharply segregated larger community.—*President, private college*

1) Lack of understanding on the part of many people in all walks of life of the real nature and purpose of the university.

2) Difficulty of persuading the Legislature to accept advanced planning and provide the funds to prepare in advance for clearly foreseen future needs in teaching, research, etc.

3) Inability to communicate adequately and effectively with both faculty and students.

4) The assumption by many people in all walks of life, including parents, that the president is personally responsible for all the thoughts, words, and acts of all employees, faculty, and students of the university and that the president somehow has the authority and power to "control" all persons connected with the University.—*President, public university*

Give the president the opportunity to be an educational statesman, not a handmaiden to every human derelict that comes down the road. May not be bad for the student to learn, the professor to teach, and the administrator to administer. The classroom quality of higher education in the United States needs immediate improvement. This improvement is long overdue, and we are all afraid to tackle the problem.—*President, public college*

IMPROVEMENTS

More Money

Chief frustrations come from lack of success in fund raising.—*President, private college*

All in all, I know of no greater boon toward "improving the attractiveness of the position of president," maintaining his morale, keeping his smile broad and warm, than that solace which an occasional large-sized development check invariably provides him.—*President, private university*

In the case of State Colleges, I can think of no more effective way of improving the attractiveness of the position of president than by giving the

State Colleges the same type of support given to state universities, in equivalent areas of educational endeavor. —*President, public college*

Improving the Financial Position of the President

To attract capable men to the presidency will demand higher salaries and larger fringe benefits. —*President, private college*

Particularly desirable is a deferred compensation plan which would provide financial base for the early retirement which may be generated by the pressures and stress of office. —*President, public college*

While the president's compensation is adequate for any given year, he has no tenure and if he must resign it is unlikely that he could step into a comparable administrative or other position. This can be a concern if he has a family dependent upon him. —*President, public university*

Also insurance against suits of any legal nature that may be initiated. — *President, public college*

I think there are many of us who find ourselves making a very high level of philanthropic investments. I think this is particularly true of the president of the independent college. As you realize, most of us are frequently sponsoring financial campaigns. Since we believe in our cause and since we are the ones that must constantly be seeking financial assistance from others, we almost invariably make sizable pledges to our own campaigns and to many other projects which are projected in our community. For instance, in the last three years I have given between 25–30% of my cash salary to charities of one type or another. —*President, private college*

Make compensation such that a person can serve his time out before age 60 and have enough money to retire comfortably. —*President, public college*

Situation of the President's Wife

College boards should be made aware that, in most instances, to appoint a president is to appoint two people: the president and his wife. Thus the college gets two for the price of one. —*President, private college*

There is another important consideration and that is the president's home should be adequately staffed. The social demands on a president and the president's wife are such that every assistance should be provided them in the presidential residence. —*President, private college*

A tension source in Presidential life stems from community expectations and taboos re: the President's wife. It is hard to do all that is necessary for a growing and active family *and* meet the many demands which the community (both town and gown) feel are normal expectations as far as the President's wife is concerned. A more business-like and less socially stratified view of the "University's First Lady" would enable our family to lead a more nearly normal life and still do far more in the way of working with students and student organizations. How this can be accomplished— particularly in a smallish university city I do not know. —*President, public university*

The President's House

House located in the middle of 6,000 students. Noise! —*President, public college*

The "president's house" is an anachronism, left over from the days when presidents were moral leaders living in small town campuses. The idea is wrong. —*President, public college*

The large university has outgrown the President's House concept. —*President, public university*

Improving the Preparation of Presidents

My lack of background and special training for some of the duties of the office. —*President, private college*

The better training and background that the President has, the more will the position be attractive generally. The internship program of the ACE has great merit in giving opportunity to see how things are done in other places, and the alternatives possible in one's own. Seminars, such as the Harvard Weeks or the one at Princeton this year, sponsored by the ACE, are fine means of having new Presidents meet and discuss ways and means of becoming better administrators. The Conference at Berkeley sponsored jointly by WICHE and the U.C. Center for the Study of Higher Education also focus on particular problems of relevance to the colleges. —*President, private college*

More Opportunity for Travel

Speaking for college presidents in general, it is my thinking that they should be given the opportunity of travel to a much greater extent than is true of many college presidents I know. I travel abroad each year, and I feel that this does a great deal to help me maintain a sense of perspective. —*President, private college*

As a veteran in office, I am particularly concerned over the lack of awareness among trustees generally of the importance of leaves for the college president. Given the host of duties . . . , it is vitally important to his health and sanity that he have occasional surcease from these pressing responsibilities. From my experience I conclude that one can escape them only by going abroad. My so-called vacations in the United States are usually merely a change of scene for work, although the change of tempo when away from the office is a gain. In other words, I believe presidents would profit greatly from occasional leaves granted for a period of from two to three months (I doubt that I would find it feasible to be away from my duties much longer than that) every four or five years. If I had the opportunity of organizing a staff from scratch, I would allow for each chief staff officer six months leave every five years. Each college officer in his own degree has problems similar to those of the president. —*President, private college*

More Authority

I suspect that a combination of the increasing attractiveness of faculty positions and the decreasing authority allowed presidents is going to make it more and more difficult to attract and keep good presidents.—*President, public college*

He should be given the authority and responsibility to administer all phases of the college programs.—*President, public college*

He must necessarily speak both on and off campus with reasonable frequency, all of which requires considerable time and preparation. We very badly need to find some way of developing a type of office through which the president does not have to be the one lone symbol of the institution.—*President, private college*

Should We Seek Attractiveness?

I am not sure that "attractiveness" is the proper description of the presidency needs. In my opinion the best presidents are those who have a dedication to the institution or to the cause which the institution represents. I have seen wonderful men accept presidencies in very unattractive circumstances. If the trustees see to it that the college has a real mission and stands for something in all probability it will be able to find men who will meet the challenge of leadership.—*President, private college*

No suggestions on "attractiveness." It's an impossible job, and any attempt to sell it any other way would be dishonest. To "make up" for its frustrations through salary or fringe or other means would not lessen the wear and tear or ease the burden of responsibility. It might help the Boards' conscience or ease the plight of the widow.—*President, private college*

I suppose you could improve the position of president by giving him all the money he needs, always agreeing with his recommendations, having the students come to learn instead of help administer, and have him surrounded by bright and capable aides who could take over his job at a moment's notice. If you did, you would remove the problems and most of the fun.—*President, public college*

The Work of Others

Most of the other administrative officers here work too hard. I have great difficulty forcing them to take time off. On those rare occasions when they do take a leave, things seem to run as well or better than when they are here.—*President, private university*

My annual salary is satisfactory, but I regret that salaries of conscientious faculty members with excellent preparation are not more closely approximate to the salary of the president.—*President, public college*

In regard to improving conditions for work in the administrative offices of the college, I feel that most deans are probably frustrated because they do not have the authority to undertake the necessary action, yet have all of the blame for the lack of performance. As an administrator in a non-presidential capacity for a number of years, I have found that most deans who have not been delegated proper authority find their positions miserable and untenable.—*President, public college*

Establish a relaxed attitude. Stay out of their hair. Be available, be sympathetic, be generous in opinions and frequent in compliments. —*President, private college*

THE QUESTIONNAIRE (a biased selection)

[Frustrations:] Trivia, and questionnaires such as this. —*President, private college*

The questionnaire opens up the areas of need. Thanks for the help. —*President, private college*

This, like so many other time-consuming questionnaires, is unnecessary. Recently a study which included three hour visits to many college presidents covered many of these items and much more.

As may be suspected by now, my chief source of frustration is the stream of questionnaires I use precious time to answer.

I have distributed the material to my fellow administrators. Best of everything. —*President, private college*

I would like to express appreciation for the study of total compensation of chief administrative officers in the U.S. colleges and universities. The study will perform an important service to the academic community. —*President, private college*

The following quotations I like either for their humor or their mellow wisdom, or both:

[No frustrations] other than those attributable to human beings acting as such. —*President, public college*

Treasurer supplies money when necessary . . . . No official budget. —*President, private college*

There is nothing in my job that could not be improved by a higher level of financial support for my institution . . . .

Instead of trying to make the President's position more attractive, I propose abolishing it in favor of the bright young men who are serving as executive assistants to, and secretaries of, legislative committees, boards, commissions and the like. These are the ones who should have the sobering, practical responsibility of management to match the authority that they have assumed. —*President, public college*

One in administration generally feels he could do better what he should be doing if he had someone else to do the things he has to do. As a battlescarred, spavined, windblown acting president, I doubt it. —*President, private college*

Conclusion—I only wish I had the time to answer this part. —*President, private college*

Lack of perspective on the part of the faculty. There is apparently a developing trade union approach. There are tensions also because of ever more strident student minorities who operate behind the façade of freedom issues. But such tensions and frustrations cannot be avoided and they must be considered an inevitable part of the responsibilities of the presidency.

The position is highly esteemed in American life and no matter how heavy the tasks that have to be performed, the President should be grateful that he has been assigned the privilege of a career in such a setting. — *President, private university*

I could write a book on this subject as could each of my colleagues in the profession. A good many of them have as you know, but none of us has quite been able to catch the strange fusion of high reward and, at times, incredible burden that goes with the job. I've been at it now for nearly twelve years and I must confess that it is deeply satisfying to me, but like everyone else I have to fight, at times, to keep my perspective in the face of a thousand partial, often ambitious, even more often self-seeking views of one superb reality. Any president who deserves the job—if any one of us does—gets his central reward from his feeling for the place and the fact that he is, in his own time and style, helping to advance it. To do so he must work with powerful voluntary support on the one hand, and powerful professional forces on another, and these days at least, equally powerful, though often nameless, forces of frustration and hunger in students. His job is a restless one and he is doomed to be a failure with some group at any given moment in his career. I do not see how this can be changed but I shall be glad to expand on it, both as a necessity and as a limiting factor of the president's job, if it seems useful to you to have me do so.

I would enter one further comment which grows from this: the physical demands of the president's job are severe and they seem to become more so every year. I do think that the Boards of Trustees would be well advised to insist on protecting their presidents to some slight extent; it seems to be difficult for us to protect ourselves. — *President, private university*

[The trustees] are well led, well disciplined, and dedicated, and in many ways are more liberal and daring than the faculty. They present constantly to the president the interesting challenge of how they can be used even more effectively than they are to move the college ahead, but this challenge is one of the excitements of the president's job.

My chief source of frustration comes in the range of my duties and the inability to pick and choose what I want to do next. The duties are ceremonial functions, housekeeping and clerical chores, student problems, academic matters, financial agonies, alumni visiting, going to off-campus meetings, entertaining "friends of the college." In one way the range makes life interesting but it also tires out a president. I suppose the job would be more attractive if small colleges could afford more administrative help, but help has to be supervised and it might only add to the president's responsibilities. The chief problem I think is the number of associations and bureaus that either send the president work to do or call him out of town. Don't misunderstand me. I do not object to this particular questionnaire; I find it clear and responsible and much good can come of it. Nor do I discount the need for inter-college cooperation. It is simply that there is too much going on that is of questionable value. Every president knows this but is almost afraid to say so on the ground that he'll offend a granting agency, a prospective donor, or an accrediting outfit and thus damage the college because of his own bad disposition. The superstructure of higher education on top of colleges and universities now is of mixed value; and until we sort out the useful from the trivial and meretricious, presidents of small colleges with small administrative staffs are going to find it harder and harder to give proper attention to their students and faculty.

But it's the most exciting job in the world and I'd almost do it for nothing.—*President, private college*

TRUSTEES

The governing board of an educational institution is a problem and an opportunity.

It is an opportunity because usually it is composed of able and unselfish men who wish to be of public service. No other group is better prepared to present the institution's needs, both for understanding and for support, to its constituents. No other group is better prepared to reflect both the criticism and the approval of an institution's public to the institution. No other group can make official the aspirations and actions of the college. There is no other group which can discuss so well within the framework of loyalty the relation between the external and the internal aspects of the college's problems. Moreover, where power resides there also resides opportunity.

The above is a bit highfaluting—so back to earth. To most institutions the question of their financial support is crucial. Few institutions could long maintain their present quality on their present budgets. Rising prices are part of the picture. So are rising expectations and the proliferation of knowledge. There is, therefore, a balance to be sought which involves quality, size, tuition charges, and other income. All agree that the quality should not decrease. There is, therefore, need to estimate what size is optimum in order to allow diversity without too great dilution; what tuition can be charged, along with granting offsetting student financial aid, to maximize income without denying educational opportunities unfettered by great debt or heavy outside work to worthy students; and finally, how much income can be secured from foundations, government, and personal giving. This estimate is not just for the present, but also for the immediate and intermediate future. The best financial judgment is needed, and good financial judgment here, as elsewhere, involves the recognition of when to gamble. Moreover, these are not matters to be settled independent of the actions of the trustees as individuals, since trustees who are willing to give or to solicit gifts, grants, or appropriations can happily alter the parameters.

But often a board of trustees is also a problem.

Its conservatism can be a problem. This conservatism arises from various sources: Trustees tend to be old; trustees tend to be well-to-do, and well-to-do persons are apt to be well adjusted to the current environment and not anxious for change; trustees tend to be alumni and alumni are nostalgic.

Trustees are a problem because they are able men. Able men frequently do not know when to be rubber stamps, and there are many matters on which they should be. That is putting it too simply. To be more accurate, there are many matters concerning which the trustees have power but in which they should leave the final decisions to the president and the faculty, and do so with such definiteness that the president and faculty will listen without resentment to the opinions of the trustees. One of the hardest things to do successfully is to advise a subordinate on a matter that has been delegated to him, without appearing to rescind the delegation. I can remember with gratitude many instances of advice from presidents of the University of Wisconsin concerning questions which were still left completely in my charge. I believe, moreover, presidents have learned better how to listen to advice from the board concerning their actions than have faculties concerning theirs.

Trustees are problems because they sometimes forget that no one of them as an individual has authority that any other individual does not have, unless the board has given it to him.

I have not touched in the above on the relatively rare abuses of trustees who want special favors.

To the president, the trustees are an especial problem because they are one of the two millstones—the faculty being the other—between which he is ground; but, to change the metaphor, the board of trustees is an opportunity like the modern telephone receiver. It is in one piece both the mouthpiece through which he may speak and the earphone through which he may listen.

Many presidents commented on the desirable composition of the board, and the way it can aid the president. In particular, they commented on the variety of types that should be on the board, on the age of its members, and on its desirable size. Perhaps, next to Truman's "if you can't stand the heat," their favorite quote is from Henry Wriston, that a trustee should bring to the board "wisdom, work or wealth" (when Wriston is around, there is also wit). To a degree, wealth and willingness to work are measurable. It is hoped by many that wisdom, at least corporate wisdom, will be maximized by a variety of backgrounds. A large number of presidents mention that boards should contain some persons from the faculties or administrations of other institutions. At least six, perhaps seven if you include faculty members, of the classes from "rich men" to "chiefs" to which children skip rope or pluck daisy petals are desired. (After writing the last sentence, I recalled some episodes when I was an infantry supply officer with rival companies in France, and concluded, considering that I am now a college trustee, that all eight types are acceptable.) In particular, many of the presidents of Catholic institutions want more lay members on their boards or are happy to report a change in this direction. This desire is sometimes shared by their colleagues in Protestant church-related colleges.

As to size, more complained that their boards are too large than that they are too small, though some are reasonably satisfied by a large board with a small executive committee. Most presidents of public institutions want rather small boards.

Many pointed out the danger of a board overbalanced with old men.

In discussing the trustees as opportunities and problems, I have reflected in a somewhat distorted mirror the comments of numerous presidents. It is clear that most presidents wish the board and its members to:

1. Be active in raising funds.
2. With proper advice, make the primary decisions in regard to finances, campus planning, and selection of presidents.
3. Involve themselves in broad policy questions and the determination of institutional objectives.
4. Bring to the institution a viewpoint less internally generated than that of the faculty and explain to the public the nature of an educational institution.
5. Leave the administration to the administrators.

6. Leave questions of curriculum to the proper persons (there is ambiguity here since some presidents believe the proper persons are the faculty and others perhaps the administration with faculty advice).

This, of course, is not a complete list of the president's desires.

Clearly, the board of trustees is a problem to itself. To be the source of authority for a free community of scholars is anomalous, but some order is necessary, for every effort to establish an unstructured free community has failed. The fact that, in my judgment, more authority should legally reside in the faculty than is now the case is of little relevance. The necessity that there be authority and this authority be used wisely is far more important. Boards, when they are intelligent, are perplexed. But they have performed a great service to American society. The opportunities and the problems will not vanish.

A list of suggestions always has a negative appearance. Most presidents are appreciative of their boards. Throughout the questionnaire we asked for comments that would lead to improving situations that often, perhaps usually, were already good. This tended to elicit criticism rather than praise. There was abundant testimony to the devotion and to the value of many trustees and even of many boards. But we must remember that the spur will get more speed from the good steed than from a nag.

May I add one special word to the trustees? The trustees must take a special interest in the president. Neither the faculty nor other administrative officers will concern themselves with his salary, his vacations, his health, or his freedom to live a normal family life. The trustees must do so. The president frequently gets a good salary when he starts, but becomes the forgotten man as inflation progresses, as other salaries rise, and as his own value increases. The trustees should be aware of this and take suitable action. They should also see to it that he has the type of personal staff and supporting administrative structure that makes it feasible for him to do his work within the normal limits of human strength. They should not expect from him the little time-consuming favors he can scarcely refuse but which are sometimes the last straw. It should be on his initiative that the lot of the rest of the staff is improved. The trustees must improve his. In other words, next to the president's wife, no one should be more solicitous of his welfare than the trustees.

REFLECTIONS

COMPOSITION OF BOARD

General

I believe that the Board should be so constructed as to always include men who can and will contribute directly and significantly to those basic tasks which are major concerns of the Board. Included among these tasks are: determination of the basic purposes and objectives of the college; general direction of campus planning; direction of endowment-fund investments; participation in the work of gift procurement; provision of assurance of good institutional management, etc.

Therefore, ideally, the Board should always include men whose competencies and interests match these tasks—educators, attorneys, men who know and understand construction; financiers; public-relations and advertising men; industrialists; research men; etc., etc. These are intended to be illustrations—not exhaustive.—*President, private college*

The Board should not be archly conservative, particularly in the time of exciting educational experimentation. I would think that a fairly wide range of professions should be present on the board, and that they should be picked for their interest in the institution rather than because they happen to believe any one set of beliefs. Clearly, the possession of money is an important consideration, but not a prime requirement, of a board member. I think that it is highly important for board members to back the president in his major interests or get someone else to whom they can give this kind of loyalty. (I do not mean an uncritical loyalty.)—*President, private college*

The only criteria for choosing members of a board that make any sense to me are intelligence, energy, dedication to the institution, time to work for it, and means with which to support it. Not all of these need to be present in each member of a board. The members of the board can aid the president by helping him shape policy and in carrying it out, and by keeping out of the internal affairs of the institution except to get rid of the president.—*President, private university*

A nice mixture of lawyers, bankers, doctors, educators and industrialists —millionaires and workers, men and women. All willing to spend time, money, and advise within the scope of their abilities. A president can never be sure he is leading his faculty, but he should be sure he is leading his Board. If not, he should resign and take a job with the federal government. —*President, private college*

. . . has sought out and elected to the Board of Trustees five highly qualified professional educators: two college presidents, the dean of student affairs at . . . , a professor of philosophy from . . . , and a professor of economics from. . . . Their advice and counsel have been invaluable both in guiding the Board and in guiding the president. And this system is far better, so it seems to me, than having the College's own faculty members serve on the Board.—*President, private college*

In church-related institutions the board of trustees ought to include laymen and laywomen as well as priests and religious. — *President, private college*

Have achieved a 50/50 balance of lay and ministerial board membership and an excellent working relationship. Wasn't easy. — *President, private college*

Age

Trustees should retire when ill, over 70, or out of step with recognized educational procedures. — *President, private college*

Secondly, we have a small Board of Trustees with more than half serving for a long period of time. Age of more than 50% is past 75 years. They have been generous with me, but also appear to lack the understanding for the changes which are being made, and changes which must be made. They accept this but with reluctance. — *President, private college*

Size

Our Board of Trustees is entirely too large. Its forty-five members make it unwieldy and it, therefore, exerts little influence in the conduct of affairs in the institution. The real work of administration is carried on by the Executive Committee of the Board, consisting of thirteen people. I find that this committee gives me excellent support and makes most of the weighty decisions which govern the future of the institution. The many members of the larger board of trustees, itself, can be much more useful to the college if they were all willing to work at their jobs. The fact of the matter is that few of them are willing to accept anything like a working concept of their position. — *President, private college*

A larger board with greater representation would enhance our operation. — *President, private college*

We have a 24-person board of trustees operating through standing committees. I feel that a board of about 12, relying more heavily on administrative recommendations instead of trustee sub-committee recommendations would be just as effective. — *President, public college*

Give me eight college-trained men and women who have won stature in the public eye and who can be objective and fair and I will get along. — *President, public university*

Duties

I do wish we could inspire a few more trustees to engage in fund-raising activities . . . . — *President, private college*

They must either give the money or get it. — *President, private college*

Committed men, willing *truly* to support the college re: fund-raising, extra-curricular offerings, *and student recruitment.* — *President, private college*

This [the question about trustees] is an invitation for an essay, but in brief:
1) Should be workers and enthusiastic, BUT temper with realism and judgment.

2) Don't meddle in management.
3) Don't try to use trusteeship for personal advantage—in getting business or in seeking honors.
4) Understand differences between "making a profit" and "education."
5) Have a good balance as to backgrounds and college needs; e.g., law, insurance, research, banking, construction, faculty, administration, organization, and, most of all, education.
6) Either have or appreciate money, and necessity to (1) get it in, and (2) spend it.
7) Understand something of colleges: academic freedom, faculty responsibility, salaries at all levels and areas and competition, college structures, histories, and trends.
8) Above all, know what they are trying to do, why, and their responsibility in seeing it is achieved, personal and dollar-wise.

To quote a trustee: "The President cannot be any bigger than the Trustee will let him be." Every trustee should be aware of this and act accordingly.—*President, private college*

They can assist the President most successfully when they take pride in the order and discipline demanded by their bylaws and when they insist upon their prerogatives.—*President, private university*

I also believe on the basis of my experience that contrary to what is being written in many quarters these days, boards of trustees can actually become too much involved in the college even in decision making and that care must be exercised in our day lest we misuse able trustees or try to get them to do that which they are not fitted for either by virtue of their position or by the background and experience which most of them have.—*President, private college*

The trustees' main job is to select a president and then to support, defend, and trust him.—*President, public university*

I'm convinced that most institutions would be better off without boards of trustees, or with boards having more restricted powers than do most college and university boards. But the reasons would require a more extended comment than I can make now.—*President, public university*

My greatest asset is my Board of Trustees, first because they number only 14 and hence are remarkably participative and, second, because each trustee has earned public prestige and stature.—*President, private university*

Care of President

I am becoming alarmed at the evidence of physical—and sometimes mental—breakdown among presidents. This cannot be solved by any single measure or series of measures—presidents must be compensated well, protected from overstrain and physical exhaustion and supported by the Board.—*President, private college*

Have a small committee of Trustees explore with the president fully and frankly his financial situation to assure that his present and future situation are in line with their expectations. I am sure Trustees want a president to be reasonably free of financial concerns and they also want him to maintain certain standards (dress, contributions, entertainment, etc.) for the sake of the college. —*President, private college*

CHAPTER 15

THE VICE PRESIDENT AND THE DEAN

The president is a man with a worried look on his dean's face.

IT seems best to cover the positions of academic vice president and the dean of liberal arts in one chapter. In many institutions only one of these titles exists, and in others one individual holds both titles. Most universities now have an academic vice president and a cluster of college deans, sometimes reporting to the president but, perhaps, more often to the vice president. This is also apt to be true in the large public colleges, many of which have the title and are rapidly assuming the character of a university.

The above is not the common picture in the small private college, where either there is no vice president or he is essentially the dean of the college—frequently a person whose coat, but not whose spots, has recently been changed.

We had planned to consider only those vice presidents who were administratively between the president and the dean, and we used such a definition in our questionnaire. But, questionnaires at best are a considerable imposition and to expect anyone to be guided by a strange definition of a familiar term is naïve. Moreover, even when the positions are distinct, the people holding the two positions seem very similar. I may mention here that a number of persons who in title are vice presidents speak of themselves as deans in describing their positions. One had better not try to divide the white from the yolk of a scrambled egg.

I approached writing this chapter as a labor of love. A score of years as dean of letters and science of the University of Wisconsin, with all the friendships created, problems shared, and understanding developed with other deans would naturally lead to such an attitude. But as I read the replies to the questionnaires, I began to realize that even if I was prepared by affection, I was not by experience. The situation of the dean of a large college in a large public university is so different from that of one in a small private college that clearly I was equipped as much with a set of false assumptions as with common experiences. So I write with warmth, but also with caution lest my analysis have an anecdotal rather than a statistical base.

The median age of male vice presidents is 51, and of liberal arts deans 49. Of the vice presidents, 71% had Ph.D.'s and 16% Ed.D.'s. The corresponding figures for liberal arts deans were 73% and 8%. Over 90% of the highest degrees of deans and vice presidents were in the following fields: social science, 26%; education, 20%; English and journalism, 14%; physical sciences, 14%; philosophy, 6%; biological sciences, 5%; and psychology, foreign languages, and religion, 4% each. Both education and commerce furnished a greater proportion of vice presidents than of deans. The reverse is notably true for foreign languages.

Twenty-three (5%) of the vice presidents were women, all but one in colleges; and there were 97 women deans (16%), all in colleges.

Nearly two-thirds of the vice presidents and deans were already at the same institution when they took their present position.

DUTIES

It is clear that the titles of vice president and dean stand for many different types of responsibilities. If there is an academic vice president, he is the chief academic officer under the president; otherwise, the dean of the college usually is. If there is both a vice president and a dean (as is usual in large universities), then the dean may be either the chief academic officer of the college, and at least theoretically reports to the vice president, or he may have a different set of duties, largely in connection with students, the vice president himself dealing directly with such questions as faculty recruitment, salary budgets, and curriculum. If there is an incipient graduate program, either of these officers may be its director.

The degree to which the president chooses to be involved in academic policy or in academic details will, of course, largely determine the duties of his immediate subordinates. Sometimes there is not much more than a hairline between neglect and intrusion. In the other direction, the president may call on the vice president or dean to play a large role in public relations and in working with the governing board or its committees.

Just as the president is in a position, sometimes uneasy, between the trustees and the public on one hand and the academic community on the other, so the dean or vice president may have an equally difficult time explaining the president's desires to the faculty and persuading the faculty to the president's point of view, while often he himself agrees with the faculty, but understands and sympathizes with the president. This duty may be especially delicate and especially important when the president has recently come from another institution. Although the situation may be so difficult that the dean is blamed by the whole community for its own as well as for his faults, there are other cases—many, I believe—where he may become trusted by the president, the board, and the faculty. DeVane of Yale was such a person; I could mention numerous living examples.

In my opinion, the dean tends to be overworked to almost as great an extent as the president. Moreover, he may have to deal with as many and as difficult personnel problems as does the president. But in two other respects his job is far less frustrating. Although routine duties may keep the dean from what he considers more important and certainly more interesting educational aspects of his work, he does not face to the same degree the dichotomy of being responsible for both external and internal leadership. Secondly, he is not constantly forced to consider what compromises he must make—not against his own conscience (a good man will resist this), but within his own conscience—between what is distasteful but may appear necessary and what is congenial to his own habits of thought.

Another major duty of the dean—who once was an expert—is to be a respected generalist trying to preserve the community aspects of a body of specialists. There are few more interesting or valuable duties in American society.

THE STAFF

Like the president, the vice president or dean needs additional staff both in his own office and throughout the college. Additional secretarial help is called for by vice presidents and deans, a call often accompanied by a tribute to the present secretary. Next, they list the need for a special personal assistant to help in whatever ways seem desirable. Frequently there is need for a person in charge of institutional research who can supply the vice president or dean with data and answer questionnaires. Help with federal programs is another theme song. An assistant dean, an associate dean, or an alter ego to aid at all times and take over when the dean has a leave is often desired. One dean called for an automation expert. Illustrations of additional administrative staff reported as needed throughout the college, other than in the administrator's office itself, are: a divisional chairman to act as subdean; a registrar (the dean now has that duty); a director of graduate study (the vice president now acts in that capacity); and better staff in the departmental offices so that the dean's secretary does not have to keep correcting the departmental payrolls, reports, and so on.

DELEGATION

Typical complaints are:

1. The president will not delegate to me matters that should be in my hands.
2. Delegation doesn't stick.
3. Just because I'm handy, I'm given too many irrelevant chores both by the president and by the faculty.
4. The staff or the departments won't take the responsibilities I give them.

Remember, although the above are typical complaints, an attitude of complaint is not itself typical.

ATTRACTIVENESS, FRUSTRATIONS, AND SUGGESTIONS

Like the presidents, the vice presidents and deans are a pretty happy group. To a greater degree than is the usual human lot, they are doing the work they like. Day by day they deal with people who know something interesting and want to tell it to them. They are discontented mostly because they would not be happy if they were contented.

However, there are reported frustrations that form a pattern; overwork, inappropriate work, or too much routine work head the list. The red tape of government or church rules seems almost, if not quite, as great a hindrance to them as to the president. In the case of laymen in Catholic institutions or Protestant church-related colleges, the difficulty in dealing with the church hierarchy may be greater for the vice president or dean than for the president who is a minister or belongs to a religious order. The problem of guidelines and effective communication is both up, down, and lateral; that is, with the president, with the faculty, and with coordinate administrative officers.

The attitude of a minority of the faculty who carp and criticize is a cross to be borne as patiently as possible. Moreover, the students and faculty members, who always wish to deal with the president, complicate the dean's work.

Perhaps the suggestions for improvement can be summarized as: remove the frustrations; increase the staff and improve its quality; grant proper and clear authority to these officers. There are, of course, a miscellaneous set of suggestions, many excellent, but so varied as to defy summary. Some of them will be quoted.

REFLECTIONS

One should note that some vice presidents call themselves deans; for example, the first and the last "reflection."

There are happy vice presidents and deans:

I love my work as academic dean. — *Vice president, private college*

The A. & S. deanship is perhaps the most attractive position in a university administration. — *Liberal arts dean, public university*

My eighteen years as Dean of the College have been filled with some achievement, and with satisfying memories that come from working with faculty, students, and alumni. — *Liberal arts dean, private college*

I do not see how my position could be made more attractive to an administrator who is, at the same time, a religious. The salary and fringe benefits are not applicable to me. The atmosphere in which I work here is most pleasant; my associates are cooperative; and the faculty and students, by and large, all seem to have the good of the University at heart. — *Vice president, private college*

Find administrative responsibilities fully as rewarding as teaching and scholarship except for longer wait to see payoff. — *Vice president, private college*

It ain't bad. — *Liberal arts dean, public college* [He must have a Webster III.]

Perhaps it is too attractive now. — *Vice president, public college*

OVERWORK AND USE OF TIME. Vice presidents and deans are over-worked and the use of their time is often inappropriate.

As it stands, the position of academic dean is certainly the achievement of history, not logic, and each year more miscellaneous functions are dropped into this office, to the further confoundment of this occupant . . . .

At the present time the academic dean of necessity spends most of her time being dean of students, and very little time being dean of the faculty. — *Liberal arts dean, private college*

I still have reservations as to whether it is an office in its own right (perhaps a reflection of my having moved from a deanship in which I had virtually complete autonomy). — *Vice president, public university*

Specify what Dean is to do and not pile things on him because things need to be done and he is efficient. — *Liberal arts dean, private college*

The cut system and many student requests might better be handled by another office. — *Liberal arts dean, private college*

I am serving as a dept. head *and* as *Dean.* I am overworked. — *Liberal arts dean, public college*

Partly overworked in detail because at present I am responsible also for admissions. — *Liberal arts dean, private college*

There is need for an assistant dean as well as a director of graduate studies who could handle the summer session and extension program.

Class scheduling and examination scheduling should be delegated to the Office of the Registrar. — *Vice president, public college*

Sorry, I'd like to fill this out — but it's 11:00 P.M., two days after this was due. I have a speech to prepare for tomorrow — a recommendation on a new Dean of Arts and Sciences — and a whole series of statements on persons to be promoted — etc., etc.

When an institution grows at the rate of 2,200 students per year with a comparable increase in administrative staff, there isn't much time to think about what you'd like to see done to eliminate frustration. — *Vice president, public college*

I would appreciate a more flexible schedule. We are expected to be in our offices from 8:00 A.M. to 5:00 P.M., Monday through Friday, and from 8:00 A.M. to noon on Saturday. There are many occasions when I work nights and on the weekends. I teach a 7:30 A.M. class and am usually at school before 7:00 but this is not considered to be any reason for leaving the office before 5:00 P.M.

I feel the position entails "a job to be done," and I'm willing to work many extra hours in order to do it well; but less rigidity concerning "time at the desk" would make the situation more pleasant. — *Vice president, private college*

The most frustrating thing about the job cannot be corrected — the necessity for spending a disproportionate amount of time on "problem" faculty members and "problem" departments. Just as the professor must neglect the good students in order to help the poor ones, the Dean must neglect the swingers to help the weak. He is punished for this, by the weak.—*Liberal arts dean, public university*

All administrators seem to me to get caught up in details that are not themselves important. I spend time in resolving small problems and doing some relatively unimportant things. I have always felt that such involvement creates a web of understanding and that one should not be wholly divorced from the trivia of one's office. I feel content with the responsibilities that come to me.—*Liberal arts dean, private college*

I think that my position could be more effective and attractive if I were not involved with the external relations of the college.—*Vice president, private college*

Like most administrative officers, I resent time spent on *pro forma* appearances at functions, welcoming groups, etc.—*Vice president, public university*

I still can't decide whether my chief role is to be stimulator or mediator. —*Liberal arts dean, private college*

As noted earlier in substance, too much time is spent taking care of the urgent to the detriment of the important.—*Vice president, private college*

Frequent interruptions with trivia because there is no other place for the faculty or students to have their problems (which they, too, recognize as not being of great importance—but still necessary) attended to. This is not being critical of them for they really have no alternative procedure available to them.—*Vice president, private college*

Being the middle man is not easy:

I get some envy, some sympathy, but more cooperation. The toughest question is how one speaks for the Faculty to the Governing Boards, and vice versa, while retaining the trust of both.—*Liberal arts dean, private university*

The chief source of frustration—and perhaps it is true of *any* dean—is that a president usually tends to think of a dean as *his* representative of the administration while the faculty thinks of him as their voice *to* administration. The job is invariably schizophrenic. What to do? Nothing. Perhaps history and higher education will someday reach a common definition of the job.—*Liberal arts dean, public college*

STAFF

In His Office
My exceptionally efficient secretary is badly overworked and needs help. —*Vice president, private college*

Very inadequate in secretarial help. I am trying to conduct the work of my office with the same secretarial help I had when our enrollment was one-fourth of the current figure. Also during the same period the faculty has grown from about 50 to 155.—*Vice president, public college*

One source of frustration to me is that all our administrative secretaries must be paid on the same scale and receive the same vacation benefits, etc. I think that a person who has a position such as mine, should be allowed to make special arrangements for his own secretary, since I have had the experience of being a Dean with inefficient secretarial assistance and now am a Dean with a very capable secretary who can cope with irate parents and faculty, the public, other members of the staff, an anxious student, etc., as well as turn out a great volume of high caliber work. A good secretary can cut one-third, at least, off the work load of an administrator.—*Liberal arts dean, private college*

An "apprentice" dean, after some experience, could make it possible for me to have a year's leave of absence to complete my Ph.D. dissertation. Under present conditions this is manifestly impossible, and lack of doctorate has been a continual frustration.—*Liberal arts dean, private college*

An assistant dean might be helpful, but I believe it would be more advantageous to continue the decentralization process, as the college grows, rather than to build up a larger staff in this office.—*Vice president, public college*

Outside His Office

More and competent secretarial help is needed for the other departments within the college so there will be less dependence upon my secretary who has little enough time to perform her many tasks.—*Liberal arts dean, public university*

Job should be divided into two: one for Dean of Academic Affairs and one Dean of Student Affairs.—*Liberal arts dean, private college*

Chief frustrations are largely in lack of parallel force in financial area at the present, that make financial studies difficult.—*Vice president, private university*

The big university is now typically under-administered. There is such a need for a number of really good educational leaders at the various levels so that no one would need to be quite as over-extended as he is now.—*Liberal arts dean, public university*

A clear definition of one's role and the proper delegation of authority are constantly desired, but not always attained:

I am in a newly created position. My duties have not been clearly defined. I find it exceedingly difficult to work not knowing fully my responsibilities and authority.—*Vice president, private college*

Inadequate adherence to lines of authority and responsibility. The effectiveness of my office is sometimes impaired by blurred lines of responsibility between my office and others (e.g., Admissions, Student Personnel, Business). There is an administrative flow-chart, but it is often ignored in the prosecution of campus affairs.—*Liberal arts dean, public college*

The duties of my office and the limits of its authority in academic matters, as opposed to those of the office of the president, have not been clearly enough delineated. Secondly, the young turks among the faculty who are anxious to participate in all decisions (which frequently means they would like to change some established *modus operandi*). These two sources tend to work together to create frustrations and tensions. Since it is not always clear that the dean has the authority to make the final decision, on occasions little effort is made to convince him. Rather, the matter is taken quickly to the president. Whether this is a problem that is peculiar to our college, or to small colleges, I do not know. It is my opinion that the dean's position would be enhanced and his frustrations lessened if the lines of authority were more clearly outlined. — *Liberal arts dean, private college*

There is a lack of delegated power which makes it difficult, if not impossible, to carry out the responsibilities. — *Vice president, private college*

Infringement on my area by other administrators, especially those in Student Personnel. There is a tendency, and increasingly so, for Student Personnel to run this University in the sense that it is exercising influence in academic matters far beyond that which is appropriate. — *Liberal arts dean, public university*

I am somewhat reluctant to mention this, but my chief frustration is lack of major budgetary control and freedom in policy making for my college . . . . If a deanship is to be no more than a chief clerk's job, then it is not worth having. — *Liberal arts dean, public university*

Clear subordination of buildings and grounds, as well as the business office, to the academic side of the University. — *Liberal arts dean, private university*

If the Division Chairmen would accept the responsibility for being "Deans" in their own areas, it would enable this office to function more efficiently. The framework for the organization is now present, but is not functioning satisfactorily. — *Liberal arts dean, private college*

One evolves into his position. I do the things I can do best and delegate what someone else can do better.

I have a very ideal job. The president gives me full latitude and backs up my decisions. If I don't like something we get together and work out a better way of doing it. Personalities make the jobs pleasant. — *Vice president, public university*

The problem of delegation is closely related to that of communication:

Usually they [the faculty] feel they are not well-enough treated. Since our salaries are not openly available to everybody, their information often is erroneous. — *Liberal arts dean, public university*

We never have any staff meetings. The President prefers to make policies and decisions himself or at best in conjunction with one staff member at a time. — *Liberal arts dean, private college*

The greater source of dissatisfaction and frustration thus far has been the lack of communication between the area of academic affairs and that of development. Many of the questions that arise on the academic level, with which I am mainly concerned, cannot be answered unless some information is provided concerning the availability of resources.—*Vice president, private college*

The chief tensions arise from poor communication, since the Board of Directors is exclusively religious (there are no laymen thereon) and planning and policy-making etc. are reserved to the Board.—*Liberal arts dean, private college*

In my opinion, it would help if top administrators could get together. Perhaps with some board members away from campus for several days for policy planning.—*Vice president, private college*

Nonetheless, there are two possible areas of uneasiness: relationships with trustees and the definition of responsibility within the administration. Although a Dean of Faculty should be present at trustee meetings and work closely with certain trustee committees, it is inadvisable, in my judgment, that he be expected to become so friendly with trustees that his position with respect to the President ever comes into question.—*Vice president, private college*

FRUSTRATIONS

The relation to external hierarchies, whether governmental or ecclesiastical, is mentioned. This sample is small, since this is a topic particularly discussed by librarians and business officers.

Regulations, controls, excessive reports and interference by state agencies are the chief sources of frustrations in the conduct of my office.—*Vice president, public college*

The problems are highlighted by the fact that, as a State school, we have to resort to the Legislature and to governmental agencies for support, although one is torn between a selfish concern for one's own problems and an overall awareness of the importance of legislative review over the activities of public institutions.—*Vice president, public college*

The chief frustrations arise in dealing with state officials and bureaus. State architects have little comprehension of *academic* requirements in planning and siting buildings.—*Vice president, public college*

We are encouraged to go into government programs, but these are frequently disappointing. They require matching funds; they divert our good staff members from teaching; and they force us to try to do things which are really outside the main mission of the University, as I see it. The financial returns are not usually enough to pay for the time and energy involved.—*Vice president, public college*

It might be better if the College would still formulate its own plans in regard to its priest teachers, regardless of what the Order does in this regard.—*Liberal arts dean, private college*

Pressures from church constituency can be trying and vexing.—*Vice president, private college*

I suppose that oneself and other people are usually our chief sources of frustration, and it may well be that vice presidents and deans are self-confident enough so that they are chiefly troubled by the others.

Temperamental and impatient faculty members along with pampered students and doting parents.—*Vice president, private college*

Conflicting demands of faculty couched in sanctimonious concern for the college when the particular department or personal sphere of work is the real problem.—*Vice president, private college*

Another source of frustration comes from faculty members who want to participate in decision making (this is good) but do not know the facts or fail to take the total view of the college either from ignorance or self-interest.—*Liberal arts dean, private college*

The inability or unwillingness of a very small minority of the faculty to make any compromise whatever between academic idealism and practical necessity.—*Liberal arts dean, public college*

The second source of difficulty, and one for which I was altogether unprepared when I took office, is what I have come to consider the plague of the academic profession: insecurity. This is not limited to those still without tenure, nor do higher salaries seem to have helped. The result, for the administrator, is to find his motives constantly misinterpreted, his suggestions viewed as threats, his proposals considered dictates.—*Liberal arts dean, private college*

I wish the faculty would cease trying to take over administrative functions and tend to their jobs of teaching.—*Liberal arts dean, public college*

My greatest disappointment in academic administration has been the growing signs of unprofessional and unethical conduct on the part of administrative officers in other institutions who seem to have little qualms of conscience in attempting to hire successful faculty members for higher salaries.—*Liberal arts dean, private college*

I suppose any position has its distasteful duties:

The least pleasant part of a dean's work is that which affects the personal well-being of individual faculty members—salaries, promotions, support of various kinds. But some decisions must be hurtful, and if one isn't willing to explain what has been or will be done in face-to-face confrontation, one should not be a dean. You get awfully tired of it though.—*Liberal arts dean, public university*

I must frequently administer and defend decisions which I did not participate in making and, at times, with which I basically disagree.—*Liberal arts dean, public college*

The great difficulty of important work is often noted:

The difficulties lie entirely in being one member of a very small group that attempts to steer an extremely complicated university. When other members are out-of-town or when conclusions to complicated problems are only forming in the President's mind, a vice president's life is not a happy one. — *Vice president, private university*

The primary frustrations of the position are associated with the lack of time to study and make well-informed decisions on the wide variety of problems which present themselves in rapid succession for consideration. This condition is a reflection of an institution experiencing rapid growth in enrollment and a developing program. It is an exciting and interesting position. — *Vice president, public college*

The main frustration comes from attempting to develop the spirit of a liberal arts college in an institution which has been a normal school and teachers' college. — *Liberal arts dean, public college*

Some take frustrations philosophically:

To eliminate the tensions and uncertain aspects of the position would be to destroy the intrigue of the work. — *Liberal arts dean, public college*

If there are frustrations and tensions, they are too trivial to get frustrated and tense about. — *Vice president, public university*

Every scholar desires to remain one:

One [frustration] that's inherent in the office. The desire and the need to continue teaching, combined with the inability to devote sufficient time to keeping up with one's field. Otherwise, frustrations and tensions distinctly limited. — *Vice president, private college*

SUGGESTED IMPROVEMENTS

Some mention preparation for their positions:

Give proper training for future administrators plus in-service training. To suddenly give a person a position of major responsibility without adequate preparation is very bad both for the man and the institution. — *Liberal arts dean, private college*

I found my year leave of absence at the University of Michigan at the Center for the Study of Higher Education refreshing, invigorating and academically stimulating. I'm convinced that whatever effectiveness I have in this office is directly related to this experience. — *Liberal arts dean, private college*

Leaves of absence are highly desirable but are practically non-existent for Deans. I would like to attend the Center for the Study of Higher Education in Michigan but who takes over my duties? — *Liberal arts dean, private college*

In spite of a chapter on leaves and vacations, some mention of them here is proper:

Leaves are important to me. I'm a geologist and cherish the few moments to look at rocks and renew my spirits. — *Liberal arts dean, public university*

In addition to summer vacation, administrators should be required to absent themselves from the office and from official duties at such times as Christmas vacation and Easter holidays. I find the pressures of office very great so that the need to get away entirely for a few days seems imperative. — *Liberal arts dean, private college*

Some suggest a fixed term of office:

College administrators (in my opinion) should be limited to 10 years with any one institution; then be given one year leave at full pay to get back into an academic field. — *Vice president, public university*

For a religious community, I would suggest that the dean should serve a stated term of years (5–10 years), after which he could be reappointed. I figure that if a dean has not done what he can do best in five years, he should be removed. — *Liberal arts dean, private university*

Some make suggestions to the faculty:

If faculty would read the *catalog* and *faculty handbook*, my time could be used more effectively. A clarification of the role of department head in recruitment of faculty would be helpful. — *Vice president, private college*

I believe faculty must demand better administrators and must be willing in the process to turn over administrative duties to their administrators, reserving only policy questions to themselves. — *Vice president, public college*

Some want even more meetings (or at least other meetings):

I would heartily welcome the opportunity of meeting for a week or longer with the deans of ten to twenty small liberal arts colleges to consider problems common to us all; e.g., curriculum and the "tone" of residence hall living. — *Liberal arts dean, private college*

And there are special suggestions:

Though I certainly do not wish to appear ungenerous toward such a product as you are about to formulate, I wonder if it can really make up for the thousands of man hours it costs. When one thinks of the hundreds of good men he knows who must be laboring away on similar questionnaires, one begins to believe that institutions ought to be reimbursed, at the rate of $50 per hour, for each administrator's time requirement in responding. Whether or not the administrators are that valuable, such projects are likely to be disruptive, and affect more than one person's schedule. Such *external* items, moreover, are less foreseeable, less controllable, and therefore more disturbing, than that which originates out of local situations. — *Vice president, private college*

The possibility of receiving tenure within my discipline would make a proper professional reluctance to be a mere "yes" man safer.—*Vice president, public college*

In my opinion, a University home on or very near the campus would not only be a financial help but more importantly would make contacts with students, faculty, and visitors easier and more effective.—*Vice president, public university*

As many industrial concerns are now doing, provision for taking one's wife or family on trips should be allowed (i.e., paid).—*Liberal arts dean, public university*

Give the present board members a trip to universities west of the Hudson River.—*Liberal arts dean, public university*

The Ford Foundation, exercising its lordly functions, has now picked out a group of small colleges and extended them matching grants to enable them to become "peaks of excellence." This is a fine thing. And these awards were made to institutions which had the ability to organize themselves for the sort of display of institutional power demanded by the Ford investigators. Another group of institutions should now be chosen. These are institutions potentially quite capable of *becoming* places of genuine excellence but which have, by virtue of their position, traditions, or past leadership, been so far incapable of mounting programs of institutional research, development, etc., which produce anything but frustration for the participants. These institutions should be given: (*a*) outright grants; and (*b*) aid in securing appropriate personnel to enable them to tool up for the future.—*Liberal arts dean, private college*

QUOTABLE AND GENERAL

I have no answer other than that either I should be twice as efficient or there should be two of me.—*Vice president, private college*

Anyone who finds my position attractive needs some advice.—*Liberal arts dean, private college*

No problems, no dean!—*Liberal arts dean, private college*

Nobody (so far as I know) wanted the job, so that I enjoy sympathy and cooperation.—*Liberal arts dean, private college*

Seriously, I know from frequent meetings with other deans that no two jobs are alike. Tradition, historical accidents, and personalities make each office function in its own way.—*Vice president, private college*

As this process has continued, there has been a tendency to insert an echelon of policy makers between the Dean's office and the President. The complexity of the multi-purpose university, no doubt, has made this development necessary and advantageous. However, as this structure is duplicated in universities of moderate size, it reduces the directness with which the perspectives of the Dean's office can be brought to bear upon the course of the university. Consequently, not only does this process alter the over-all role of the Dean, but it threatens to remove policy-making levels from direct contact with the instructional program and academic needs of students.—*Liberal arts dean, private college*

But if one happens to believe that in assembling a faculty (or a student body) one should aim at bringing together, and holding together, as disparate a group as possible, it appears that some such centripetal function must be the inevitable lot of the dean.—*Vice president, private college*

This expanse of white paper invites me to unburden a vast weight of divine (or mundane) discontent. Strange to say, I have none to unburden. My experience as dean has involved working with a reliable and co-operative group of administrators; a president of integrity and understanding; a talented, challenging, recalcitrant, fighting, delightful faculty; and generous compensation. Of course there are frustrations and tensions: the stiff and growing competition for superior teachers; the struggle to maintain a stable yet flexible curriculum; the daily trouble-shooting to minimize interdepartmental jealousies and fancied loss of status. But these are proper parts of the job. Eliminate tension, and the educational process flattens out into routine repetition. Except in cases of illness I see no crying need for leaves of absence. Now that I am approaching the end of my administrative experience, I would not have wanted to miss a day of it. The rest of the paper must remain white.—*Vice president, private college*

The Dean of Faculties should be a lively intellectual, not necessarily a publishing scholar, but one who knows scholarship and teaching and spends his time with other deans and faculty promoting the scholarly atmosphere of the institution. He should work constantly on ideas for experimentation and improvement in teaching, in encouraging research and curricular development and in the development of attractive personnel policies for faculty (academic freedom, leaves, pay fringe benefits). As a budget officer he should be concerned with policy but relieved of trivia and detailed budget changes. He definitely needs time for travel and study.—*Vice president, private university*

CHAPTER 16

THE GRADUATE DEAN

THE graduate dean comes closer to being a typical faculty leader than does any of the other administrators considered in this book. He is usually picked from the institution's most productive investigators. He has shown capacity for leadership, at least within his department. Those faculty members who wish to enhance the scholarly standing of the institution are likely to consider him their champion.

The median age of male graduate deans is 52. Seventy-six percent hold a Ph.D. degree (92% in universities and 66% in colleges), while 16% have a degree of Ed.D. (5% in universities, 34% in public colleges, and 10% in private colleges). Over 80% have their work for their highest degree in the following fields: education, 25% (5% in universities, 50% in public colleges, and 25% in private colleges); social sciences, 18%; physical sciences, 12% (27% in universities, where it leads all other fields); English and journalism, 10%; biological sciences, 8%; psychology, 5%; mathematics and statistics, 4%.

Nineteen of the graduate deans were women, one of these being in a public university, four in public colleges, and fourteen in private colleges. Seventy-two percent of the graduate deans (78% in universities) were serving their present institution when they became dean.

It should be remembered that we asked the presidents to distribute the questionnaires by function rather than by title. Many of those answering in the section "graduate dean" have the title of "director of graduate studies." The range of duties and the magnitude of work differ greatly from place to place. In universities with extensive Ph.D. programs, the graduate deanship is a full-time position, although some incumbents—through extraordinary effort—teach a class, and many continue a research program involving the guiding of graduate students in their thesis work. In many colleges where there is graduate work, the major emphasis is on the master's degree, frequently in education. At times, the program consists almost entirely of summer work for teachers.

In universities, the obtaining of outside grants for research and the allocation of research funds frequently center in the graduate office. Moreover, in these institutions the fellowship and graduate scholarship programs are usually extensive and the responsibility for them is located in the graduate dean's office.

In connection with the foregoing, it must be remembered that in a large university much administrative responsibility rests in the departments, the chairmen of which complain that it really lies in the numerous private empires of the recipients of federal and foundation grants. The administration of research and its related teaching in a major university are like an intricate oriental rug, which has a pattern, and yet in each portion of it the pattern becomes lost in the details. However, if the design is good and the knots are tight enough, the whole has quality and yields aesthetic pleasure.

The duties of the graduate dean are to maintain standards and facilitate scholarship. In some institutions it is up to him to see that the prestige to be derived from unreasonable standards does not impair the usefulness of the department. He frequently believes that the means at his disposal in funds, in staff, and particularly in authority are not adequate for him to perform his duties.

STAFF

His chief suggestions as to staff are the usual ones concerning more and better secretarial help, and in the large institution, the need for an assistant dean.

The graduate dean often fills other positions in addition to that of dean, especially that of departmental chairman or director of some program such as the summer school. In other cases he may be the vice president, or the college dean, and is likely to wish to retain that position and have a separate director of graduate studies appointed.

Some of the staff needs mentioned are for a person to write proposals for the NSF and other agencies and a graduate admissions officer.

LACK OF AUTHORITY

With the possible exception of being overworked, the chief complaint of graduate deans is that they do not have the authority to accompany their responsibility: "How can one help raise scholarly standards if one has no influence in the appointment and promotion of faculty members?" Some graduate deans believe their influence is scant because the faculty salaries are in the college budgets. Some would like to see created a graduate faculty with its own salary budget. Others would like veto power on appointments or at least veto power on who teaches graduate courses.

GOVERNMENT RELATIONS

The graduate dean probably is less frustrated by state rules than are other administrators, but there are few in the institution so greatly affected by the research programs of federal agencies—such as NSF, NASA, NIH, NFAH, and other alphabetical arrangements—as he is. No other person, except perhaps the business officer, is so compressed between dilatory departments and government deadlines.

Graduate deans complain less about the faculty than do other administrators, except in some places where the faculty drag their feet in initiating graduate programs. This occurs only in colleges with an historical and primary commitment to undergraduate teaching.

REFLECTIONS

All the quotations in this section are from graduate deans.

I think that most graduate deans like their work; I pick only one quotation:

I love my job!—*Public college*

In some places the graduate dean is too much of a handyman and he, too, is overworked:

Teacher, chairman of department of education, director of summer session and director of graduate study. Director of graduate study is sufficient for one man.—*Public college*

At present I have too many duties—Acting Director of Graduate Studies; Chairman, Department of Chemistry; Teaching (10 contact hours) and research.—*Private college*

Besides operating as director of graduate studies without portfolio I serve as director of the following programs: *a*) Summer school; *b*) Evening Graduate Program; *c*) Summer Institute for Secondary School Physics Teachers; *d*) Summer Institute for Secondary School Science Teachers.

My secretary and I comprise the entire administrative staff for these operations which constitute the bulk of my load. In addition to these administrative duties I carry a half-time teaching load.—*Private university*

Too damn much work (I'm writing this after 8:00 P.M.—after being on the job since 8:00 A.M. with 1½ hours off during the day).—*Public college*

STAFF

. . . very understaffed. The secretary acts as my secretary, receptionist, final validator of degree requirements, faculty secretary, and in general does the work of 3 persons. There needs to be an associate dean and an assistant academic dean.—*Private college*

If I were not a rather good secretary myself, the office work would be farther behind than it is.—*Public college*

The single item which would make it still more attractive would be a better pay scale for certain key supporting persons below the dean's rank. —*Public university*

Student wives are great help but they do not stay long.—*Public university*

FRUSTRATIONS

I must say that I believe the position I now occupy is attractive as it is presently constituted—except that it leaves virtually no time to be spent with one's family or in any recreational activity.—*Public university*

Responsibility and Authority

Absence of a graduate faculty as a well-defined statutory body. This leads, among other problems, to unsatisfactory process of approving ad hoc graduate teachers and courses.—*Public university*

I do think that the Graduate Dean needs greater control over faculty appointments than has been the situation in the past. He should at least have a veto over those considered for graduate instruction even though the salary and contract are in the College of Arts and Science.—*Private university*

The responsibility, *without* the authority to back it, to strive for excellence in graduate education has been continually frustrating. I do not know of the appointment or promotion of a faculty member who will be intimately involved in graduate education until I read it in the local press. I scrounge for funds for program improvements in a temporarily tolerated way. My office has a major share of responsibility for the research activity of the entire campus, for *all* higher degrees, for all faculty activities in higher degree programs—and as such is the only office other than that of the Chief Campus Officer involved in such an overview; yet I am not a part of the Administration as it *should* be organized and I must conduct my office as a relatively personal relationship with it, with no basis in the regulations of the Academic Senate or Administration. It is, regrettably, an irregular position on a regular basis.—*Public university*

Relation to Students

Lack of any disciplinary control over graduate students.—*Private university*

The rapid growth of interest in, and demand for, graduate education—often resulting in an expectation on the part of unqualified students that they *must* go on to graduate school and that they *should* be admitted to our own school.—*Public university*

Faculty and Administrative Attitudes

A large percentage (85%) of our graduate students are in education. However, at times the graduate council—some of which are antagonistic to education—act in opposition to recommendation of Chairman of Education Department or Dean of School of Education. This sometimes creates problems.—*Public college*

At my University, graduate work is looked on as a secondary endeavor to a very considerable extent. Many members of faculty react with suspicion to the whole area, fearing a deterioration of the undergraduate programs, or, perhaps, a modernization of the undergraduate offerings. (Is that unduly cynical?)—*Private college*

Frustrations and irritations arise mainly because my faculty colleagues often take too lightly the responsibility for adequate programming and counseling of doctoral students. Their amiable indifference to administrative detail causes problems that are simply unnecessary.—*Private university*

My chief source of irritation or frustration is coming from certain academic departments which are recommending for admission students who are not admissible. I expect to be able to cope with this situation more competently in the near future.—*Public university*

Of course there are frustrations and tensions. The main ones arise in relations with faculty members who seek special privileges and exemptions for their doctoral students. But, by and large, cooperation between administration and faculty is good and it is possible to uphold good standards while maintaining warm relationships with the faculty.—*Private university*

The chief sources of frustrations and tensions come from the development office, and have to do with promises or statements from public-relations personnel who attempt to interfere with the academic areas of the institution. The development office feels the pressures of our various publics and attempts to apply these pressures to academicians. In any confrontation the academicians usually win, but it is unpleasant to have to deal with such problems.—*Private college*

SUGGESTIONS

Better Preparation

There is an assumption that academic accomplishments qualify academicians to service as administrators. In my experience the good administrators drawn from this group are the exceptions. But it is heresy to suggest that courses and seminars should be provided to enable university executives to perform more effectively and to make use of modern technology in administrative management.—*Public university*

And here is a good package:

If I ever start shedding tears about the scholarly accomplishments that I am passing by because of my job, I hope I have the courage to get out of administration. In *my* case, however, I find that I can be a dean, do a limited amount of teaching, and still get an occasional article done.

My suggestions for further improvement: 1) arrange for more creative use of summer months, the only time of the year that I could be away from the office without hurting the institution unduly; 2) while there is no tenure in administrative positions, I think that three-year contracts would give me (and my colleagues in similar positions) the freedom to make long-range plans; 3) the institution should not expect every administrative officer to spend many evenings at banquets, testimonials, awards assemblies, etc. A representative from the administration at each of these time-consuming functions is enough!—*Private college*

And one final suggestion:

Further, I am frequently struck by the anti-intellectual attitude taken by some of my administrative associates, both at . . . and elsewhere. This makes the problem of administration an enterprise which, for better or worse, is devoted to intellectual ends, considerably more difficult. The best way to improve this position is, to my mind, to abolish it and every other administrative position that does not concern itself with the supervision of routine operations. The highest purely administrative position ought to be office manager. Decisions of policy, etc., ought to be formed by those upon whom the consequences of decision have the greatest effect.—*Private college*

THE QUESTIONNAIRE

Incidentally, this has been a most enjoyable experience and an excellent opportunity to take a personal inventory.—*Public college*

QUOTABLE AND GENERAL

From conversations with fellow Graduate Deans I believe I share the problems common to the position—but I seem to have one advantage many of them lack: a budget.—*Private college*

Often enough I feel that running a graduate school is like driving through jello.—*Private university*

When one is my age he knows few frustrations and tensions. He has learned to take things calmly. If he had not, he would not be living. [Age 69.]
—*Private university*

As for ways of making the position more attractive, probably the most important would be provision for time in which to carry on the Dean's own scholarly research. I believe that if at all possible, the Dean should continue actively to participate in some graduate teaching, either by offering a seminar, participating in colloquia and the like in his own field. Such an arrangement, again, means he must be free for some percentage of his time and energy from administrative duties. Basically, a Dean must depend for his effectiveness as a leader in graduate education upon the respect he commands among graduate faculty. If he clearly becomes a "has-been" in his own field of scholarly endeavor, he is likely to exhaust the reservoir of good will and respect fairly rapidly.—*Private college*

Were the operation merely one of carrying on the routine of a long and well-established graduate program in a University that is primarily or to a large extent involved in past B.A. instruction, the task might be simplified. But, to be deeply involved in the detail of an operation and, at the same time, to provide leadership in assisting an institution whose commitment is primarily to undergraduate instruction, to come to terms with its graduate commitment is a fascinating, challenging, time-consuming and frustrating experience. A tremendous amount of time and energy is expended in developing understanding, in enlisting cooperation, in writing proposals and recommendations, and in helping the faculty to achieve a consensus. Moreover, especially in the field of teacher education, the "race" to keep up with deadlines for proposals to foundations and the state and federal governments has become an almost full-time task in itself. I cannot say that the Director of Graduate Studies is somewhere "out in left field" administratively because lines of responsibility and means of operating are clear. And yet, as related to the main task of the University (undergraduate work), there is a slight element in the job of being an outside "intruder" endeavoring to capture the concern and interest of the faculty as a whole. This is inevitable in an "exploratory" and somewhat pioneering effort to define the precise obligation of an undergraduate liberal arts college to graduate study.—*Private college*

Not being a budget dean he has to lead from experience and knowledge and character for he has neither a carrot or a stick . . . . [The graduate deanship] is the most individualistic and in some ways the loneliest administrative job on a campus. More than any other administrative post it depends upon what you are.—*Private university*

CHAPTER 17

THE DIRECTOR OF LIBRARIES

IN 93% of the universities and 64% of the public colleges the directors of libraries are men. In private colleges, 52% are women. The median age of the male directors of libraries is 49 (55 in universities; 47 in colleges), while the median age of women holding these positions is 55.

Fourteen percent of the directors of libraries hold the Ph.D. degree and 1% the degree of Ed.D. However, in universities, 37% have a Ph.D. The highest degree in 69% of the cases is the master's. Sixty-five percent did their work for their highest degree in library science. This is almost uniform for all types of institutions except for private universities, where the figure is 53%. The only other subjects with strong representation are social studies, 11%; English and journalism, 10%; and education, 6%.

About two-thirds of the librarians came to their present position from another institution; however the proportion is under one-half in private universities.

STAFF

Although many librarians need additional clerical help in their own office, their chief desire is for more adequate general staff. A few librarians report that their greatest need is for nonprofessional staff to relieve the professional staff of inappropriate duties, but a far greater number give priority to an increase in the professional staff. Catalogers are, perhaps, mentioned most frequently, although circulation, reference, and acquisition librarians are often wanted. In small libraries any second professionally-trained librarian would provide a great relief.

Excessive reliance on student help is a major cause of complaint.

A number of librarians expressed dissatisfaction with the maintenance and janitorial service afforded the library.

The long periods during which the library is open appears, at times,
to be the chief reason for a shortage of staff, and to cause undue strain
on the professional librarians, some of whom must always be present.
Several librarians spoke vehemently of the "unjustified" demands of students and of faculty for long library hours—hours which proved to be
both costly and productive of undue hardship. The shortage of staff is
frequently worsened by the double duties performed by librarians,
such as teaching in the library course, being chairman of the department of library science, or giving lectures in English literature. There
are also cases of sheer imposition, such as expecting librarians to
handle tickets for athletic events.

AUTHORITY

Librarians often stated that they preferred to report to the president
rather than to anyone else.

Interference by a dean or by the business office is sometimes alleged. However, the chief complaint in regard to authority is concerning the librarian's relation to the faculty library committee. In some
places this committee appears to have been given or to have assumed
power to direct the librarian. Librarians believe, I think rightly, that
these committees should be advisory. Of course, if the committee's
advice is never heeded, it may appeal to the president.

COMMUNICATION AND STATUS

A major frustration of librarians is lack of information concerning
matters that vitally concern their work. Among the more important
are curriculum, reserved book lists, and the budget. The planning of
courses or curricula with neither the budgetary provisions nor the
time to allow the library to fulfill its part is absurd; yet it is one of the
commonest absurdities. Likewise, reserve books are not brought together by magic.

Librarians believe that to keep in touch with what is going on they
should participate in the work of faculty curriculum committees and
be on the "administrative council." Here status is relevant. The likelihood of being on faculty committees is increased by having faculty

rank or, at least, faculty status. To be on the administrative council, a position akin to that of a dean reporting to the president or to the vice president helps. If faculty status brings sabbatical privileges, so much the better.

RELATIONS TO GOVERNMENT

Government red tape is particularly hard on librarians. There is less complaint concerning relations with the federal government than in the cases of the president, the graduate dean, the registrar, or the business officer; but state procedures concerning both purchases of books and civil service appointments sometimes can scarcely be endured.

Several librarians, while recognizing the importance of computer techniques, correctly warn against considering them a cure-all or a money-saver.

Often the chief frustration of the librarian is the library building itself; and often the chief joy is a new one.

I have had the privilege of serving on the council and the board of the Center for Research Libraries, both under its present name and when it was the Midwest Inter-Library Center. I prized the opportunity to become well acquainted with some of the leading university librarians. Serving on this board was especially valuable because of the mixture of positions represented, including not only librarians but faculty members, graduate deans, college deans, vice presidents, and business officers. All of these persons quickly won each other's respect and the non-librarians came to realize the complexity of libraries and the intelligence as well as the hard work that librarians devote to their problems. Perhaps more than others, librarians are a breed apart—but a splendid breed.

REFLECTIONS

All the quotations in this section are from librarians.

The following is a sample from the many librarians who like their positions:

The position of Librarian at . . . College is a very satisfying one. The Library has never been treated as a step-child, being the first to be cut when finances are tight, and has also been appreciated by the faculty, who in the right sense feel they "own" it. —*Private college*

Most of all for nine years I have worked with an administration which believes in the library and have worked even harder to get the money for all requests—these factors make one very scrupulous about not asking for more than a fair share of the College's resources for the Library.—*Private college*

In general, I should say that I am overpaid, and not really overworked. The problems of the position are perhaps more of my making than inherent in the job itself. Of course, one would always wish for a fresh new building (though I am not sure one should wish for the job of creating it) and a staff that consists wholly of dedicated people who never worry about how long or how hard they are worked. But in the real world, things are not bad here.—*Private college*

OVERWORK AND INAPPROPRIATE WORK

Many librarians are badly overworked:

I have been so damn busy trying to patch up a decrepit library for the past six years that a leave of absence hasn't even entered my mind (except that occasionally I entertained the tho't of coming down with some rare disease that would put me out of commission for a month or so!)—*Private college*

Activities have expanded beyond available secretarial help; consequently I answer the telephone, write some letters in longhand, search for faculty and students for telephone calls, etc. I have even been asked to prepare and serve coffee to college guests.—*Private college*

Shortage of staff requires that I do all sorts of little things nobody else has time to do, such as opening heavy boxes, sorting junk mail, evaluating gifts, and fixing broken equipment. Big things are avoided so all the little things can be kept under control.—*Private university*

The institution has a generous policy in regard to books, and we spend more on books in proportion to income and number of students than almost any other university in the country. However, the personnel budget is always lagging, for the administration is not really convinced that it costs as much—and often more—to order, process and maintain a book as it does to pay the purchase price.—*Private university*

I am also Director of Alumni Relations and Editor of the Magazine.—*Private college*

Administrative officers should not, as we are, be expected to sell and take tickets at ball games during the year.—*Public college*

The jobs I do other than library-related are: Peace Corps Liaison Officer, Foreign Student Advisor & Fulbright Advisor. I also perform student counseling and act as independent studies advisor and culminating study advisor from time to time. I have taught a seminar on War and Peace (1964) and I have two committee responsibilities. I do not find my duties onerous and they fit my style rather well.—*Private college*

STAFF

Overworked people need more staff:

Adequate funds have been provided for acquisition of materials but staff positions at both the professional and clerical levels have not been provided in keeping with added enrollment, increased book budget, and increased responsibilities and demands inherent in curricular developments, specifically a growing graduate program. Staff shortage precipitates a chain reaction of inadequate service, faculty and student dissatisfaction, and staff frustration. Faculty and student expectations are sometimes unreasonable but never without reason, and our inability, or lack of staff time, even to communicate adequately is a major source of frustration and mutual irritation.

An added and related source of frustration and tension, of course, is the extreme scarcity of qualified librarians. —*Public college*

Since our college has a work program for all students, the library utilizes the services of students for clerical jobs and employs no non-student full-time clerical help. Obviously, this creates a problem of continually training new students as each academic quarter begins. Probably within the next year or two, the library will have to add some full-time or part-time clerical personnel who are not students. —*Private college*

Problems also arise from the never-ending demand to extend hours of opening. In the face of the mounting costs of a college education, it would seem reasonable to expect students and faculty alike to regulate their study time to take advantage of already adequate library hours. Simply extending hours at every request without a close examination of the operational costs and other problems involved is unwise. Most staff problems in a library are caused by working conditions resulting from long opening hour schedules. —*Private college*

FRUSTRATIONS

As in other positions, the desire for clear guidelines, proper authority, and adequate communication is stressed:

The necessity of re-arguing with the Business Manager proposals that have already been approved by the Dean of Faculty. —*Private college*

Probably common in some degree to the office of chief librarian of any large university are the frustrations of his ambiguous relationship to faculty and the campus administration. He is the head of a very expensive enterprise, highly important to the scholarly economy of his institution, the operations of which are woven into the daily lives of faculty and students. Yet the library is beside, rather than in, the main stream of interchange between faculty and administration out of which policy decisions grow and which affect many of his library's operations. Whereas faculty have each other in a department and a departmental chairman and a dean to hear their problems and with the assurance of the understanding of a fellow worker, the chief librarian really has no innately sympathetic ear available to him . . . .—*Public university*

My work would be more effective if I reported directly and only to the President.—*Private college*

Responsibility for policy decisions in the Library has been given to the Senate Library Committee. In my opinion, this Committee should be advisory in nature.—*Public college*

I think most people in a position like mine would like to see librarians achieve a larger voice in educational and administrative policy. The librarian very often is neither fish nor fowl—the faculty regard him as an administrator and the administration, in some connections, regard him as faculty, a situation which often makes it difficult for him to perform at maximum capacity. It hampers him in everything from maintenance department services to consultation with faculty on instructional use of the library and the development of the collection. I suppose all administrators tend to feel they should have more authority and standing, but I feel the librarians have a legitimate problem here and that their contribution is seriously reduced as a result.—*Private college*

In general, the position of Chief Librarian suffers from isolation from the basic planning processes of the institution. The sadness here is two-fold: (1) the institution loses the benefit of the knowledge of the librarian with respect to the basic needs of the institution as a whole; and (2) the library program suffers from a lack of intimate knowledge of institutional goals as conceived by other officers of central administration. This double handicap is multiplied in the more complex multi-faculties universities, because the incompleteness of communication at the central level (libraries and university) is duplicated with the major professional schools and other faculties and their counterpart librarians. Furthermore, the cumulative effect of incomplete or poor communication all too frequently leads to dissatisfaction with the library program and concomitant weakening of the librarian's position, even to the point of a "no confidence" situation. True—the incumbent librarian himself may be a contributor to this breakdown. Nevertheless, I would assert on the basis of more than 30 years of study, reflection and participation in the process of managing library programs that the responsibilities assigned to the position of Chief Librarian are frequently in excess of the real authority granted to the position.—*Private university*

The inadequacy of buildings and book budgets is often cited:

I am personally satisfied with my salary. My office is a butler's pantry with tile walls and floors which I detest.—*Private college*

Chief sources of frustration are lack of space, lack of money to build a good collection, lack of staff to service the needs of the students, the faculty and the collection.—*Public college*

The chief problems now relate to the need for more money for books, periodicals and binding. The growing Ph.D. and Research programs make it essential that such funds be substantially increased. — *Private university*

The chief source of frustration arises from the rapid growth of the university and the change from a college to a university without sufficient time to build an adequate collection of materials. — *Public college*

The library has its problems with (also blessings from) the church and the government.

The following six quotes regarding government relations are from different states:

The federal government, until now, has not made money available to college libraries, and private foundations and other donors are generally unwilling to give money to state colleges. — *Public college*

But we have created, at least in state supported schools, a system of controls intended, apparently, to keep us honest rather than to promote efficient operation. Our business offices, our civil service systems are controlled by persons off campus, with a tendency to believe that education can be purchased in carload lots. — *Public college*

A regulation . . . prohibits hiring personnel on a full-time permanent professional level if they lack American citizenship. — *Public university*

Because of state civil service restrictions, I am forced to have many classified employees who are second rate. — *Public university*

Generally, it is the "system" with which we are forced to deal . . . the "state" purchasing pattern is most cumbersome and often negates the energy and good intentions of doing a good job or having some bit of pride in any type of accomplishment. — *Public college*

Fellow bureaucrats get in my hair, as I get in theirs. Rear guard actions take too much of my time and energy, as does compliance with red tape (some of it inescapable) and finding my way through, around, and under or over it. — *Public university*

And these are from both Protestant and Catholic institutions:

Being supported by a church, there are duties which I must perform which I feel do not really belong to me as a librarian. — *Private college*

Lay leaders are not among the "in" group in a Catholic institution. — *Private university*

Faculty and students may be difficult or pleasant:

A continuing frustration is the assignment of topics for research without knowledge, or any attempt to gain any, on the part of many of the faculty as to what the strengths and weaknesses in the Library's collections are. — *Private college*

A great frustration is the simple fact that some faculty members order books already catalogued and on the shelves; others have no appreciation of a Departmental Budget, and order without regard to ultimate cost —

when a little bookkeeping would help control such budgets. —*Private college*

The acceptance of librarians by their faculty colleagues here at this institution is a happy and agreeable one. —*Public college*

A place in key groups:

The librarian should, I believe, be an ex-officio, though non-voting member, of all college curriculum committees. With such participation the librarian could advise curriculum planners of the library's ability to meet the bibliographical needs of new courses or programs and could make advance plans for meeting such needs. —*Public college*

The only condition that could improve the librarian's position would be for the librarian to be on the administrative council. Many items concerning the library are discussed, planned, and carried out by the council before the librarian knows about them. This is embarrassing to the library and its staff. —*Private college*

Faculty and administrative status:

As college librarian I feel that professional librarians should have faculty status and should have virtually the same privileges (e.g., sabbatical leaves, tenure, salary increments equated with teaching faculty, etc.) as do faculty. Without these it is increasingly difficult to recruit staff members and morale suffers as a result also. —*Public college*

Two packages to improve the "attractiveness"—one centering on the work of the director, the other discussing the library as a whole:

Ways of improving attractiveness of the position have already been mentioned.

1. Secretarial staff (at least ½ time for Director).
2. Removal of supervision of student assistants to another staff member.
3. Replacement of part of student help with full-time clerks.
4. Work week of Director not to include regular evening hours or on weekends.
5. Academic vacations during the winter, plus one month in the summer.
   —*Public college*

Keeping in mind that we are a small school, only about 1000 students a year, the improvements I'd ask for are as follows:

1. An adequate book budget to build up our book collection faster.
2. A small but good full-time staff. In some positions, I'd use business trained people, such as for bookkeeping, book ordering, typing, etc.
3. Trained librarians for cataloging—but here again, I'd use Library of Congress catalog cards whenever obtainable, to cut down on the cost of cataloging.

4. A really good reference librarian to work with the students and faculty.
5. A conference room for students, and faculty.
6. A music room for the recording machines to be placed there with the records and scores.
7. A typewriting room for the use of students and their typewriters.
8. Sufficient money to bind up all the unbound periodicals which should be bound.
9. Wall peg boards for art exhibits, etc.
10. Space and locked cases when advisable for the showing and use of our archives.
11. A full-time maid—not to be shared with another building.
12. Since the administrative officers are sympathetic and interested in library development, a larger budget for our college as a whole.—*Private college*

Some miscellaneous suggestions:

My own view, perhaps not a commonly held one, is that fringe benefits that tend to tie one to an institution, cause one to be fearful of making change (to value security more than satisfaction, competence, achievement) is a disadvantage for the human being and the institution. TIAA plans may be sufficiently universal so that the individual is not disadvantaged, and changes are made quite freely by faculty without concern for these matters.—*Private college*

Some of our staff would restrict service exclusively to persons formally connected with the College, and others of us believe in extending to alumnae, visiting scholars, the clergy, the press, radio station personnel and other responsible townspeople library facilities and privileges, as long as the interests of our students and faculty are not jeopardized.—*Private college*

Librarians should allow themselves time to read for pleasure, at least in the intervals between questions, when on duty at the reference desk.—*Private college*

There should be in the library budget, necessary money for items needed to provide attractiveness, such as flowers, etc. An attractive atmosphere is conducive to studying.—*Public college*

It would be of inestimable value, in my judgment, if accrediting bodies would give college presidents firm and clear standards for their use in attempts to obtain funds to implement his college officers' requests.—*Public college*

My major concern at this time is to increase the book collection from 30,000 to 50,000 volumes in order to meet the prescribed standards as set forth by the American Library Association.—*Private college*

The role of automation is on the minds of many librarians, although they are less hopeful about it than are outsiders:

The most difficult problem is to counter, without seeming reactionary, the absurd and misleading publicity about "push button libraries." Technology has caught up with librarians—perhaps it is more accurate to turn the phrase around—but computerization of the book world is not a matter for unilateral action, nor will it reduce library costs, nor can it be had now for the asking. It is coming, probably faster than most universities will be able to raise the money to pay for it, but probably not in the way most people expect from the science-fiction they have been reading about it. In the meantime librarians are again stereotyped as unimaginative and obsolete because they insist that planning, working, and building for tomorrow do not eliminate the necessity for living with today on today's terms. Furthermore, to do effective planning and building for tomorrow require highly skilled staff in very short supply who add considerably to the salaries budget.—*Private university*

The work of a large university library covers the whole spectrum of human knowledge. To try and cope with all knowledge in every conceivable form of publication and in all languages at an increasing volume is humanly impossible at the present time and the panaceas promised by automation are remote, in fact to date have seemed to compound the problem rather than to alleviate it.—*Private university*

QUOTABLE AND GENERAL

[Frustration:] Currently, producers of library literature who see librarianship as an exercise in information retrieval; and/or define moral courage in terms of how many copies of Henry Miller you have available!—*Private college*

To the Administrator, the head librarian is a faculty member; to the faculty member, the head librarian is an administrator.—*Private college*

The only suggestion I would care to make for improving my position is this: If it is a library matter you are concerned with, Mr. President, please talk to me, not your favorite old crony.—*Private college*

I consider that anything necessary for the functioning of the library is my duty, and that no work that is useful or needed is beneath my dignity. I belong to the old school which believes in work and not the mere supervision of people who do the work.—*Private college*

People need to be reminded occasionally that the world will still revolve without their willing it to continue.—*Public college*

The following is excerpted from an extremely thoughtful and well written essay which I wish the author would amplify and publish:

First, this college is changing fairly rapidly, in my view, where the roles of its various segments are concerned. Many of the subjective questions asked in this inquiry have never been asked of us within the institution. This is not a criticism of the college but simply an indication that we all seem to be breathlessly busy with other concerns. Thus it seems a bit disloyal to sound off on any frustrations, problems, and recommendations to an outside agency before these have been considered locally.

. . . .

The librarian here, I think, will always feel there is less difference between his position and the positions of his first and second level aides than would be the case for other administrators here. There is much more logic in a fairly hierarchical structure in most other administrators' offices than in mine.

My primary concern is to build a strong library staff. Part of this requires that there be minimal gaps between my position and its privileges and the positions of the upper part of this staff. I don't want to pull down the position of the librarian in this effort; I do want to pull up the positions of other staff members. Thus I can't talk about vacation, leaves, benefits, etc., only as I see them pertaining to myself in comparison with the privileges of other administrators. I always see them in comparison with those of the library staff as well.

. . . .

Often I've wished there were some way to deflect my salary increases to raise other library salaries. A study I recently made of 1964 figures suggests that assistant librarians, for instance, are commonly paid a salary equivalent to about 75% of the chief librarian's salary. We are a long way from that, and an even longer way from paying generally good salaries to all staff.

. . . .

Faculty support has always been strong, good-natured, and heartwarming. Administrative understanding and support have been good, but because of a great many changes in incumbents in major administrative posts, this is a difficult matter on which to generalize. Our top administrators are, I suspect, overburdened and harried. Communication with them is erratic and often superficial.

. . . .

The chief frustrations are, as perhaps in all administrative posts, the simple wear and tear of trying to explain all things to all people all of the time. In short, communications . . . To keep our library genuinely related to all the moving parts of the college calls for more involvement of library staff. It's an impossible (and terribly time-consuming) assignment for one person, working outward into the academic community and inward to the staff. It is also a worrisome responsibility for one person to try to interpret so much to each element of the community.

I started out life loving people and books. Sometimes, by Friday night I hate people and books. So maybe occupational fatigue is setting in. If so, as with so many things one enjoys griping about, I may have to do a bootstrap job to remodel my professional life.

. . . .

The position I hold is attractive. Frankly, it's never very hard to find head librarians, especially in a "good" college where the library itself is an interesting one.

. . . The real problem comes in getting and holding other staff, for [this] is a stepping-stone library to greener pastures.

. . . .

The relations with the upper echelons of administration are complicated. In part this grows out of the very independence of the library from that busy-bodyness I've mentioned. We are trusted to define our work and get on with it. But this can create a kind of vacuum. Lines of authority—and we all need them just to do the daily round—are confused. Consultation between librarian and other administrators occurs all too often only when there is a crisis or an urgency or an isolated need for information or action, and all too rarely when the air is clear and there might be time for what colleges and their inmates are supposed to be good at—cerebration, philosophizing, and concerted planning.—*Private college*

CHAPTER 18

THE BUSINESS OFFICER

NO one could have read the many responses to the questionnaire without a deepening respect for college and university administrators. The replies of the business officers were to me particularly revealing.

My background, of course, was that of a faculty member, but my administrative work had close contacts with the business office. These were delightful because of the intelligence, devotion, and courtesy of the business staff from top to bottom. In spite of this I was not prepared, as probably I should have been, for the quality of the replies from the chief business officers. First of all their answers to factual questions were the clearest, and as far as I could check through external and internal evidence, the most accurate of those from any officers. Secondly, by and large they showed no rancor or greed, but a poignant desire that their motives be understood by the faculty. Thirdly, they showed tremendous institutional loyalty—a loyalty that sometimes made it difficult for them to understand the loyalty of faculty members to a department or to a field of scholarship.

This is a group which I admire.

The median age of male business officers is 48. There were 73 women (10%) among those responding, one in a public college, and 72 in private colleges, many in Catholic women's colleges.

Four percent had the Ph.D. degree and 2% the degree of Ed.D., while 42% had a master's degree as the highest one attained. The major subjects for their highest degree were: business and commerce, 49%; education, 15%; social studies, 9%; mathematics and statistics, 4%. No other subject accounted for as much as 3%.

Sixty-three percent of the chief business officers were already serving at the same institution when they assumed their position.

STAFF

The business offices of our universities and colleges are swamped with work. In a few cases, this may be inappropriate work, but in general it is not. However, it is both diverse and technical, and many institutions are badly understaffed, sometimes needing specialists and sometimes clerical help. This is illustrated by the business officer of a state college who says he needs (in addition to present staff) an assistant business manager, a purchasing agent, and twenty clerks.

Aside from secretarial help of a higher order and the appointment of an assistant business manager, some of the positions which should be established or filled are: a purchasing agent, budget analyst, superintendent of buildings and grounds, personnel officer, cashier, director of student aid, bookstore manager, director of auxiliary enterprises, and a person to handle federal programs. These positions are all those of specialists and not interchangeable, but often the business manager in addition to his central duties is handling the work of one or more of these positions. Moreover, in addition to these middle management positions, there is great need for such highly trained people as accountants and computer programmers.

In addition to personnel, the desire to have better business machine equipment is often voiced. Some suggest that surveys including computer feasibility analyses should be made.

Seldom could a fair-minded faculty member claim that the business office spends too much on itself.

DELEGATION AND GUIDELINES

Although a number of business managers state that they do not have sufficient authority, and even more complain that the guidelines are not clear, there seems to be less confusion than in the case of the vice president or dean. Probably fewer presidents feel capable of handling the business affairs of the college than wish to assume a leadership role in academic matters. In the case of the business office, neglect is the trouble more often than intrusion.

In some institutions there is both a chief business officer or manager and a treasurer, the treasurer sometimes being a member of the board designated to fill this office. The relation between such an official and the business officer can be decidedly complicated. Such a treasurer must depend on the business officer to care for most of the routine work, while the business officer hardly knows what authority he himself has. I suspect that in some cases the treasurership was created to give aid and guidance to the president of a small college which had no other business officer. The president may have been called from a ministry of a church with a similar financial structure. It would seem now that in many cases either the position of treasurer should be abolished or should be transformed into the chairmanship of the board's financial committee concerned chiefly with financial and investment policy and perhaps fund raising, leaving the fiscal administration of the institution to the business officer.

RELATIONS WITH GOVERNMENT AND CHURCH

Although many officers are entangled in government procedure, there is no other who must unwind as much red tape as the business manager. He not only is involved in the securing of funds but also in the fearsome task of accounting for their expenditure. The varied rules for auditing depend not only on the nature of the expenditure, but also on the source of the money and can make one doubt whether the labyrinth has an exit. In the "Reflections" at the end of this chapter, I have given more extensive quotations on this subject than in the chapters concerning other officers.

ATTITUDE OF OTHERS

A man with managerial responsibilities and orderly business habits working within an academic community, even under the best of conditions, merits our sympathy. But often he does not work under the best of conditions. The president may care about and even be skillful in getting money but pay little attention and have little talent for using it efficiently. He may make promises with no regard to the realities of the budget, but often with the encouragement of a faculty member or a dean; then there is indignation, disguisedly righteous, when the business officer does not immediately provide the wherewithal. I presume that for every president who is lavish with money, there are several who are spendthrifts with the time of their fiscal officers. Business officers are expected to "pass miracles" on a week's notice, the time being short because the preceding committee deliberations were long.

But for the business officer, the most trying group is likely to be the faculty. For a man who has slaved to attain goals set by the faculty, which in turn refuses to be interested in the financial facts of life, to be blamed for any shortcomings in the results is bad enough. To have both his intelligence and his motives questioned is intolerable.

Fortunately, neither a hostile faculty nor a financially incompetent president is typical; but I fear that lack of understanding of the intricacies of a business office is almost universal.

It must be admitted that there are also matters that the business officer is likely not to appreciate. If the value system of a humanist is not understood by the physicist, or that of the physicist by the historian, is it unexpected that both the minds and the ways of many scholars are a mystery to the accountant?

Frequently the committee is a special aggravation to the business officer. If our purpose is rapidly to reach reasonable decisions, the committee is a horrendous way to go about it. This, the business officer sees clearly. What he does not comprehend is that for a community of scholars to truly function there must not only be decisions but a high degree of consensus and mutual understanding. The committee is by no means a failure as a means for the adult education necessary to such understanding. I believe a business officer is often mistaken when he complains of the waste of time in committees. He has reason to complain when, as is sometimes the case, he is excluded from the institution's committee structure.

LEAVES AND VACATIONS

Business officers often do not think of leaves in the same terms as faculty members. Not only are there many who believe they do not need leaves, but their idea of what a leave is differs widely from, for instance, that of the dean of the graduate school. Anything beyond a standard vacation may be considered a leave by a business officer; a leave of a single day was reported.

REFLECTIONS

The quotations in this section are all from business officers.

ATTRACTIVENESS OF WORK

I have been in this job for three years after having been 15 years in industrial financial work and in most ways have found it the most satisfactory and fulfilling job I have ever had. The salary levels are more than adequate—perhaps not on a level with similar industrial administrative positions but there are offsetting advantages.

1. The working conditions are superior. The surroundings are pleasanter. There are no parking or commuting problems.
2. There is an atmosphere of freedom and more receptiveness to new ideas.
3. The retirement program is equal or superior to most industrial plans.
4. The vacation program is considerably more liberal than comparable industry plans.
5. Other fringe benefits—group insurance, automobiles, expense allowances—are roughly comparable to industrial benefits.

But perhaps the greatest single source of satisfaction is the respect and hearing provided to individuals, opinions and ideas.—*Private college*

. . . is most fortunate to be the kind of institution where the administrative officers of the College are considered faculty. We are small enough so that we all know each other on the staff and this helps to give a real community spirit. There is good give and take between administration and teaching faculty. Very seldom, if ever, does one faction take sides against the other. In my job as Business Manager I have been given all the freedom in the world to run the job as I think it should be done. Sometimes I wonder if I don't have too much freedom.—*Private college*

The position of a chief administrative officer in a small residential liberal arts college, such as . . . , is one of the most pleasant job opportunities I can imagine. Being an alumnus of the institution adds to the general spirit and atmosphere of the work and instills an added feeling of pride of such accomplishments as are achieved. These plus the ideal conditions of living for myself and family offset whatever there may be in sacrifice of monetary compensation that might otherwise be attained.—*Private college*

The college is situated in a small rural area, rich in historic tradition, surrounded by a beautiful countryside, which makes for a pleasant place to live. The program of the college is progressive and therefore stimulating to those who participate in its development. Being a small college with a relatively small enrollment, small endowment, and lacking adequate funds, there are obvious shortcomings. For the present these shortcomings are not serious. As the college continues to grow it will become increasingly important to raise the necessary funds to carry on this fine educational program.—*Private college*

Few generalizations can be made about a career in college business administration, but it is probably true that the rewards available, both financial and other, are at least equal to those available in business and industry for those willing to work for them and to seek them out.—*Private college*

As ridiculous as it may sound, I would request no improvements in the attractiveness of the position which I now occupy.—*Private university*

I would not want to see the position so attractive that its appeal to selfish ambition would be as great as the appeal to the man's dedication to the goals of the institution. — *Private college*

We hire low salaried, inefficient people for vital spots of maintenance-purchasing office functions and think we are saving money when in reality we are wasting it with inferior work and rapid turnover plus time loss for harried administrators. — *Private college*

We need badly a position on campus to handle the many relationships with the Federal Government. [The college] participates in the National Defense Student Loan Fund, the Appalachian Program, the Work-Study Program, Economic Opportunity Grants, Language Laboratory, Library, National Science Foundation, etc., etc. This requires a specific knowledge of government procedure and takes a tremendous amount of time, and the amount of money involved is most substantial. — *Private college*

State centralized data processing is going to require additional staff for developing of data transmission procedures between state and local offices. — *Public university*

The first of the following quotations gives an outline of the work of many business officers:

The Comptroller is *inter alia* responsible for the following:
A. All financial matters.
B. All non-faculty and non-library personnel.
C. Control and maintenance of physical plant. There is some degree of assurance that a superintendent of plant and buildings will be appointed in 1968.
D. Faculty housing.
E. Presentation of budgets, both revenue and capital, financial reports, etc. to Board of Managers.
F. Long-term financial and budgetary requirement reports. — *Private college*

Perhaps the most unpleasant duty that has reached this office is that of transportation — seeing that our students get to and from bus station, train station and airport — this is very unpleasant at times. — *Private college*

Many times the duties required of me are not related to my job. Certain public functions held on the campus have been my complete responsibility. We do not have a public relations officer, nor do we have a vice president to whom duties of this type would normally be delegated at other institutions. — *Public college*

The chief source of frustrations and tensions is the seemingly endless time it takes to get results because: (1) of red tape involving doing business with various Federal agencies. This is increasing. (2) of red tape involving the State Government. This continues to increase. (3) of time and effort explaining to the faculty matters they could read for themselves but refuse to.—*Public university*

FRUSTRATIONS

Attitude of Others
Unfortunately the chief business officer is still considered an outsider in the academic community. There should be more appreciation of what he and his staff accomplish and more realization that he contributes to the success or failure of the educational institution.—*Private college*

The lack of a business-like approach by academic personnel and the lack of understanding of the daily activities within the University by some trustees are the chief sources of frustration.—*Private college*

My chief frustrations: 1) Indecision by superiors and confrers; 2) Faculty *vs.* nonacademic personnel conflict; 3) Administration being considered unessential by faculty and students; 4) Lack of understanding of detail required (red tape) to do job.—*Private college*

I take a dim view of the changing attitudes of the faculty. Teaching is less important, and the age of dedication in the profession is passing. The "smell of money" is not making the profession stronger in areas of responsibility.—*Private college*

Communication
Chief source of frustration—learning second-hand information that should be channeled to top officers first.—*Private college*

While regular staff meetings tend to become too lengthy, I know of no substitute to keep everyone as informed as possible and coordinated in action.—*Private college*

RELATIONS WITH GOVERNMENT AND CHURCH

Federal
In Federal contract relationships we should be audited by the organizations with whom we contract rather than some auditor that knows nothing about the program.—*Public college*

A further difficulty with the federal programs is the insistence on detailed and minute control elements. Presumably, such elements are necessary to satisfy the trust concept attaching to the expenditure of public funds but one cannot [help] wonder as to their necessity or economy.—*Private university*

The chief source of frustration is the multiplicity of federal programs and federal agencies with which we deal, each one of which has a unique set of contracting procedures, forms, controls, and reporting requirements. —*Public college*

The paper work connected with the erection of a building with funds from the Housing and Urban Development consumes endless time and energy. In addition, we now have the Higher Education and Facilities Act of 1963 which includes and entails grants and loans.—*Private college*

The Federal programs with aid to the student and to the college could be set up in format with reference index and stated in such a manner as to be understandable to the average person. There is no limit of confusion on several of the Federal Aids as published.—*Public college*

State

It would seem that the primary function of the Civil Service Commission would be to recruit, but such is not the case in . . . . We find in most instances we have to do our own recruiting, and the Commission serves primarily as a policing body.—*Public university*

We fall under the direction of so many state offices, with so many different directives, that many a day produces nothing . . . . By law, I may purchase up to $10 without approval by state officials. *Frustration.*—*Public college*

I consider that the compensations and the conditions of work at . . . University are satisfactory as far as the internal operations of the University are concerned. However, my work would be more effective and more pleasant if the University had more autonomy in the areas of: employing of nonteaching personnel; in purchasing supplies and materials, in planning and erecting buildings; and flexibility in allocating and using funds made available to the university.

One of the major sources of frustrations and tensions is trying to make the most effective use of university resources when arbitrary and unrealistic restraints are placed upon the university by State and Federal agencies outside of the university. Some examples are: (1) The requirement that all non-faculty personnel be employed under state classified civil service when many of the classifications and specifications for these positions are either not broad enough or not interpreted on a flexible enough basis to be applicable to the duties of the positions required; also, the salaries of many jobs are too low which prevents the university from employing and retaining competent employees to support the administrative, research and teaching staff in an effective and efficient manner. (2) The requirement that all material and supplies be purchased through the state purchasing director many times results in slow delivery of scientific supplies and apparatus or unsatisfactory substitutions. (3) Too many restrictions are imposed upon the university in the use of its funds for remodeling, construction of small research facilities, and the construction of streets, sidewalks and parking areas. It is not possible for a multi-university to plan 18 to 24 months in advance and get legislative authority for every small capital improvement that is needed within the university. The needs for teaching and research are continually changing and the university must be authorized to reallocate its resources without waiting for detailed legislative authorization for small capital improvements to meet the faculty's needs. (4) The requirement that all accounting and fiscal procedures be uniform for all state agencies large and small including the universities results in some inappropriate record keeping and reporting for the universities. With the increased support for higher education provided by the Federal government, which must be administered in accordance with the diverse regulations promulgated by the many different agencies and departments of the Federal government that control and distribute these Federal funds, it is time consuming, frustrating and almost impossible to comply with the financial and accounting procedures superimposed upon the university by the State and Federal governments which many times are both overlapping and conflicting.

An ever-expanding teaching and research program staffed by vigorous, highly trained, ambitious and dedicated personnel in a university such as . . . University demands that the administrative officers of the university have the freedom to adopt procedures and make the necessary administrative decisions to meet these needs without undue outside interference.—*Public university*

Church

I will state that I am sure McNamara could not operate this facility with greater economy than the Brothers and Priests achieve with or without modern techniques.—*Private college*

Church related institutions are inclined to use an employee's church dedication in holding their personnel rather than to pay them professional salaries which are competitive. Too frequently an institution may lose a good administrator because they do not pay professional competitive salaries and turn right around and pay more to replace the person they just lost.—*Private college*

OTHER FRUSTRATIONS

I feel my salary could definitely be higher. I think the tendency by a large University system is to treat the campus business staffs as a subordinate staff to the system business staff, consequently, putting an unreal salary level on the campus officers.—*Public university*

If any frustration exists, it is the fact that the financial affairs of the college's business function are related to the Development Office. I believe it important that both offices work independently as far as function.—*Private college*

I think one of the most frustrating things to happen is when the administration makes decisions without regard to the financial implications. I do not imply that every decision should be based on financial ability, but I do say that those making the decision should be aware of the financial implications.—*Private university*

Failure to have lines of authority and areas of responsibility defined as clearly as possible.—*Public college*

Locals are always active and sometimes unreasonable.—*Public college*

It is hard to have faculty and other staff realize that the business manager needs time to think, read, study, plan. Constant interruptions are frustrating and prevent best use of time. — *Private college*

During a typical four-week period, I tabulated the number of interruptions encountered in my office. During a 38-hour work week, I had an average of 142 people come to my office, was called out of the office 35 times and received 42 telephone calls or a total of 219 interruptions—an average of one every 10 minutes. I think this takes care of item (*b*) [frustrations and tensions] above! — *Private college*

We made one mistake at this college that is impossible to correct. Three years ago we built a separate unit for the administration, which, while improving the office conditions, separated us from the academic areas.

We formerly had been scattered. Now, it is much easier for me to reach my fellow administrators, but I am convinced that we have paid for this convenience by deterioration in our relationship with the faculty and students. I was opposed to this move from the start and I am convinced I was right. — *Private college*

IMPROVEMENTS

Eliminate committee mode of government and its subsequent demands for excessive time consumption in extremely non-productive operations. If the faculty taught and the administration administered, heaven would be achieved. — *Private college*

Chairmen of academic departments should be chosen based upon administrative competence as well as academic competence and leadership. — *Private university*

If there is any one thing that would improve the position, I believe it would be a sympathetic understanding on the part of the faculty (and students) that the business officer's actions are taken in the sincere belief that they are the best measures for the good of the whole institution. — *Private college*

If the Business Officer is to maintain the close interest in and association with the faculty that his position requires, then, he should have faculty rank. — *Private college*

Because to the best of my knowledge I have served the institution well for many years, some arrangement equal to academic tenure appears in order. — *Private college*

Time must be provided for involvement in outside affairs. There should be deliberate attempts on the part of the Presidents, Trustees, Alumni and the like to involve their top business and financial officers in corporate directorships, advisory boards for the Government, and Foundations. This should have the effect of broadening the perspective of an individual who is intimately involved in the destiny of higher education. — *Private university*

Our own institution separates the Treasurer's office from the Business Office with overlapping responsibilities and misunderstandings. Considerable effort is still required to clarify working relationships. There is no doubt that a preferred relationship is one in which the Business Manager and Treasurer are one and the same person.—*Private college*

A professional program of education should go far beyond the mere technical knowledge he needs in his work. This program should involve a complete preparation in terms of liberal education without which the business officer is helpless in understanding the academic mind.—*Private college*

THE QUESTIONNAIRE

It is good to see someone concerned about the parts played by ten administrators. We were, for a while, generalists with the most fascinating jobs in our society! Today we are increasingly circumscribed in power, conditioned in activity, reduced to specialties in the modern arena. I doubt that regeneration will occur and certainly generous fringe benefits won't compensate for the loss of fraternal feelings. Just to know that we might become "a problem" is heartwarming.—*Public college*

Most of the questions you ask could be summarized by "What can the college do to help administrators fulfill their positions effectively?" While the questions that need to be asked and answered should be of the type: "What can administrators do to fulfill the aims of the College?" In other words, the less I am concerned with the answers to the questions you ask, the more effective an administrator I'll be.—*Private college*

God bless you in the project.—*Private college*

QUOTABLE AND GENERAL

Human appreciation for work well done.—*Public college*

Dealing with people is an art and this art must be mastered before a full degree of satisfaction can be obtained from one's work.—*Private college*

Need more trained competent administrators and fewer promoted faculty, exiled military experts and tired business men. This is a profession and we should train people for this type of responsibility.—*Private university*

Have always worked hard, enjoy it and am happy in my present position. —*Private college*

Many business officers seem to frustrate themselves trying to attain "faculty status."—*Public college*

The compensation is realistic and compatible with the other vice presidents. The dignity, stature, authority and responsibility of the position are placed at the same level as the other vice presidents except the Vice President for Academic Affairs (which is top and second to the President). I feel this is a sound structure and administratively places the Vice President for Business Affairs in a solid executive position.—*Public college*

Because many decisions involve choices in the expenditure of funds, the financial officer frequently finds it difficult to avoid making a decision because the educational officer is dilatory or indecisive. In his efforts to obtain decisions from educational officers, the financial officer should be constantly alert to prevent his personal prejudices and value judgments from unduly influencing such decision.—*Public university*

As long as the basic security and needs of a man's family are met he should be willing to dedicate his whole life to the cause of education and be willing to accept whatever hardships come his way as long as the true end or goal of his efforts is not frustrated.—*Private college*

What makes any position of responsibility attractive? Isn't it the opportunity to improve the functions administered by the position for the betterment of the institution and the resulting impact on its students? To aid your staff members in their growth in experience and responsibility is most rewarding.—*Private college*

Among the chief sources of frustrations and tensions I would list Trustee relations, faculty relations and adequate staffing to provide time for planning and developing of programs and/or buildings. The chief frustration with Trustees is the lack of understanding on the part of Trustees with the overall purposes of an educational institution. Most Trustees at . . . and any other college are businessmen and not educators and unfortunately look at everything in terms of the business operation and the profit and loss situation and fail to fully appreciate what a quality college should be doing. There is also a strong tendency for Trustees to get into operational matters and not stick to strictly policy matters. I feel that for a Business Manager I have very good overall relations with the faculty. However, it does bother me that quite a few faculty still think of me as the Business Manager and, therefore, one who has to be contended with rather than a friend and colleague. There is probably no way to overcome this situation but I keep hoping that there might be. As pointed out earlier there is also the frustration of not having adequate time to plan and develop new programs and generally oversee the operation instead of being wrapped up in day to day decisions. I am not implying that the person in this position should do nothing but long range planning, and supervise, but certainly a significant part of his time should be spent on these aspects of his job. I don't believe even in the best of situations at other institutions that there is probably enough time given to this phase of the business officer's job.—*Private college*

Among the chief causes of frustration and tension is the very character of the university—a collection of individual enterprises assembled loosely in almost autonomous departments, schools, and colleges served by a centralized operating staff with management and administrative authority diluted among the many components, but with responsibility fairly well fixed. Competing objectives and purposes for restricted funds and space make for an impossible situation at times, particularly when the conflicting motivations are all noble and worthy. The cumulative impact of federal programs has intensified this problem.—*Public university*

CHAPTER 19

THE DEAN OF STUDENTS

"DEAN of students" is an ill-defined term. Some are perhaps primarily disciplinary officers, and others are in charge of a vast complex of activities including counseling, dormitories, aptitude testing, financial aid, the student union, and parking. Some are called deans of men, deans of women, or assistants to the president for student affairs, while others are vice presidents. Some report to the president, some to the academic dean, and one unfortunate to the director of development. My statistics, therefore, concern those people who, the president felt, came nearest being described by the designation "dean of students."

The median age of male deans of students is 45, and of the 10% who are women, 49. Twenty-one percent had a Ph.D. degree, 18% the degree of Ed.D., the master's degree was highest for 49%. In universities the majority held one of the two doctoral degrees. Three-quarters had the work of their highest degree in the following four fields: education, 40%; psychology, 15%; social science, 14%; and English and journalism, 8%. Less than 4% came from any other single area. The dominance of education and psychology (often, I presume, educational psychology) was striking in public colleges, where these two fields accounted for 74%.

Two general aspects of the work of dean of students present difficulty: its twenty-four-hour nature and the ambivalence in the responsibilities of counselor and disciplinary officer.

Trouble in the form of public disturbance or of a student in personal difficulty may erupt at any time and dealing with it cannot be put off. Moreover, one who wishes to participate in the life of students must be prepared for strange hours.

There is no doubt that the large majority of faculty members and probably of most administrators, including presidents, expect the primary burden of handling student misconduct to fall upon the dean of students, the dean of men, or the dean of women. It is, of course, true that most deans of students, both by desire and training, are more inclined to put emphasis on counseling and the development of programs of student activities than on discipline. Most students are not involved in misconduct; but certain behavior on the part of a few appears far less serious to other students than it does to the administration or the public. Hence, forceful disciplinary action may alienate many students with whom the dean of students otherwise could readily work.

The reliance of the faculty upon the dean of students to preserve the tranquility of the campus, without appreciating the skill it takes to do so, is gall and wormwood to these deans.

In addition to the extensive complex of student-related functions of an administrative nature, many deans of students teach one or more classes; others have odd jobs thrust upon them, such as the headache of handling parking.

DELEGATION AND GUIDELINES

There is less complaint by deans of students concerning the problem of delegation than by other officers; but this is balanced by the disciplinary function concerning which wailing is loud and long. One can never seem to hit the happy medium. The dismissal of a student may not stick, for the parents, other students, and the minister bring such pressure on the president that the student is reinstated. The converse of this picture also occurs. The public or the academic dean demands an example, and the scapegoat is an individual the dean of students believes can be successfully worked with inside the institution without harming others. When the faculty gets in on the act, tension builds up.

May I add that although the view of the dean of students is understandable, so are those of the president, the academic dean, and the faculty. I, for one, believe that in these questions the responsibility properly belongs to the faculty.

LEAVES AND VACATIONS

It is easy to realize why deans of students, perhaps even more than other administrators, desire leaves of absence. Aside from the tensions of their work and its night and day demands is the fact that more of them than of those in other positions are candidates for the doctor's degree and are anxious to complete this work.

THE STAFF

Staff needs, of course, depend on the definition of the position and the complexity of the organization of which it is the keystone.

Like other administrators, the dean of students wants more and better secretarial help and many desire an associate or an assistant dean who can act as deputy on many occasions and, in particular, make it possible for the dean to take leaves. Aside from this, the more frequent demands are to add a dean of men or dean of women, a director of security with an adequate staff, a staff including a director of housing to operate the dormitories, a person in charge of financial aid for students, a person in charge of orientation (sometimes the title of "dean" is suggested), enlarged student health services, and most of all, professional staff in the areas of counseling, vocational guidance, testing, psychology, and psychiatry. Besides these, there are less frequent calls for directors of student activities, placement directors, directors for the Union, and file clerks for confidential materials.

STATUS AND SALARY

I think it is fair to report that deans of students have greener eyes and appear to be more dissatisfied with their status than other officers. If they do not have faculty status, they want it. Some desire to be vice presidents or at least have the status and salary of an academic dean. The business officers and the deans of students differ widely in their view of their role and its relation to faculty status. The business officer believes rightly that the faculty and sometimes the rest of the administration do not justly recognize the value of his work. He understands that it is ancillary to the purpose of the institution. His is a service function and both he and the faculty recognize it as such, although the importance they attach to it may be different. However, the dean of students believes that his is a central educational function, and many faculty members simply do not agree. He is unwilling to settle for performing a vital service function. In the case of the business officer, it is the question of assigning due weights to the importance of his service, and my experience would indicate that the faculty has often been rather cavalier about the matter. One's view on the role of dean of students involves one's educational philosophy, and I have not seen many deans of students or faculty members change their opinions concerning this role. There may even be a few institutions where the dean of students takes himself seriously because no one else has. However, riots may have changed any such misguided attitude on the part of his colleagues.

REFLECTIONS

The quotations in this section are all from deans of students.

Most deans of students enjoy their work:

We work hard, have fun, and think we are making some progress.

Our students appear well pleased, too. Student, faculty, and administration rapport is pretty good. Our doors are always open to faculty and students.

I am proud to be a part of this organization and hope that we instill this type of attitude in our students.—*Public college*

I imagine any Dean of Students is subject to long and irregular hours. Because our college is religiously and denominationally oriented, we attract, proportionately, students who are morally superior to those of most other schools. We also have a fine system of Student Government (with which I work). Nevertheless there are still problems that have to be dealt with and many hours are spent in counselling. The work is difficult but the personal awards are very great.—*Private college*

Like other administrators, deans of students are overworked. Many, also, feel that many of their duties are inappropriate:

Off hours telephone calls from students who expect you to be in your office and available at any hour. The persistence of students to get their way—a growing trend. The anytime interruptions which make many evenings of work a necessity.—*Private college*

My policy is to be available to any and all students at any time—but on occasion it is too demanding.—*Private college*

Time completely occupied by duties resulting in neglect of family. This condition could be improved by additional staff.—*Public university*

Inordinate amount of time spent working with students in problem areas (disciplinary) as compared with the amount of time spent with those students who are making satisfactory adjustment.—*Private college*

I am required to teach 9 hours which is not fair to a student personnel program.—*Private college*

The chief source of frustrations and tensions arises from the fact that you are not getting a chance to do what is usually considered to be the dean of students' function, see students. Perhaps this is caused by the new trend "a

dean of students seldom sees students, but refers them to other agencies."
—*Public university*

This is, perhaps, the only position where there was as much complaint about the relationship of the institution with the church as with the government:

I prefer to remain in elementary education and feel that my abilities lie more at this—rather than a college—level. However, as a religious, we are appointed to various duties.—*Private college*

Make a clear-cut policy distinction between: The University as a university, and the University as a place where a religious order lives, runs and teaches in. This latter problem, seems to me, is a crucial one for the future of higher education in Catholic Universities run by religious orders.—*Private college*

There is evidence here as elsewhere that the problem of communication is not solved:

Not knowing about most developments on campus (such as administrative decisions) until after students or others have been told about them.—*Private college*

Poor dissemination of vital information to key administrators results not only in confusion, but quite frequently in embarrassing contradiction; leaving students, faculty, and administrators faced with sometimes critical and dangerous frustrations.—*Private university*

The expectation of students, their parents, and the community are in some ways frustrating because they are based so totally on different perceptions of the University and unreal hopes for change. Universities might act here to detail the pictures of their functional goals and operations rather than broad brushing of an image with warm colors.—*Public university*

Lack of clear definition of responsibilities makes it difficult to know who should make decisions and thus often delays solution of pressing problems. —*Private college*

Too much faculty involvement in policy decisions.—*Public college*

I do feel that if a dean of students were given full and final authority in the dismissal of students it would . . . ease the tension somewhat.—*Private college*

There should be a more uniform way of dealing with discipline. Should have a committee to work on all cases—not a Dean only. This will be changed next year.—*Private college*

[The university] is extremely wise in allowing its administrative officers to develop in their own way. No precise duties and responsibilities are defined. One simply administers under broad basic policy, but one is allowed considerable leeway and knows he will be supported by higher authority.—*Private university*

The dean of students and the faculty frequently do not see eye to eye and they also find fellow administrators difficult:

I think the main problem today confronting Deans of Students is the growing reluctance of faculty members to assume partial responsibility for non-academic student affairs. Their reluctance is owing to their increasing professional commitment, and this attitude is quite understandable. Unfortunately, the growth in administration to cope with the problem is frequently met with faculty criticism.—*Private college*

The chief source of tension is lack of faculty support in certain decisions on rules which are made by the faculty.—*Private college*

A title such as Division of Student Development would be more descriptive. The stereotype of the "disciplinary dean" adhered to by both academicians and non-university people is a source of frustration indicating the University has done a poor job of interpreting the role of their several problems.—*Public university*

Some difficulty arises from the duality of my duties—trying to be general counselor, friend, and advocate of the student and at the same time being the chief disciplinary officer of the college. The lack of clearly-stated policies, the friction between students and faculty, and the desire of some faculty members to stir up controversies among students for the sake of controversy and to furnish themselves with some student causes to champion.—*Public college*

Disciplinary measures. Especially when such measures are too severe because of established policy and do not reflect the progress made in recent years in student personnel work.—*Public college*

There is a certain intellectual snobbery that is affected by some faculty members who believe that the *only* important activity of a college student is his attendance in a classroom.—*Private college*

All too often student personnel are viewed as agencies for "wild life management" or as purely service-oriented organizations with no relationship to the educational purpose of higher education. This commonly held view, in turn, affects the educational services of this division, which, in turn, affects the quality and spirit of the student body, quality and type of residence halls and activity programs, extent of financial aid provided students, nature and quality of counseling, etc.—*Public college*

Living in an era when the cry of "rights" comes from many sources, including faculty colleagues, with the suggestion that college administrators are culprits designed to infringe upon the "rights of students" instead of being able to make a strong contribution to the individuals "growing up," or maturing process.—*Private college*

Unreasonable expectations of higher administrators regarding student behavior.—*Private college*

My primary difficulties are with fellow administrators, many of whom regard students as objects to be feared and controlled and are forever disagreeing with my tactics. Because they're administrative types, they don't recognize their own limitations to make judgment in matters of this sort. What we need in colleges and universities is fewer administrators, and the ones that are necessary should be carefully trained and screened for their attitudes toward and handling of academic tradition and values, and civil liberties.

Keep other administrators (non-academic administrators, that is) out of my hair. — *Private college*

But:

The attractiveness of the office lies in the general respect given to this position, as a faculty member and as an administrator. Because I have made a serious effort to communicate with the faculty, I am accepted by them as a co-worker who is ready to assist them in any way and to present their view to the student body. — *Private college*

Although many deans of students are happier with students than with faculty, not everything is sweetness and light:

My principal bone of contention is with the philosophy espoused on our campuses by NSA propagandists having to do with the concept that students are autonomous. Too often, in my opinion, autonomy promotes irresponsibility and makes the maintenance of proper discipline almost impossible.

In this same connection, the widespread trend toward greater permissiveness in social and other matters by students leads me to wish for the "good old days" when persons in my position really acted *in loco parentis*. — *Public university*

Perhaps the only answer is a change in the climate of the times. — *Private college*

The chief source of frustration and tension is the problem of disciplining those students who fail to comply and cooperate with the College's rules and regulations. In dealing with today's student who is restless for reform of just about everything, one must constantly prevent oneself from telling these individuals that if they do not like our type of school why don't they go elsewhere. Instead one attempts to work with them and remind them that real progress stems from "evolution not revolution." — *Private college*

Our chief frustrations come out of problems with students who are involved in sex and alcohol situations. Another big frustration is the failure of students to know the printed matter which now exists on campus. — *Public college*

Very often the immature acts are explained away by such phrases as "I didn't know." "Nobody told me." "Why can't I be treated as a grown-up?" "This college leaves no room for initiative." "We are old enough to fight, why aren't we old enough to drink?" — *Private college*

The only sources of any frustration would be in student apathy in participation in school activities and S.B. administration, and in lack of faculty involvement in student affairs and student activities. —*Private college*

As a psychologist, I am tempted often to try to "treat" rather than "administer". . . . —*Public university*

The chief sources of frustration are the maintaining of acceptable standards of behavior and convincing of parents that they must help shoulder some of the financial responsibility of their children. —*Public college*

Same student problems year after year. —*Private college*

IMPROVEMENTS

Status

More general acceptance of the importance of student services in the overall educational framework—recognition that the process begun in the classroom must be carried over to student activities, residence halls, to living in general if the true value of education is to be realized. —*Private college*

I believe that deans of students and other student personnel officers should have faculty status and be permitted to teach an occasional class in their particular discipline. This is the practice at this institution. —*Private college*

It is my feeling that the title of vice president would be more in keeping with the actual nature of the responsibility and would thereby enhance the prestige of the position. —*Private university*

I object to the compensation being less than that of the average full professor's (which rank I have) for 11 months' work compared with their 9 months' time. —*Private college*

There is no direct communication between the Dean of Students and the Board of Trustees (the Vice-President for Academic Affairs, the Vice President for Development and Public Relations, and the Business Manager all have *direct* communication with a committee of the Board). —*Private college*

I can think of only one situation which has a degree of uncomfortableness for me and that is the academic procession in which I march with the faculty rather than in front with the President, the Dean of the College, and the Dean of the Faculty. —*Private college*

Tenure

The one suggestion I have for improving my position is the inclusion of tenure for administrators. At the moment most administrators are on annual contracts, which gives a sense of insecurity. It would help to be able to look forward to tenure and would give an administrator not only a sense of permanency, but an increased sense of loyalty as well to the Institution. —*Private college*

After years tell him he'll be kept somehow if humanly possible [as a substitute for tenure]. —*Private college*

Miscellaneous

This idea of a leave of absence for administrative officers is a very desirable one. The problem of filling the office for this length of time should not be impossible. Could retired *Deans* be a source of replacement as retired professors are for faculty?—*Private college*

Consideration might be given to some sort of personal liability insurance since my work does expose me to the possibility of legal action when students may challenge disciplinary action, etc.—*Private college*

It is becoming increasingly necessary that the Dean of Students be advised on the legal implications involved in whatever actions he may be compelled to implement wherever the "rights of students" may be involved.—*Private college*

Eliminate the telephone!—*Private college*

I believe for too long too much emphasis has been placed on professional personnel administrators and not enough emphasis on attracting bright, well-educated individuals from various disciplines to concern themselves with the problems presently facing individuals responsible for extra-curricular life at a university. Although I believe Student Personnel training programs are certainly important for many aspects of Student Affairs, I believe that many fresh ideas and new approaches are overlooked by having too many individuals from the same training classrooms, looking too much like each other, making decisions that all agree to.—*Public university*

QUOTABLE AND GENERAL

Many things can be done to make his life more comfortable, but only the dean himself can make it more rewarding—so why gripe?—*Public university*

I am often torn between my loyalty to my job and my loyalty to my family.—*Private college*

We are basically a conservative institution dealing with a changing constituency (students included) which is in both subtle and open opposition to many of the values the College wants to keep.—*Private college*

Deans of Students are generally involved in a broader and more complex administrative post than are other college administrators, with the possible exception of the president of the college.—*Public college*

One tension and frustration is also a bonus. Having a chancellor who is very much interested in students, there seems to be a tendency of being invaded. On the other hand, it is this interest in students that makes my job easier and my goals more easily explained.—*Public university*

I am sure leaves of absence are just as desirable for administrative officers as they are for teaching faculty members, but the nature of our staffing is such that acceptance of the deanship means giving up the possibility of leave; decision to seek a leave virtually requires resignation from the deanship. I am speaking here not of university policy but of the sense of obligation of a responsible administrator.

The second source of frustrations and tensions is the combination of immature and unreasonable student demands and demonstrations, and insecure and unreasonable reactions to them by administrative colleagues and members of the faculty and Board of Trustees. I see little that can be done about this problem, since playing the middle man in these conflicts is one of the chief excuses for the existence of the Dean of Students.—*Private college*

CHAPTER 20

THE REGISTRAR AND THE DIRECTOR OF ADMISSIONS

SINCE in a number of institutions the registrar and the director of admissions are the same person, and in some institutions one reports to the other (the practice not being clear as to which takes precedence), it seems best to treat the two positions in one chapter.

Clearly, in a narrow sense, the functions of a registrar are distinct from those of an admissions officer; yet the same person may supervise both operations and, in addition, have such duties as caring for financial aid. It would be difficult to write about the two positions separately. However, in considering them together one must often make distinctions between them; not only because of real differences in some of their duties, but also because the statistics concerning them were tabulated separately.

The median age for male directors of admissions is 43 and of females, 50. The registrars are about two years older. Eighty-two percent of the directors of admissions and 59% of the registrars are male. In the case of private colleges, 53% of the registrars are female.

Taking the two positions together, 8% hold a Ph.D. and 7% an Ed.D. The master's degree is the highest degree in 52% of the cases. The work toward the highest degree for three-fourths of the registrars and directors of admissions was in the following fields: education, 35%; social science, 15%; English and journalism, 10%; and psychology, business, or commerce, 7% each.

STAFF

There is the usual demand for secretarial and clerical help and for an assistant or deputy to be the second person in the office. Connected with an admissions function, there is need for admissions counselors, "professionals" to visit high schools or junior colleges, and recruiters. In the registrar's office, the need is mentioned for persons to take charge of checking on the fulfillment of graduation requirements.

Registrars, almost as much as librarians, have problems with part-time student help.

In many cases, better computing equipment and better organization of the computing service are desired. Along with this is the demand for more and better trained personnel to handle these voracious machines. Microfilm equipment is often needed.

The range of financial levels at which these offices operate is illustrated by the registrar who wanted better access to the "360" system and the registrar who would be glad to receive a used adding machine from anyone.

FRUSTRATIONS

There are two special annoyances that these officers have in addition to those which they share with others; namely, pressures to accept students whom the admissions officer believes should be excluded, and late grade reports from the faculty.

The pressures on the admissions officer may be from parents, alumni, ministers, and donors. They may also be internal: to fill the dormitory, to favor one college over another within an institution, or to boost the fortunes of the football team. Life becomes pretty hectic for the admissions officer if a president tries to deal with individual cases. There is a contrast between the college that needs more students to balance a budget and the one that turns away several times as many qualified students as it admits. Both situations are not without tensions. The situation where all students are expected to live in dormitories and these are to be filled, has its own exacting perils for the admissions officer.

As for late grades, a tiny minority of faculty members can hold up the completion of transfers, of probationary or dropping actions, or certification for graduation. The problem of the administrator is increased if the dilatory professor is distinguished, mentally ill, or both.

The registrar or the director of admissions is naturally bitter when he is not consulted on matters about which he knows more than anyone else.

The lack of good office facilities and especially private offices is mentioned more frequently by registrars and admissions officers than by others.

A number of admissions officers and registrars protest strongly against being under the dean of students, their first choice being to report directly to the president, and if that is not granted, at least to report to an "academic" officer. Even worse is the arrangement under which the director of admissions reports to the development officer.

There are those who suggest that graduate schools should have special courses to prepare those who wish to become admissions officers or registrars.

REFLECTIONS

ATTRACTIVENESS OF POSITION

The registrar's position can be attractive only to the person who does not mind detail work, to the one who can be very patient, and who is resilient enough to change with the educational structure and rigid enough to keep from bowing to every whim. The attractiveness of the position is enhanced only by understanding and consideration of those about him. Happily, for me, the position is very attractive. — *Registrar, private college*

Just getting used to my position. After the headaches of public school administration it's so nice I just can't find anything to complain about. — *Registrar, private college*

I have found the work mysterious, exciting, and rewarding. I have been given the funds and equipment required to do the kind of work I consider essential. The Presidents I have served (3) have given me full support. I have been overpaid. I have no complaint. Would that all workers could have the feelings I have toward my job and my employers. — *Director of admissions, private college*

The working conditions are excellent; I have the respect of my colleagues and have the opportunity of serving on three of the top four administrative committees.

Besides, the parking fees are reasonable!! — *Registrar, public university*

I can only say that my thirty-three years of service to one institution evidences satisfaction not only on my part, but also on the part of . . . College. — *Registrar, private college*

OVERWORK AND EXTRA DUTIES

I am answering while riding on the Seaboard Railroad. Please excuse my hand. — *Director of admissions, private college*

But in this job I am more than a Registrar for I serve as co-director of Summer School, Head of the History and Political Science Departments, and Professor of History. — *Registrar, private college*

One duty which we have does not seem to belong to a Registrar's office.

This is the receiving of students' excuses for absence and the recording of cuts.—*Registrar, private college*

In addition to my main responsibility in Admissions, I am also Director of Alumni Relations. I feel frustrated between two major responsibilities.—*Director of admissions, private college*

I think that supervision of the duplicating service requires an undue proportion of my time; however, at the present time there is no other logical place for this service.—*Registrar, private college*

Present conditions demand that I spend approximately one-half of my time traveling out-of-state for periods of two to three weeks. This works a hardship on one's family life, and I hope to cover most of this function with young single men.—*Director of admissions, private college*

Most welcome of all, however, would be just a little of that highly touted leisure time that we keep reading about so that we could spend a beautiful Sunday in spring engaged in pursuits other than in writing a report for the Association of American Colleges.—*Registrar, private college*

STAFF

My position as Director of Admissions could be vastly improved by the addition of a field representative with the authority to recruit students and grant scholarships.—*Director of admissions, private university*

My family is neglected; I have almost no time for recreation and rest. Consequently, my efficiency on the job is greatly diminished. A sufficient number of able, well-trained assistants would greatly ease this situation. The University has now made provisions for four full-time administrative assistants for this office. If we can only keep these people here *after* they are trained, life will be infinitely more pleasant for the Director of Admissions. We *must* find ways to make their jobs more attractive by providing opportunities for increasing responsibilities, attractive salary raises, and increased prestige within this office.

Thank you for listening to me.—*Director of admissions, public university*

The position of admissions director would be much more attractive if the Admissions Office budget and personnel were removed from control and entanglement with the records and registration personnel, so that the director could manage his own staff and operations in the way that seems best to him.

If the administration could discover that it takes more budget, more staff, and more physical space and equipment to admit 15,000 students than it used to take to admit 7,000, that would help immensely, too.—*Director of admissions, public university*

Presently I am also Chairman of the Financial Aid Committee. We do not have a Director of Financial Aid, which is sorely needed to coordinate consistent administration of the various forms of financial aid which are now handled in four different offices here!—*Director of admissions, private university*

The whole staff of the Registrar and Admissions Office would work more effectively if it were not necessary to remain open on Saturday mornings. Little is accomplished on Saturdays, and the staff could profit more from the rest and relaxation. —*Director of admissions, public university*

The Registrar's Office should not use student help unless such students can give as much as three hours at a time. —*Registrar, private college*

We need another full-time secretary, but the administration prefers us to use part-time help because it is not then liable for fringe benefits. —*Director of admissions, private college*

There is no reason to change. We are blessed with a hard-working loyal staff! —*Director of admissions, private college*

GUIDELINES, COMMUNICATION, AND DELEGATION

This office should fall directly under the responsibility of the President— not the Academic Dean. —*Director of admissions, private college*

It is difficult to accept responsibility for decisions one must make without guidelines from an overall plan. —*Director of admissions, private college*

For reasons of efficiency and promptness it is preferable for the Dean of Admissions to have the authority to accept or reject all applications he deems clear cut. —*Director of admissions, private college*

The chief frustrations develop because of the complete inadequacy of communication on our campus. Most important decisions are heard about through the grapevine. —*Director of admissions, private college*

As for communication, we all want and need to be involved in the decision-making process affecting our work and our lives. —*Registrar, public college*

Being restricted from participation in the policy-making level of the administration is frustrating. After 20 years of administrative experience, I feel I could contribute something at this level. —*Director of admissions, private university*

I wish those who made the regulations would support those who have the responsibility for the enforcement of them. —*Registrar, private college*

RELATIONS TO GOVERNMENT AND CHURCH

It's a shame, however, that state appropriations have to be made on the basis of enrollment. This keeps the pressure on all the time. We're doing all right in this regard, but this business is competitive in many ways, regardless of what anyone says. —*Director of admissions, public college*

Positions left open until former employee's vacation and overtime expire. —*Director of admissions, public college*

I am appalled at the encroachment of government agencies demanding official certifications of various sorts, and am thankful this is a women's college not greatly affected by Selective Service in addition. —*Registrar, private college*

Laymen can be, on occasions, treated as less than equals in administrative positions (as well as other faculty positions) and this, of course, can be one source of lack of communication. — *Director of admissions, private college*

THE ATTITUDE OF OTHERS (especially faculty and students)

In dealing with the public and professional secondary school personnel, our patience is sometimes taxed to the fullest. But I am the first to admit they are probably saying the same about us. It is impossible to please all of the people all of the time, yet our public seems to demand this some of the time. Fortunately for us, the President is understanding and has supported us in every quarter. — *Director of admissions, private college*

1. The inability to communicate objectively with some parents concerning their children.

2. The attitude of some alumni that their children and friends are special cases. These alumni appeal from personal pride rather than reasonableness. They may be unaware of the real need of the child and may not understand a decision in the child's best interest. — *Director of admissions, private college*

The chief tension of the first year in this position at this institution is the obtainment of a quality freshman class in sufficient quantity to enable the institution to meet expenses. Having taken the administration and faculty seriously in their stressing quality, I find myself in a very poor position regarding numbers.

Most colleges need to do a more thorough job of self analysis. Faculties must realize that not all could or should compete with the most prestigious institutions. Each college has a role that is unique, however, each needs to more adequately define that role. — *Director of admissions, private college*

Our frustrations and tensions do *not* come from our administrative relations or from lack of facilities. They come from faculty members who want strict admissions requirements enforced for everyone except their own friends. — *Director of admissions, public university*

Our students are wonderful people and I honestly do not feel my work could be made more pleasant. — *Director of admissions, private college*

In addition to the above, my chief frustrations result from an inadequate advising system. This is a system which attempts to use the entire faculty for advising so as not to have to count this duty in anyone's work load. Many faculty members do a poor job of advising, and the problems usually end up in the Registrar's Office. — *Registrar, private college*

Every exam schedule, room schedule, etc., draws a barrage of complaints such as "Why did you have to put my exam on Friday? Why can't I combine all my sections? Why did you put me in room 400? I *always* taught in room 450!" Such criticism, while it is expected, is discouraging—maybe it boils down to the fact that many faculty members simply don't realize how much is involved in creating schedules, and the like. — *Registrar, private college*

The chief sources of frustrations are the failure of faculty to meet grade reporting deadlines and the failure of students to complete records carefully and legibly. (Being realistic, these frustrations will be ever with us!) —*Registrar, private college*

Delay in returning "Grade Cards" on time. (The same faculty each semester.) —*Registrar, private college*

The chief source of frustration lies in the area of faculty relations . . . . The other large group with which this office works is the student body which presents no problems. —*Registrar, private university*

FRUSTRATIONS

Pressures to Admit

My biggest problem is keeping out one, two, or three unqualified applicants each year who have connections or money—or both. Really, it is not a big problem. However, I try to run the office with integrity so that when I talk to a boy or parents and tell them that there is no chance for acceptance (I give good, specific reasons), I do it seriously and with the intent of being fair to all applicants. However, on occasion a boy much poorer qualified than most applicants will be accepted by the president without regard to his standing in the same school relative to boys we have already rejected. To put it mildly, this burns me up, for it makes all the conscientious discussions I have had with other applicants seem misleading.

I am a firm believer in a person's making it on his own—for his own good. I do not like to have the president guarantee someone's acceptance and then come and tell me about it. —*Director of admissions, private college*

Most frustrations revolve around special interest pressures—in particular the interests of the athletic department. However, in talking with other admissions officers it is apparent that our experience is not unique! —*Director of admissions, private college*

We accept certain students to fill quota—students who do not fit the qualification we request of counselors and other persons in our contact work. —*Director of admissions, private college*

In any Admissions Office the chief sources of frustrations and tensions stem from the rejection of candidates. Sometimes I believe that more tension is connected with the rejection of unqualified applicants, as angry parents fight in defense of their spoiled darlings. When such parents call upon the help of influential alumni, they rarely give the facts of the case. As a result so much time is needed for explanations calculated to soothe injured feelings and, of course, there never is enough time.

In this whole situation I have been very pleasantly surprised by the extraordinary understanding and cooperation of our faculty. So often they are asked to put in a good word for an applicant; almost always they state what they know and add something like "the decision of course lies entirely with the Admissions Committee." It is a pleasure to count such blessings. —*Director of admissions, private college*

Problems of Selection

In a selective college, the task of admission, unfortunately, is to say "no" more frequently than "yes," with progressive difficulty in justifying the decision, since many of the applicants could achieve satisfactorily if given an opportunity.—*Director of admissions, private college*

Miscellaneous

Sources of frustrations and tensions:

1) Not being able to obtain *definite* information necessary in planning student and faculty schedules.
2) The constant changes made by students in course selection. The number is unbelievable!
3) Questionnaires.—*Registrar, private college*

The chief source of frustation I think is rooted in the trimester calendar under which we presently operate—especially the third one. I never felt quite the pressures under the semester system.—*Director of admissions, private college*

The fact that one must advertise education to the American public much the same as one must "sell" a commodity. Such competition goes beyond the healthy kind that stimulates.

The panic created in students by adults from all areas that *a*) college is an *absolute* necessity for one's fulfillment and that *b*) there are just not enough colleges to take care of students. This panic causes endless and needless frustration in young people.—*Director of admissions, private college*

The following, though wide-ranging, is a thoughtful outline:

The chief sources of frustrations and tensions, if any, that arise in the conduct of your office:

1. Unnecessary courses:
   a) Proliferation as applied to course offerings in some departments.
   b) The introduction of highly specialized courses based on narrow doctoral theses.
   c) "Empire building" in some departments.
   d) Duplication in course content within and between some departments.
   e) The numerous one and two credit courses.
2. Academic regulations:
   a) Advisers and instructors who either ignore or forget about academic regulations.
   b) The introduction of graduation requirements rarely found in similar institutions.
   c) The retention of academic regulations to which frequent exceptions are made.
   d) The tendency on the part of some groups and committees to assume responsibilities originally assigned by the faculty to the

individual faculty member or to certain standing committees of the faculty.

3. Research and current practices:
   a) The limited use made of research reports relating to academic matters.
   b) The lack of interest in awarding advanced academic credit to students who receive high ratings on the Advanced Placement Examinations of the College Entrance Examination Board.
   c) Wide variations in teaching loads and costs per unit of instruction.

4. Space utilization:
   a) The rather low utilization of classroom space on Saturday mornings and the still lower utilization of laboratory space in some sciences on Saturday mornings.
   b) The freshman course in General Biology—three two-hour lecture-laboratory periods per week—which must be scheduled so as to leave the labs open during the three weekly lecture periods for possible use whenever the lectures are less than 50 minutes in length. (The three weekly lab periods are scheduled immediately after the three lecture periods. Since we have four sections in General Biology, the corresponding labs remain closed to other use 12 periods per week.)

5. The admission of too many freshmen and transfers whose past records indicate that their chances of graduating are close to nil.

6. The failure of significant segments of the faculty to recognize the importance of academic programs for the large number of students who do not go directly to graduate schools on scholarships, assistantships, or fellowships.

7. The lack of interest in lecture-demonstration courses in science designed for the non-science majors as opposed to the highly specialized individual laboratory courses for non-science majors.—*Registrar, private college*

IMPROVEMENTS

Administrative Structure

Most frustrations and tensions arise from leaving the post of Director of Admissions subservient to and responsible to the University Registrar (a somewhat archaic and provincial administrative alignment).—*Director of admissions, private university*

The Director of Admissions reports directly to the President and if any change is made due to growth it is hoped the line will be through the academic dean which seems more appropriate than through Student Personnel.—*Director of admissions, public college*

Two years ago the responsibility for recruitment of students was transferred to the Development Office. There are certain advantages to this move, but a major disadvantage is that too much emphasis is placed on the quantity of enrollment rather than the quality.—*Director of admissions, private college*

Status

My plea is: Give Registrars the recognition they deserve. The Registrar is not just a keeper of records—he is an executive.—*Registrar, private college*

Elevate the office to: Executive Vice President and Registrar.—*Registrar, private college*

One possibility would be change of title from Registrar to Dean of Admissions and Records, or some other more appropriate title.—*Registrar, public college*

Tenure

After an administrative officer has shown competency and is the type of individual the college desires, *tenure* should be considered for him. Security is equally important to teaching and non-teaching faculty members.—*Director of admissions, private college*

Uncertainties surrounding the question of tenure are a matter of concern.—*Director of admissions, public college*

The position of Registrar in any institution should carry with it the privilege of voting on academic matters, if not full faculty status. Since I do not favor the principle of tenure for anyone I certainly do not recommend tenure for any administrative position, but other faculty privileges should be extended to my successor.—*Registrar, private college*

Miscellaneous

I would like to see the director's office decor improved—floor covering and wall treatment as well as certain furniture changes would, again, enhance the position and its image in the eyes of the public and colleagues. When persons who are upset, because they have a complaint, wish to see the director the office should be somewhat different from the counselors and/or assistants who have already seen the person, so it can be *felt* by the person that he is finally in the office of the responsible head.—*Director of admissions, public university*

I think there are not enough women college admissions officers on the official boards of organizations. Men seem to be taking over so many of the responsible positions—several titles under one office—and then the clerical work is delegated to staff consisting of women.—*Director of admissions, private college*

Another male staff member should be added. I am the only one in the office.—*Director of admissions, private college*

It seems to me that no other person in the administration, the President excepted, so needs to know *all* about the institution.—*Director of admissions, private college*

I believe that at . . . we have an excellent solution to the definition of a Registrar—a man *with faculty experience* who is in a central position of maintenance of standards and curricular policy formation, as well as being in charge of record-keeping.—*Registrar, private college*

The Registrar is the chief academic conscience of an institution and as such should be consulted by all departments and deans on proposed changes in curricula and courses.—*Registrar, public college*

I feel that the recent cry for more so-called "fringe benefits" is uncalled for. Basic compensation for the job performed should be adequate enough for the individual to provide the "extras" as he sees fit. Aside from a reasonable retirement program, provision of group health and life insurance policies (paid for by the individual), and an adequate vacation period, an employer has no other responsibilities in this area.—*Registrar, public university*

I get a bit tired of professional people in education asking for increased salary, benefits, etc. or asking for increased attractiveness of working conditions, reduced class loads or extra administrative help, (and administrators asking for additional assistants and so forth). No one ever questions these requests—we all assume they are our due. None of us are ever questioned about our efficiency or about the contribution we make to the overall objectives of our institutions. In short we do very little to justify the demands we make. I very much fear we are becoming a nation of spoiled educators, who in thinking of ourselves only, forget that our purpose is to help or serve someone else. Many of us seem to have the notion that students get in our way and keep us from our truly productive resources. I hope this is not true, but it has been that kind of day so far—and it is only the middle of the afternoon.—*Registrar, private college*

Financial aid should be a part of the admissions office. Centralization is crucial and its logical location is in admissions. Financial aid complements the admissions effort and the needs of the total student body, and its economic diversity must be the continuing concern of admissions. In addition, because of their technical skills and knowledge of the total educational scene, admissions personnel are apt to be aware of developing sources of funds for financial aid.—*Director of admissions, private college*

To be able to meet students at the junior high school and high school levels and again when they are seniors in high school; interview them in order to provide financial aid and answer admissions questions; to continue through the four years of college providing further financial assistance, part-time job opportunities and employment counseling, is additionally satisfying. We visit some 100 high schools throughout the state and find that our problem rather than recruitment must of necessity deal more with motivation and then financial aid. Because of the types of homes and communities from which the majority of our students come, the need for motivation is uppermost. Finally, after they have entered and as they approach graduation, to be able to arrange interviews and make contacts with various industries, organizations and agencies provide a culminating experience that is even more satisfying. Remembering the experiences with these youngsters and then to later have contact and be able to assist them when needed to change from one position of employment to another produces a type of professional compensation which tends to overcome any lacking in financial compensation. — *Director of admissions, public college*

THE QUESTIONNAIRE

It is against my better judgment to budget the needed time to complete this form. However, I am doing so at the request of the President of the College. — *Registrar, private college*

May I say that having to complete this questionnaire has made me think a little more about the job, its frustrations, and its potentialities? I have an idea I can solve most of the problems, for they're really minor. We have complete administrative cooperation, no real supervision, and plenty of leeway to make whatever improvements we can devise. — *Registrar, private college*

Thank you for this opportunity for personal expression. — *Director of admissions, private college*

I deeply appreciate the questions that have been advanced in this questionnaire. — *Registrar, public college*

Was the booklet [questionnaire] for admissions officers labeled "Section 8" by accident? At any rate, it has had certain cathartic value. — *Director of admissions, public college*

CHAPTER 21

THE DIRECTOR OF DEVELOPMENT

THERE are two distinct types of positions whose incumbents are called directors of development or given some similar title. In almost all private institutions and in some public ones the director of development is, next to the president, the chief money raiser. In a number of large public institutions this title is used for the campus planner, the person who is in charge of locating buildings, roads, walks, and so on, as well as the person who deals with architects and contractors.

Those who suggested that this study cover the director of development were clearly thinking of the first definition and in my comments I will stick to it, except to insert here a list of duties given in response to the questionnaire by a person holding the second type of position:

1. Preparation of all material on space projections and utilization.
2. Preparation of architectural programs (space statements) and equipment lists for all new buildings.
3. Supervision of college maintenance staff.
4. Liaison with state officials and architects on all new facility projects.
5. College liaison with local property owners affected by land acquisition program.
6. Supervision of renovation projects for existing facilities.

However, I know of no way of unraveling the statistics for these two types of positions.

The median age of male directors of development is 46. All except 19 of those who responded are male. Sixty-four percent were already at their present institution when appointed to the position. The median number of years already in office is three—the least of any of the positions studied.

Ten percent hold the Ph.D. degree and 6% the degree of Ed.D. The highest degree of 31% was the master's and of 45% the bachelor's. Of the ten positions covered in this study, this has the largest percent with no degree beyond the bachelor's. Over three-fourths had their work for their highest degree in the following fields: social sciences, 22%; education, 20%; English and journalism, 15%; business and commerce, 13%; and religion, 7%.

The director of development often has many duties depending on the local situation. Sometimes these are added to his central duties of raising funds. In other cases, raising funds has been added to some other duty such as that of alumni relations or publicity which still demands his major attention. Perhaps an idea of the variety of these duties is in part indicated by the various staff requirements that are mentioned.

STAFF

Of course, like all other administrators, directors of development wish good secretarial assistance and frequently a deputy. Quite often it is suggested that a director of development be appointed so that the present incumbent may fulfill other functions which he is now also carrying and which are more to his taste.

Frequently, the chief staff positions desired are defined by the group they are to work with (perhaps it would be more accurate as well as more grammatical to omit the "with"). Each group may need the attention of a full-time person. Some of these are: alumni, parents, corporations, foundations, government agencies, the church, and those making wills.

In addition, public relations experts, skilled writers, field representatives, and institutional research personnel are mentioned. An indication of the diversity of duties is the desire at one place to add a person in charge of teacher placement.

Additional equipment such as auto-typewriters, or even data processing equipment for alumni records and records of gifts, occasionally are said to be needed.

GUIDELINES AND COMMUNICATION

Where communication is inadequate, and such inadequacy is widespread, the development officer is severely handicapped. Government agencies, foundations, and intelligent donors wish to know about the program of an institution before they give to it. Not only when a program is formulated but also during the process of its development and continual revision, the development officer should know what is going on. Hence, it is natural that they want not only clear guidelines for their work and authority within their bailiwick, but above all, information.

In some cases certain academic functions, such as admissions, have been put under the development officer. These are hard to distinguish from the cases where money raising has been put under an academic officer. These are exceptions. I would say that in general the first is malign and the second futile.

STATUS AND SALARY

Development officers are perhaps more salary-conscious than other administrators. In many cases, especially considering their short service, they are well-paid, but this is by no means uniformly true. Moonlighting, for instance on TV, was reported.

The question of status is different for directors of development than for other administrators. For others, the question is one of internal status; but many development officers want a position that will appear sufficiently important to outsiders. Some believe that a corporation executive or a foundation officer wishes to deal with a person holding at least the title of vice president, or a designation clearly indicating that he is the deputy of the president. Club memberships and larger expense accounts are desired by some for similar reasons.

Belief in the value of leaves is not as overwhelming among development officers as among administrators in other positions. In fact, there were many who oppose such leaves and, being business oriented, did so on the ground that leaves were not common in the business world. Others, of course, believed that leaves would increase their effectiveness.

There were a number who advocated more formal training as well as more apprenticeships than exist at present for development officers.

Before making my final comments, it is only fair to state that although I have had close and collaborative relations with persons in the other nine positions which are the subject of this study, I have had no such relationship with development officers as defined above. I have worked closely with a number of campus planners. Whether this lack of contact means that I write in ignorance or with a fortunate lack of bias, I will not presume to say.

The relationship of development officers to the rest of the institution ranges over a surprisingly long spectrum.

At one extreme there is a small but not negligible minority who have no comprehension of the purpose of academic freedom, who would model an institution of higher learning after an industrial corporation, and who are essentially anti-intellectual.

In the middle of the spectrum is a group of useful persons with faith in their institutions, but mildly perplexed by the academic community.

And then there are a goodly number who understand not only the goals of higher education but also the *modus vivendi* of their own institutions, whose intellectual interests are both wide and intense, and who find excitement in a faculty or in a group of alert business-men—more perhaps than either of these two do in each other. Such officers are among education's most valuable servants.

Although I staunchly hold that the faculty should be the primary body to determine educational policy, I believe it is done more wisely when the faculty is exposed to public opinion, especially the opinion of the institution's own public. The federal government should not interfere in educational matters, but the National Science Foundation, for instance, has wide experience which should not be ignored. Foundations should not determine the actions of colleges but among foundation officers there is much wisdom to be tapped. The insurance executive on the board, the local banker, or the lawyer for the Civil Liberties Union have viewpoints that are not irrelevant to the clash of opinions between the professor of engineering and the Shakespeare scholar.

The good development officer, and there are many, has wealth other than financial to bring to an open-minded institution. I would not increase the power of the development officers; sometimes I would decrease it. But their influence should be greater.

REFLECTIONS

All the quotations in this section are from directors of develop-ment.

ATTITUDE TOWARD THEIR WORK

No complaints. It's a good job.—*Private college*

Any man working in development now would go to Siberia for pleasure! —*Private college*

DIVERSITY OF WORK

My duties in the Development Office are appropriate to its function, I believe. However, continuing responsibility for supervising studio courses in the art department consumes a portion of my time.—*Private college*

On several occasions there are circumstances that arise which force me to move into other areas which are somewhat removed from my regular function. A typical example is the duty of Veterans Adviser.—*Private college*

My interest is in deferred gifts. Our lack of a Director of Development makes it necessary for me to spend too much time at home to do the job I want to do on the field.—*Private college*

Legislative relations have taken an increasing amount of time, and I feel that it would be in the best interests of the University and the position if the basic responsibility for this function can be turned over to another member of the University staff.—*Public university*

We are responsible for all income for the University. Thus, we have responsibility for student recruitment (tuition, room, and board income), public relations (media, special events, and publications), alumni relations, fund-raising (current, capital, endowment).—*Private university*

I do need more time to devote to the work and in the future we hope to delete the admissions responsibilities from this office. It is related to the academic and probably needs to be under the direction of the admissions office of the college.—*Private college*

STAFF

I am paid a high salary and then sufficient secretarial help is denied. I am given *a student* for ten hours a week. This is wholly untenable.—*Private college*

Proper staffing in other areas would eliminate some of the peripheral activity that deprives development officers from concentrating on their primary obligations.—*Private college*

We believe in a lean administrative staff. Our major need ahead is for a trained estate-planning officer, and there will be no difficulty in funding that position when we are ready. We can't prove it but we suspect that a fair number of the college development offices are overstaffed.—*Private college*

GUIDELINES AND COMMUNICATIONS

Frustrations that arise are mainly due to top administrative personnel (above level of this administrator) who delegate authority and responsibility but fail to remember to whom that authority is delegated. Or who delegate but hang onto authority in actuality.—*Private college*

Over-supervision by the president, who is my immediate superior. There is a tendency on his part to tell me not only what he wants done, but how to do it.—*Private college*

In a small school which did not have a Development Office prior to my coming, the rest of the administration is not quite sure what they want from the Development Officer, nor are they aware of how to help this officer.—*Private college*

Inadequate direct communication with Board of Regents.—*Private college*

RELATIONS WITH CHURCH AND STATE

The quest for available government funds is beginning to take its toll as far as time is concerned. I anticipate more and more time being spent in learning about the public fund programs and in applying for the available funds.—*Private college*

Some few of the personnel determining the future of the State Colleges are competent professionals, but they are definitely in the minority.—*Public college*

This writer is worried about the tendency of private foundations, for example, to withdraw their support from areas into which the Federal government has moved. The probable danger of venture capital being removed from the university-foundation relationship is a serious one indeed.—*Public university*

The most frustrating feature of my position is the fact that my superiors, as well as faculty associates (mostly religious women), are totally naïve as to what public relations and development is—and therefore have difficulty in measuring results. Public relations does not begin on Monday and end on Friday. Furthermore, it cannot guarantee immediate results in terms of major financial support.

But we are making progress in improving this understanding!—*Private college*

Most of the religious tend to regard the lay board of trustees only as fund raisers. The unwillingness to involve the trustees in other critical areas of college administration diminishes the enthusiasm of some of these key personnel. I do believe that this concept is beginning to change, but very, very slowly.—*Private college*

FRUSTRATIONS

Faculty

My chief concern right now is that educational institutions should be looking for ways to educate or provide an education. Instead, they are providing bases for propaganda—or a one-sided presentation of a subject or an issue. Academic freedom has become, instead, academic bigotry. This is an extremely difficult "product" to sell, and will only become more difficult in the future. As academic bigotry becomes obvious, the public relations job, and the development job, will become more difficult. —*Public college*

Too many departments in the University want to "get in the act" and sponsor fund programs of their own. This detracts from the development fund drive; and many alumni have the idea we are treating them like milk cows—stripping them dry. Specifically aimed drives, if any, should be correlated with the major drives through this office and/or handled by the development fund office. —*Public university*

If teaching hours were reduced, perhaps our faculty would have more time for research programs. Until this is accomplished, foundation money for curriculum development, for instance, isn't forthcoming. —*Private college*

Status and Salary

Here the director of development is not listed in the catalog as an officer of administration, chiefly I think because to do so would mean listing several others whose presence on the list is not desired—a foolish reason. This grieves me, in any event, though not enough to force the issue. —*Private college*

I feel all staff officers should receive the same rights and privileges as faculty, have sabbatical leaves, etc., as our work in the College is just as important to the College as the teaching part. —*Private college*

The main frustration is that I am not involved in any major policy decisions. At times, I get the feeling that I am a valet for the president. —*Private college*

Development function generally lacks security. Seems to be a general feeling that instability in development positions is a good thing. In spite of my liking for this work, this factor is the one thing that may some day drive me from this field. —*Private college*

To do the work effectively, you have to have access to the decision-making people in foundations, corporations, etc. In a sense you have to be their equal, or near to it. That means that under our present setup, they're willing to talk only with the president. We can't afford that much of his time.

I know of companies that appoint vice presidents simply to get their sales personnel into the right doors. I shouldn't have any hesitancy, if I were president, to do precisely the same thing.

I'm in a competitive business. I need every legitimate advantage I can get. —*Private college*

More money—a better car—a house—a more appropriate title—and the acceptance on the part of the faculty as well as the Trustees that a Development Officer can help mould the destiny of the institution. —*Private college*

Compensation for all administrative staff must be kept above level of faculty division heads or else the president of the college is going to settle for a mediocre staff. This is a built-in disciplinary device to demand performance or get someone who is worthy of such compensation. —*Private college*

The promotional area—Public Relations and Development, I refer to as the promotional entity of the University. Such an area should be budgeted differently than the Academic as it is competitive with business—not education. It needs its own set of specifics as to budget, secretarial salaries. (Our correspondence is with businessmen and firms. They expect correspondence and phone handling to be on a par with their everyday business competition.)

Possibly I am saying that there exists an academic philosophy that attempts to fit this area into the same groove and pattern that is good and necessary for the academic area, but which stifles, frustrates and at times defeats the very thing this department is attempting to achieve.—*Private university*

I should be spending more time in direct contact with potential donors:

The position of Director of Development in a University should be made as prestigious as possible in order better to permit development personnel to deal on more equal terms with those in the community who make the dollar decisions.—*Public university*

I am persuaded that the effective development officer is soon appreciated by the "people who fully matter." And since the superior development man is at such a high premium presently, he can—let's face it—write his own ticket. The tragedy is that so many not worth a tinker's damn are able with superficial charm to do the same thing. Of course, such folks cannot fool either the public or the president for too long a time—but the development—public relations—alumni relations segment of educational administration suffers as a result.—*Private college*

A key development officer should in time reach a state of trust and maturity where the most confidential internal facts and figures can be routinely shared. Subsequently, he could be invited to meet with the Board of Trustees, at least some of the time, as do some other administrative officers.—*Private college*

Fund Raisers

Unrealistic comprehension of fund raising problems on the part of the Board of Trustees, unwillingness to contribute as individuals, and unwillingness to participate individually and as a group in the fund raising efforts.—*Private college*

Chief frustration is difficulty of getting alumni to feel need of giving and realizing that state-supported schools need money beyond Legislative appropriations and student fees.—*Public university*

Although considerable improvement has been achieved, the University still does not have the volunteer leadership it needs for the successful execution of the very ambitious development program under way.—*Private college*

The Questionnaire

I do not like studies which are directed to the care and feeding of individuals.—*Private university*

By this time I have lost interest in this peculiar line of questioning.

What is the purpose of all this fluff? If [attractiveness] is representative of the goals of development, I'm a total misfit. —*Private college*

IMPROVEMENTS

If it were possible to remove University budget considerations from my thinking, I would advocate University sponsorship of the development officer's membership or memberships in the leading private clubs of the community and I also would support University provision of an attractive home for the development officer. Such a home should be adequate for entertaining and should be located in a center of community influence and affluence. My questionnaire responses do not indicate this thinking because of budget considerations. —*Private college*

I think a logical extension of development work is to move into the area of government-sponsored research and contract programs. There is great duplication and overlapping of work and operating costs in having a separate office dealing with support from governmental sources, and from a practical standpoint, university development is going to depend more and more on federal programs. The work of preparing proposals and acting as a liaison between the campus and the benefactor is quite similar whether the support comes from governmental or private sources. Extension of university development work into the area of governmental support of private education seems not only practicable but inevitable. —*Private university*

One minor suggestion would be the possibility of a non-residential club membership in New York City for a means of insuring attractive, dignified surroundings for cultivation of major gift prospects. I believe the benefits to my institution could more than justify the expense of such a membership. —*Private college*

More voice in Trustee selection. —*Private college*

The chief frustration which I have found is the inability to convince the president and the chairman of the board of the necessity, as I view it, of making basic changes in the composition of the board and its more intensive involvement in the development program of the college. This would include, for example, an increase in the number of directors and a change in the area from which they could be elected. It would also include the establishment of a strong Development Council (primarily drawn from the board) which would commit itself to an active deferred gifts and bequests program and corporate solicitation on a long range basis. —*Private college*

In closing I would like to list some dangers the development officer must constantly guard against.

1) Becoming trapped in the office with paper shuffling. As much time as possible must be spent in servicing committees of volunteers and in making personal calls.

2) Making optimistic promises of "big money being just around the corner."

3) Attending too many development and public relations conventions.

These are costly and rarely creative. However, good workshops and convocations can be very beneficial. — *Private college*

QUOTABLE AND GENERAL

Public relations administration must be particularly on guard not to let themselves give in to the temptation to bypass faculty completely at times. — *Private college*

I believe the time is here in an institution of our type and size when there must be a single concept of money. The divided concept of one staff group with its supporting committees deciding what are the needs and how the money is to be spent and another staff group and supporting committees deciding how the money is to be obtained is antiquated in light of the many new sources of funds which are available to institutions which did not exist twenty years ago when the principal financial sources were tuition and gifts. And long range planning is so necessary now for any institution regardless of its type or size. It might be possible to achieve integration, but I firmly believe that the one who spends the money should also be fully aware of how the money is to be raised. This is particularly true of supporting committees of the board of trustees. — *Private college*

It was discovered [in industry] that an intelligent, well-educated man could do many different jobs well, providing he had motivation and was willing to become a student of his work. This, I believe, is also true of college and university administrative work. Too often it is assumed that the administrator cannot possibly serve efficiently without a teaching background. Such logic renders a disservice to the entire process of education. — *Private university*

As director of development and public relations my communication with every aspect of the college's life is essential. I am interested in all these aspects and the knowledge I get by being party to many meetings within the college gives me the background I need for public relations activities in behalf of the college. Frankly, however, my *real* job is raising money. I know it. The President knows it. The Board knows it. People in my position tend to rationalize that they are doing great things for the College by making it better known to its publics, making lots of friends for the College and that sort of thing. While this is necessary, of course, in the process of cultivation of donor prospects, my time would be best spent by concentrating on direct fund-raising, utilizing businesslike and scientific means rather than hoping that my speeches or brochures or Parents Day activities are going to rally a lineup of impatient donors at my office threshold. — *Private college*

Our college has a long tradition of solid church support. Prior to the 1950's the Church provided almost all the gift support. The job of developing support outside of church sources depends, to a great extent, on the academic reputation. While we have made important strides in this direction, we are behind some of the private colleges in our area. We do not have Phi Beta Kappa. Our record has not been strong in producing graduates attaining to the Ph.D. degree nor have we had the number of Woodrow Wilson, Fulbright, Rhodes (etc.) scholars to make an impressive record. When a more impressive academic reputation is attained, I feel the job of development officer here will be as attractive as at any small private college anywhere. — *Private college*

The faculty is the more dominant factor in the University and the administration the less important — as it ought to be. But, this relationship ought not to suppose that administration is as easily accomplished by "John" as by "Joe." Rather, the University ought to be as particular in its standards and as exacting in its expectations with its administrative staff as it is with its faculty — and, ought to assure for the administrative officers comparable release time so that their overall effectiveness will prove to be of the highest quality. — *Public university*

A. Whitney Griswold, the late president of Yale, once told me that the only way to beat the problem is to marry for money and teach or administer for love . . . . The single most important danger I see on the university landscape in the United States is the tendency to bring in hired Hessians and, worse, development officers who do not possess the most rigid set of criteria for membership in the academic community. Such individuals, in my judgment, do not reflect the important values of the University and, therefore, cannot translate them to the external world. Further, they communicate, perhaps inadvertently, a kind of anti-intellectualism which is destructive to the total mission of the institution. There is some evidence, too, that some development officers have thrown their weight around to the resultant muting of academic powers of deans and chairmen. Happily, none of the foregoing obtains here at . . . . What I am suggesting for all universities is a conscious effort to recruit development officers from within the academy and from among teachers and scholars. Such a linkage is not only important but fundamental to the good health of the university. — *Public university*

CHAPTER 22

REMARKS AND CONCLUSIONS

ASIDE from the fact that this chapter concludes with a section giving my assessment of the relative importance of certain benefits, it has little structure. Yet, I have had more fun writing it than any other.

THE PROBLEM OF OVERWORK

Overwork, including inappropriate work, is perhaps the most crucial problem concerning academic administration today. It applies to all levels. Secretaries are often overworked. Department chairmen are usually overworked. It would be only a slight exaggeration to say that those who hold the ten positions covered in this study are always overworked—the president, like the captain, "worst of all."

To some degree this derives from inadequate facilities and insufficient staff in administrative offices. To a greater extent it comes from the administrative structure of our institutions. The lack of reasonably clear and sensible assignment of responsibilities is often at fault; sometimes the trouble is lack of capacity and of responsiveness to one's duties. Perhaps even more often there is unwillingness or inability to delegate what other capable persons are willing to perform.

However, more important than these difficulties is the fact that tradition and public expectation force the chief administrative officers to do more and other things than they should be doing. This applies especially to the president who is expected to be an internal educational leader, a constant speaker before the alumni (who clearly still need educating), and both a policy consultant and a mendicant in his relation to governmental agencies and foundations. But he is not the only officer with ill-defined duties or overburdened with public expectations. For instance, the dean of students is often expected to see, without using compulsion, that students behave the way their elders wish them to, rather than the way their elders did or do behave; to keep the police off the campus, but to see that ample force is available to insure order; and in many places tactfully to tell students that they cannot live in already full dormitories, or in other places to be certain that the dormitories are full and that the students do not live elsewhere. Other illustrations are given by quotations in the chapters devoted to the separate positions.

Aside from major duties, sometimes misplaced, there are the exasperating demands of trivia—also at times misplaced and often not necessary at all:

The president should not be expected to look into the freshman grades of a donor's son.

The vice president should not have to rescue the president's secretary from a student who believes that the president, who is closeted with the governor, should see him at once.

The college dean should not be importuned by a legislator who believes that a certain athlete should be eligible. (I will say for the solon that all he usually wants is to have his constituent know that he tried.)

The graduate dean should not need to entertain a foundation representative who, in turn, would rather spend his time with the psychologist.

The librarian should not be asked to personally expedite the gathering together of the books on the reserved list tardily provided by a faculty member.

The business officer should not be asked to collect money owed to a hardware dealer by a teaching assistant.

The dean of students should not have a bucket of water poured over him during a panty raid. (I regret, however, that I did not witness the outrage.)

The admissions officer should not have to explain to a professor why the professor's daughter was not admitted.

The registrar should not have to repeat to students day after day the rules which have been clearly printed and given to them in advance.

The development officer should not have to get football tickets for an alumnus.

None of these examples is imaginary. A number of them stem from the quirk of human nature which finds one's self-esteem enlarged if one deals with important people, even if one gets a "no." Such demands can keep an important person from being an effective person.

A warning note against a nonexistent danger: If our administrators were suddenly released from routine and from emergencies to do all the planning they declare they would like to do, the overplanning and undermanaging would be catastrophic.

RELATIONS WITH THE FACULTY

In reading the comments of administrative officers, I was disturbed by the evidence of frayed relationships with the faculty. Of course, there was also a great deal of evidence of extremely cordial and healthy relations between the administrators and the faculty. However, any considerable unhappiness in this regard is to be regretted.

Many of the complaints arise from four types of difficulties:

1. The alleged existence of a small group in many faculties who are irresponsible in their actions and dilatory in performance of their duties.
2. The conflict of authority consisting of: (*a*) the desire of the faculty for what the administration believes is undue authority; (*b*) the unwillingness of the faculty to recognize the difference between participation in policy-making, and interfering in administrative details.
3. The belief by some administrative officers that their compensation and privileges are less than they should be in comparison with the faculty's.
4. Lack of faculty appreciation of the administrative role.

Of course the weights placed on these difficulties vary greatly according to position. The president may be most sensitive to imprudent statements; the registrar to late grade-cards; the dean of students to administrative interference; the librarian to salary inequities; and the development officer to belittlement.

Where does justice lie? There is no general answer, for it must be determined locally.

Have we any hunches that might cover many cases? Yes, we have.

Few faculties are free from fools. It is natural and right that their actions which embarrass the college or its administration should be resented. But fools must be suffered, even if impatiently. The nonconformity of the seer, especially when accompanied by a loud voice and lack of courtesy, can easily be mistaken for the nonconformity of the fool. Of course, there are many more fools than seers. But I would not silence one seer to throttle ten fools. It is hard to ask the one man, the president, who suffers most from the abuses of academic freedom to be its staunchest defender. But that he must be. Usually, but not always, the president's or the dean's irritation is justified. I advocate every protection of academic freedom, but we need not lean so far backwards as to use idiocy as a reason to promote one who is both an unproductive scholar and a poor teacher.

On the matter of dilatory performance of duties, the fault can be more clearly located. It is usually the faculty member's. Persuasion must be our chief weapon. I fear that the distinguished scholar is as likely to delay getting in grades or timetable copy as is the lesser light. If there were penalties, equity would demand like treatment. The results might be disastrous.

Hence, regarding items of type 1, I would guess that in over half the cases the faculty member is at fault, but that 99+% of the time, little should be done about it. (You see what you get for asking an ex-officer of the AAUP to write a book.)

Let us consider the complaints of type 2, listed above. I believe that in most institutions the role of the faculty in academic government should be increased. It is conceivable that it could be excessive, but it seldom is. Until the goals set forth in the "Statement on Government of Colleges and Universities," published in the *AAUP Bulletin* (Winter, 1966) by the American Association of University Professors, the American Council on Education, and the Association of Governing Boards of Universities and Colleges, are more nearly attained, I shall tend to side with the faculty. But a clear distinction between policy determination and administration must be made. When all parties— faculty, administration, and governing board—have reached agreement, both the governing board and the faculty must leave much to the administration. Otherwise, the institution is hobbled. Someone should admit a student, usually not a committee; someone should order a book or an adding machine, usually not a committee; someone should assign rooms, usually not a committee; and someone should be able to authorize quick expenditures, never a committee.

As to comparison of compensation, my sympathy is with neither party but with the president and dean who must make the key decisions. In general, when the faculty salary scale is good, so is the administrative scale; and when an institution is impoverished, all suffer together—often with less complaint.

Misunderstanding by the faculty of the administrative role, especially the role of a so-called "unacademic" administrator, is almost universal and completely unjustified. In many cases it is matched by the administrative lack of understanding of the work of the scholar. The hard worker works hard wherever he is. An administrator who is driven by conscience and circumstances to put in long hours and to take little vacation should not assume that faculty members are not equally driven by conscience and circumstances. The longer vacation, often used for work by faculty members, and the fact that the faculty member is not always visible in classroom or in office but may be studying at home or in the library, deceive even such ex-faculty members as graduate deans. When I changed from being a teaching professor to being a dean, I worried less about how matrices behaved and more about how people behaved than before, but I noticed little difference in the arduousness of the work.

The problem of faculty-administrative relations is not solvable, but it can be ameliorated by good will and attempts on the part of the amenable few to understand one another. Like education, there is always a new crop. We do not give up because every baby is born a barbarian. We even hope that the proportion of those who reach retirement with an understanding mind may be increased.

FACULTY STATUS FOR ADMINISTRATORS

Many administrators desire faculty status. In some cases they want rank as a professor. In other cases they are not concerned with rank but wish to have faculty privileges, often primarily the right to participate and vote in faculty meetings and to be on faculty committees. They argue that their work is as important, takes as much intelligence, and is more demanding than that of the faculty. Moreover, they point out that they must be fully aware not only of the result of faculty actions but of its rationale, and that they, too, have information which, if shared by the faculty, would lead to wiser decisions.

I agree with most of these arguments and some of the conclusions. I have no doubt that the importance of the work of an administrator and the ability it requires is as great as that of a faculty member—except for that rare person, a truly great scholar or teacher.

I also believe that the faculty could gain much from the administrator's knowledge. Hence, I think that the faculty often would be wise to add the chief administrators to the roster of participants in its activities.

Moreover, it is a narrow-minded faculty member, usually an undistinguished one, who believes that the work of the administrator is less important than that of himself and his colleagues. The administrator should get as clear recognition as the faculty member; but two things of equal importance may be different in kind, and the rank of professor should stand for scholarly accomplishment and teaching skill. These are not of themselves shown by being a successful development officer, a successful business officer, or even a successful president. For some positions, such as deanships, a person unqualified for a professorship is rarely selected. Moreover, all major administrative positions are frequently filled by faculty members who should not lose their rank upon accepting administrative posts. The justice of according the business officer as much recognition as a professor of mathematics is reason for doing so, but not for blurring descriptive distinctions or playing fast and loose with the English language. Academic rank will not procure respect; it may incite resentment. If prestige (an ugly word) is sought, some title, such as "Member of the President's Council," could be devised. Such a council could well include faculty representatives. If the thrust is toward egalitarianism, doing away with academic rank—not beclouding its meaning—is a preferable solution which I would heartily applaud.

TENURE

It would be unwise to accord tenure to administrative officers in their positions as administrators. However, as much as possible should be done to give them a sense of security. A man works best if his financial worries are reduced to a minimum. He will act more courageously if it takes less courage to do so. A president should be ready on occasions to oppose a governing board. Moreover, it is unfortunate to continue regularly carrying out policies with which one disagrees. A man should relinquish a job in which he no longer works with zest.

Throughout a deanship which I thoroughly enjoyed, I still found comfort in regarding the pleasures of a professorship of mathematics to which I could return.

In Table 11 and in chapters 3 and 13 facts about the faculty tenure of administrative officers are discussed. There seems to be little difficulty in granting faculty tenure to academic vice presidents, liberal arts deans, and graduate deans. Since almost any library needs more than one professional librarian, continued employment after a probationary period could well be guaranteed to librarians. Considering the demands for teachers, counselors, and testers, the situation of the dean of students and the admissions officer would seem to be similar to that of librarians. The problem for registrars should be only slightly more difficult. The president whose background is nonacademic and the development officer may present a problem. There is, of course, no universal formula but there is almost always a need to stabilize employment as much as possible and certainly to bring men to recognize the stability that in most cases actually exists. Baseless jitters are no less nerve-racking than justified anxieties and hence are equally harmful to one's effectiveness.

RELATION OF BENEFITS FOR
FACULTY AND ADMINISTRATORS

The question often arises as to how closely salaries and various fringe benefits for administrators should be meshed with those of the faculty. This is not a question on which one can be dogmatic, since not only differences of opinion are legitimate, but varying circumstances dictate varying decisions. This does not mean that general discussion is useless.

First of all, there are certain provisions that can be most economically obtained through group action and in which all members of the group are treated alike. These include group life insurance, group medical insurance (both major and basic), and group disability insurance.

There are certain provisions in which it will usually be wise to treat the administrator the same as the faculty, or if there is a difference, to favor the faculty. Instances of these follow.

1. Retirement age. It may be wise to have retirement ages as early as 65 for administrators and as late as 70 for faculty members.

2. Children's education. In some institutions it may well be more embarrassing to have the child of the president or dean enroll than the child of a faculty member.
3. Tenure. The administrator, in general, should not have tenure as an administrator, and at times it may be difficult to provide tenure for him in any subordinate position or in a department.
4. Leaves. Although improved provisions should be made for leaves for administrators, in many places it will be a long time before there are as ample leave provisions for the administrator as for the faculty member. This is no excuse for discontinuing favorable conditions for the faculty.

There are benefits in which the administrator should be treated more favorably than the faculty and in which distinctions may be made between different administrative positions. Some instances are:

1. The provision of entertainment allowances for the president, the development officer, and the dean of students. Related to these are special housing arrangements for the president and special aid for his wife.
2. Allowances that clearly recognize that travel is a central activity of many administrators. Certain officers may also be assigned cars for their exclusive use.
3. Retirement provisions could reflect more than at present any difference in normal retirement age between administrators and faculty and any insecurity on the part of the administrators because of lack of tenure. For instance, the institution might make additional contributions toward retirement annuities for administrators which would provide, some five years before the retirement age for the faculty, as large annuities relative to salaries as the faculty members receive upon retirement. Special provisions would not be necessary for those who either in law or in practice have the same security and the same retirement age as does the faculty.

OFT REPEATED SUGGESTIONS

Some items about which we did not ask questions kept cropping up.

LIABILITY INSURANCE. The value of liability insurance was pointed out by a number of officers, especially deans of students. In contrast to faculty members who are particularly concerned about liability arising from laboratory accidents or accidents on field trips, the chief worry of administrative officers in this regard seemed to be connected with possible suits due to disciplinary actions whether for misconduct or for academic failure.

SATURDAY MORNING. The requirement, often by the state, that employees work on Saturday morning seems to many administrators to place them in an unfavorable competitive position for securing staff, as well as making it difficult for the administrator himself to take a long weekend or to have a half day alone in an office, which can itself be productive, especially if the telephone is quiet.

RELATIVE IMPORTANCE OF MATTERS CONSIDERED

There are four items I believe are of prime importance. Three of them have large financial implications. The fourth, though as difficult to attain, is only tangentially financial. The first three are: salary, retirement provisions, and facilities for effective work. I do not try to rate these three, for in the absence of affluence a college must seek the best balance possible between them rather than place one above the other in a doctrinaire fashion. At least as important as these three is the fourth: a congenial atmosphere for one's work. Some of its components are: mutual understanding between oneself and others of one's role, appreciation of one's work, the freedom to do it, and as much security as the nature of an administrative job will permit.

I will not rediscuss salaries at this point.

The financial retirement provisions should be rationally related to salary, normal retirement age, and perhaps the degree of security in one's position. Facilities for effective work beyond retirement without salary should be furnished to both faculty and administrators. Although local conditions are important, there are standards which are generally accepted in the academic world concerning retirement. These are now being reviewed jointly by the AAC and the AAUP, but even before the review is complete one can have good guidance on these questions through the 1958 statement of these two organizations and through the wise counsel of TIAA.

The absurdity of expecting good administration when it is understaffed, underequipped, and poorly housed is recognized by nearly all administrators, but too many do not act on this recognition. Often faculty, legislative, or public criticism is feared. While every effort should be made to allay such criticism by means of clear explanation of needs, there must be determination to furnish what is necessary for

effective administration. This does not mean that penny-pinching ti-
midity must be replaced by plush defiance. We may approve austerity
—not paucity. The desk may need an expensive calculator, but the
floor no rug.

The personal relations involved in one's work are as essential to its
effectiveness as compensation and facilities. It is important that there
be a close correspondence between what one considers are one's
duties and what others believe them to be. Few persons are so self-sufficient as not to derive pleasure from the appreciation of others.
Tax-free praise can be as great an incentive as the clipped dollar.
Moreover, the administrator worth his salt wants to do a good job and
do it in his own way. In the case of most of the principal administrators, the understanding, the praise, and the freedom must come chiefly
from the president and from the faculty; in the case of the president,
from the faculty, his administrative colleagues, and the board. This
requires intelligent comprehension, not just good-natured tolerance.

After these four essentials, I would perhaps place first vacations and
leaves. The usual formal regulations in regard to vacations and frequently the regulations concerning leaves are adequate. However, the
definition of one's role (often self-determined) is likely to be so
burdensome and the staff and facilities so inadequate as to curtail any
real opportunity for respite.

There are many other important items, among the chief of which
are: major medical insurance, group life insurance, provision for income during disability, health services, and housing for certain officers
(dependent on local conditions; especially in the case of the president,
this may at times belong far higher on the list).

ONE LAST WORD

For two years, through replies to the questionnaire, I have lived
closely with more college administrators than I know in the flesh. I
like their company.

APPENDIX

QUESTIONNAIRE

A photocopy of the questionnaire sent to presidents follows this note. The questionnaires sent to other officers were identical to each other except for varying designations of positions and the corresponding identifying position numbers and colors.

They differed from the questionnaire sent to the president as follows:

1. The directions as to distributions were omitted.
2. The individual's name and title was requested on page 1.
3. The wording was adjusted to suit positions other than the president's. For example: Question 27 for presidents which reads "Are the retirement age provisions for the president the same as for the faculty?" became "Are the retirement age provisions for your position the same as for the faculty?" and Question 28 where the word "president" is replaced by "officers."
4. The following from the president's questionnaire were omitted:
   a) Questions on page 1 concerning the institution.
   b) All of page 2.
   c) Questions 14, 68, 69, 70, 71, 72, 86, 92, 94, 95, 97, 98, 99, that portion of 84 in box, and *d* and *e* on page 15.
5. The following were substituted for the first three items in Question 25:

   33– 1—Has another position on this campus.

   33– 2—Is on leave from this campus.

   33– 3—Has a college position elsewhere.
6. Of course, the questions have different numbers and the sections different letters.

Section 1

Commission on College Administration
of the Association of American Colleges

President

**STUDY OF TOTAL COMPENSATION OF CHIEF ADMINISTRATIVE OFFICERS
IN U.S. COLLEGES AND UNIVERSITIES**

Association of American Colleges
Teachers Insurance and Annuity Association
730 Third Avenue   New York, N. Y.   10017

TO THE PRESIDENT - REQUEST FOR INFORMATION

This study seeks information on the *total compensation* and conditions of work of ten college and university administrative positions. The purpose of the study, which is being conducted by AAC/TIAA under a grant from the Esso Education Foundation, is to aid those concerned with policies of educational administration in planning effectively for the future staffing of college and university administrative positions.

A separate questionnaire is enclosed for each of the ten positions covered by the study.

The information supplied in the questionnaire will not be identified by name of individual or institution. Information will be published in summary statistical tables, within which categories will be kept large enough to prevent the identification of figures from any given institution.

INSTRUCTIONS CARD 0 (IN 1)	A. GENERAL QUESTIONS
1. Please fill out all the pages of this questionnaire. This is the president's section. A copy is enclosed for your files.	1. Name and Address of Institution:

2. Please distribute the other sections of the questionnaire (2 through 10) to the officers of your institution listed on the next page. The title of the officer who is to fill out each section is shown on the section's first page. Some institutions will not have all the positions listed, and exact titles may differ, of course, among institutions. File copies are enclosed for each officer.	2 – 8:
	2. Student Enrollment: (Full-time equivalent, Fall 1965)
	
	9–1 ☐ Below 500 –4 ☐ 2,500 - 4,999
	  –2 ☐ 500 - 999 –5 ☐ 5,000 - 9,999
	  –3 ☐ 1,000 - 2,499 –6 ☐ 10,000 & over

3. Administrative officers of Catholic institutions, whether lay or not, are asked to fill out the questionnaire. When a particular question does not apply, write in NA (not applicable).	3. Does your Institution Have Any Other Branches or Campuses? ☐ NO ☐ YES IF YES, please list those — INCLUDED in this report
4. A business reply envelope is enclosed for each section so that an officer may return his questionnaire as soon as completed. We recommend this method. However, all sections may be returned in one envelope from the president's office, if you prefer.	EXCLUDED from this report

Please complete and return, if possible, before May 15, 1966

B. SALARIES OF CHIEF ADMINISTRATIVE OFFICERS

Col. 1:   For each position at your institution, please give the name and exact title of the person holding the position. This will permit any necessary correspondence or follow-up. If position exists but is currently vacant, write in "vacant" in place of name.

Col. 2, 3, 4:   In reporting on whether you have the positions, *please consider the nature of the services performed* rather than the particular titles listed here or at your institution, since the terminology of titles varies greatly. If a person has duties falling under more than one function, report under the administrative position which engages his major effort or responsibility, and whether his employment in this position is part- or full-time. If the same title is used for more than one position, such as two or more registrars in different branches or colleges, report the position with the highest salary.

Col. 5:   Please show the individual's total current salary for all duties. Exclude institutional contributions to fringe benefits. If total salary is for less than full-time, add PT after salary. If the position is occupied on a *contributed service* basis, write CS in the salary space.

Col. 6, 7:   Please check whether the salary shown in Colum 5 is for work on a 9-10 or an 11-12 months basis.

Catholic Institutions: For each administrative officer, please indicate after the name whether he is: Lay – L; Diocesan – D; or in a Religious Order – R. If the salary is a contributed service, indicate the amount of this if officially determined and add CS.

1	2	3	4	5	6	7
POSITION Give NAME of each officer Give TITLE if different than as printed	Do Not Have Position	Is This Position		Total Current Annual Salary	9-10 Mos. Work Basis	11-12 Mos. Work Basis
		Part-Time	Full-Time			
4. PRESIDENT	10-1	-2	-3	$ 11 15	16-1	-2
5. ACADEMIC VICE PRESIDENT (or Dean of Faculties, an academic position between the President and the Dean of Liberal Arts College)	17-1	-2	-3	$ 18 22	23-1	-2
6. DEAN OF THE LIBERAL ARTS COLLEGE	24-1	-2	-3	$ 25 29	30-1	-2
7. DEAN OF THE GRADUATE SCHOOL (not professional schools such as Law, Medicine, Business, etc.)	31-1	-2	-3	$ 32 36	37-1	-2
8. DIRECTOR OF LIBRARIES	38-1	-2	-3	$ 39 43	44-1	-2
9. CHIEF BUSINESS OFFICER (Financial Vice-President, etc.)	45-1	-2	-3	$ 46 50	51-1	-2
10. DEAN OF STUDENTS	52-1	-2	-3	$ 53 57	58-1	-2
11. DIRECTOR OF ADMISSIONS	59-1	-2	-3	$ 60 64	65-1	-2
12. REGISTRAR	66-1	-2	-3	$ 67 71	72-1	-2
13. DIRECTOR OF DEVELOPMENT	73-1	-2	-3	$ 74 78	79-1	-2

If R following name, zone x over next col. (10, 17, 24, etc.).
If D following name, zone y over next col. (10, 17, 24, etc.).

If PT, zone x over units.
If CS or CS-PT, zone y over units.   80 – 1

14. What is the AVERAGE salary (arithmetic mean) for full professors in your institution, stated on a 9-month academic year basis?
(Exclude institutional contributions to fringe benefits.)

$ _____
(Average salary)
10   14

C. PERSONAL DATA

15. What is your age *(last birthday)*? _____
(Years)
15   16

16. Your sex?

17-1 ☐ Male
  -2 ☐ Female

17. Please indicate your highest earned academic degree.

18-1 ☐ Bachelor's
  -2 ☐ Master's
  -3 ☐ Ed. D
  -4 ☐ Ph. D.
  -5 ☐ Other (Describe, e.g., M.D., LL.B., etc.):
_____

18. What is the academic field in which your highest academic degree was obtained?

19 _____

19. Do you hold a faculty rank in your institution?

20-1 ☐ NO
  -2 ☐ YES | IF YES, do you have tenure status in this faculty rank?
             | 21-1 ☐ NO
             | -2 ☐ YES

20. For how long have you been president of your institution?

_____
(Years)
22   23

21. What was your position (title) just prior to the one you now hold?

24
_____

22. Did you come to your present position from another institution?

25-1 ☐ NO
  -2 ☐ YES | IF YES,
            | a. Where was your previous position?
            | *(Give organization, city, and state.)*
            |
            |
            |
            |
            | b. Were your moving expenses paid by your present institution?
            | 26-1 ☐ NO
            | -2 ☐ In full
            | -3 ☐ In part IF in part, approximately what per cent of expenses was paid?
            | %
            | 27   28

23. How many years did your immediate predecessor serve as president? *(Do not count interim or acting appointments.)*

_____
(Years)
29   30

NOTE: If you are the first occupant of the position check here: ☐ and skip to question 26.
ZONE X-30

24. What was your immediate predecessor's age when he left the presidency?
_____
(Age)
31   32

25. What is the present status of your immediate predecessor? He is now *(Check one)*:

33-1 ☐ A college president
  -2 ☐ A college faculty member
  -3 ☐ On leave
  -4 ☐ Retired
  -5 ☐ Other *(Specify)*:
_____

  -6 ☐ Deceased

D. RETIREMENT

26. Is there a stated retirement age for the president?

34-1 ☐ NO

-2 ☐ YES │ IF YES, what is the stated retirement age?

_____
35   *(Age)*   36

When the president reaches this stated age, may his period in office be extended beyond it?

37-1 ☐ NO

-2 ☐ YES IF YES,

    a. Who decides on an extension?

_____

    b. Is there an age beyond which such extensions in the presidency are not allowed?

    38-1 ☐ NO

    -2 ☐ YES IF YES, what age?

_____
(Age)
39   40

27. Are the retirement age provisions for the president the same as for the faculty?

41-1 ☐ NO │ IF NO, what is the difference?

-2 ☐ YES

28. In your opinion, do you believe that the retirement age for college presidents should be fixed at a stated age, or should it be flexible, with Board action necessary for extensions beyond a stated age? *(Check one and explain.)*

42-1 ☐ Retirement should be at a fixed age

-2 ☐ Retirement should be flexible with Board extensions possible

Summarize reasons for either choice:

29. Do you participate in the regular faculty retirement annuity plan?

43-1 ☐ NO │ IF NO, explain

-2 ☐ YES

30. Are the institution's retirement contributions for the president made on the same basis (same rate) as contributions made for the faculty?

44-1 ☐ NO │ IF NO, explain the difference:

-2 ☐ YES

31. If you left your position as president, assuming you had not yet reached the faculty retirement age, could you continue at your institution as a faculty member?

45-1 ☐ NO

-2 ☐ YES

-3 ☐ DON'T KNOW

E. GROUP LIFE INSURANCE

32. Are you covered under an institutional group life insurance plan?

46-1 ☐ NO

-2 ☐ YES │ IF YES,

    a. What is the amount of your insurance benefit under the plan, or what is the benefit formula?

    b. Are faculty members also covered under the same group life insurance plan?

    47-1 ☐ NO

    -2 ☐ YES

33. Does your institution have a travel accident insurance policy that covers the president while on institutional business?

48-1 ☐ NO
-2 ☐ YES │ IF YES,
a. What is the insurance amount?

$ _____
49   54

b. To whom is the insurance payable?

55-1 ☐ A beneficiary of your choice
-2 ☐ Institution

34. Does your institution reimburse you for travel accident insurance (for example, air travel insurance) you purchase while traveling on institutional business?

56-1 ☐ NO
-2 ☐ YES

35. In addition to the insurance described in questions 32 through 34, does your institution contribute to the purchase of any other insurance on your life?

57-1 ☐ NO
-2 ☐ YES │ IF YES,
a. What is the insurance amount?

$ _____
58   63

b. What is the type of policy?

c. To whom is the insurance payable?

64-1 ☐ A beneficiary of your choice
-2 ☐ Institution

F. SALARY, DEFERRED SALARY, AND RELATED COMPENSATION

36. In addition to your *regular salary* as president (as shown in Question 4), do you receive any *other salary* because of your position as president of the institution, or from any other office that is held by you as president of the institution?

65-1 ☐ NO
-2 ☐ YES │ IF YES, what is the amount per year of the additional compensation?

$ _____
66   70

For this additional compensation, in what capacity (or capacities) do you serve?

37. Are you currently utilizing the salary reduction provisions of the Technical Amendments Act of 1958, providing for tax deferred annuity contributions under the Salary-or-Annuity Option?

71-1 ☐ NO
-2 ☐ YES

38. Do you have any arrangements (other than Salary-or-Annuity Option) in effect by which part of your financial compensation is being deferred until after you leave office or retire?

72-1 ☐ NO
-2 ☐ YES │ IF YES, please describe the deferred arrangement:

39. What is your institution's policy regarding retention of lecture fees received by the president?

73-1 ☐ Lecture fees are turned over to the institution
-2 ☐ Lecture fees are retained by the president
-3 ☐ No policy stated

40. What is your institution's policy regarding retention of consulting fees received by the president?

74-1 ☐ Consulting fees are turned over to the institution
-2 ☐ Consulting fees are retained by the president
-3 ☐ No policy stated

G. COLLEGE EDUCATION OF CHILDREN

41. Does your institution provide *a waiver of undergraduate tuition* for the children of the president?

75-1 ☐ NO
-2 ☐ YES

IF YES,
a. Is the waiver *(Check one)*:
76-1 ☐ Full tuition
-2 ☐ Partial tuition
IF PARTIAL state per cent:
___%___
77   78
b. Is the waiver for *(Check one)*:
79-1 ☐ Sons only
-2 ☐ Daughters only
-3 ☐ Both sons and daughters
80-1

CARD 2 (IN 1) DUP 2-9

42. Does your institution provide for *cash grants* for payment of part or all of the undergraduate tuition of children of the president who attend another college?

10-1 ☐ NO
-2 ☐ YES

43. Are the provisions described in questions 41 and 42 for your children *the same* as for children of faculty members?

11-1 ☐ NO IF NO, what is the difference?

-2 ☐ YES

H. HEALTH

44. Does your institution make any provision for a periodic physical examination for the president?

12-1 ☐ NO
-2 ☐ YES

IF YES
a. How often is the examination made?
13-1 ☐ Annually
-2 ☐ Other: *(Please state frequency)*:
b. Is the physical examination required or voluntary?
14-1 ☐ Required
-2 ☐ Voluntary
c. Who pays for the physical examination?
15-1 ☐ Institution
-2 ☐ President
-3 ☐ Cost is shared
d. Is the health information derived from the examination made available to anyone other than yourself?
16-1 ☐ NO
-2 ☐ YES

45. For the following health service items, please show if your institution has the service described (either for students or faculty), whether as president you may use it, and whether or not you are charged for the service.

	Does College Have Service	Available to you?	When Available, Free or with Charge?
a. Annual Physical Examination	17-1 ☐ NO -2 ☐ YES	18 ☐ NO ☐ YES	19 ☐ Free ☐ Chg.
b. Doctor's Consultation	20-1 ☐ NO -2 ☐ YES	21 ☐ NO ☐ YES	22 ☐ Free ☐ Chg.
c. Emergency Medical Treatment	23-1 ☐ NO -2 ☐ YES	24 ☐ NO ☐ YES	25 ☐ Free ☐ Chg.
d. Regular Medical Treatment	26-1 ☐ NO -2 ☐ YES	27 ☐ NO ☐ YES	28 ☐ Free ☐ Chg.
e. Infirmary Bed	29-1 ☐ NO -2 ☐ YES	30 ☐ NO ☐ YES	31 ☐ Free ☐ Chg.

46. Does your position make you eligible for a basic group hospital-surgical-medical plan (e.g., Blue Cross-Blue Shield, etc.)?

32-1 ☐ NO
-2 ☐ YES | IF YES, who pays for the coverage?
(*Please check one under both a and b.*)
a. **For your Own Coverage**

    33-1 ☐ Institution pays total cost
    -2 ☐ Individual and institution share the cost
    -3 ☐ Individual pays whole cost

b. **For Dependents' Coverage**

    34-1 ☐ Institution pays total cost
    -2 ☐ Individual and institution share the cost
    -3 ☐ Individual pays whole cost

47. Does your position make you eligible for a group major medical expense insurance plan?

35-1 ☐ NO
-2 ☐ YES | IF YES, who pays for the coverage?
(*Please check one under both a. and b.*)

a. **For Your Own Coverage**

    36-1 ☐ Institution pays total cost
    -2 ☐ Individual and institution share the cost
    -3 ☐ Individual pays whole cost

b. **For Dependents' Coverage**

    37-1 ☐ Institution pays total cost
    -2 ☐ Individual and institution share the cost
    -3 ☐ Individual pays whole cost

48. Please suggest the measures, if any, that you believe ought to be taken by a college or university to promote the continuing good health of the person with your responsibilities.

I. SHORT-TERM DISABILITIES

Short-term disabilities are defined here as illnesses or injuries that cause absences from work of from 1 to 2 days to perhaps as long as 6 months.

Salary Continuation or Sick Pay
(Excludes Disability Insurance Plans)

49. Would your institution continue salary (or provide sick pay) to the president during short-term absences due to illness or injury?

38-1 ☐ NO | IF NO, *skip to Question 51.*
-2 ☐ YES

50. Are your institution's provisions for the continuation of your salary during short-term absences due to illness or injury (or for sick pay) formally stated as to amount and duration of payments, or are they arranged for on an informal, *ad hoc* basis? (*Check one.*)

39-1 ☐ Informal —*ad hoc* basis | IF informal, *skip to Question 51.*

    -2 ☐ Formal — i.e., amount and duration of salary continuation (or of sick pay) is stated in advance.

IF PLAN IS FORMAL, please indicate the portion of salary that is continued, and the duration of payments. (*Check one or both, and indicate duration of payments.*)
☐ Full salary is continued for _____
40-1 during disability   41 (*Weeks, mos., etc.*) 42
☐ Partial salary is continued for_____
43-1 during disability   44 (*Weeks, mos., etc.*) 45
ZONE X IN UNITS IF MONTHS

Short-Term Disability Insurance

51. Does your institution provide you any short-term disability income benefits through a group insurance plan? (*Include only plans administered under a group insurance policy.*)

46-1 ☐ NO
-2 ☐ YES | IF YES, please state the amount and duration of insurance benefits.
Amount: $ _____
    47   50
Duration: (*Weeks, mos etc.*)

    51   52
ZONE X IN UNITS IF MONTHS

J. LONG–TERM (TOTAL AND PERMANENT) DISABILITY INCOME

A long-term total disability is defined here as a disability that renders a person unable to work for a period longer than 6 months. Such disabilities may last 10, 15, or 20 years or longer.

52. Does your institution have a formal plan that will provide you a continuing income during long-term total disability?

53-1 ☐ NO | IF NO, *skip to Question 57*
-2 ☐ YES | IF YES, what type of total disability plan is in effect? *(Check one)*

    54-1 ☐ Part of a public employee or state teacher *retirement system*

    -2 ☐ A TIAA group long-term disability insurance plan

    -3 ☐ A commercial company's group long-term disability insurance plan

    -4 ☐ Other *(Describe)*:

IF YOU participate in a TIAA Group Disability Income plan, please skip to Question 57.

53. Please indicate the benefit payable under your long-term total disability plan. *(Check one and fill in)*

    55-1 ☐ Per cent of monthly salary at time of disability

    ————————————— %

    -2 ☐ Formula based on length of service :

    —————————————————

    —————————————————

    -3 ☐ Other *(Explain)*:

54. For persons eligible for disability benefits, is the duration of benefit payments dependent on length of service before the disability occurred?

    56-1 ☐ NO
    -2 ☐ YES

55. How long is the disability income benefit payable under the plan?

    57   58

56. Does the long-term disability plan provide for continuation of retirement annuity premiums during disability?

    59-1 ☐ NO
    -2 ☐ YES

57. Are administrative officers at your institution covered under the Federal Social Security system?

    60-1 ☐ NO
    -2 ☐ YES

58. Please comment on the adequacy, for your position, of your institution's arrangements for income, both short-term and long-term, during periods of sickness and disability.

K. VACATION

59. To how much vacation per year are you entitled?

Length of vacation in weeks: _____
61

☐ No stated policy

ZONE X IN 61

60. How many weeks of vacation did you take in each of the last three years?

1965 _____
62   63
1964 _____
64   65
1963 _____
66   67

ZONE X IN UNITS IF DAYS

61. Please comment on the adequacy of the vacation provisions for your position.

L. LEAVES OF ABSENCE

62. Which of the following types of leaves of absence are you eligible to take? *(Check under both the WITH PAY and WITHOUT PAY headings and check as many as apply.)*

a. With Pay from the College or University

68-1 ☐ Sabbatical leave
69-1 ☐ Leave for research or study
70-1 ☐ Leave of absence for health reasons (not covered under disability insurance or sick-pay provisions)
71-1 ☐ Other *(Specify):* _____
72-1 ☐ No stated policy

b. Without Pay from the College or University

73-1 ☐ Leave for research or study
74-1 ☐ Leave of absence for public service
75-1 ☐ Leave of absence for health reasons (not covered under disability insurance or sick-pay provisions)
76-1 ☐ Other *(Specify):* _____
77-1 ☐ No stated policy

63. Are the leave of absence provisions for faculty members the same as for your position?

78-1 ☐ NO | IF NO, please explain differences:

-2 ☐ YES   79 BLANK. 80—1
CARD 3 (IN 1) DUP 2—9

64. Under present conditions, for how long a period do you believe it would be feasible to take a leave of absence from your position for the following purposes within the next five years? *(Check under both the WITH PAY and WITHOUT PAY headings and check as many as apply.)*

a. With Pay from the College or University

	Not Feasible	Feasible Length of Time *(Please estimate maximum you could take)*
(1) Research or study in your own academic field	10-1 ☐	-2 ☐ _____
(2) Research or study in college administration	11-1 ☐	-2 ☐ _____
(3) Public service	12-1 ☐	-2 ☐ _____
(4) Rest and renewal	13-1 ☐	-2 ☐ _____
(5) Other *(Explain):*	14-1 ☐	-2 ☐ _____

(Continued.)

64. *(Leave of absence feasibility—continued.)*

b. Without Pay from the College or University

	Not Feasible	Feasible Length of Time *(Please estimate maximum you could take)*
(1) Research or study in your own academic field	15-1 ☐	-2 ☐ _____
(2) Research or study in college administration	16-1 ☐	-2 ☐ _____
(3) Public service	17-1 ☐	-2 ☐ _____
(4) Rest and renewal	18-1 ☐	-2 ☐ _____
(5) Other *(Explain)*:	19-1 ☐	-2 ☐ _____

65. Have you taken any leaves of absence (other than sick leave) since you have held your present position?

20-1 ☐ NO
-2 ☐ YES | IF YES, *please specify:*

  a. How many?
  21

  b. Purpose of each:

  c. Length of each:

  d. Whether with or without pay in each case:

M. HOUSING

66. Do you live in a house owned or provided by your institution?

22-1 ☐ NO | IF NO, *please answer a. and b. and then skip to Question 73:*

  a. Do you receive a housing allowance?

  23-1 ☐ NO
  -2 ☐ YES - Adequate
  -3 ☐ YES - Inadequate

  b. Do you believe that the institution should provide a house for the president?

  24-1 ☐ NO
  -2 ☐ YES

-2 ☐ YES

67. Do you pay rent for this house?

25-1 ☐ NO
-2 ☐ YES

68. Does this house provide overnight accommodation for official guests?

26-1 ☐ NO
-2 ☐ YES IF YES, for how many?

27 _____ *(Number of guests)* 28

69. Do you feel that this house is adequate for your official entertaining?

29-1 ☐ NO | IF NO, *please explain:*

-2 ☐ YES

70. For this house does the institution furnish *(Check as many as apply)*:

30-1 ☐ Furniture - all
31-1 ☐ Furniture - in part
32-1 ☐ Utilities
33-1 ☐ Heating
34-1 ☐ Air conditioning
35-1 ☐ Maintenance and repair of the house
36-1 ☐ Grounds maintenance
37-1 ☐ Garage
38-1 ☐ Telephone - local service
39-1 ☐ Maid service
40-1 ☐ Houseman service
41-1 ☐ Cook
42-1 ☐ Food or food allowance (other than for official entertainment)

71. Would you prefer to provide your own housing if reasonable financial adjustments were made?

43-1 ☐ NO
-2 ☐ YES
-3 ☐ DON'T KNOW

72. Please comment on the suitability of the housing provided you by the college.

N. OFFICIAL ENTERTAINMENT

73. Do you have an entertainment allowance?

44-1 ☐ NO   IF NO, *skip to Question 75*

-2 ☐ YES   IF YES,

    a. Please give the amount of the entertainment allowance budgeted for the current fiscal year:

         $ _____
            45   **48**

    b. Is this amount:

       49-1 ☐ Adequate

         -2 ☐ Inadequate

74. May this fund be used for *(Answer in all four of a, b, c, and d below)*

    a. Entertainment in your home   **50**-1 ☐ NO   -2 ☐ YES

    b. Entertainment on the campus   **51**-1 ☐ NO   -2 ☐ YES

    c. Entertainment in town   **52**-1 ☐ NO   -2 ☐ YES

    d. Entertainment out of town   **53**-1 ☐ NO   -2 ☐ YES

75. Have you spent your own money (in addition to any entertainment allowance) for official entertainment during 1965.

54-1 ☐ NO

-2 ☐ YES   IF YES, approximately how much?

         $ _____
            55   **58**

76. If you have no entertainment allowance, or it is inadequate, please explain needs:

59-1

77. May you use the institution's food services for entertaining? *(Answer both a and b below)*

    a. In your home   **60**-1 ☐ NO   -2 ☐ YES

    b. On the campus   **61**-1 ☐ NO   -2 ☐ YES

    IF YES to a or b, are you charged personally for the use of these services?

    a. In your home   **62**-1 ☐ NO   -2 ☐ YES

    b. On the campus   **63**-1 ☐ NO   -2 ☐ YES

78. Does your institution pay for your professional society memberships?

64-1 ☐ NO

-2 ☐ YES

79. Does your institution pay for any of your club memberships?

65-1 ☐ NO

-2 ☐ YES - SOME

-3 ☐ YES - ALL   IF YES, please indicate which memberships are paid for. *(List)*

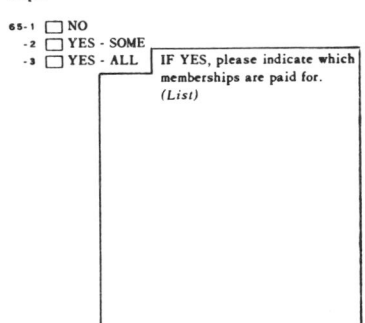

O. AUTOMOBILE, ETC.

80. Does your institution have an airplane which is available to you when needed?

66-1 ☐ NO

-2 ☐ YES

81. Does your institution charter an airplane for your use on institutional business?

67-1 ☐ NO

-2 ☐ YES

82. Does your institution reimburse you for rental of automobiles used on institutional business?

68-1 ☐ NO

-2 ☐ YES

-3 ☐ Rented cars not used

83. Are you provided with, or do you have use of, an institutionally-owned automobile?

69-1 ☐ NO   IF NO, *skip to Question 88.*

-2 ☐ YES

84. Is the institutionally-owned automobile (or automobiles) specifically assigned to you as president or is it a car that, while not specifically assigned to you and may be used by others, is available when needed?

70-1 ☐ Specifically assigned to the president

-2 ☐ Available when needed

IF SPECIFICALLY ASSIGNED, *please answer both a and b below:*
a. Are you assigned more than one automobile?
71-1 ☐ NO -2 ☐ YES IF YES, how many?
72 _____   (Number)
b. What is the make, type (sedan, station wagon, limousine, etc.) and year of the automobile(s)?
Make:
Type:
Year:

85. Are the following expenses for the institutionally-owned automobile(s) paid for by you or by the institution? *(Please check the appropriate boxes in a, b, and c below)*

	By Institution	By You	Shared
a. Gas and oil	73-1 ☐	-2 ☐	-3 ☐
b. Maintenance	74-1 ☐	-2 ☐	-3 ☐
c. Insurance	75-1 ☐	-2 ☐	-3 ☐

86. Are you provided with a chauffeur without charge to you?

76-1 ☐ NO

-2 ☐ YES	IF YES, is driving the chauffeur's only official duty?
	77-1 ☐ NO -2 ☐ YES

87. May you make personal use of the institutionally-owned automobile(s)?

78-1 ☐ With charge
-2 ☐ Without charge
-3 ☐ Personal use not permitted

88. Does the institution reimburse you for the use of your own automobile when used on institutional business?

10-1 ☐ NO
-2 ☐ DO NOT USE own automobile on institutional business

-3 ☐ YES	IF YES, what reimbursements are made to you. *(Check as many as apply.)*
	11-1 ☐ Auto license
	12-1 ☐ Auto insurance
	13-1 ☐ Auto liability insurance
	14-1 ☐ Auto maintenance
	15-1 ☐ Depreciation allowance *(Give amount):*
	16-1 ☐ Auto purchase allowance *(Give amount):*
	17-1 ☐ Mileage reimbursement *(Give formula):*
	18-1 ☐ Other *(Explain):*

P. TRAVEL EXPENSES

89. When traveling on *official institutional duties* are you reimbursed in full, in part, or not at all for the following travel expenses? *(Check type of reimbursement for each expense.)*

	Extent of Reimbursement		
	Full	Partial	None
a. Transportation	19-1 ☐	-2 ☐	-3 ☐
b. Hotel	20-1 ☐	-2 ☐	-3 ☐
c. Meals	21-1 ☐	-2 ☐	-3 ☐
c. Tips	22-1 ☐	-2 ☐	-3 ☐

90. When traveling in connection with *your own professional academic field* (e.g., classics) are you reimbursed by the institution in full, in part, or not at all for the following expenses? *(Check type of reimbursement for each expense.)*

	Extent of Reimbursement		
	Full	Partial	None
a. Transportation	23-1 ☐	-2 ☐	-3 ☐
b. Hotel	24-1 ☐	-2 ☐	-3 ☐
c. Meals	25-1 ☐	-2 ☐	-3 ☐
d. Tips	26-1 ☐	-2 ☐	-3 ☐

27-1 ☐ No occasion for such travel

91. For travel expenses other than transportation, does your institution pay on a *per diem* basis?

    28-1 ☐ NO
      -2 ☐ YES IF YES, how much per day?

        $ _____
          29   30

92. Are travel expenses for your wife paid by the institution when: *(Answer in both a and b below)*

    a. She accompanies you on official business?

      31-1 ☐ NO
        -2 ☐ YES

    b. She represents you or the institution in your absence?

      32-1 ☐ NO
        -2 ☐ YES

93. Please comment on the adequacy of present provisions for your travel expenses:

Q. ADDITIONAL ALLOWANCES

94. Are any institutional funds budgeted for gifts to charitable organizations that are made in your name?

    33-1 ☐ NO
      -2 ☐ YES | IF YES, how much was budgeted for such gifts in 1965?

        $ _____
          34   38

95. Does your institution provide you with an annual expense allowance intended to cover the items not reported in normal expense accounting?

    39-1 ☐ NO
      -2 ☐ YES | IF YES, please give amount budgeted in 1965:

        $ _____
          40   44

R. YOUR OWN OFFICE

96. Please check below as to whether you believe your office facilities are *satisfactory* or *unsatisfactory* in the following respects: *(Check for each item, a through f.)*

	Satis-factory	Unsatis-factory	Not Considered Important
a. Floor space and layout	45-1 ☐	-2 ☐	-3 ☐
b. Physical attractiveness	46-1 ☐	-2 ☐	-3 ☐
c. Furnishings	47-1 ☐	-2 ☐	-3 ☐
d. Office equipment	48-1 ☐	-2 ☐	-3 ☐
e. Location on campus	49-1 ☐	-2 ☐	-3 ☐
f. Conference rooms	50-1 ☐	-2 ☐	-3 ☐

97. Is your wife provided with secretarial help in connection with aiding you in your official duties, social or otherwise?

    51-1 ☐ NO
      -2 ☐ YES - A LITTLE
      -3 ☐ YES - MODERATE
       4 ☐ YES - SUBSTANTIAL

98. Do you have a *personal assistant* or *executive assistant* assigned to your office?

    52-1 ☐ NO
      -2 ☐ YES IF YES, please give title and assignment: *(If more than one give title and assignment of each.)*

99. How many *officers* of your institution report directly to you? *(Answer both items.)*

    a. Regularly and formally: _____
                  53 *(Number)* 54

    b. Occasionally or informally: _____
                  55 *(Number)* 56

100. Do you believe your own office is now staffed in such a way as to enable you to make reasonably satisfactory use of your time? *(Please comment.)*

102. Do you think that the duties that circumstances force upon you are reasonably close to those you should be performing? *(Please comment.)*

101. What additions or changes do you think might be desirable in the organization or staffing of your own office? *(Please comment.)*

CONCLUSION

The answers to the preceding questions form the substance from which good appendices are made, but the real judgements derived from the study must be the distillation of the wisdom of those who live with the administrative problems of our colleges and universities. Hence we are particularly anxious for you to comment on the topics of this study, including, but not limited to, the following:

a. Your compensation and conditions of work and on any means by which your work might be made pleasanter and more effective.

b. The chief sources of frustrations and tensions, if any, that arise in the conduct of your office.

c. The desirability of leaves of absence for the college president.

d. Suggested methods of improving the conditions of work for the other administrative officers of the college.

e. The desirable composition of the board of trustees and the ways the trustees can aid the president.

f. Ways of improving the attractiveness of the position of president.

(Please use additional pages if you wish.)

We appreciate your cooperation in answering this questionnaire and I believe it will be of value to higher education.

Sincerely,

Mark H. Ingraham, Director
Study for the AAC Commission on College Administration

AAC/TIAA
730 Third Avenue
New York, N. Y. 10017

SUMMARY TABLES

The tables which follow are derived from a very much larger and more detailed set produced from the tabulation of replies to the questionnaire. They follow the order of the questions in the questionnaire, but the replies to many were summarized in the text rather than through tables.

The complete tabulations are available to those who have reason to refer to them either extensively or concerning particular items.

Percentages are based on the numbers given in Table 1 unless the title, body, or footnote of the table indicate otherwise.

TABLE 1: NUMBER OF OFFICERS RESPONDING TO THE STUDY QUESTIONNAIRE
Questionnaire Sect. A, Q. 1

		All Institutions			Public Institutions			Private Institutions	
	Total	Univ.	Col.	Total	Univ.	Col.	Total	Univ.	Col.
1. President	813	134	679	268	90	178	545	44	501
2. Academic V.P.	465	123	342	223	86	137	242	37	205
3. Liberal Arts Dean	599	116	483	188	75	113	411	41	370
4. Graduate Dean	304	121	183	179	76	103	125	45	80
5. Librarian	735	125	610	241	82	159	494	43	451
6. Business Officer	734	126	608	239	82	157	495	44	451
7. Dean of Students	718	124	594	237	81	156	481	43	438
8. Dir. Admissions	670	112	558	208	67	141	462	45	417
9. Registrar	689	110	579	216	71	145	473	39	434
10. Dir. Development	548	98	450	141	59	82	407	39	368
11. Total	6,275	1,189	5,086	2,140	769	1,371	4,135	420	3,715

TABLE 2: NUMBER OF SALARIES REPORTED AND PERCENT OF THESE WHICH WERE
CONTRIBUTED SERVICES—FULL-TIME POSITIONS, 11–12 MONTHS
Questionnaire Sect. B, Q. 1–13

		All Institutions			Public Institutions			Private Institutions	
	Total	Univ.	Col.	Total	Univ.	Col.	Total	Univ.	Col.
President									
1. Salaries Reported	734	129	605	254	88	166	480	41	439
2. Contributed Services	13%	9%	14%	...	...	...	20%	27%	20%
Academic V.P.									
3. Salaries Reported	393	115	278	209	80	129	184	35	149
4. Contributed Services	6%	7%	6%	...	...	...	13%	23%	11%
Liberal Arts Dean									
5. Salaries Reported	528	113	415	173	76	97	355	37	318
6. Contributed Services	17%	10%	19%	...	...	...	25%	30%	25%
Graduate Dean									
7. Salaries Reported	249	115	134	163	78	85	86	37	49
8. Contributed Services	6%	3%	7%	...	...	...	16%	11%	20%
Librarian									
9. Salaries Reported	631	122	509	227	82	145	404	40	364
10. Contributed Services	11%	4%	13%	...	...	...	18%	13%	18%
Business Officer									
11. Salaries Reported	706	122	584	240	81	159	466	41	425
12. Contributed Services	11%	7%	13%	...	...	...	17%	20%	17%
Dean of Students									
13. Salaries Reported	618	116	502	228	80	148	390	36	354
14. Contributed Services	12%	7%	14%	...	...	...	20%	22%	19%
Dir. Admissions									
15. Salaries Reported	599	117	482	201	78	123	398	39	359
16. Contributed Services	8%	4%	9%	...	...	...	12%	13%	12%
Registrar									
17. Salaries Reported	564	92	472	172	52	120	392	40	352
18. Contributed Services	9%	1%	10%	...	...	...	13%	3%	14%
Dir. Development									
19. Salaries Reported	520	97	423	136	60	76	384	37	347
20. Contributed Services	4%	3%	4%	...	...	...	5%	8%	5%

The actual percent of contributed services is somewhat higher than indicated above
because some of those in religious orders whose services were contributed did not so report.

TABLE 3: SALARY DISTRIBUTION (IN DOLLARS)—FULL-TIME POSITIONS, 11–12 MONTHS
Questionnaire Sect. B, Q. 4–13

	All Institutions			Public Institutions			Private Institutions		
	Total	Univ.	Col.	Total	Univ.	Col.	Total	Univ.	Col.
President									
1. Number Reported	637	118	519	254	88	166	383	30	353
2. Highest	55,000	55,000	44,500	47,000	47,000	36,000	55,000	55,000	44,500
3. Ninth Decile	30,000	40,000	26,500	32,000	36,000	26,268	30,000	40,000	27,000
4. Average	21,729	30,527	19,728	23,460	28,853	20,602	20,580	35,436	19,318
5. Median	20,000	29,500	19,200	23,000	27,500	19,664	20,000	35,000	18,750
6. First Decile	14,000	23,000	13,000	16,500	23,000	16,170	12,000	25,000	12,000
Academic V. P.									
7. Number Reported	369	107	262	209	80	129	160	27	133
8. Highest	40,000	40,000	35,000	35,000	35,000	26,000	40,000	40,000	35,000
9. Ninth Decile	25,100	28,668	21,000	25,100	27,500	21,000	25,000	31,000	20,400
10. Average	18,616	23,575	16,591	19,564	23,137	17,347	17,379	24,871	15,858
11. Median	18,000	23,200	16,500	18,950	23,000	17,000	16,500	25,000	15,500
12. First Decile	12,500	18,000	12,000	14,766	18,000	13,729	10,812	18,000	10,500
Liberal Arts Dean									
13. Number Reported	438	102	336	173	76	97	265	26	239
14. Highest	30,000	30,000	28,000	29,100	29,100	24,850	30,000	30,000	28,000
15. Ninth Decile	22,000	25,000	18,200	22,900	25,000	18,810	19,200	24,000	18,000
16. Average	15,914	20,595	14,494	18,253	20,660	16,367	14,388	20,404	13,734
17. Median	15,600	20,000	14,500	17,772	20,500	16,400	13,900	20,000	13,200
18. First Decile	10,725	16,000	10,000	14,000	16,500	14,000	10,000	15,400	9,800
Graduate Dean									
19. Number Reported	235	111	124	163	78	85	72	33	39
20. Highest	29,500	29,500	26,000	28,300	28,300	26,000	29,500	29,500	25,000
21. Ninth Decile	23,700	25,100	18,200	23,600	25,000	18,500	24,000	25,500	17,500
22. Average	17,732	20,186	15,535	18,222	20,532	16,103	16,621	19,368	14,296
23. Median	17,000	20,000	15,600	17,750	20,000	16,030	15,500	19,000	14,000
24. First Decile	13,000	15,400	12,000	14,000	16,500	13,000	10,500	13,500	10,230
Librarian									
25. Number Reported	559	117	442	227	82	145	332	35	297
26. Highest	27,000	27,000	22,000	26,500	26,500	22,000	27,000	27,000	19,500
27. Ninth Decile	16,600	21,000	14,911	18,600	20,950	16,200	14,500	23,000	13,000
28. Average	11,626	15,953	10,480	13,585	15,992	12,225	10,285	15,861	9,628
29. Median	10,800	15,750	10,000	13,008	16,000	11,760	9,500	15,500	9,100
30. First Decile	7,500	11,300	7,200	9,250	11,500	8,800	7,000	9,500	7,000

(continued on next page)

TABLE 3 (continued)

	All Institutions			Public Institutions			Private Institutions		
	Total	Univ.	Col.	Total	Univ.	Col.	Total	Univ.	Col.
Business Officer									
31. Number Reported	625	114	511	240	81	159	385	33	352
32. Highest	40,000	40,000	35,000	37,500	37,500	25,000	40,000	40,000	35,000
33. Ninth Decile	21,500	30,500	18,000	23,000	26,000	17,772	20,500	32,500	18,000
34. Average	14,738	21,563	13,215	16,019	20,323	13,826	13,939	24,609	12,939
35. Median	13,756	20,400	12,500	15,315	19,992	13,950	12,500	22,000	12,400
36. First Decile	9,200	15,000	9,000	10,200	14,200	9,744	8,700	17,325	8,500
Dean of Students									
37. Number Reported	541	108	433	228	80	148	313	28	285
38. Highest	28,500	28,500	26,000	28,500	28,500	26,000	23,000	21,000	23,000
39. Ninth Decile	17,772	21,000	16,000	19,250	21,000	17,772	15,000	20,000	14,000
40. Average	12,649	16,563	11,673	14,917	16,953	13,817	10,997	15,447	10,559
41. Median	12,000	16,400	11,300	14,700	16,700	13,300	10,500	14,300	10,000
42. First Decile	8,400	12,000	8,000	11,000	13,000	10,032	7,650	11,000	7,500
Dir. Admissions									
43. Number Reported	552	112	440	201	78	123	351	34	317
44. Highest	20,750	20,750	18,025	20,750	20,750	18,025	19,000	19,000	15,750
45. Ninth Decile	14,622	18,000	13,500	16,120	18,040	14,250	13,400	16,500	12,300
46. Average	10,819	13,831	10,052	12,654	14,174	11,690	9,768	13,043	9,417
47. Median	10,500	13,500	10,000	12,704	13,920	11,840	9,500	13,500	9,200
48. First Decile	7,500	9,700	7,200	9,000	11,000	8,700	7,000	8,000	6,800
Registrar									
49. Number Reported	514	91	423	172	52	120	342	39	303
50. Highest	20,850	20,850	20,850	20,850	20,850	20,850	19,500	19,500	16,400
51. Ninth Decile	13,280	16,780	12,000	15,000	17,040	13,650	11,650	14,500	11,000
52. Average	9,508	12,712	8,819	11,256	13,384	10,334	8,630	11,816	8,220
53. Median	9,000	12,480	8,600	11,000	13,008	9,948	8,385	11,500	8,000
54. First Decile	6,200	9,500	6,000	7,600	9,660	7,200	6,000	8,500	5,750
Dir. Development									
55. Number Reported	500	94	406	136	60	76	364	34	330
56. Highest	33,000	33,000	30,750	30,750	30,750	26,000	33,000	33,000	30,750
57. Ninth Decile	20,000	26,000	17,772	20,000	21,500	17,772	19,380	28,000	17,600
58. Average	13,984	18,582	12,919	15,224	16,876	13,919	13,520	21,593	12,689
59. Median	13,200	18,000	12,500	14,700	17,000	13,611	13,000	21,000	12,300
60. First Decile	8,700	12,500	8,500	10,000	11,500	9,800	8,500	14,500	8,400

TABLE 4: SALARY DISTRIBUTION (IN DOLLARS)—FULL-TIME POSITIONS, 11–12 MONTHS—
BY SIZE OF INSTITUTION (STUDENT ENROLLMENT)
Questionnaire Sect. B, Q. 4–13

	Public Institutions				Private Institutions				
	1,000–2,499	2,500–4,999	5,000–9,999	10,000 & Over	500–999	1,000–2,499	2,500–4,999	5,000–9,999	10,000 & Over
President									
1. Number Reported	58	56	67	55	156	147	23	14	12
2. Highest	27,500	30,000	37,500	47,000	40,000	55,000	40,000	40,000	55,000
3. Ninth Decile	24,000	25,020	30,000	37,500	24,000	30,000	37,500	40,000	40,000
4. Average	18,854	21,265	24,560	30,132	17,423	21,738	27,578	31,275	35,968
5. Median	18,000	21,000	25,000	30,000	17,000	21,000	30,000	32,500	37,500
6. First Decile	15,000	17,000	18,000	23,000	12,000	14,000	15,175	21,600	20,000
Academic V.P.									
7. Number Reported	38	44	65	50	54	58	19	13	10
8. Highest	23,500	24,900	32,000	35,000	23,000	35,000	32,000	32,500	40,000
9. Ninth Decile	18,660	20,806	24,000	28,000	18,300	20,800	29,000	31,000	32,000
10. Average	15,665	17,964	19,884	23,931	13,872	17,099	20,342	23,506	27,005
11. Median	15,236	17,599	19,596	24,000	13,500	16,500	19,250	21,000	26,000
12. First Decile	12,992	15,000	16,000	18,660	9,600	12,500	14,350	18,000	17,450
Liberal Arts Dean									
13. Number Reported	25	35	54	51	107	95	18	12	10
14. Highest	18,000	22,900	27,100	29,100	19,200	28,000	24,000	24,000	30,000
15. Ninth Decile	17,300	19,000	22,000	25,200	16,000	19,000	22,000	24,000	29,500
16. Average	14,944	16,763	17,983	21,317	12,915	14,836	16,626	19,250	22,780
17. Median	14,750	16,400	17,500	21,000	12,920	15,000	16,500	18,250	23,000
18. First Decile	13,020	15,000	14,000	17,772	9,800	10,230	11,000	15,400	13,900
Graduate Dean									
19. Number Reported	16	37	55	52	9	21	15	16	10
20. Highest	25,500	23,600	25,900	28,300	25,000	21,000	27,000	25,500	29,500
21. Ninth Decile	15,900	18,000	22,300	26,000	14,850	16,400	24,000	23,000	26,000
22. Average	14,804	16,076	17,990	20,994	13,466	14,180	16,472	18,694	21,955
23. Median	14,450	16,100	17,580	20,508	13,000	14,000	15,100	17,500	21,000
24. First Decile	12,076	13,500	14,500	17,300	10,000	10,230	12,000	14,000	15,300
Librarian									
25. Number Reported	52	44	64	51	121	135	25	19	10
26. Highest	16,200	18,000	20,950	26,500	16,000	17,800	23,000	20,100	27,000
27. Ninth Decile	13,611	15,000	18,200	21,500	12,000	13,000	19,000	18,000	26,000
28. Average	10,664	12,397	13,876	17,815	8,938	10,232	12,726	13,300	20,830
29. Median	10,200	12,310	13,500	16,920	8,500	10,000	11,500	12,000	18,900
30. First Decile	8,148	10,000	10,532	14,540	6,900	7,600	9,500	9,300	15,000

(continued on next page)

TABLE 4 (continued)

	Public Institutions				Private Institutions				
	1,000- 2,499	2,500- 4,999	5,000- 9,999	10,000 & Over	500- 999	1,000- 2,499	2,500- 4,999	5,000- 9,999	10,000 & Over
Business Officer									
31. Number Reported	54	54	66	49	155	147	24	17	11
32. Highest	19,950	22,000	26,000	37,500	22,000	35,000	32,000	40,000	37,000
33. Ninth Decile	17,616	18,000	21,500	28,000	15,500	18,600	30,000	30,000	32,500
34. Average	12,466	14,010	17,163	21,678	11,774	14,389	18,582	22,024	27,072
35. Median	11,508	13,916	16,500	21,000	11,600	13,600	16,560	20,000	27,300
36. First Decile	9,011	10,432	13,000	16,200	8,400	9,600	11,000	16,700	15,500
Dean of Students									
37. Number Reported	49	51	65	49	120	126	24	14	9
38. Highest	17,760	20,000	22,000	28,500	15,000	20,000	23,000	20,000	21,000
39. Ninth Decile	14,911	16,509	19,000	22,080	12,000	14,500	18,000	20,000	20,840
40. Average	12,082	14,102	15,388	18,511	9,678	11,401	13,313	14,110	17,326
41. Median	12,000	14,000	15,000	17,800	9,600	11,000	13,000	13,000	18,000
42. First Decile	9,300	12,000	12,000	15,000	7,200	8,500	8,000	6,200	12,500
Dir. Admissions									
43. Number Reported	33	45	59	51	134	140	26	17	10
44. Highest	14,911	15,587	18,240	20,750	15,000	17,500	16,500	15,000	19,000
45. Ninth Decile	13,920	14,622	16,120	18,400	11,000	12,750	15,250	14,500	17,000
46. Average	11,052	11,658	12,689	14,843	8,779	10,157	11,253	11,765	14,606
47. Median	11,000	12,168	12,500	14,250	8,600	10,200	10,930	12,500	14,000
48. First Decile	8,500	8,500	9,700	11,750	6,700	7,400	8,385	7,500	8,000
Registrar									
49. Number Reported	41	38	49	32	127	136	25	22	10
50. Highest	14,050	14,603	19,300	20,850	12,300	16,400	14,000	17,250	19,500
51. Ninth Decile	12,500	13,650	14,500	17,800	9,700	11,500	12,000	13,250	17,400
52. Average	9,288	10,651	11,864	14,125	7,668	8,878	9,933	10,909	13,765
53. Median	9,500	10,116	12,000	14,000	7,700	8,712	10,500	10,300	12,500
54. First Decile	5,270	8,100	8,640	9,948	5,500	6,500	7,500	7,900	11,000
Dir. Development									
55. Number Reported	21	25	38	45	130	148	22	21	10
56. Highest	17,772	17,772	25,500	30,750	21,000	33,000	26,500	31,500	30,000
57. Ninth Decile	14,400	17,000	20,000	23,500	16,000	18,500	23,000	28,000	26,500
58. Average	11,568	13,737	15,352	17,692	12,070	13,385	17,254	20,421	22,500
59. Median	11,500	13,700	14,250	17,500	12,000	12,600	16,000	19,000	22,500
60. First Decile	8,500	10,240	10,500	12,600	8,500	8,845	12,020	14,500	16,000

About 15 public institutions below 1,000 in size and about 30 private institutions below 500 were omitted from this table.

TABLE 5: RATIO OF SALARIES IN 11—12 MONTH ADMINISTRATIVE POSITIONS TO
          AVERAGE FULL PROFESSORS' SALARIES ADJUSTED TO 11—12 MONTH BASIS
Questionnaire Sect. B, Q. 4—14

	All Institutions			Public Institutions			Private Institutions		
	Total	Univ.	Col.	Total	Univ.	Col.	Total	Univ.	Col.
President									
1. Number Reported	559	97	462	225	73	152	334	24	310
2. Ninth Decile	2.00	2.32	1.89	1.98	2.14	1.80	2.01	2.51	1.93
3. Average	1.59	1.84	1.54	1.59	1.78	1.50	1.59	2.03	1.56
4. Median	1.54	1.82	1.49	1.54	1.77	1.47	1.53	2.07	1.52
5. First Decile	1.25	1.40	1.23	1.27	1.33	1.23	1.23	1.49	1.22
Academic V.P.									
6. Number Reported	326	91	235	188	69	119	138	22	116
7. Ninth Decile	1.59	1.71	1.48	1.56	1.69	1.40	1.60	1.72	1.52
8. Average	1.29	1.45	1.23	1.32	1.44	1.24	1.25	1.46	1.21
9. Median	1.26	1.40	1.19	1.29	1.38	1.22	1.21	1.40	1.17
10. First Decile	1.01	1.21	1.00	1.09	1.25	1.06	.97	1.20	.94
Liberal Arts Dean									
11. Number Reported	386	88	298	157	65	92	229	23	206
12. Ninth Decile	1.37	1.45	1.34	1.37	1.47	1.30	1.35	1.31	1.37
13. Average	1.16	1.26	1.14	1.21	1.28	1.16	1.13	1.19	1.13
14. Median	1.17	1.26	1.12	1.21	1.27	1.17	1.11	1.20	1.10
15. First Decile	.96	1.10	.94	1.03	1.14	.99	.93	.95	.93
Graduate Dean									
16. Number Reported	216	96	120	149	67	82	67	29	38
17. Ninth Decile	1.37	1.44	1.27	1.37	1.49	1.25	1.37	1.41	1.29
18. Average	1.15	1.25	1.08	1.18	1.27	1.10	1.10	1.19	1.03
19. Median	1.15	1.24	1.09	1.16	1.28	1.11	1.07	1.12	1.02
20. First Decile	.92	1.04	.86	.96	1.07	.91	.87	1.01	.82
Librarian									
21. Number Reported	498	102	396	206	72	134	292	30	262
22. Ninth Decile	1.08	1.20	1.01	1.15	1.21	1.08	1.01	1.16	.94
23. Average	.84	.96	.80	.91	.97	.88	.78	.94	.76
24. Median	.81	.97	.78	.90	.97	.87	.76	.93	.74
25. First Decile	.65	.72	.64	.70	.77	.69	.63	.68	.63
Business Officer									
26. Number Reported	550	97	453	215	70	145	335	27	308
27. Ninth Decile	1.41	1.67	1.31	1.48	1.61	1.27	1.37	1.92	1.32
28. Average	1.08	1.32	1.03	1.08	1.26	1.00	1.08	1.45	1.05
29. Median	1.05	1.27	1.00	1.05	1.23	.97	1.05	1.38	1.03
30. First Decile	.79	.92	.77	.76	.92	.74	.80	1.05	.80
Dean of Students									
31. Number Reported	477	94	383	209	70	139	268	24	244
32. Ninth Decile	1.18	1.27	1.14	1.25	1.28	1.22	1.11	1.12	1.11
33. Average	.94	1.02	.92	1.01	1.05	1.00	.87	.92	.87
34. Median	.93	.98	.91	.99	1.05	.99	.86	.93	.85
35. First Decile	.72	.77	.71	.79	.81	.79	.67	.58	.67
Dir. Admissions									
36. Number Reported	484	99	385	180	69	111	304	80	274
37. Ninth Decile	1.00	1.14	.97	1.08	1.17	1.05	.94	1.00	.94
38. Average	.79	.85	.77	.84	.88	.82	.75	.77	.75
39. Median	.79	.85	.78	.85	.88	.83	.76	.77	.76
40. First Decile	.58	.62	.58	.63	.67	.62	.57	.55	.57
Registrar									
41. Number Reported	463	80	383	161	47	114	302	33	269
42. Ninth Decile	.94	.97	.91	.98	.99	.97	.87	.93	.87
43. Average	.70	.77	.69	.76	.81	.74	.67	.72	.67
44. Median	.70	.78	.69	.78	.79	.74	.67	.76	.67
45. First Decile	.48	.58	.47	.50	.60	.46	.47	.51	.47
Dir. Development									
46. Number Reported	446	80	366	127	53	74	319	27	292
47. Ninth Decile	1.35	1.50	1.27	1.27	1.38	1.20	1.35	1.68	1.29
48. Average	1.03	1.12	1.01	1.01	1.03	.99	1.04	1.29	1.01
49. Median	1.01	1.08	1.00	.99	1.03	.97	1.02	1.20	1.01
50. First Decile	.74	.75	.74	.72	.64	.72	.75	.99	.74

Since both the officer's salary and the salary of the full professor are needed to produce a ratio, the numbers involved in this table are less than in Table 3.

Since a few institutions reported average salaries of full-time staff rather than of full professors, the ninth deciles given above are probably slightly high.

TABLE 6: RATIO OF SALARIES IN 11—12 MONTH ADMINISTRATIVE POSITIONS
TO SALARY OF PRESIDENT
Questionnaire Sect. B, Q. 4—13

	All Institutions			Public Institutions			Private Institutions		
	Total	Univ.	Col.	Total	Univ.	Col.	Total	Univ.	Col.
Academic V.P.									
1. Number Reported	355	107	248	206	80	126	149	27	122
2. Ninth Decile	.94	.91	.94	.93	.91	.94	.94	.88	.94
3. Average	.79	.79	.79	.81	.81	.82	.75	.71	.76
4. Median	.79	.79	.79	.81	.80	.81	.76	.77	.76
5. First Decile	.66	.67	.66	.71	.70	.71	.61	.56	.63
Liberal Arts Dean									
6. Number Reported	419	101	318	170	76	94	249	25	224
7. Ninth Decile	.90	.85	.91	.91	.86	.95	.88	.76	.90
8. Average	.74	.70	.75	.76	.73	.78	.73	.71	.74
9. Median	.75	.72	.76	.76	.74	.76	.74	.60	.75
10. First Decile	.60	.53	.61	.61	.61	.63	.57	.45	.60
Graduate Dean									
11. Number Reported	227	109	118	160	78	82	67	31	36
12. Ninth Decile	.86	.86	.86	.88	.86	.88	.81	.74	.81
13. Average	.69	.68	.70	.72	.72	.73	.61	.58	.64
14. Median	.70	.70	.70	.71	.72	.71	.60	.55	.63
15. First Decile	.50	.49	.53	.61	.60	.61	.42	.40	.45
Librarian									
16. Number Reported	525	114	411	224	82	142	301	32	269
17. Ninth Decile	.68	.66	.68	.72	.68	.73	.64	.61	.64
18. Average	.53	.53	.53	.58	.56	.59	.49	.47	.49
19. Median	.53	.54	.53	.58	.57	.60	.49	.45	.49
20. First Decile	.40	.39	.39	.44	.44	.45	.36	.28	.36
Business Officer									
21. Number Reported	597	114	483	237	81	156	360	33	327
22. Ninth Decile	.84	.89	.83	.83	.84	.83	.84	.95	.83
23. Average	.68	.71	.68	.68	.70	.67	.68	.71	.68
24. Median	.68	.69	.68	.68	.70	.67	.68	.68	.68
25. First Decile	.53	.55	.52	.53	.56	.52	.52	.51	.52
Dean of Students									
26. Number Reported	516	107	409	225	80	145	291	27	264
27. Ninth Decile	.77	.73	.78	.79	.74	.81	.76	.56	.76
28. Average	.59	.56	.60	.64	.59	.67	.56	.46	.57
29. Median	.60	.56	.60	.65	.61	.67	.56	.44	.57
30. First Decile	.43	.41	.43	.50	.46	.53	.40	.33	.41
Dir. Admissions									
31. Number Reported	519	109	410	198	78	120	321	31	290
32. Ninth Decile	.67	.63	.68	.69	.66	.73	.63	.50	.64
33. Average	.50	.47	.51	.53	.50	.55	.48	.39	.49
34. Median	.49	.47	.50	.54	.49	.55	.47	.37	.48
35. First Decile	.36	.32	.37	.39	.36	.41	.36	.26	.37
Registrar									
36. Number Reported	485	88	397	169	52	117	316	36	280
37. Ninth Decile	.63	.55	.64	.65	.60	.65	.62	.44	.63
38. Average	.45	.42	.45	.48	.46	.49	.43	.35	.44
39. Median	.44	.42	.44	.48	.46	.49	.41	.34	.42
40. First Decile	.30	.29	.30	.34	.35	.34	.28	.27	.29
Dir. Development									
41. Number Reported	474	93	381	134	60	74	340	33	307
42. Ninth Decile	.83	.79	.86	.80	.76	.81	.86	.80	.86
43. Average	.65	.60	.66	.61	.58	.64	.66	.63	.66
44. Median	.64	.60	.65	.61	.59	.64	.65	.60	.65
45. First Decile	.46	.43	.48	.44	.42	.46	.47	.43	.48

Since both the officer's salary and the salary of the president are needed to produce a
ratio, the numbers involved in this table are less than in Table 3.

Appendix

TABLE 7: AGE DISTRIBUTION—MALE
Questionnaire Sect. C, Q. 15

	All Institutions			Public Institutions			Private Institutions		
	Total	Univ.	Col.	Total	Univ.	Col.	Total	Univ.	Col.
President									
1. Number Reported	723	133	590	264	90	174	459	43	416
2. Highest	74	68	74	69	68	69	74	67	74
3. Ninth Decile	63	64	63	64	64	64	62	62	62
4. Median	54	56	53	55	56	55	52	54	52
5. First Decile	43	46	43	44	46	43	43	46	43
6. Lowest	33	39	33	33	39	33	33	42	33
Academic V. P.									
7. Number Reported	428	119	309	218	84	134	210	35	175
8. Highest	71	68	71	69	68	69	71	65	71
9. Ninth Decile	61	62	60	62	62	62	60	63	60
10. Median	51	52	50	52	52	53	50	54	49
11. First Decile	40	41	39	41	41	41	39	43	38
12. Lowest	29	37	29	36	38	36	29	37	29
Liberal Arts Dean									
13. Number Reported	493	116	377	185	75	110	308	41	267
14. Highest	69	69	69	69	69	67	69	63	69
15. Ninth Decile	62	63	62	63	64	62	61	58	61
16. Median	49	51	48	51	53	51	47	49	47
17. First Decile	39	42	38	40	42	39	38	42	38
18. Lowest	29	36	29	34	36	34	29	36	29
Graduate Dean									
19. Number Reported	278	116	162	170	71	99	108	45	63
20. Highest	72	70	72	70	65	70	72	70	72
21. Ninth Decile	64	64	63	63	64	62	64	64	64
22. Median	52	53	52	52	52	52	53	54	51
23. First Decile	42	44	41	42	42	42	42	46	40
24. Lowest	29	33	29	33	33	35	29	38	29
Librarian									
25. Number Reported	432	116	316	178	76	102	254	40	214
26. Highest	67	67	67	65	65	65	67	67	67
27. Ninth Decile	60	62	58	61	62	58	59	61	58
28. Median	49	54	47	50	54	47	47	53	47
29. First Decile	36	41	34	39	42	37	33	41	33
30. Lowest	25	36	25	27	37	27	25	36	25

(continued on next page)

TABLE 7 (continued)

	All Institutions			Public Institutions			Private Institutions		
	Total	Univ.	Col.	Total	Univ.	Col.	Total	Univ.	Col.
Business Officer									
31. Number Reported	649	122	527	234	81	153	415	41	374
32. Highest	72	68	72	69	65	69	72	68	72
33. Ninth Decile	60	61	60	60	60	60	61	62	60
34. Median	49	52	48	50	52	49	48	52	48
35. First Decile	37	40	36	37	38	36	36	43	36
36. Lowest	24	28	24	28	28	30	24	39	24
Dean of Students									
37. Number Reported	575	119	456	220	78	142	355	41	314
38. Highest	71	66	71	71	66	71	66	64	66
39. Ninth Decile	57	61	56	59	61	59	56	60	54
40. Median	45	48	44	48	48	48	43	48	43
41. First Decile	34	37	33	36	37	36	33	38	33
42. Lowest	26	30	26	28	30	28	26	30	26
Dir. Admissions									
43. Number Reported	545	105	440	189	64	125	356	41	315
44. Highest	73	68	73	67	65	67	73	68	73
45. Ninth Decile	59	60	59	59	60	59	58	58	59
46. Median	43	48	42	46	49	44	42	43	42
47. First Decile	30	34	29	31	36	30	29	32	29
48. Lowest	25	26	25	25	30	25	25	26	25
Registrar									
49. Number Reported	407	95	312	176	64	112	231	31	200
50. Highest	71	66	71	70	66	70	71	62	71
51. Ninth Decile	61	60	62	61	61	61	62	57	62
52. Median	46	46	46	47	46	47	46	46	45
53. First Decile	33	36	32	34	36	32	32	35	32
54. Lowest	24	26	24	26	26	27	24	31	24
Dir. Development									
55. Number Reported	520	97	423	137	58	79	383	39	344
56. Highest	73	73	71	70	66	70	73	73	71
57. Ninth Decile	58	59	58	59	57	59	58	61	58
58. Median	46	48	45	47	48	47	45	47	45
59. First Decile	34	36	33	35	33	35	33	37	33
60. Lowest	24	24	24	24	24	24	27	33	27

For the purposes of studying the age distributions, we divided males and females. We did not make a combined table. Since the variations between the two groups were slight, we are publishing only the male table.

In age distribution the averages are almost identical with the medians.

TABLE 8: AGE DISTRIBUTION OF ADMINISTRATIVE OFFICERS ACCORDING TO SALARY
Questionnaire Sect. C, Q. 15

					Salary				
	5,000- 9,999	10,000- 14,999	15,000- 19,999	20,000- 24,999	25,000- 29,999	30,000- 34,999	35,000- 39,999	40,000- 44,999	45,000- 49,999
President									
1. Average Age	50	51	53	53	53	53	53	55	57
2. Median Age	51	52	54	54	54	53	54	55	60
Academic V. P.									
3. Average Age	47	50	49	52	51	57	52	. . .	. . .
4. Median Age	44	50	50	53	51	60	50	. . .	. . .
Liberal Arts Dean									
5. Average Age	48	49	50	51	54	45	. . .	. . .	. . .
6. Median Age	50	48	49	51	55	45	. . .	. . .	. . .
Graduate Dean									
7. Average Age	47	50	53	51	49	. . .	. . .	. . .	. . .
8. Median Age	45	52	54	51	51	. . .	. . .	. . .	. . .
Librarian									
9. Average Age	42	48	52	56	56	. . .	. . .	. . .	. . .
10. Median Age	42	49	53	56	53	. . .	. . .	. . .	. . .
Business Officer									
11. Average Age	45	47	49	51	53	51	57	51	. . .
12. Median Age	44	46	50	52	54	54	57	51	. . .
Dean of Students									
13. Average Age	42	44	48	50	43	. . .	. . .	. . .	. . .
14. Median Age	41	44	49	50	40	. . .	. . .	. . .	. . .
Dir. Admissions									
15. Average Age	40	44	49	64	. . .	. . .	. . .	. . .	. . .
16. Median Age	38	44	48	64	. . .	. . .	. . .	. . .	. . .
Registrar									
17. Average Age	43	47	52	62	. . .	. . .	. . .	. . .	. . .
18. Median Age	44	47	55	57	. . .	. . .	. . .	. . .	. . .
Dir. Development									
19. Average Age	43	44	47	50	52	47	. . .	. . .	. . .
20. Median Age	43	45	49	49	50	47	. . .	. . .	. . .

Those with salaries below $5,000 were omitted.

TABLE 9: ADMINISTRATIVE OFFICERS—PERCENT MALE
Questionnaire Sect. C, Q. 16

	All Institutions			Public Institutions			Private Institutions		
	Total	Univ.	Col.	Total	Univ.	Col.	Total	Univ.	Col.
1. President	90%	100%	88%	99%	100%	98%	86%	100%	84%
2. Academic V. P.	93	97	92	98	98	99	89	85	88
3. Liberal Arts Dean	82	100	78	99	100	98	75	100	72
4. Graduate Dean	92	97	89	96	95	96	86	100	79
5. Librarian	59	93	52	74	93	64	52	93	48
6. Business Officer	89	100	87	98	100	97	85	100	83
7. Dean of Students	80	96	77	94	96	92	74	95	72
8. Dir. Admissions	82	95	79	91	96	89	77	93	76
9. Registrar	59	86	54	81	90	77	49	79	47
10. Dir. Development	95	100	95	99	100	99	95	100	94

Practically all respondents answered this question.

TABLE 10: HIGHEST EARNED ACADEMIC DEGREE HELD—PERCENT HOLDING DEGREE
Questionnaire Sect. C, Q. 17

	All Institutions			Public Institutions			Private Institutions		
	Total	Univ.	Col.	Total	Univ.	Col.	Total	Univ.	Col.
President									
1. Bachelor's	4%	4%	4%	2%	3%	1%	5%	7%	5%
2. Master's	18	8	19	7	7	7	23	11	24
3. Ed.D.	11	4	12	22	3	31	5	5	5
4. Ph.D.	59	77	55	63	80	54	57	70	55
5. Other	8	7	9	6	7	5	10	7	10
Academic V.P.									
6. Bachelor's	0	1	...	0	1	...	...	...	...
7. Master's	8	4	10	6	3	7	11	5	12
8. Ed.D.	16	3	20	21	5	31	11	...	13
9. Ph.D.	71	85	66	70	85	60	72	86	70
10. Other	4	7	3	3	6	1	5	8	4
Liberal Arts Dean									
11. Bachelor's	0	...	0	...	...	...	0	...	0
12. Master's	15	4	17	5	1	7	19	10	21
13. Ed.D.	8	...	10	7	...	12	8	...	9
14. Ph.D.	73	91	69	86	96	80	68	83	66
15. Other	3	4	2	2	3	1	3	7	3
Graduate Dean									
16. Bachelor's	...	...	...	...	...	...	...	...	...
17. Master's	2	1	3	1	...	2	4	2	5
18. Ed.D.	16	5	23	21	4	34	9	7	10
19. Ph.D.	76	92	66	76	96	61	77	84	73
20. Other	4	2	5	2	...	3	8	7	9
Librarian									
21. Bachelor's	9	5	10	6	5	7	11	5	11
22. Master's	69	51	72	61	51	66	72	51	74
23. Ed.D.	1	...	1	3	...	5	0	...	0
24. Ph.D.	14	37	10	23	37	16	10	37	7
25. Other	7	7	6	5	7	4	7	7	7
Business Officer									
26. Bachelor's	39	33	41	39	37	41	39	25	41
27. Master's	42	48	40	43	49	39	41	45	41
28. Ed.D.	2	1	2	3	1	4	1	...	1
29. Ph.D.	4	10	3	5	9	3	3	11	2
30. Other	7	7	7	5	4	6	8	14	7
Dean of Students									
31. Bachelor's	9	10	8	4	9	2	11	14	11
32. Master's	49	36	51	34	31	35	56	47	57
33. Ed.D.	18	17	18	33	17	41	10	16	9
34. Ph.D.	21	35	18	27	43	19	18	21	17
35. Other	3	1	4	2	...	3	4	2	5
Dir. Admissions									
36. Bachelor's	27	14	30	12	12	12	34	18	36
37. Master's	53	51	53	57	42	64	51	64	50
38. Ed.D.	7	16	6	16	24	13	3	4	3
39. Ph.D.	8	16	6	13	19	10	6	11	5
40. Other	2	1	3	...	...	...	3	2	3
Registrar									
41. Bachelor's	30	22	32	20	18	21	35	28	36
42. Master's	51	47	51	56	49	59	48	44	48
43. Ed.D.	6	14	4	11	17	8	3	8	3
44. Ph.D.	7	13	6	9	14	6	6	10	6
45. Other	2	2	2	1	1	1	3	3	3
Dir. Development									
46. Bachelor's	45	47	44	28	47	13	51	46	51
47. Master's	31	33	31	35	31	39	30	36	29
48. Ed.D.	6	3	6	14	5	21	3	...	3
49. Ph.D.	10	7	10	18	8	24	7	5	7
50. Other	7	9	6	4	7	2	7	13	7

Although practically all responded to this question, the percents will not quite add up to
100. The difference measures the "No Response" group.

TABLE 11: PERCENT OF ADMINISTRATIVE OFFICERS REPORTING HOLDING FACULTY RANK
WITH TENURE
Questionnaire Sect. C, Q. 19

	All Institutions			Public Institutions			Private Institutions		
	Total	Univ.	Col.	Total	Univ.	Col.	Total	Univ.	Col.
1. President	26%	46%	22%	33%	53%	22%	23%	32%	22%
2. Academic V.P.	67	78	63	73	83	66	62	68	61
3. Liberal Arts Dean	64	84	59	81	91	75	56	73	54
4. Graduate Dean	84	83	85	87	87	86	81	78	83
5. Librarian	47	60	44	52	62	47	45	56	43
6. Business Officer	16	25	15	21	26	18	15	23	14
7. Dean of Students	37	40	36	51	48	53	30	26	30
8. Dir. Admissions	23	30	22	33	34	32	19	24	18
9. Registrar	28	22	29	34	23	39	25	21	26
10. Dir. Development	15	14	15	34	12	50	9	18	8

Some of the "No Responses" probably represent persons with faculty rank with tenure. The "No Responses" were under 10% for all positions except "Librarians" where they were about 15%.

TABLE 12: YEARS IN PRESENT POSITION
Questionnaire Sect. C, Q. 20

	All Institutions			Public Institutions			Private Institutions		
	Total	Univ.	Col.	Total	Univ.	Col.	Total	Univ.	Col.
President									
1. Highest	31	31	31	31	31	31	31	20	31
2. Ninth Decile	17	16	17	18	16	19	17	16	17
3. Median	6	6	6	6	6	6	6	7	6
4. Percent less than 1 year	14%	13%	14%	15%	12%	16%	13%	16%	13%
Academic V.P.									
5. Highest	28	18	28	28	18	28	20	9	20
6. Ninth Decile	12	9	13	13	10	16	11	8	11
7. Median	4	4	4	4	3	5	4	5	3
8. Percent less than 1 year	24%	28%	23%	25%	29%	22%	24%	24%	23%
Liberal Arts Dean									
9. Highest	34	27	34	32	25	32	34	27	34
10. Ninth Decile	15	13	15	16	17	15	14	12	14
11. Median	4	4	4	4	4	4	4	4	4
12. Percent less than 1 year	21%	19%	21%	22%	19%	24%	20%	20%	20%
Graduate Dean									
13. Highest	28	28	28	28	28	28	23	14	23
14. Ninth Decile	13	12	13	14	16	13	9	11	9
15. Median	4	4	4	4	4	4	4	4	3
16. Percent less than 1 year	18%	18%	19%	17%	20%	15%	21%	16%	24%
Librarian									
17. Highest	45	45	40	45	45	37	40	33	40
18. Ninth Decile	22	22	22	22	23	21	22	20	23
19. Median	7	12	6	8	13	7	6	10	6
20. Percent less than 1 year	13%	6%	14%	12%	6%	14%	13%	7%	14%
Business Officer									
21. Highest	41	36	41	41	34	41	36	36	36
22. Ninth Decile	20	19	20	21	19	23	19	19	18
23. Median	7	8	7	8	8	9	7	10	6
24. Percent less than 1 year	12%	11%	13%	12%	12%	11%	13%	9%	13%
Dean of Students									
25. Highest	29	24	29	29	24	29	27	19	27
26. Ninth Decile	13	14	13	15	14	15	13	15	12
27. Median	4	4	4	4	3	5	3	4	3
28. Percent less than 1 year	22%	23%	22%	19%	21%	19%	23%	28%	23%
Dir. Admissions									
29. Highest	47	26	47	26	26	26	47	19	47
30. Ninth Decile	16	17	15	16	17	14	15	15	15
31. Median	5	6	4	5	6	4	5	5	5
32. Percent less than 1 year	15%	15%	15%	16%	13%	17%	15%	18%	14%
Registrar									
33. Highest	50	39	50	50	29	50	46	39	46
34. Ninth Decile	20	19	21	18	18	18	21	19	22
35. Median	6	6	6	6	6	5	6	7	6
36. Percent less than 1 year	14%	13%	14%	12%	13%	12%	15%	13%	15%
Dir. Development									
37. Highest	27	24	27	25	24	25	27	21	27
38. Ninth Decile	10	14	9	11	14	10	9	13	9
39. Median	3	3	3	3	3	3	3	3	3
40. Percent less than 1 year	27%	24%	28%	30%	27%	33%	26%	21%	26%

TABLE 13: PERCENT OF OFFICERS WHOSE PREVIOUS POSITION WAS AT ANOTHER INSTITUTION
Questionnaire Sect. C, Q. 22

	All Institutions			Public Institutions			Private Institutions		
	Total	Univ.	Col.	Total	Univ.	Col.	Total	Univ.	Col.
1. President	54%	55%	53%	65%	61%	66%	48%	43%	49%
2. Academic V.P.	35	28	38	32	27	35	39	30	40
3. Liberal Arts Dean	35	28	36	30	33	28	37	20	39
4. Graduate Dean	26	20	31	27	20	33	25	20	28
5. Librarian	66	63	66	73	72	73	62	37	64
6. Business Officer	36	24	38	31	20	36	39	32	39
7. Dean of Students	45	28	48	43	32	49	46	21	48
8. Dir. Admissions	38	31	39	44	28	51	35	36	35
9. Registrar	30	25	31	31	24	34	30	28	31
10. Dir. Development	36	27	38	24	14	32	40	46	39

Practically all respondents answered this question.

TABLE 14: PAYMENT OF MOVING EXPENSES IF COMING FROM ANOTHER INSTITUTION—
PERCENT PAID IN FULL; PERCENT PAID IN PART
Questionnaire Sect. C, Q. 22b

	All Institutions			Public Institutions			Private Institutions		
	Total	Univ.	Col.	Total	Univ.	Col.	Total	Univ.	Col.
1. President									
Full	50%	55%	49%	28%	49%	19%	65%	74%	64%
Part	7	12	6	9	11	8	6	16	5
2. Academic V.P.									
Full	26	29	25	10	22	4	38	45	37
Part	20	29	18	15	30	8	23	27	23
3. Liberal Arts Dean									
Full	28	21	30	9	16	3	36	38	36
Part	15	21	14	11	24	...	17	13	17
4. Graduate Dean									
Full	11	13	11	...	...	...	29	33	27
Part	14	21	11	10	20	6	19	22	18
5. Librarian									
Full	11	13	11	5	10	3	14	20	14
Part	11	10	11	3	7	2	15	20	15
6. Business Officer									
Full	23	13	24	4	...	5	30	29	31
Part	13	7	14	7	...	9	15	14	15
7. Dean of Students									
Full	18	20	18	4	8	3	25	56	24
Part	18	37	16	16	35	10	19	44	18
8. Dir. Admissions									
Full	12	14	12	5	21	1	16	6	17
Part	10	9	11	1	...	1	15	19	15
9. Registrar									
Full	10	14	9	9	24	4	10	...	11
Part	10	18	8	3	6	2	13	36	11
10. Dir. Development									
Full	35	50	33	9	25	4	40	61	38
Part	18	23	17	15	38	8	19	17	19

"No Responses" were 8% of the total, varying considerably by position.

TABLE 15: YEARS OF SERVICE OF OFFICER'S IMMEDIATE PREDECESSOR
Questionnaire Sect. C., Q. 23

	All Institutions			Public Institutions			Private Institutions		
	Total	Univ.	Col.	Total	Univ.	Col.	Total	Univ.	Col.
President									
1. Highest	57	33	57	37	27	37	57	33	57
2. Ninth Decile	23	22	24	23	20	25	23	24	22
3. Average	11	11	11	12	10	13	11	13	10
4. Median	9	10	9	11	7	12	9	12	8
5. First Decile	3	4	3	3	3	3	3	4	3
Academic V.P.									
6. Highest	43	30	43	43	27	43	30	30	28
7. Ninth Decile	20	16	23	24	16	25	18	18	17
8. Average	8	7	9	9	6	10	8	8	8
9. Median	6	5	6	5	5	8	6	7	6
10. First Decile	2	2	2	2	2	1	2	2	2
Liberal Arts Dean									
11. Highest	50	31	50	31	31	30	50	25	50
12. Ninth Decile	18	20	18	20	20	18	17	15	18
13. Average	8	9	8	9	10	7	8	7	8
14. Median	6	8	6	7	8	5	6	7	6
15. First Decile	2	2	2	2	2	1	2	1	2
Graduate Dean									
16. Highest	34	34	27	34	34	25	27	20	27
17. Ninth Decile	16	19	15	17	20	15	15	15	13
18. Average	7	8	6	8	9	6	7	7	6
19. Median	5	6	5	6	7	4	5	6	5
20. First Decile	2	3	1	2	3	1	1	2	1
Librarian									
21. Highest	49	48	49	48	48	45	49	37	49
22. Ninth Decile	27	30	26	30	30	30	26	27	25
23. Average	11	15	11	13	14	12	11	16	10
24. Median	9	12	7	10	12	9	8	13	7
25. First Decile	2	3	2	2	2	2	2	5	2
Business Officer									
26. Highest	50	44	50	49	44	49	50	30	50
27. Ninth Decile	30	31	28	33	33	30	25	24	25
28. Average	11	13	11	14	14	14	10	11	10
29. Median	8	10	7	12	11	12	7	10	7
30. First Decile	2	2	2	2	2	2	2	3	2
Dean of Students									
31. Highest	30	30	27	26	26	25	30	30	27
32. Ninth Decile	11	16	10	15	18	10	10	10	10
33. Average	5	7	5	6	8	5	5	5	5
34. Median	4	5	4	5	6	4	4	4	4
35. First Decile	2	2	2	2	2	2	2	1	2
Dir. Admissions									
36. Highest	40	40	40	40	40	40	40	40	40
37. Ninth Decile	20	32	17	30	32	30	17	28	15
38. Average	8	11	7	10	13	8	7	9	6
39. Median	5	7	4	5	8	4	4	5	4
40. First Decile	2	2	1	1	2	1	2	2	2
Registrar									
41. Highest	50	50	45	50	50	44	50	50	45
42. Ninth Decile	30	34	28	33	34	31	27	36	26
43. Average	11	14	10	13	15	11	10	12	10
44. Median	7	10	7	9	12	7	7	6	7
45. First Decile	2	2	2	2	2	2	2	2	2
Dir. Development									
46. Highest	38	38	28	38	38	28	27	21	27
47. Ninth Decile	10	15	8	15	16	15	8	11	8
48. Average	4	7	4	6	8	5	4	5	3
49. Median	3	5	3	4	5	3	3	4	3
50. First Decile	1	1	1	1	2	1	1	1	1

TABLE 16: AGE OF OFFICER'S IMMEDIATE PREDECESSOR ON LEAVING OFFICE
Questionnaire Sect. C, Q. 24

	All Institutions			Public Institutions			Private Institutions		
	Total	Univ.	Col.	Total	Univ.	Col.	Total	Univ.	Col.
President									
1. Highest	93	72	93	80	70	80	93	72	93
2. Ninth Decile	70	70	70	70	69	70	70	70	70
3. Median	60	61	60	62	60	63	59	62	58
4. First Decile	45	46	45	45	46	45	45	45	44
5. Lowest	31	38	31	33	38	33	31	42	31
Academic V.P.									
6. Highest	74	71	74	70	68	70	74	71	74
7. Ninth Decile	66	65	66	67	65	67	65	65	65
8. Median	53	54	53	54	54	56	52	54	52
9. First Decile	42	43	42	42	44	42	42	41	42
10. Lowest	34	35	34	34	39	34	35	35	35
Liberal Arts Dean									
11. Highest	82	70	82	82	70	82	75	69	75
12. Ninth Decile	65	65	65	66	66	68	65	65	65
13. Median	52	53	51	56	57	55	51	52	51
14. First Decile	40	43	40	41	42	39	40	44	40
15. Lowest	30	38	30	37	38	37	30	40	30
Graduate Dean									
16. Highest	72	70	72	70	70	68	72	70	72
17. Ninth Decile	67	68	67	67	69	65	68	65	68
18. Median	54	55	54	55	58	52	53	53	54
19. First Decile	42	41	42	44	44	44	39	40	38
20. Lowest	30	35	30	30	40	30	33	35	33
Librarian									
21. Highest	80	75	80	71	71	70	80	75	80
22. Ninth Decile	68	69	68	68	68	68	68	70	68
23. Median	52	54	51	51	52	50	52	56	51
24. First Decile	34	38	32	35	36	35	33	41	32
25. Lowest	20	31	20	24	31	24	20	37	20
Business Officer									
26. Highest	90	74	90	74	74	73	90	72	90
27. Ninth Decile	68	68	68	68	69	68	68	67	68
28. Median	50	55	50	53	55	50	50	56	50
29. First Decile	36	41	35	36	41	34	36	42	35
30. Lowest	27	30	27	30	30	30	27	39	27
Dean of Students									
31. Highest	70	70	70	70	70	69	70	68	70
32. Ninth Decile	62	65	60	65	65	60	60	65	60
33. Median	44	48	43	45	48	45	43	47	43
34. First Decile	34	38	33	35	38	35	33	38	33
35. Lowest	24	31	24	30	32	30	24	31	24
Dir. Admissions									
36. Highest	72	70	72	72	70	72	71	67	71
37. Ninth Decile	65	65	65	66	65	66	65	65	63
38. Median	42	52	41	46	54	42	42	44	41
39. First Decile	30	35	30	31	35	30	30	34	30
40. Lowest	22	28	22	27	28	27	22	29	22
Registrar									
41. Highest	78	74	78	70	70	70	78	74	78
42. Ninth Decile	66	68	66	65	67	65	66	68	66
43. Median	50	50	50	50	52	48	50	46	50
44. First Decile	33	35	32	33	39	29	32	32	32
45. Lowest	20	30	20	22	33	22	20	30	20
Dir. Development									
46. Highest	78	72	78	70	66	70	78	72	78
47. Ninth Decile	64	65	62	66	65	68	62	67	61
48. Median	45	47	45	50	46	50	45	47	45
49. First Decile	33	37	32	34	35	30	33	36	32
50. Lowest	25	33	25	25	33	25	25	35	25

TABLE 17: RETIREMENT AGE AND EXTENSIONS—PERCENT UNDER VARIOUS PROVISIONS
Questionnaire Sect. D, Q. 26

	All Institutions			Public Institutions			Private Institutions		
	Total	Univ.	Col.	Total	Univ.	Col.	Total	Univ.	Col.
President									
1. No stated retirement age	35%	16%	39%	7%	8%	7%	49%	32%	50%
2. No response to above	3	1	3	1	1	1	3	...	4
3. When retirement age stated, extensions not permitted	33	37	32	42	37	45	24	37	23
4. No response to above	5	1	6	2	...	4	7	3	7
5. When extensions permitted, no specified age limit	40	44	38	31	40	26	46	56	45
6. No response to above	9	17	7	9	19	2	10	11	10
Academic V.P.									
7. No stated retirement age	16	11	18	6	3	8	26	27	25
8. When retirement age stated, extensions not permitted	35	42	32	48	45	50	21	35	18
9. When extensions permitted, no specified age limit	33	34	33	24	30	21	40	44	40
Liberal Arts Dean									
10. No stated retirement age	24	9	27	9	4	12	31	20	32
11. When retirement age stated, extensions not permitted	35	54	29	52	56	50	24	52	21
12. When extensions permitted, no specified age limit	38	34	39	32	32	32	40	36	40
Graduate Dean									
13. No stated retirement age	12	7	15	4	4	4	22	11	29
14. When retirement age stated, extensions not permitted	47	50	44	51	52	49	39	46	33
15. When extensions permitted, no specified age limit	20	25	16	16	26	9	26	24	28
Librarian									
16. No stated retirement age	17	6	19	5	4	5	23	12	24
17. When retirement age stated, extensions not permitted	29	39	27	44	46	43	20	24	19
18. When extensions permitted, no specified age limit	26	18	27	14	17	13	31	19	32
Business Officer									
19. No stated retirement age	21	9	23	5	4	6	28	18	29
20. When retirement age stated, extensions not permitted	30	37	28	46	44	47	19	20	19
21. When extensions permitted, no specified age limit	33	26	35	23	21	24	37	33	38
Dean of Students									
22. No stated retirement age	25	10	28	7	2	9	34	23	35
23. When retirement age stated, extensions not permitted	35	38	34	43	37	46	29	39	28
24. When extensions permitted, no specified age limit	28	24	29	22	19	23	32	35	32
Dir. Admissions									
25. No stated retirement age	25	12	28	8	6	9	33	20	35
26. When retirement age stated, extensions not permitted	35	43	33	55	53	55	23	26	23
27. When extensions permitted, no specified age limit	32	26	33	19	24	16	37	28	38
Registrar									
28. No stated retirement age	21	5	25	8	4	10	27	8	29
29. When retirement age stated, extensions not permitted	35	42	33	56	53	57	22	20	22
30. When extensions permitted, no specified age limit	28	26	28	19	28	15	31	24	32
Dir. Development									
31. No stated retirement age	25	11	28	11	12	11	30	10	32
32. When retirement age stated, extensions not permitted	27	36	24	44	42	45	19	26	18
33. When extensions permitted, no specified age limit	40	32	41	25	22	26	44	42	44

For analysis derived from this table see Chapter 3. A sample of the percentage of
"No Responses" to this question is given under "President."

TABLE 18: RETIREMENT AGE—PERCENT OF INSTITUTIONS WITH A STATED AGE
           BY SIZE OF INSTITUTION (STUDENT ENROLLMENT)
Questionnaire Sect. D, Q. 26

	Public Institutions				Private Institutions				
	1,000– 2,499	2,500– 4,999	5,000– 9,999	10,000 & Over	500– 999	1,000– 2,499	2,500– 4,999	5,000– 9,999	10,000 & Over
President	94%	86%	94%	95%	43%	54%	58%	50%	77%
Academic V.P.	88	88	95	98	76	73	79	61	82
Business Officer	90	90	100	96	63	72	81	74	83

These figures were developed only for the positions of president, vice president, and business officer. From this table about 15 public institutions below 1,000 in size and about 55 private institutions below 500 were omitted.

TABLE 19: RETIREMENT AGE—PERCENT REPORTING SAME AGE AS FOR FACULTY
Questionnaire Sect. D, Q. 27

	All Institutions			Public Institutions			Private Institutions		
	Total	Univ.	Col.	Total	Univ.	Col.	Total	Univ.	Col.
1. President	53%	54%	53%	60%	59%	61%	50%	45%	50%
2. Academic V.P.	69	59	73	65	60	69	73	54	77
3. Liberal Arts Dean	68	60	70	68	60	73	68	61	69
4. Graduate Dean	70	67	72	70	66	74	70	69	70
5. Librarian	78	74	79	79	71	83	78	81	77
6. Business Officer	72	66	73	72	67	74	72	64	73
7. Dean of Students	71	65	72	74	63	80	69	67	69
8. Dir. Admissions	73	67	74	72	61	77	73	76	73
9. Registrar	73	73	73	75	69	79	71	79	71
10. Dir. Development	76	77	76	76	69	80	76	87	75

"No Responses" averaged about 10%.

TABLE 20: OPINION ON FIXED VERSUS FLEXIBLE RETIREMENT AGE FOR POSITION OCCUPIED—
           PERCENT OF TOTAL FAVORING FLEXIBLE RETIREMENT AGE
Questionnaire Sect. D, Q. 28

	All Institutions			Public Institutions			Private Institutions		
	Total	Univ.	Col.	Total	Univ.	Col.	Total	Univ.	Col.
1. President	53%	40%	55%	45%	40%	47%	57%	41%	58%
2. Academic V.P.	51	40	54	41	40	42	60	41	63
3. Liberal Arts Dean	58	38	62	48	33	58	62	46	64
4. Graduate Dean	61	50	67	56	51	60	66	49	76
5. Librarian	69	49	73	63	46	72	71	53	73
6. Business Officer	62	46	66	49	41	53	69	55	70
7. Dean of Students	67	59	69	64	54	69	69	67	69
8. Dir. Admissions	70	58	73	59	51	62	75	69	76
9. Registrar	67	56	69	56	48	61	71	72	71
10. Dir. Development	68	58	70	62	59	65	70	56	72

"No Responses" averaged about 5%.

TABLE 21: PARTICIPATION IN THE REGULAR FACULTY RETIREMENT ANNUITY PLAN—
PERCENT PARTICIPATING

Questionnaire Sect. D, Q. 29

		All Institutions			Public Institutions			Private Institutions	
	Total	Univ.	Col.	Total	Univ.	Col.	Total	Univ.	Col.
1. President	74%	86%	72%	95%	92%	96%	64%	73%	63%
2. Academic V.P.	86	88	85	96	97	96	76	68	78
3. Liberal Arts Dean	73	91	69	96	99	95	63	76	61
4. Graduate Dean	88	95	84	96	97	95	78	91	70
5. Librarian	76	90	74	90	90	91	69	88	68
6. Business Officer	76	88	73	85	90	82	71	84	70
7. Dean of Students	73	89	69	89	91	88	64	84	62
8. Dir. Admissions	74	83	72	84	81	86	69	87	68
9. Registrar	74	89	72	88	90	87	68	87	66
10. Dir. Development	82	92	80	90	92	89	80	92	79

In public institutions, a number of positions are frequently covered by a public employers' retirement system rather than by a system covering faculty. A number of administrative officers are not participating in the plan because they have not met the waiting period requirement. In Catholic institutions, those in religious orders have either reported not participating or did not respond to the question.

TABLE 22: COVERAGE OF COLLEGE AND UNIVERSITY OFFICERS UNDER INSTITUTIONAL GROUP
LIFE INSURANCE PLAN—PERCENT OF OFFICERS COVERED (BY SALARY LEVEL)

Questionnaire Sect. E, Q. 32

	Salary								
	5,000-9,999	10,000-14,999	15,000-19,999	20,000-24,999	25,000-29,999	30,000-34,999	35,000-39,999	40,000-44,999	45,000-49,999
1. President	22%	54%	57%	65%	75%	72%	83%	88%	100%
2. Academic V.P.	50	55	64	69	83	86	100	...	...
3. Liberal Arts Dean	42	51	67	76	100	100	...	...	...
4. Graduate Dean	33	49	68	77	77	...	...	...	...
5. Librarian	56	65	69	73	100	...	...	...	...
6. Business Officer	45	62	74	78	94	100	100	100	...
7. Dean of Students	52	67	71	83	33	...	...	...	...
8. Dir. Admissions	60	65	82	100	...	...	...	...	...
9. Registrar	61	71	84	...	...	...	...	...	...
10. Dir. Development	55	69	75	86	71	100	...	...	...

Percentages based on those whose salaries were reported. Those whose salaries were below $5,000 were omitted.

TABLE 23: TRAVEL ACCIDENT INSURANCE—PERCENT PROVIDED INSURANCE
Questionnaire Sect. E, Q. 33

		All Institutions			Public Institutions			Private Institutions		
		Total	Univ.	Col.	Total	Univ.	Col.	Total	Univ.	Col.
1.	President	33%	43%	31%	24%	39%	16%	37%	50%	36%
2.	Academic V.P.	27	32	25	19	26	15	34	46	32
3.	Liberal Arts Dean	22	29	21	19	23	17	24	41	22
4.	Graduate Dean	24	31	20	23	30	17	26	33	23
5.	Librarian	23	37	20	26	35	21	22	40	20
6.	Business Officer	30	42	28	26	40	18	33	45	31
7.	Dean of Students	27	31	26	25	27	24	28	40	27
8.	Dir. Admissions	29	36	28	25	37	20	31	33	31
9.	Registrar	22	33	20	22	30	18	22	38	21
10.	Dir. Development	30	39	29	21	37	10	34	41	33

TABLE 24: AVERAGE AMOUNT (IN DOLLARS) OF TRAVEL ACCIDENT INSURANCE
PROVIDED IN INSTITUTIONS WITH SUCH COVERAGE—
BY SIZE OF INSTITUTION (STUDENT ENROLLMENT)
Questionnaire Sect. E, Q. 33a

	Public Institutions				Private Institutions				
	1,000–2,499	2,500–4,999	5,000–9,999	10,000 & Over	500–999	1,000–2,499	2,500–4,999	5,000–9,999	10,000 & Over
President	$52,500	$68,500	$73,916	$97,750	$60,937	$67,946	$81,333	$64,444	$128,571
Academic V.P.	12,500	53,000	43,909	96,000	45,555	67,000	52,272	37,500	87,500
Business Officer	53,333	56,000	34,000	80,721	44,113	56,318	61,538	44,000	75,000

Public institutions below 1,000 in enrollment and private institutions below 500 were omitted.

TABLE 25: INSTITUTIONAL PURCHASE OF LIFE INSURANCE OTHER THAN GROUP LIFE OR
TRAVEL ACCIDENT—PERCENT PROVIDED INSURANCE
Questionnaire Sect. E, Q. 35

		All Institutions			Public Institutions			Private Institutions		
		Total	Univ.	Col.	Total	Univ.	Col.	Total	Univ.	Col.
1.	President	12%	8%	12%	6%	6%	6%	14%	14%	15%
2.	Academic V.P.	8	10	7	7	10	5	8	8	8
3.	Liberal Arts Dean	7	11	6	6	9	4	8	15	7
4.	Graduate Dean	8	10	7	5	4	6	12	20	8
5.	Librarian	8	12	7	7	12	4	8	12	8
6.	Business Officer	7	10	6	8	11	6	6	7	6
7.	Dean of Students	8	14	7	7	12	4	9	16	8
8.	Dir. Admissions	8	13	7	5	10	2	9	18	8
9.	Registrar	8	8	7	5	6	4	9	13	9
10.	Dir. Development	9	14	8	9	12	6	10	18	9

TABLE 26: SALARY REDUCTION PROVISIONS OF THE TECHNICAL AMENDMENTS ACT OF 1958—
PERCENT UTILIZATION
Questionnaire Sect. F, Q. 37

	All Institutions			Public Institutions			Private Institutions		
	Total	Univ.	Col.	Total	Univ.	Col.	Total	Univ.	Col.
1. President	30%	43%	27%	33%	48%	26%	28%	32%	28%
2. Academic V.P.	29	45	23	31	44	23	26	46	22
3. Liberal Arts Dean	21	29	19	26	32	21	19	24	18
4. Graduate Dean	26	40	17	26	39	17	26	40	18
5. Librarian	19	30	17	21	29	16	18	30	17
6. Business Officer	25	36	23	21	29	17	27	48	25
7. Dean of Students	19	32	16	21	31	15	18	35	16
8. Dir. Admissions	19	29	16	15	24	11	20	38	18
9. Registrar	19	35	16	17	28	12	19	46	17
10. Dir. Development	23	39	20	18	24	13	25	62	21

TABLE 27: SALARY REDUCTION PROVISIONS OF THE TECHNICAL AMENDMENTS ACT OF 1958—
PERCENT UTILIZATION BY SALARY LEVEL
Questionnaire Sect. F, Q. 37

	Salary								
	5,000-9,999	10,000-14,999	15,000-19,999	20,000-24,999	25,000-29,999	30,000-34,999	35,000-39,999	40,000-44,999	45,000-49,999
1. President	11%	26%	27%	31%	39%	40%	52%	35%	60%
2. Academic V.P.	38	14	25	34	60	57	50	...	...
3. Liberal Arts Dean	10	21	25	28	67	...	...	...	...
4. Graduate Dean	33	16	25	33	46	...	...	...	...
5. Librarian	17	18	26	60	50	...	...	...	...
6. Business Officer	16	24	29	38	50	67	33	...	...
7. Dean of Students	15	20	22	30	67	...	...	...	...
8. Dir. Admissions	17	19	33	100	...	...	...	...	...
9. Registrar	16	24	47	...	...	...	...	...	...
10. Dir. Development	17	18	22	50	57	60	...	...	...

Percentages based on those whose salaries were reported. Those whose salaries were below $5,000 were omitted.

TABLE 28: INSTITUTIONAL POLICY REGARDING RETENTION OF LECTURE FEES—
           PERCENT WITH VARIOUS POLICIES
Questionnaire Sect. F, Q. 39

	All Institutions			Public Institutions			Private Institutions		
	Total	Univ.	Col.	Total	Univ.	Col.	Total	Univ.	Col.
President									
1. Turned over to institution	10%	4%	11%	2%	2%	2%	13%	9%	14%
2. Retained by officer	37	42	37	42	41	43	35	43	34
3. No policy stated	49	52	48	55	56	55	46	45	46
4. No response	4	1	5	0	1	...	6	2	6
Academic V.P.									
5. Turned over to institution	2	...	2	...	...	...	3	...	4
6. Retained by officer	66	73	63	74	78	71	59	62	58
7. No policy stated	27	21	30	25	20	28	30	24	31
8. No response	5	6	5	2	2	1	8	14	7
Liberal Arts Dean									
9. Turned over to institution	5	2	6	...	...	...	7	5	8
10. Retained by officer	55	72	51	70	76	66	48	66	46
11. No policy stated	33	24	35	28	23	32	35	27	36
12. No response	7	2	8	2	1	2	9	2	10
Graduate Dean									
13. Turned over to institution	2	1	2	...	...	...	4	2	5
14. Retained by officer	76	79	73	82	83	81	67	73	64
15. No policy stated	19	18	20	17	16	18	22	22	21
16. No response	4	2	5	1	1	1	7	2	10
Librarian									
17. Turned over to institution	4	...	5	0	...	1	5	...	6
18. Retained by officer	45	66	40	57	67	52	39	65	36
19. No policy stated	40	26	43	37	24	43	42	30	43
20. No response	11	7	12	6	9	4	14	5	15
Business Officer									
21. Turned over to institution	4	2	5	1	2	...	6	...	7
22. Retained by officer	43	64	38	54	63	50	37	66	34
23. No policy stated	44	29	47	40	30	45	46	27	48
24. No response	9	5	10	5	4	6	11	7	11
Dean of Students									
25. Turned over to institution	5	1	6	0	1	...	7	...	8
26. Retained by officer	49	65	45	61	64	59	43	67	41
27. No policy stated	38	31	39	37	32	39	38	28	39
28. No response	8	3	10	2	2	2	12	5	12
Dir. Admissions									
29. Turned over to institution	3	1	3	1	1	1	3	...	4
30. Retained by officer	43	60	40	57	63	55	37	56	35
31. No policy stated	43	33	45	36	31	38	46	36	47
32. No response	11	6	12	6	4	6	14	9	14
Registrar									
33. Turned over to institution	3	...	3	0	...	1	4	...	4
34. Retained by officer	41	62	37	51	66	43	36	54	34
35. No policy stated	37	29	39	37	28	41	38	31	38
36. No response	19	9	21	12	6	14	22	15	23
Dir. Development									
37. Turned over to institution	3	2	3	1	2	...	4	3	4
38. Retained by officer	44	53	42	60	61	59	38	41	38
39. No policy stated	47	38	49	33	31	34	52	49	52
40. No response	7	7	6	7	7	7	6	8	6

The responses concerning retention of consulting fees were so similar to those concerning lecture fees that the table covering them is omitted.

TABLE 29: WAIVER OF UNDERGRADUATE TUITION FOR ADMINISTRATIVE OFFICERS' CHILDREN—
PERCENT PROVIDING WAIVER (NON-RESPONDENTS NOT INCLUDED)
Questionnaire Sect. G, Q. 41

		All Institutions		Public Institutions			Private Institutions		
		Total	Univ.	Col.	Total	Univ.	Col.	Total	Univ.	Col.
1.	President	62%	41%	66%	13%	21%	10%	91%	89%	91%
2.	Academic V.P.	54	40	59	15	20	12	95	97	95
3.	Liberal Arts Dean	66	46	71	17	21	14	94	95	94
4.	Graduate Dean	43	44	41	13	17	10	93	93	93
5.	Librarian	62	45	67	14	19	12	92	95	91
6.	Business Officer	65	45	69	13	20	10	94	93	94
7.	Dean of Students	63	43	69	13	16	11	95	95	95
8.	Dir. Admissions	65	47	69	12	17	9	94	95	93
9.	Registrar	63	44	67	12	18	9	92	95	91
10.	Dir. Development	74	48	80	13	20	8	96	92	96

TABLE 30: CASH GRANTS FOR PAYMENTS OF PART OR ALL OF UNDERGRADUATE TUITION
OF ADMINISTRATIVE OFFICERS' CHILDREN—PERCENT PROVIDING GRANT
(NON-RESPONDENTS NOT INCLUDED)
Questionnaire Sect. G, Q. 42

		All Institutions		Public Institutions			Private Institutions		
		Total	Univ.	Col.	Total	Univ.	Col.	Total	Univ.	Col.
1.	President	21%	10%	23%	. . .	. . .	1%	34%	35%	33%
2.	Academic V.P.	16	8	18	. . .	. . .	. . .	32	30	33
3.	Liberal Arts Dean	18	8	21	1	. . .	1	28	23	29
4.	Graduate Dean	10	12	9	1	3	. . .	26	29	24
5.	Librarian	20	10	22	. . .	1	. . .	32	29	32
6.	Business Officer	22	12	24	. . .	1	. . .	34	33	34
7.	Dean of Students	21	11	24	1	. . .	1	34	33	34
8.	Dir. Admissions	21	9	23	. . .	. . .	. . .	32	24	33
9.	Registrar	20	9	22	. . .	. . .	. . .	31	28	31
10.	Dir. Development	25	9	28	. . .	. . .	. . .	34	24	35

TABLE 31: PERIODIC HEALTH EXAMINATION—PERCENT PROVIDED EXAMINATION
Questionnaire Sect. H, Q. 44

		All Institutions		Public Institutions			Private Institutions		
		Total	Univ.	Col.	Total	Univ.	Col.	Total	Univ.	Col.
1.	President	11%	17%	10%	6%	9%	4%	13%	34%	12%
2.	Academic V.P.	10	14	9	9	9	8	12	24	10
3.	Liberal Arts Dean	11	8	12	6	4	8	13	15	13
4.	Graduate Dean	12	13	11	10	7	13	15	24	10
5.	Librarian	9	12	8	7	9	6	10	19	9
6.	Business Officer	8	11	8	7	5	8	9	23	8
7.	Dean of Students	10	10	10	6	5	6	13	21	12
8.	Dir. Admissions	7	8	7	6	6	6	7	1	7
9.	Registrar	9	12	9	8	8	8	10	18	9
10.	Dir. Development	8	16	6	8	8	7	8	28	5

TABLE 32:   HEALTH SERVICE—ANNUAL PHYSICAL EXAMINATION—PERCENT AVAILABLE
            AND PERCENT FREE
Questionnaire Sect. H, Q. 45

		All Institutions			Public Institutions			Private Institutions		
		Total	Univ.	Col.	Total	Univ.	Col.	Total	Univ.	Col.
1.	President—available	12%	15%	12%	10%	8%	12%	13%	30%	12%
2.	—free	9	10	9	6	3	8	11	23	10
3.	Academic V.P.—available	12	17	10	9	14	6	15	24	13
4.	—free	6	6	6	4	5	4	8	11	8
5.	Liberal Arts Dean—available	11	16	10	7	8	7	13	29	11
6.	—free	7	6	7	3	1	4	9	15	8
7.	Graduate Dean—available	12	21	7	9	16	4	18	31	10
8.	—free	6	8	5	3	4	3	10	16	8
9.	Librarian—available	8	10	8	6	5	7	9	21	8
10.	—free	4	5	4	3	1	4	5	12	5
11.	Business Officer—available	9	13	9	6	6	6	11	27	10
12.	—free	5	6	5	2	. . .	3	7	18	6
13.	Dean of Students—available	10	13	10	8	11	6	11	16	11
14.	—free	6	5	7	3	2	3	8	9	8
15.	Dir. Admissions—available	11	17	10	9	12	7	12	24	10
16.	—free	5	4	5	2	. . .	4	6	9	6
17.	Registrar—available	9	14	9	8	7	9	10	26	9
18.	—free	5	5	5	2	. . .	3	6	15	6
19.	Dir. Development—available	10	18	8	10	12	9	10	28	8
20.	—free	5	8	4	5	5	5	4	13	4

Those who did not respond were treated as if the service was neither available nor free.

TABLE 33:   HEALTH SERVICE—DOCTOR'S CONSULTATION—PERCENT AVAILABLE AND
            PERCENT FREE
Questionnaire Sect. H, Q. 45

		All Institutions			Public Institutions			Private Institutions		
		Total	Univ.	Col.	Total	Univ.	Col.	Total	Univ.	Col.
1.	President—available	32%	35%	31%	25%	26%	24%	35%	55%	33%
2.	—free	20	21	20	15	13	16	23	36	22
3.	Academic V.P.—available	26	24	27	15	17	14	36	38	36
4.	—free	13	11	14	7	5	8	19	27	18
5.	Liberal Arts Dean—available	25	23	26	13	13	13	31	41	30
6.	—free	14	9	16	4	. . .	7	19	24	18
7.	Graduate Dean—available	28	26	28	20	18	20	39	40	39
8.	—free	14	9	17	11	5	15	18	16	20
9.	Librarian—available	23	18	23	18	12	21	25	30	24
10.	—free	13	11	13	10	6	11	14	21	14
11.	Business Officer—available	22	22	22	15	12	16	25	41	24
12.	—free	13	11	13	7	2	10	15	27	14
13.	Dean of Students—available	27	21	28	18	12	21	31	37	31
14.	—free	16	10	18	10	2	13	20	26	19
15.	Dir. Admissions—available	28	27	28	21	16	23	31	42	30
16.	—free	15	14	15	12	6	16	16	27	15
17.	Registrar—available	27	28	27	19	17	19	31	49	29
18.	—free	14	15	14	9	7	10	17	28	16
19.	Dir. Development—available	27	31	26	23	25	22	28	38	27
20.	—free	13	12	13	11	5	15	14	23	13

Those who did not respond were treated as if the service was neither available nor free.

TABLE 34: HEALTH SERVICE—EMERGENCY MEDICAL TREATMENT—PERCENT AVAILABLE
AND PERCENT FREE
Questionnaire Sect. H, Q. 45

		All Institutions			Public Institutions			Private Institutions		
		Total	Univ.	Col.	Total	Univ.	Col.	Total	Univ.	Col.
1.	President—available	59%	70%	57%	60%	68%	57%	58%	75%	57%
2.	—free	39	43	38	42	41	43	37	48	37
3.	Academic V.P.—available	62	63	62	61	67	57	63	54	65
4.	—free	44	38	46	40	37	42	47	41	48
5.	Liberal Arts Dean—available	58	61	57	56	57	56	59	68	58
6.	—free	37	35	37	36	31	40	37	44	36
7.	Graduate Dean—available	60	60	60	59	55	61	62	69	58
8.	—free	36	30	39	36	30	41	34	29	38
9.	Librarian—available	54	57	54	54	56	53	54	58	54
10.	—free	37	38	37	39	38	40	36	37	35
11.	Business Officer—available	62	68	61	61	65	59	63	75	61
12.	—free	43	40	43	40	33	43	44	55	43
13.	Dean of Students—available	57	62	56	59	63	57	56	60	56
14.	—free	39	35	40	40	30	45	39	47	38
15.	Dir. Admissions—available	55	56	55	52	46	55	57	71	55
16.	—free	31	29	32	33	19	39	31	42	30
17.	Registrar—available	53	58	52	53	51	54	53	72	51
18.	—free	32	32	32	31	25	34	33	44	32
19.	Dir. Development—available	57	62	56	59	56	61	57	72	55
20.	—free	36	33	37	35	27	40	37	41	36

Those who did not respond were treated as if the service was neither available nor free.

TABLE 35: HEALTH SERVICE—REGULAR MEDICAL TREATMENT—PERCENT AVAILABLE
AND PERCENT FREE
Questionnaire Sect. H, Q. 45

		All Institutions			Public Institutions			Private Institutions		
		Total	Univ.	Col.	Total	Univ.	Col.	Total	Univ.	Col.
1.	President—available	17%	21%	16%	9%	11%	7%	21%	41%	20%
2.	—free	9	7	10	3	2	4	12	18	12
3.	Academic V.P.—available	14	19	13	8	16	3	20	24	20
4.	—free	4	4	4	1	2	1	7	8	6
5.	Liberal Arts Dean—available	14	16	13	6	9	4	18	27	16
6.	—free	6	4	6	1	1	. . .	9	10	8
7.	Graduate Dean—available	12	14	10	7	12	3	19	18	20
8.	—free	4	2	5	1	1	1	8	4	10
9.	Librarian—available	14	10	14	8	5	10	16	21	16
10.	—free	6	4	6	2	. . .	3	8	12	8
11.	Business Officer—available	12	11	12	5	6	5	16	20	15
12.	—free	5	2	5	0	. . .	1	7	7	7
13.	Dean of Students—available	17	12	18	8	10	6	22	16	22
14.	—free	9	2	10	2	. . .	3	12	7	12
15.	Dir. Admissions—available	15	12	16	8	7	8	18	20	18
16.	—free	4	3	5	1	. . .	1	6	7	6
17.	Registrar—available	14	12	15	7	6	8	18	23	17
18.	—free	6	4	6	. . .	. . .	. . .	8	10	8
19.	Dir. Development—available	13	16	12	8	12	5	14	23	14
20.	—free	5	3	5	1	. . .	1	6	8	6

Those who did not respond were treated as if the service was neither available nor free.

TABLE 36: HEALTH SERVICE—INFIRMARY BED—PERCENT AVAILABLE AND PERCENT FREE
Questionnaire Sect. H, Q. 45

	All Institutions			Public Institutions			Private Institutions		
	Total	Univ.	Col.	Total	Univ.	Col.	Total	Univ.	Col.
1. President—available	16%	18%	16%	12%	14%	11%	18%	25%	18%
2. —free	11	6	11	5	3	6	13	11	13
3. Academic V.P.—available	13	14	12	9	13	7	16	16	16
4. —free	6	2	8	4	1	6	9	5	9
5. Liberal Arts Dean—available	15	14	15	9	9	8	17	22	17
6. —free	10	6	10	4	1	6	12	15	12
7. Graduate Dean—available	12	16	10	9	13	6	18	20	16
8. —free	6	7	4	3	7	1	9	9	9
9. Librarian—available	14	8	15	7	4	9	17	16	17
10. —free	8	2	10	5	...	8	10	7	10
11. Business Officer—available	12	9	12	9	7	10	13	11	13
12. —free	8	2	9	5	...	7	9	5	10
13. Dean of Students—available	14	12	15	8	11	6	17	14	18
14. —free	9	3	10	2	...	3	12	9	12
15. Dir. Admissions—available	16	14	16	8	9	7	19	22	19
16. —free	9	3	10	2	...	4	12	7	12
17. Registrar—available	14	9	15	7	6	8	17	15	18
18. —free	8	2	9	2	...	3	11	5	12
19. Dir. Development—available	13	17	12	11	14	9	14	23	13
20. —free	7	4	8	4	2	5	9	8	9

Those who did not respond were treated as if the service was neither available nor free.

TABLE 37: BASIC GROUP HOSPITAL-SURGICAL-MEDICAL PLAN—PERCENT COVERED
            UNDER VARIOUS PAYMENT ARRANGEMENTS
Questionnaire Sect. H, Q. 46

	All Institutions			Public Institutions			Private Institutions		
	Total	Univ.	Col.	Total	Univ.	Col.	Total	Univ.	Col.
Business Officer									
1. Percent covered	89%	90%	88%	95%	89%	98%	85%	93%	85%
When covered:									
2. Institution pays cost	19	10	21	6	8	5	26	12	27
3. Cost shared	36	38	36	40	38	41	34	37	34
4. Individual pays cost	41	46	40	50	47	51	37	46	36
5. Institution pays for dependents' coverage	5	3	6	0	1	...	8	5	8
6. Dependents' coverage cost shared	26	29	25	26	29	25	26	29	25
7. Individual pays for dependents' coverage	59	59	59	66	60	68	55	56	55

Since this is a group coverage, the replies were relatively uniform and the business officer was picked as typical. If the non-response had been eliminated, these percentages would be somewhat higher.

TABLE 38: GROUP MAJOR-MEDICAL EXPENSE INSURANCE PLAN—PERCENT COVERED
UNDER VARIOUS PAYMENT ARRANGEMENTS
Questionnaire Sect. H, Q. 47

	All Institutions			Public Institutions			Private Institutions		
	Total	Univ.	Col.	Total	Univ.	Col.	Total	Univ.	Col.
Business Officer									
1. Percent covered	78%	92%	75%	91%	94%	90%	71%	89%	70%
When covered:									
2. Institution pays cost	33	27	35	9	18	4	48	44	48
3. Cost shared	39	42	38	36	43	33	40	41	40
4. Individual pays cost	24	25	24	50	32	59	9	10	9
5. Institution pays for dependents' coverage	16	10	18	2	6	...	25	18	25
6. Dependents' coverage cost shared	30	33	29	25	32	21	32	33	32
7. Individual pays for dependents' coverage	46	48	45	66	52	73	34	41	33

Since this is a group coverage, the replies were relatively uniform and the business officer was picked as typical. If the non-response had been eliminated, these percentages would be somewhat higher.

TABLE 39: LONG-TERM TOTAL AND PERMANENT DISABILITY INCOME PLANS—
PERCENT COVERED UNDER VARIOUS TYPES
Questionnaire Sect. J, Q. 52

	All Institutions			Public Institutions			Private Institutions		
	Total	Univ.	Col.	Total	Univ.	Col.	Total	Univ.	Col.
Business Officer									
1. Percent plan in effect	43%	64%	39%	50%	68%	40%	40%	57%	38%
When plan in effect:									
2. Public retirement system	25	38	20	64	54	73	1	4	1
3. TIAA	41	22	47	7	11	3	61	48	63
4. Commercial	24	21	25	18	21	16	27	20	28
5. Other	9	17	6	8	13	5	10	28	7

Since this is a group coverage, the replies were relatively uniform and the business officer was picked as typical. If the non-responses had been eliminated, these percentages would be somewhat higher.

TABLE 40: LONG-TERM TOTAL AND PERMANENT DISABILITY INCOME PLANS—
PERCENT OF OFFICERS COVERED (BY SALARY LEVEL)
Questionnaire Sect. J, Q. 52

	Salary								
	5,000-9,999	10,000-14,999	15,000-19,999	20,000-24,999	25,000-29,999	30,000-34,999	35,000-39,999	40,000-44,999	45,000-49,999
1. President	44%	27%	28%	45%	53%	55%	78%	53%	60%
2. Academic V.P.	25	34	41	55	60	43	50	...	...
3. Liberal Arts Dean	23	25	41	54	56	100	...	...	...
4. Graduate Dean	33	41	49	36	62	...	...	...	...
5. Librarian	32	41	55	80	50	...	...	...	...
6. Business Officer	24	40	54	66	81	56	67	...	...
7. Dean of Students	26	37	38	52	100	...	...	...	...
8. Dir. Admissions	32	40	51	...	...	...	...	...	...
9. Registrar	36	45	58	...	...	...	...	...	...
10. Dir. Development	25	39	48	54	57	60	...	...	...

This includes disability provisions of public employee and state teacher retirement systems, of the TIAA disability income plan, and of commercial insurance companies' plans. Percentages are based on those whose salaries were reported. Those whose salaries were below $5,000 were omitted.

TABLE 41: LENGTH OF VACATION ENTITLEMENT AND LENGTH OF VACATION TAKEN IN 1965 —
PERCENT WITH VARIOUS LENGTHS
Questionnaire Sect. K, Q. 59, 60

	All Institutions			Public Institutions			Private Institutions		
	Total	Univ.	Col.	Total	Univ.	Col.	Total	Univ.	Col.
President—Entitlement									
1. 1-3 weeks	14%	5%	16%	22%	8%	30%	10%	...	11%
2. 4 weeks or 1 month	42	58	38	53	69	44	36	36	36
3. Over 1 month	4	6	4	3	7	1	5	5	5
4. No stated policy	37	28	38	21	16	24	44	55	43
President—Taken									
5. 1 day to 3 weeks	52	43	53	53	46	56	51	36	52
6. 4 weeks or 1 month	21	29	19	22	32	16	21	23	21
7. Over 1 month	9	13	9	7	10	5	11	20	10
8. No vacation reported	18	15	19	19	12	22	18	20	17
Academic V.P.—Entitlement									
9. 1-3 weeks	21	8	26	30	10	43	13	3	14
10. 4 weeks or 1 month	57	73	52	58	76	47	57	68	55
11. Over 1 month	5	6	5	5	7	4	5	3	6
12. No stated policy	12	11	13	5	5	5	19	24	19
Academic V.P.—Taken									
13. 1 day to 3 weeks	56	57	56	65	64	66	48	41	49
14. 4 weeks or 1 month	19	21	18	13	17	9	25	30	24
15. Over 1 month	8	8	8	6	6	6	10	16	9
16. No vacation reported	17	13	18	17	13	19	17	14	18
Liberal Arts Dean—Entitlement									
17. 1-3 weeks	20	9	23	24	11	33	19	7	20
18. 4 weeks or 1 month	51	76	45	60	77	49	46	73	43
19. Over 1 month	5	6	5	5	7	4	5	5	5
20. No stated policy	18	6	21	7	3	10	23	12	24
Liberal Arts Dean—Taken									
21. 1 day to 3 weeks	50	47	51	57	53	59	47	34	49
22. 4 weeks or 1 month	20	28	18	18	21	16	20	39	18
23. Over 1 month	9	13	8	10	9	10	9	20	8
24. No vacation reported	21	13	23	15	16	15	23	7	25
Graduate Dean—Entitlement									
25. 1-3 weeks	21	7	30	26	9	39	13	2	19
26. 4 weeks or 1 month	55	74	43	59	78	45	50	67	40
27. Over 1 month	9	10	8	7	9	6	11	11	11
28. No stated policy	10	8	11	6	3	8	17	18	16
Graduate Dean—Taken									
29. 1 day to 3 weeks	50	50	50	52	53	51	46	44	48
30. 4 weeks or 1 month	22	25	20	20	17	21	25	38	18
31. Over 1 month	10	9	10	11	12	11	8	4	10
32. No vacation reported	19	17	20	17	18	17	21	13	25
Librarian—Entitlement									
33. 1-3 weeks	15	11	16	20	11	24	13	12	13
34. 4 weeks or 1 month	52	68	48	57	72	50	49	60	48
35. Over 1 month	16	14	16	12	15	11	17	14	17
36. No stated policy	10	6	11	5	1	7	12	14	12
Librarian—Taken									
37. 1 day to 3 weeks	38	54	35	46	57	41	34	47	33
38. 4 weeks or 1 month	28	32	27	26	29	25	28	37	27
39. Over 1 month	16	10	18	14	10	16	18	12	18
40. No vacation reported	18	4	21	14	4	19	20	5	22

(continued on next page)

TABLE 41 (continued)

	All Institutions			Public Institutions			Private Institutions		
	Total	Univ.	Col.	Total	Univ.	Col.	Total	Univ.	Col.
Business Officer—Entitlement									
41. 1-3 weeks	27%	11%	30%	32%	13%	42%	24%	7%	26%
42. 4 weeks or 1 month	54	68	51	57	72	50	53	61	52
43. Over 1 month	5	10	4	5	12	2	5	7	5
44. No stated policy	9	9	9	3	2	3	12	20	12
Business Officer—Taken									
45. 1 day to 3 weeks	65	60	66	72	71	73	62	41	64
46. 4 weeks or 1 month	13	17	12	8	13	6	15	23	14
47. Over 1 month	6	10	5	6	7	6	5	16	4
48. No vacation reported	17	13	17	13	9	15	18	20	18
Dean of Students—Entitlement									
49. 1-3 weeks	23	14	25	29	14	37	20	14	21
50. 4 weeks or 1 month	52	74	48	57	78	47	50	67	48
51. Over 1 month	7	7	6	5	6	5	7	9	7
52. No stated policy	12	4	14	6	2	8	15	7	16
Dean of Students—Taken									
53. 1 day to 3 weeks	47	52	46	59	54	62	41	49	40
54. 4 weeks or 1 month	23	27	22	18	26	14	25	28	25
55. Over 1 month	9	10	9	8	7	8	9	14	9
56. No vacation reported	22	11	24	15	12	17	25	9	26
Dir. Admissions—Entitlement									
57. 1-3 weeks	26	16	27	30	12	38	24	22	24
58. 4 weeks or 1 month	59	73	57	61	76	53	59	69	58
59. Over 1 month	4	6	3	4	7	3	3	4	3
60. No stated policy	7	2	8	2	. . .	3	9	4	10
Dir. Admissions—Taken									
61. 1 day to 3 weeks	54	55	54	60	61	59	52	47	53
62. 4 weeks or 1 month	25	27	24	17	21	16	28	36	27
63. Over 1 month	6	8	6	8	7	8	6	9	5
64. No vacation reported	15	10	16	15	10	18	14	9	15
Registrar—Entitlement									
65. 1-3 weeks	26	10	30	27	7	37	26	15	27
66. 4 weeks or 1 month	54	82	49	63	83	52	51	79	48
67. Over 1 month	3	7	3	5	10	2	3	3	3
68. No stated policy	10	1	11	4	. . .	6	12	3	13
Registrar—Taken									
69. 1 day to 3 weeks	58	61	57	64	68	62	55	49	56
70. 4 weeks or 1 month	19	23	18	11	14	10	22	38	21
71. Over 1 month	8	9	8	10	8	10	7	10	7
72. No vacation reported	16	7	17	15	10	18	16	3	17
Dir. Development—Entitlement									
73. 1-3 weeks	26	17	28	33	19	43	24	15	25
74. 4 weeks or 1 month	60	70	58	57	71	46	61	69	60
75. Over 1 month	5	6	4	4	5	4	5	8	4
76. No stated policy	6	2	7	3	. . .	5	7	5	8
Dir. Development—Taken									
77. 1 day to 3 weeks	55	59	54	60	61	59	54	56	53
78. 4 weeks or 1 month	23	18	24	13	15	12	26	23	26
79. Over 1 month	5	7	5	9	10	7	4	3	4
80. No vacation reported	17	15	18	18	14	22	17	18	17

The "No Responses" are not shown.

"No vacation reported" consists chiefly of persons who took no vacation. There are some "No Responses" in this group and there are some persons serving their first year in the position.

TABLE 42: LEAVES OF ABSENCE WITH OR WITHOUT PAY FROM THE COLLEGE OR UNIVERSITY—
PERCENT ELIGIBLE
Questionnaire Sect. L, Q. 62

	All Institutions			Public Institutions			Private Institutions		
	Total	Univ.	Col.	Total	Univ.	Col.	Total	Univ.	Col.
President									
1. Sabbatical with pay	16%	17%	16%	24%	21%	26%	12%	9%	13%
2. Research or study with pay	9	11	8	12	12	12	7	9	7
3. Research or study without pay	13	17	12	28	21	31	6	9	5
4. Public service without pay	13	22	11	30	28	31	5	11	4
Academic V.P.									
5. Sabbatical with pay	37	31	39	42	38	45	31	14	35
6. Research or study with pay	23	24	22	28	31	26	18	8	20
7. Research or study without pay	39	41	38	55	50	58	24	19	24
8. Public service without pay	37	44	35	54	53	54	22	22	22
Liberal Arts Dean									
9. Sabbatical with pay	33	41	32	47	52	44	27	20	28
10. Research or study with pay	19	28	17	24	28	22	17	27	16
11. Research or study without pay	37	55	33	62	67	58	26	34	25
12. Public service without pay	34	57	29	61	71	54	22	32	21
Graduate Dean									
13. Sabbatical with pay	49	49	50	51	51	51	46	44	48
14. Research or study with pay	28	25	30	33	26	38	21	22	20
15. Research or study without pay	57	53	59	66	58	72	43	44	43
16. Public service without pay	53	52	54	64	59	68	37	40	35
Librarian									
17. Sabbatical with pay	39	40	38	45	44	46	35	33	36
18. Research or study with pay	24	30	23	29	32	27	22	28	21
19. Research or study without pay	42	57	39	66	67	66	30	37	29
20. Public service without pay	31	52	26	52	60	48	20	37	18
Business Officer									
21. Sabbatical with pay	11	14	10	17	18	17	8	7	8
22. Research or study with pay	7	10	7	13	12	13	5	5	5
23. Research or study without pay	13	17	12	27	22	29	7	9	6
24. Public service without pay	13	24	10	26	28	25	6	16	5
Dean of Students									
25. Sabbatical with pay	28	35	27	43	42	44	21	21	21
26. Research or study with pay	19	23	18	27	27	28	15	16	14
27. Research or study without pay	32	47	29	60	62	60	18	19	18
28. Public service without pay	27	48	22	51	62	46	15	23	14
Dir. Admissions									
29. Sabbatical with pay	21	21	21	37	28	40	15	11	15
30. Research or study with pay	13	12	13	18	15	19	10	7	11
31. Research or study without pay	24	29	23	44	37	48	15	16	14
32. Public service without pay	21	27	20	37	34	38	13	16	13
Registrar									
33. Sabbatical with pay	19	25	18	28	28	28	15	18	15
34. Research or study with pay	13	15	13	20	15	22	11	13	10
35. Research or study without pay	23	28	22	40	30	46	15	26	14
36. Public service without pay	17	26	16	34	30	36	10	21	9
Dir. Development									
37. Sabbatical with pay	15	15	14	30	17	40	9	13	9
38. Research or study with pay	10	17	9	20	20	20	7	13	7
39. Research or study without pay	19	26	18	46	36	54	10	10	10
40. Public service without pay	18	30	16	48	39	54	8	15	7

TABLE 43: LEAVE OF ABSENCE PROVISIONS—PERCENT SAME AS FOR FACULTY
Questionnaire Sect. L, Q. 63

	All Institutions			Public Institutions			Private Institutions		
	Total	Univ.	Col.	Total	Univ.	Col.	Total	Univ.	Col.
President									
1. Same	33%	34%	33%	45%	40%	47%	27%	20%	28%
2. No response	10	6	11	3	3	3	13	11	14
Academic V.P.									
3. Same	57	53	58	70	66	72	44	22	48
4. No response	8	6	8	1	1	1	14	16	14
Liberal Arts Dean									
5. Same	56	62	55	77	76	77	47	37	48
6. No response	12	6	13	1	3	. . .	16	12	17
Graduate Dean									
7. Same	73	72	74	80	78	83	62	62	63
8. No response	6	3	8	2	3	1	13	4	18
Librarian									
9. Same	64	69	63	78	78	79	57	51	58
10. No response	16	6	18	7	4	9	20	12	21
Business Officer									
11. Same	29	25	30	37	33	39	26	11	27
12. No response	10	5	12	4	2	4	14	9	14
Dean of Students									
13. Same	52	54	52	75	68	79	41	28	42
14. No response	15	10	16	4	5	3	21	19	21
Dir. Admissions									
15. Same	42	46	41	64	55	69	32	31	32
16. No response	17	9	19	7	6	7	22	13	23
Registrar									
17. Same	42	45	41	58	49	63	34	36	34
18. No response	20	10	22	12	7	14	24	15	25
Dir. Development									
19. Same	32	28	34	55	34	70	25	18	26
20. No response	11	3	13	5	. . .	9	14	8	14

TABLE 44: LEAVE OF ABSENCE (OTHER THAN FOR SICK LEAVE)—PERCENT HAVING TAKEN LEAVE CLASSIFIED BY LENGTH OF SERVICE
Questionnaire Sect. L, Q. 65

	All Institutions			Public Institutions			Private Institutions		
	Total	Univ.	Col.	Total	Univ.	Col.	Total	Univ.	Col.
President									
1. 2 to 5 years	7%	7%	8%	13%	7%	16%	5%	8%	5%
2. 6 to 10 years	15	10	16	18	14	20	14	. . .	14
3. 11 to 15 years	27	29	27	19	20	19	31	44	29
4. 16 years or over	36	22	39	38	23	44	35	20	37
Academic V.P.									
5. 2 to 5 years	7	6	7	6	8	5	7	. . .	8
6. 6 to 10 years	19	10	23	21	7	27	18	12	20
7. 11 to 15 years	35	40	35	33	40	31	38	. . .	38
8. 16 years or over	30	. . .	31	27	. . .	29	33	. . .	33
Liberal Arts Dean									
9. 2 to 5 years	9	6	10	8	11	7	10	. . .	11
10. 6 to 10 years	20	29	18	21	29	16	20	29	19
11. 11 to 15 years	21	27	20	15	18	11	25	50	22
12. 16 years or over	28	30	27	21	38	9	31	. . .	33
Graduate Dean									
13. 2 to 5 years	12	18	9	10	15	7	16	22	13
14. 6 to 10 years	18	13	23	13	11	14	25	14	33
15. 11 to 15 years	38	27	47	39	17	50	38	40	33
16. 16 years or over	53	38	64	47	38	57	75	. . .	75
Librarian									
17. 2 to 5 years	9	4	10	5	6	4	11	. . .	12
18. 6 to 10 years	23	27	22	25	33	21	21	14	22
19. 11 to 15 years	35	42	33	41	36	44	32	50	29
20. 16 years or over	45	52	43	58	58	58	38	38	38
Business Officer									
21. 2 to 5 years	9	6	9	8	8	8	9	. . .	9
22. 6 to 10 years	7	11	7	8	17	3	7	. . .	8
23. 11 to 15 years	4	7	3	6	7	5	3	7	2
24. 16 years or over	12	5	13	10	7	11	13	. . .	14
Dean of Students									
25. 2 to 5 years	10	9	11	10	6	12	10	14	10
26. 6 to 10 years	17	9	18	22	8	28	14	10	15
27. 11 to 15 years	25	25	24	27	31	24	23	. . .	25
28. 16 years or over	33	18	37	36	14	47	30	25	30
Dir. Admissions									
29. 2 to 5 years	6	6	6	7	10	5	6	. . .	6
30. 6 to 10 years	15	21	14	13	21	9	17	20	16
31. 11 to 15 years	16	17	15	6	20	. . .	20	14	21
32. 16 years or over	16	6	19	21	8	33	14	. . .	15
Registrar									
33. 2 to 5 years	8	6	8	9	5	10	8	9	8
34. 6 to 10 years	12	17	11	21	27	19	8	. . .	9
35. 11 to 15 years	17	11	18	14	9	17	18	14	19
36. 16 years or over	20	9	22	14	13	15	22	. . .	23
Dir. Development									
37. 2 to 5 years	4	2	4	4	4	3	4	. . .	4
38. 6 to 10 years	6	. . .	6	4	. . .	6	6	. . .	6
39. 11 to 15 years	4	13	. . .	13	25	. . .	. . .	. . .	. . .
40. 16 years or over	12	. . .	22	13	. . .	33	11	. . .	17

TABLE 45: INSTITUTION-OWNED HOUSING—PERCENT OCCUPYING RENT-FREE
Questionnaire Sect. M, Q. 67

	All Institutions			Public Institutions			Private Institutions		
	Total	Univ.	Col.	Total	Univ.	Col.	Total	Univ.	Col.
1. President	71%	81%	69%	71%	88%	62%	71%	68%	71%
2. Academic V.P.	11	8	12	2	3	1	19	19	20
3. Liberal Arts Dean	16	6	18	1	...	1	23	17	24
4. Graduate Dean	3	2	4	1	1	...	7	4	9
5. Librarian	8	2	9	...	...	...	12	7	12
6. Business Officer	11	6	13	2	1	3	16	14	16
7. Dean of Students	15	10	16	4	5	3	21	19	21
8. Dir. Admissions	6	2	7	...	...	...	8	4	9
9. Registrar	6	...	8	...	...	...	9	...	10
10. Dir. Development	3	3	3	1	...	1	4	8	3

TABLE 46: PRESIDENT'S HOUSE—PERCENT CONSIDERED ADEQUATE FOR OFFICIAL
ENTERTAINING AND PERCENT PROVIDING OVERNIGHT GUEST ACCOMMODATIONS
Questionnaire Sect. M, Q. 68, 69

	All Institutions			Public Institutions			Private Institutions		
	Total	Univ.	Col.	Total	Univ.	Col.	Total	Univ.	Col.
1. Considered adequate for official entertaining	75%	77%	74%	77%	78%	77%	73%	74%	73%
2. Provides overnight guest accommodations	68	63	69	65	64	65	69	58	70

TABLE 47: PRESIDENT'S HOUSE—PERCENT OF INSTITUTIONS PROVIDING HOUSING (BOTH
RENT-FREE AND OTHERWISE) AND PERCENT WHICH ALSO PROVIDE VARIOUS ITEMS
Questionnaire Sect. M, Q. 70

	All Institutions			Public Institutions			Private Institutions		
	Total	Univ.	Col.	Total	Univ.	Col.	Total	Univ.	Col.
1. Number of houses provided	636	112	524	216	81	135	420	31	389
2. Percent of institutions providing houses	78%	84%	77%	81%	90%	76%	77%	70%	78%
3. Furniture—all	19	21	18	13	19	10	22	29	21
4. Furniture—in part	61	73	59	75	75	75	55	68	53
5. Utilities	90	96	88	97	98	97	86	94	85
6. Heating	91	96	90	98	98	99	87	94	86
7. Air conditioning	48	62	45	58	59	57	43	68	41
8. Maintenance and repair	96	98	96	99	99	99	95	97	95
9. Grounds maintenance	91	97	90	97	98	97	88	97	87
10. Garage	86	96	83	95	98	94	80	90	80
11. Telephone—local	71	79	70	81	78	84	66	81	65
12. Maid service	53	81	47	61	79	50	49	87	46
13. Houseman service	21	41	17	23	41	12	20	42	18
14. Cook	27	52	21	25	48	12	27	61	25
15. Food (other than for official entertainment)	14	7	15	5	1	7	18	23	18

TABLE 48: PRESIDENTS OCCUPYING INSTITUTIONALLY PROVIDED HOUSING—
PERCENT PREFERENCES AS TO PROVIDING OWN HOUSING
IF REASONABLE FINANCIAL ADJUSTMENTS WERE MADE
Questionnaire Sect. M, Q. 71

	All Institutions			Public Institutions			Private Institutions		
	Total	Univ.	Col.	Total	Univ.	Col.	Total	Univ.	Col.
1. Do not prefer to provide own housing	60%	69%	59%	55%	63%	50%	63%	84%	61%
2. Prefer to provide own housing	17	16	17	28	19	34	11	10	11
3. Don't know	14	9	16	13	12	13	15	...	16
4. No response	8	6	9	4	6	2	10	6	11

TABLE 49: ENTERTAINMENT ALLOWANCE—PERCENT PROVIDED ALLOWANCE
Questionnaire Sect. N, Q. 73

	All Institutions			Public Institutions			Private Institutions		
	Total	Univ.	Col.	Total	Univ.	Col.	Total	Univ.	Col.
1. President	66%	81%	63%	60%	80%	49%	69%	84%	68%
2. Academic V.P.	34	43	31	19	34	10	48	65	45
3. Liberal Arts Dean	32	34	31	13	19	10	40	63	37
4. Graduate Dean	24	36	16	13	22	7	39	58	29
5. Librarian	10	18	9	6	9	5	12	35	10
6. Business Officer	19	29	17	11	23	4	24	41	22
7. Dean of Students	30	45	27	18	36	9	36	63	33
8. Dir. Admissions	21	14	23	2	1	3	30	33	30
9. Registrar	7	11	6	2	3	1	9	26	7
10. Dir. Development	48	59	46	27	46	13	56	79	53

TABLE 50: OFFICIAL ENTERTAINMENT DURING 1965—PERCENT SPENDING OWN FUNDS
Questionnaire Sect. N, Q. 75

	All Institutions			Public Institutions			Private Institutions		
	Total	Univ.	Col.	Total	Univ.	Col.	Total	Univ.	Col.
1. President	50%	54%	50%	74%	68%	76%	39%	25%	40%
2. Academic V.P.	60	70	56	74	83	69	46	41	47
3. Liberal Arts Dean	46	67	41	68	85	57	36	34	36
4. Graduate Dean	53	62	48	63	74	54	40	42	39
5. Librarian	31	61	25	49	68	38	22	47	20
6. Business Officer	38	56	34	58	71	51	28	27	29
7. Dean of Students	50	68	46	69	81	63	41	42	40
8. Dir. Admissions	31	45	28	41	51	37	27	36	26
9. Registrar	18	35	15	28	34	25	13	36	11
10. Dir. Development	46	57	44	62	66	59	41	44	41

TABLE 51: USE OF THE INSTITUTION'S FOOD SERVICES FOR OFFICIAL ENTERTAINING—
PERCENT FREE AND PERCENT CHARGE
Questionnaire Sect. N, Q. 77

	All Institutions			Public Institutions			Private Institutions		
	Total	Univ.	Col.	Total	Univ.	Col.	Total	Univ.	Col.
President									
1. In home—no charge	46%	49%	45%	43%	49%	40%	47%	48%	47%
2. In home—charge	15	22	14	19	23	17	13	20	12
3. On campus—no charge	69	63	70	62	62	62	72	66	72
4. On campus—charge	16	24	15	22	24	21	14	23	13
Academic V.P.									
5. In home—no charge	8	10	8	4	9	...	13	11	13
6. In home—charge	16	20	15	18	21	17	14	16	14
7. On campus—no charge	52	52	51	43	49	39	60	59	60
8. On campus—charge	28	29	28	37	33	40	20	22	20
Liberal Arts Dean									
9. In home—no charge	10	9	10	2	3	2	14	20	13
10. In home—charge	10	12	9	13	15	12	8	7	8
11. On campus—no charge	47	46	47	31	32	31	54	71	52
12. On campus—charge	26	37	23	40	47	36	19	20	19
Graduate Dean									
13. In home—no charge	5	7	3	2	4	1	8	11	6
14. In home—charge	10	13	8	12	13	11	8	13	5
15. On campus—no charge	42	44	41	32	34	30	57	60	55
16. On campus—charge	33	36	31	41	43	40	22	24	20
Librarian									
17. In home—no charge	3	2	4	1	1	1	5	5	5
18. In home—charge	7	8	7	8	7	8	7	9	6
19. On campus—no charge	32	32	32	20	23	18	38	49	37
20. On campus—charge	31	43	29	48	55	44	23	21	23
Business Officer									
21. In home—no charge	5	8	5	3	6	2	6	11	6
22. In home—charge	10	17	9	11	20	7	10	14	9
23. On campus—no charge	45	38	46	32	29	34	50	55	50
24. On campus—charge	23	33	21	32	38	29	19	23	19
Dean of Students									
25. In home—no charge	10	10	10	4	6	3	13	16	12
26. In home—charge	15	26	12	19	28	14	13	21	12
27. On campus— no charge	44	35	46	27	26	28	52	53	52
28. On campus—charge	29	43	26	43	49	40	22	30	21
Dir. Admissions									
29. In home—no charge	5	3	6	1	3	1	7	2	7
30. In home—charge	7	11	6	6	7	6	7	16	6
31. On campus—no charge	51	38	54	31	22	35	60	60	60
32. On campus—charge	20	33	17	30	40	25	15	22	14
Registrar									
33. In home—no charge	3	...	4	1	...	1	4	...	4
34. In home—charge	7	13	6	7	14	4	7	10	7
35. On campus—no charge	29	25	30	18	17	18	34	41	33
36. On campus—charge	27	40	24	38	48	33	22	26	21
Dir. Development									
37. In home—no charge	14	14	14	8	15	2	16	13	17
38. In home—charge	6	11	5	11	14	10	4	8	4
39. On campus—no charge	64	55	66	48	44	50	69	72	69
40. On campus—charge	15	27	13	26	32	22	11	18	11

Those who did not respond were treated as not having the service available.

TABLE 52: CLUB MEMBERSHIP—PERCENT PROVIDED MEMBERSHIP BY INSTITUTION
Questionnaire Sect. N, Q. 79

	All Institutions			Public Institutions			Private Institutions		
	Total	Univ.	Col.	Total	Univ.	Col.	Total	Univ.	Col.
1. President	38%	45%	37%	19%	29%	13%	48%	77%	46%
2. Academic V.P.	10	11	10	5	8	3	15	19	14
3. Liberal Arts Dean	10	7	11	2	1	3	14	17	13
4. Graduate Dean	4	6	3	...	...	...	10	16	8
5. Librarian	4	4	4	0	1	...	6	9	5
6. Business Officer	16	16	16	5	7	4	21	32	20
7. Dean of Students	9	4	10	1	1	1	13	9	13
8. Dir. Admissions	8	3	9	2	3	2	11	4	11
9. Registrar	4	3	4	2	1	3	5	5	5
10. Dir. Development	30	36	29	13	19	9	36	62	33

TABLE 53: REIMBURSEMENT FOR RENTAL OF AUTOMOBILES USED ON INSTITUTIONAL BUSINESS—
PERCENT REIMBURSED
Questionnaire Sect. O, Q. 82

	All Institutions			Public Institutions			Private Institutions		
	Total	Univ.	Col.	Total	Univ.	Col.	Total	Univ.	Col.
President									
1. Reimbursed	71%	81%	69%	67%	80%	60%	74%	84%	73%
2. Rented cars not used	18	13	19	22	16	25	17	9	17
Academic V.P.									
3. Reimbursed	69	86	63	68	88	55	71	81	69
4. Rented cars not used	20	7	25	21	8	28	19	5	22
Liberal Arts Dean									
5. Reimbursed	61	83	56	55	81	38	64	85	62
6. Rented cars not used	24	14	27	30	16	40	22	10	23
Graduate Dean									
7. Reimbursed	56	72	45	52	72	37	62	71	56
8. Rented cars not used	25	17	31	27	14	37	22	20	23
Librarian									
9. Reimbursed	38	61	34	35	57	24	40	67	37
10. Rented cars not used	32	18	35	35	23	41	31	7	33
Business Officer									
11. Reimbursed	71	91	67	66	89	54	74	95	72
12. Rented cars not used	19	7	21	24	10	32	16	2	18
Dean of Students									
13. Reimbursed	57	69	54	51	73	40	59	63	59
14. Rented cars not used	27	17	29	30	17	37	25	16	26
Dir. Admissions									
15. Reimbursed	66	75	64	49	61	43	74	96	71
16. Rented cars not used	21	16	22	31	24	35	17	4	18
Registrar									
17. Reimbursed	48	65	45	43	58	35	50	77	48
18. Rented cars not used	30	26	30	36	34	37	27	13	28
Dir. Development									
19. Reimbursed	78	86	76	65	83	51	83	90	82
20. Rented cars not used	16	9	18	24	8	35	14	10	14

Percentages not shown are for "No Response" and "No Reimbursement," the latter being the more numerous.

TABLE 54:   INSTITUTION-OWNED AUTOMOBILE—PERCENT HAVING USE OF
Questionnaire Sect. O, Q. 83

	All Institutions			Public Institutions			Private Institutions		
	Total	Univ.	Col.	Total	Univ.	Col.	Total	Univ.	Col.
1. President	81%	90%	79%	85%	92%	81%	79%	86%	78%
2. Academic V.P.	64	66	63	77	74	78	52	46	53
3. Liberal Arts Dean	56	48	58	66	61	69	51	24	54
4. Graduate Dean	57	54	59	75	70	79	31	27	34
5. Librarian	54	55	54	73	76	72	44	16	47
6. Business Officer	66	75	65	77	84	74	61	59	61
7. Dean of Students	60	51	62	73	69	76	54	16	58
8. Dir. Admissions	61	52	63	75	70	77	55	24	58
9. Registrar	52	53	52	71	72	70	43	18	45
10. Dir. Development	59	58	60	76	71	79	54	38	55

TABLE 55:   INSTITUTION-OWNED AUTOMOBILE—PERCENT SPECIFICALLY ASSIGNED
            AUTOMOBILE
Questionnaire Sect. O, Q. 84

	All Institutions			Public Institutions			Private Institutions		
	Total	Univ.	Col.	Total	Univ.	Col.	Total	Univ.	Col.
1. President	68%	91%	63%	69%	89%	57%	67%	95%	65%
2. Business Officer	15	24	13	10	20	3	18	35	17
3. Dir. Admissions	16	12	17	5	6	5	23	36	22
4. Dir. Development	25	25	25	8	17	3	33	47	32

The number of assigned cars for other positions was relatively small.

TABLE 56: INSTITUTIONAL REIMBURSEMENT OF OFFICER FOR USE OF OWN AUTOMOBILE
ON INSTITUTIONAL BUSINESS—PERCENT OF OFFICERS REIMBURSED
Questionnaire Sect. O, Q. 88

	All Institutions			Public Institutions			Private Institutions		
	Total	Univ.	Col.	Total	Univ.	Col.	Total	Univ.	Col.
President									
1. No reimbursement	5%	6%	5%	5%	8%	3%	5%	2%	6%
2. Own auto not used	27	40	25	21	36	13	30	50	29
3. Reimbursement made	57	48	58	74	57	82	48	30	50
4. No response	11	6	12	1	...	1	16	18	16
Academic V.P.									
5. No reimbursement	3	2	3	2	1	2	4	5	3
6. Own auto not used	6	7	5	2	2	2	9	16	7
7. Reimbursement made	86	88	85	96	97	95	76	68	78
8. No response	6	3	7	0	...	1	11	11	11
Liberal Arts Dean									
9. No reimbursement	3	3	3	4	1	6	2	5	2
10. Own auto not used	8	5	8	4	4	4	9	7	9
11. Reimbursement made	76	90	73	91	95	88	69	80	68
12. No response	13	3	16	1	...	1	19	7	20
Graduate Dean									
13. No reimbursement	2	1	3	2	1	2	2	...	4
14. Own auto not used	7	8	7	6	4	7	10	16	6
15. Reimbursement made	83	87	80	91	92	89	71	78	68
16. No response	8	4	11	2	3	2	17	7	23
Librarian									
17. No reimbursement	4	3	4	4	2	4	4	5	4
18. Own auto not used	8	8	8	4	2	4	10	19	9
19. Reimbursement made	76	85	74	92	94	91	68	67	68
20. No response	12	4	14	1	1	1	18	9	19
Business Officer									
21. No reimbursement	2	2	2	1	1	1	2	2	2
22. Own auto not used	8	10	7	4	4	4	9	20	8
23. Reimbursement made	82	86	82	95	94	95	77	70	77
24. No response	8	3	9	0	1	...	12	7	12
Dean of Students									
25. No reimbursement	3	3	4	4	4	4	3	2	3
26. Own auto not used	6	4	6	3	2	3	7	7	7
27. Reimbursement made	79	89	77	91	93	90	74	81	73
28. No response	12	4	13	3	1	3	16	9	17
Dir. Admissions									
29. No reimbursement	1	...	1	1	...	1	1	...	1
30. Own auto not used	7	4	7	3	3	4	8	7	8
31. Reimbursement made	84	93	82	93	94	93	79	91	78
32. No response	9	3	10	2	3	2	11	2	12
Registrar									
33. No reimbursement	3	2	3	2	1	3	3	3	3
34. Own auto not used	9	2	10	6	1	8	10	3	10
35. Reimbursement made	78	95	75	90	97	87	73	92	71
36. No response	10	1	12	1	...	2	15	3	16
Dir. Development									
37. No reimbursement	2	3	2	4	2	5	2	5	2
38. Own auto not used	7	11	6	7	10	5	7	13	6
39. Reimbursement made	88	86	89	88	88	88	88	82	89
40. No response	3	...	3	1	...	2	3	...	3

TABLE 57: REIMBURSEMENT FOR TRAVEL ON OFFICIAL INSTITUTIONAL DUTIES—
PERCENT OF OFFICERS REIMBURSED
Questionnaire Sect. P, Q. 89

	All Institutions			Public Institutions			Private Institutions		
	Total	Univ.	Col.	Total	Univ.	Col.	Total	Univ.	Col.
President									
1. Transportation—in full	94%	96%	93%	94%	94%	93%	94%	98%	93%
2. —in part	2	3	2	6	4	7	1	...	1
3. Hotel—in full	87	80	88	74	71	75	93	98	93
4. —in part	7	13	6	20	20	20	1	...	1
5. Meals—in full	86	81	87	72	72	71	93	98	92
6. —in part	8	13	7	22	19	24	1	...	1
7. Tips—in full	75	68	76	41	53	35	91	98	91
8. —in part	6	8	5	16	12	17	1	...	1
Academic V.P.									
9. Transportation—in full	93	96	92	92	95	91	94	97	93
10. —in part	2	1	3	4	1	7	...	...	...
11. Hotel—in full	79	75	81	64	65	63	94	97	93
12. —in part	14	18	12	29	26	31	...	...	...
13. Meals—in full	76	71	78	59	62	57	92	92	92
14. —in part	17	22	16	34	29	37	2	5	1
15. Tips—in full	64	63	65	37	49	29	89	95	88
16. —in part	9	11	9	18	14	20	1	3	1
Liberal Arts Dean									
17. Transportation—in full	94	97	93	95	96	94	94	100	93
18. —in part	2	1	2	3	1	4	1	...	1
19. Hotel—in full	86	79	87	68	69	67	94	98	94
20. —in part	9	13	7	26	20	30	0	...	1
21. Meals—in full	83	74	85	62	63	62	93	95	92
22. —in part	10	16	9	31	25	35	1	...	1
23. Tips—in full	73	63	76	37	45	32	90	95	89
24. —in part	7	11	5	18	17	19	1	...	1
Graduate Dean									
25. Transportation—in full	92	96	90	91	93	88	95	100	93
26. —in part	4	2	5	7	3	10	...	...	...
27. Hotel—in full	76	75	77	63	62	64	94	98	93
28. —in part	16	17	16	28	26	29	...	...	...
29. Meals—in full	73	74	72	60	62	59	91	96	89
30. —in part	19	17	20	30	26	33	2	2	3
31. Tips—in full	56	57	56	34	37	31	89	91	88
32. —in part	14	12	15	22	20	24	2	...	3
Librarian									
33. Transportation—in full	83	96	80	87	95	83	81	98	79
34. —in part	6	4	7	9	5	11	5	2	5
35. Hotel—in full	72	78	71	59	70	53	79	93	77
36. —in part	14	18	13	32	23	36	5	7	5
37. Meals—in full	68	72	67	53	63	47	75	88	74
38. —in part	17	22	16	38	29	43	7	9	7
39. Tips—in full	57	58	56	31	44	25	69	86	67
40. —in part	9	14	8	19	18	19	4	7	4

(continued on next page)

TABLE 57 (continued)

	All Institutions			Public Institutions			Private Institutions		
	Total	Univ.	Col.	Total	Univ.	Col.	Total	Univ.	Col.
Business Officer									
41. Transportation—in full	93%	95%	92%	91%	94%	90%	94%	98%	93%
42. —in part	3	1	3	6	1	9	1	...	1
43. Hotel—in full	85	77	86	67	66	67	94	98	93
44. —in part	9	16	8	27	24	29	1	...	1
45. Meals—in full	82	74	84	61	61	61	93	98	92
46. —in part	12	19	10	33	29	35	1	...	1
47. Tips—in full	73	60	76	36	40	34	91	98	91
48. —in part	6	11	4	14	17	13	1	...	2
Dean of Students									
49. Transportation—in full	93	97	92	91	96	88	94	98	94
50. —in part	3	2	3	6	2	8	1	...	1
51. Hotel—in full	85	74	87	67	63	69	93	95	93
52. —in part	10	20	8	27	30	26	1	2	1
53. Meals—in full	82	70	84	62	58	64	91	93	91
54. —in part	13	23	10	32	33	31	3	5	3
55. Tips—in full	69	59	71	36	42	33	85	91	85
56. —in part	8	11	7	17	17	17	3	...	3
Dir. Admissions									
57. Transportation—in full	93	96	93	93	93	93	94	100	93
58. —in part	2	3	2	5	4	5	1	...	1
59. Hotel—in full	86	79	87	68	64	70	94	100	94
60. —in part	9	15	7	27	25	28	0	...	0
61. Meals—in full	83	76	84	61	60	61	93	100	92
62. —in part	12	18	10	34	30	36	2	...	2
63. Tips—in full	72	60	74	32	36	30	90	96	89
64. —in part	7	13	6	20	19	20	2	2	2
Registrar									
65. Transportation—in full	89	96	87	88	94	85	89	100	88
66. —in part	4	1	4	7	1	12	2	...	3
67. Hotel—in full	80	76	81	63	66	62	88	95	87
68. —in part	12	18	10	30	25	32	3	5	3
69. Meals—in full	78	75	78	59	65	57	86	95	86
70. —in part	13	19	12	34	27	37	4	5	4
71. Tips—in full	63	56	64	27	37	22	79	92	78
72. —in part	8	13	8	19	18	20	3	3	3
Dir. Development									
73. Transportation—in full	96	96	96	89	93	87	98	100	98
74. —in part	3	2	3	8	3	11	1	...	1
75. Hotel—in full	89	82	90	62	69	57	98	100	98
76. —in part	8	13	7	30	22	35	0	...	1
77. Meals—in full	86	78	87	54	63	48	97	100	96
78. —in part	11	17	10	38	29	45	2	...	2
79. Tips—in full	81	69	83	35	49	24	97	100	96
80. —in part	6	8	5	19	14	23	1	...	1

The remaining percentages (not shown) are "No Reimbursement" and "No Response."

The number that reported "No Reimbursement" was much less than the number of "No Responses," except in the matter of "Tips" where in the public institutions somewhat over one-third reported "No Reimbursement" and slightly more than one-tenth made no response.

TABLE 58: REIMBURSEMENT FOR TRAVEL IN CONNECTION WITH OFFICER'S PROFESSIONAL
ACADEMIC FIELD—PERCENT OF OFFICERS REIMBURSED
(The officers who replied that they had "no occasion for such travel" are
excluded from the base.)
Questionnaire Sect. P, Q. 90

	All Institutions			Public Institutions			Private Institutions		
	Total	Univ.	Col.	Total	Univ.	Col.	Total	Univ.	Col.
President									
1. Transportation—in full	68%	77%	67%	73%	76%	72%	66%	78%	65%
2. —in part	7	4	8	7	4	8	7	4	8
3. Hotel—in full	62	64	61	55	57	55	65	78	64
4. —in part	11	10	11	18	13	21	7	4	8
5. Meals—in full	60	65	59	54	59	52	63	78	62
6. —in part	12	9	13	20	11	23	9	4	9
7. Tips—in full	52	52	52	30	39	26	62	78	61
8. —in part	10	5	11	14	6	18	8	4	8
Academic V.P.									
9. Transportation—in full	65	79	61	72	85	64	59	66	58
10. —in part	18	10	21	13	8	16	22	14	24
11. Hotel—in full	48	50	47	44	47	42	52	59	51
12. —in part	28	29	28	33	33	33	24	17	26
13. Meals—in full	45	48	45	40	43	38	50	59	49
14. —in part	31	32	31	36	38	36	26	17	27
15. Tips—in full	37	39	36	25	31	22	48	59	46
16. —in part	21	21	21	21	24	20	21	14	22
Liberal Arts Dean									
17. Transportation—in full	67	78	65	72	81	66	65	74	64
18. —in part	18	11	20	19	7	26	18	18	18
19. Hotel—in full	53	49	53	47	46	47	55	53	56
20. —in part	25	23	26	35	25	42	21	18	21
21. Meals—in full	49	44	50	40	40	39	53	50	53
22. —in part	28	26	28	41	31	48	21	15	22
23. Tips—in full	44	37	46	26	30	24	53	50	53
24. —in part	20	19	20	22	22	22	19	12	19
Graduate Dean									
25. Transportation—in full	69	79	64	66	75	60	74	85	69
26. —in part	15	7	20	19	10	26	10	3	14
27. Hotel—in full	50	52	48	39	41	37	65	72	62
28. —in part	26	21	29	37	32	40	10	3	14
29. Meals—in full	48	50	46	37	40	35	64	69	61
30. —in part	27	22	29	38	34	41	10	3	14
31. Tips—in full	37	40	35	21	26	17	59	64	57
32. —in part	19	15	21	27	22	30	8	3	11
Librarian									
33. Transportation—in full	64	79	61	70	81	64	61	76	59
34. —in part	17	8	19	15	10	18	18	3	19
35. Hotel—in full	50	56	49	44	53	40	53	65	52
36. —in part	24	21	25	35	27	39	19	6	20
37. Meals—in full	46	52	45	39	47	34	50	62	49
38. —in part	28	24	28	40	32	44	21	6	23
39. Tips—in full	37	38	37	21	31	17	45	56	44
40. —in part	18	16	19	22	21	23	16	6	17
Business Officer									
41. Transportation—in full	57	61	57	59	63	58	57	58	57
42. —in part	11	4	13	12	4	16	11	4	12
43. Hotel—in full	50	40	52	41	33	44	55	54	55
44. —in part	16	19	16	26	24	27	11	8	12
45. Meals—in full	48	40	50	38	33	40	54	54	54
46. —in part	18	19	18	29	24	31	12	8	13
47. Tips—in full	43	35	44	23	24	23	53	54	53
48. —in part	12	9	12	11	10	12	12	8	12

(continued on next page)

TABLE 58 (continued)

	All Institutions			Public Institutions			Private Institutions		
	Total	Univ.	Col.	Total	Univ.	Col.	Total	Univ.	Col.
Dean of Students									
49. Transportation—in full	64%	67%	64%	64%	65%	64%	65%	71%	64%
50. —in part	13	13	13	14	13	14	12	13	12
51. Hotel—in full	55	50	56	44	43	44	60	65	60
52. —in part	18	25	17	29	28	29	13	19	13
53. Meals—in full	52	48	53	41	42	41	58	61	58
54. —in part	20	26	18	31	28	33	14	23	13
55. Tips—in full	44	42	45	25	35	19	54	58	54
56. —in part	13	11	13	15	11	18	11	10	11
Dir. Admissions									
57. Transportation—in full	63	71	61	66	75	62	61	65	61
58. —in part	10	8	10	11	10	11	9	6	10
59. Hotel—in full	57	58	57	49	54	46	61	65	61
60. —in part	13	16	13	23	21	24	8	6	9
61. Meals—in full	55	54	55	44	48	43	60	65	60
62. —in part	15	18	14	27	25	28	9	6	9
63. Tips—in full	47	41	48	23	29	20	59	61	58
64. —in part	12	16	11	18	21	17	9	6	9
Registrar									
65. Transportation—in full	56	74	53	65	78	60	51	65	50
66. —in part	12	6	13	9	6	10	14	5	15
67. Hotel—in full	48	55	46	46	55	42	48	55	48
68. —in part	18	20	18	26	24	27	14	10	15
69. Meals—in full	45	52	44	43	51	40	46	55	45
70. —in part	20	22	19	28	27	29	15	10	15
71. Tips—in full	35	36	35	21	31	17	42	50	41
72. —in part	14	12	14	13	14	12	14	5	15
Dir. Development									
73. Transportation—in full	61	62	61	65	59	69	59	67	58
74. —in part	7	2	8	11	3	15	5	...	6
75. Hotel—in full	53	52	53	43	41	45	57	67	56
76. —in part	11	9	12	25	15	30	5	...	6
77. Meals—in full	49	44	50	34	28	36	56	67	54
78. —in part	15	17	15	35	28	38	7	...	7
79. Tips—in full	45	41	46	20	23	19	56	67	55
80. —in part	10	11	10	20	18	22	5	...	6

- -

Percent of all respondents reporting "No occasion for such travel"									
President	31%	40%	30%	31%	40%	27%	31%	39%	31%
Academic V.P.	14	18	12	14	16	12	14	22	12
Liberal Arts Dean	10	13	10	9	11	7	11	17	11
Graduate Dean	10	12	8	9	11	9	10	13	8
Librarian	7	10	6	5	5	6	7	21	6
Business Officer	34	40	32	29	40	24	36	41	35
Dean of Students	17	17	17	13	11	13	19	28	18
Dir. Admissions	28	26	29	23	22	23	31	31	30
Registrar	29	37	27	25	31	22	30	49	29
Dir. Development	33	33	33	20	34	10	38	31	38

TABLE 59: TRAVEL EXPENSES OF PRESIDENT'S WIFE—PERCENT OF PRESIDENTS REIMBURSED
Questionnaire Sect. P, Q. 92

	All Institutions			Public Institutions			Private Institutions		
	Total	Univ.	Col.	Total	Univ.	Col.	Total	Univ.	Col.
When accompanying president on official business:									
1. Expenses not paid	48%	47%	49%	81%	61%	92%	32%	18%	33%
2. Expenses paid	31	41	29	16	36	7	38	52	37
3. No response	21	12	23	2	3	2	30	30	30
When representing president or institution:									
4. Expenses not paid	38	45	36	72	61	78	21	11	21
5. Expenses paid	34	37	33	17	31	10	42	50	42
6. No response	28	18	30	10	8	12	37	39	37

TABLE 60: ANNUAL EXPENSE ALLOWANCE FOR PRESIDENT FOR ITEMS NOT REPORTED
           IN NORMAL EXPENSE ACCOUNTING—PERCENT PROVIDED ALLOWANCE
Questionnaire Sect. Q, Q. 95

	All Institutions			Public Institutions			Private Institutions		
	Total	Univ.	Col.	Total	Univ.	Col.	Total	Univ.	Col.
Allowance provided	14%	18%	13%	10%	17%	7%	15%	20%	15%

TABLE 61: OFFICE FACILITIES—PERCENT OF OFFICERS CONSIDERING VARIOUS ASPECTS
AS UNSATISFACTORY
Questionnaire Sect. R, Q. 96

	All Institutions			Public Institutions			Private Institutions		
	Total	Univ.	Col.	Total	Univ.	Col.	Total	Univ.	Col.
President									
1. Floor space and layout	15%	12%	16%	18%	10%	21%	14%	16%	14%
2. Physical attractiveness	10	7	10	12	6	15	9	11	9
3. Furnishings	8	4	9	10	2	13	7	9	7
4. Office equipment	5	3	5	5	3	6	5	2	5
5. Location on campus	6	3	7	4	3	5	7	2	7
6. Conference rooms	33	19	36	31	19	37	34	18	36
Academic V.P.									
7. Floor space and layout	19	15	21	20	17	22	18	8	20
8. Physical attractiveness	14	8	16	13	9	15	15	5	17
9. Furnishings	8	6	9	7	7	7	9	3	10
10. Office equipment	5	2	6	4	2	4	6	. . .	7
11. Location on campus	4	1	5	3	1	4	5	. . .	5
12. Conference rooms	37	29	40	37	31	40	37	24	40
Liberal Arts Dean									
13. Floor space and layout	27	33	26	32	37	28	25	24	25
14. Physical attractiveness	19	22	19	20	19	20	19	27	18
15. Furnishings	14	8	15	11	7	13	15	10	16
16. Office equipment	11	4	12	8	4	11	12	5	13
17. Location on campus	5	3	6	4	3	5	5	2	6
18. Conference rooms	38	41	37	43	44	42	36	34	36
Graduate Dean									
19. Floor space and layout	36	37	35	42	39	44	27	33	24
20. Physical attractiveness	21	18	23	26	20	31	14	16	14
21. Furnishings	15	15	16	16	14	17	14	16	14
22. Office equipment	12	7	15	11	7	14	14	7	18
23. Location on campus	6	6	6	6	5	6	6	7	6
24. Conference rooms	44	42	45	46	41	50	40	44	38
Librarian									
25. Floor space and layout	29	18	31	21	16	24	33	23	34
26. Physical attractiveness	20	16	21	18	13	21	21	21	22
27. Furnishings	18	13	20	15	13	15	20	12	21
28. Office equipment	16	6	18	12	6	15	18	5	19
29. Location on campus	5	2	5	5	1	6	5	5	5
30. Conference rooms	34	33	34	36	32	38	33	35	33
Business Officer									
31. Floor space and layout	31	19	34	32	22	37	31	14	32
32. Physical attractiveness	21	10	23	18	11	22	22	7	23
33. Furnishings	13	5	15	12	7	14	14	. . .	15
34. Office equipment	8	. . .	10	5	. . .	7	10	. . .	11
35. Location on campus	6	4	6	2	2	2	7	7	8
36. Conference rooms	38	33	39	41	38	43	37	25	38
Dean of Students									
37. Floor space and layout	30	35	29	41	41	41	25	23	25
38. Physical attractiveness	20	22	20	27	25	28	17	16	17
39. Furnishings	16	17	16	22	20	23	13	12	13
40. Office equipment	11	10	12	15	10	18	10	9	10
41. Location on campus	8	6	8	8	6	10	7	7	8
42. Conference rooms	43	48	43	57	58	57	37	28	37

(continued on next page)

TABLE 61 (continued)

	All Institutions			Public Institutions			Private Institutions		
	Total	Univ.	Col.	Total	Univ.	Col.	Total	Univ.	Col.
Dir. Admissions									
43. Floor space and layout	46%	55%	44%	59%	54%	62%	40%	58%	38%
44. Physical attractiveness	31	32	31	40	27	47	27	40	26
45. Furnishings	25	27	25	29	28	29	23	24	23
46. Office equipment	17	17	16	20	15	22	15	20	15
47. Location on campus	7	10	6	10	10	9	5	9	5
48. Conference rooms	47	57	45	57	54	58	43	62	41
Registrar									
49. Floor space and layout	47	61	45	63	69	60	40	46	40
50. Physical attractiveness	32	38	31	42	39	43	28	36	27
51. Furnishings	26	24	27	31	30	32	24	13	25
52. Office equipment	21	16	22	22	15	26	21	18	21
53. Location on campus	4	5	4	4	6	3	5	5	5
54. Conference rooms	41	45	40	48	49	48	37	36	37
Dir. Development									
55. Floor space and layout	31	35	30	35	34	37	29	36	28
56. Physical attractiveness	24	14	26	19	12	24	26	18	27
57. Furnishings	16	10	17	16	12	18	16	8	17
58. Office equipment	13	7	14	13	10	15	13	3	14
59. Location on campus	11	8	11	9	5	11	12	13	11
60. Conference rooms	34	31	34	39	31	45	32	31	32

With the exception of conference rooms, few officers considered any of these aspects unimportant. In many cases less than 1% or no officers so reported. On the matter of conference rooms, the percent reporting that they considered these unimportant ranged from 1% in the case of presidents to 17% in the case of registrars.

TABLE 62: PROVISION OF SECRETARIAL HELP FOR WIFE OF PRESIDENT—
PERCENT RECEIVING VARIOUS LEVELS OF HELP

Questionnaire Sect. R, Q. 97

	All Institutions			Public Institutions			Private Institutions		
	Total	Univ.	Col.	Total	Univ.	Col.	Total	Univ.	Col.
1. No help provided	55%	48%	57%	71%	57%	79%	47%	30%	49%
2. A little help provided	19	25	18	21	27	17	18	23	18
3. Moderate help provided	5	13	4	6	14	1	5	11	5
4. Substantial help provided	1	4	0	1	2	1	1	9	0
5. No response	19	9	21	1	...	2	28	27	28

TABLE 63: NUMBER OF OFFICERS REPORTING DIRECTLY TO THE PRESIDENT REGULARLY
AND FORMALLY—PERCENT BY NUMBER

Questionnaire Sect. R, Q. 99a

	All Institutions			Public Institutions			Private Institutions		
	Total	Univ.	Col.	Total	Univ.	Col.	Total	Univ.	Col.
1. 4 and under	30%	16%	33%	20%	10%	25%	35%	27%	36%
2. 5-9	55	60	54	60	59	61	52	61	51
3. 10-14	7	13	5	11	18	8	5	5	5
4. 15-19	1	4	1	2	3	1	1	7	0
5. 20 and over	1	4	1	3	7	1	1	...	1
6. No response	6	2	7	4	3	4	7	...	7

INDEX

This index does not cover the Appendix. References are given at the end of each chapter to the relevant portions of the Appendix.